Kindling the Spark

KINDLING THE SPARK

Recognizing and Developing Musical Talent

Joanne Haroutounian

OXFORD

UNIVERSITY PRESS

2002

OXFORD
UNIVERSITY PRESS

Oxford   New York
Athens   Auckland   Bangkok   Bogotá   Buenos Aires   Cape Town
Chennai   Dar es Salaam   Delhi   Florence   Hong Kong   Istanbul   Karachi
Kolkata   Kuala Lumpur   Madrid   Melbourne   Mexico City   Mumbai   Nairobi
Paris   São Paulo   Shanghai   Singapore   Taipei   Tokyo   Toronto   Warsaw

and associated companies in
Berlin   Ibadan

Copyright © 2002 by Oxford University Press

Published by Oxford University Press, Inc.
198 Madison Avenue, New York, New York 10016

Oxford is a registered trademark of Oxford University Press

Library of Congress Cataloging-in-Publication Data
Haroutounian, Joanne.
Musical talent—kindling the spark : recognizing and developing
musical talent / Joanne Haroutounian.
   p. cm.
Includes bibliographical references (p.) and index.
ISBN 0-19-512948-2; 0-19-515638-2 (pbk.)
1. Music—Instruction and study—Psychological aspects.   2. Musical ability.
I. Title: Kindling the spark.   II. Title.

ML3838 .H27 2002
781'.11—dc21   2001037038

9 8 7 6 5 4 3 2 1

Printed in the United States of America
on acid-free paper

FOR WILLY AND JENNIFER

who taught me that love is beyond what words can express

ACKNOWLEDGMENTS

Kindling the Spark was inspired by the many students who taught me so much over the decades of my musical life. This book may answer the questioning looks I received as I stood in silence watching them work or posed puzzling musical problems for them to solve. Many will surely recognize themselves in these pages. Sharing years of music in a private studio is a uniquely intimate experience. I am quite fortunate.

The research at the heart of this book was the result of a decade of reestablishing myself painstakingly in the educational climate beyond the studio door. My thanks to Carolyn Callahan for allowing me to work in my own way and guiding me in finding ways to communicate across musical and education domains. Thanks to Enid Zimmerman and Gil Clark, whose pioneering book on artistically talented students sat on a nearby shelf as a constant reminder of the need of a comparable book on musical talent to sit beside it. Close colleagues who share my passion about talented students in the arts helped me develop the ideas in these combined fields. My thanks to the Arts Division of the National Association for Gifted Children (NAGC), with a hug to Jeanie Goertz, who was my personal sounding board at times in this project.

I am grateful to Oxford University Press for recognizing the importance of the book, with ample credit to Maribeth Payne and Jessica Ryan for meticulously editing and honing the book for production. Reviews of the first draft by Sue Ann Kahn, Louise Lepley, and Marienne Uszler helped refocus and enrich the book. Thanks to Marienne Uszler and Wilma Machover for assisting in this Oxford connection.

Many knowledgeable people bring their insightful ideas and pertinent resources to the pages of this book. My thanks to Edwin Gordon, Peter Webster, Lloyd Davidson, Scott McBride Smith, Marienne Uszler, and Barry Oreck for offering their expert perspectives. A simple e-mail response from

Sharon Libero enlightened me about the unique talent of persons with Williams Syndrome. The valuable information from colleagues in early childhood organizations, specialized high schools, and Governor's School programs is much appreciated. Thanks to the Levine School, Chris Keller at McKinley School, the SEPIA program, and the studios of Lynn Grimm, Ed Johonott, and Rosita Kerr Mang for allowing us to photograph their students.

Finally, this book would not be possible without the ongoing support of my close friends and family. Martha Owens provided valuable educational feedback from a dear friend. My daughter Jennifer and her husband Sam spurred me on when I reached points when the process seemed overwhelming. My fascination with talented young musicians stems from my experience as parent of a vibrantly talented young woman. My husband, Willy, was my constant supporter, there to listen, ponder, and prod me to stop working in the wee hours of the morning. His photographs help bring these pages to life.

During the final stages of the first draft, my husband and I were nestled in a Colorado ski lodge, immersed in reading and taking notes as the sky opened up in a thunderous storm. We were drawn to the orange glow of the receding storm, only to discover a magnificent rainbow hovering over the white peaks outside. The resulting rush of picture-taking brought to a close our reflective review of the developing chapters and left an intimate memory from this writing experience that I will long cherish.

CONTENTS

PHOTOGRAPHS

Photography by William Haroutounian.

Chapter 1 Grand Canyon.

Chapter 2 Audience attending a concert. Child listening. Alexandria, Virginia.

Chapter 3 Teenagers with violins. Courtesy University of Virginia's Summer Enrichment Program in the Arts.

Chapter 4 Student singers. Courtesy of Levine School of Music.

Chapter 5 Girl with drum. Children singing and moving. Courtesy of Levine School of Music. Girl composing. Courtesy of University of Virginia's Summer Enrichment Program in the Arts.

Chapter 6 Pianist and teacher. Courtesy of the studio of Rosita Kerr Mang. Piano concerto recital. Alexandria, Virginia.

Chapter 7 Grand Canyon.

Chapter 8 Children playing Orff instruments. Courtesy of McKinley Elementary School, Arlington, VA.

Chapter 9 Children moving in a music class. Courtesy of McKinley Elementary School, Arlington, Virginia.

Chapter 10 Boy with drum. Children moving. Boy with guitar and teacher. Courtesy of Levine School of Music.

Chapter 11 Children and teacher in music classroom. Courtesy of McKinley Elementary School, Arlington, Virginia.

Chapter 12 Baby and father. Toddler at piano. Haroutounian family photos.

INTRODUCTION

The young pianist enters the stage adorned in satin, with a large velvet bow affixed to the back of her long hair. With her first movements at the keyboard, the audience and judges are impressed with the confidence and clarity of her performance. She is obviously well trained and sensitive to the style and interpretive detail of the music. She is a winner—a musical talent.

Everyone in the church is transfixed as the teenage soloist, with eyes closed, sings in front of the gospel choir. Her connection with the music seems to come straight from the heart as she freely winds her way around the simple melody of the hymn. The congregation glances at one another with an approving nod—a musical talent.

Enter the toddler, marching with a toy drum dangling from his neck and chanting in singsong style as he rhythmically travels in circles through the kitchen, living room, and dining room. Again, and again he marches and sings, entranced with the sound of the beat-beat-beat of the drum. Mom smiles at her son—a musical talent.

As vicarious listener, can you imagine the *spark* of musical talent in these three different performances? We have all experienced the type of aesthetic awareness that draws one into a musical performance—the shivers-down-the-spine feeling that makes you listen intently and savor the sounds you hear. The polished confidence of the well-trained pianist, the free improvisation of the gospel singer, and the musical "play" of the toddler create this talent connection in different ways between the music, the performer, and the listener.

This spark of musical talent is relatively easy to recognize yet remains an enigma to define. Are certain people born with musical talent? Can anyone have musical talent with proper training? How do we recognize students who have musical potential and have not had formal training? What, exactly, is musical talent?

I have been on a personal quest in search of the answer to those questions for over a decade. This quest grew from over thirty years of experience living through music and witnessing, time and again, evidence of young children or young artists truly communicating to me through sound. Each time I sit behind a judge's table listening to student performances, I am intrigued by the potential spark of talent that emanates from even the most untrained student and is recognizable to the musician's ear. Is this spark also discernible to the untrained ear? While working with talented students in my private studio, I continually listen, observe, and explore to discover exactly *how* they learn. How can teachers learn to challenge these promising students to excel technically while allowing them to explore musically? After years of study and research, my quest has brought me to these pages.

A Musical Spark

This book presents musical talent as a spark, eager to be recognized, kindled, and nurtured throughout life. Recognition of this spark depends on a person's individual perspective of what constitutes musical talent. A scientific perspective seeks measurement of sensory capacities. Psychologists observe developing behaviors from birth to expertise levels of musical ability. Musicians and music teachers mold these emerging abilities; what do they realize in this process? Parents are eager to discover why their child is captivated with sound and music as a continual plaything. This book examines musical talent from these different perspectives, synthesizes ideas to discover the underpinnings that define this talent, and offers ways to recognize and develop musical potential.

The topic of musical talent has been examined, researched, and debated by experts across the fields of music performance, music psychology, and music education since the turn of the century, and well before. Even Plato and Aristotle had opposing views. If you are seeking a heated discussion between colleagues in music, simply bring up the subject of musical talent—then sit back and listen. Gathering these different perspectives into a single volume makes it possible to compare, contrast, and synthesize ideas to develop our own individual perspective of this difficult-to-define spark. This book adds fuel to the fire of future discussion and debate.

There is a voluminous amount of research on the perception of sound and its measurement, and another mountain of studies measures the development of musical abilities at different ages. I gratefully bow to Seashore, Gordon, Sloboda, Hargreaves, and Shuter-Dyson and Gabriel for the rich resources they have provided in the field of music psychology. I have attempted to filter pertinent information from these sources and other talent-related studies and present them in easily readable terms for the wider audience of music teachers, students, and parents.

Music teachers in studios and school classrooms are drawn to students who show musical potential. There is a mixture of excitement and wonder (and sometimes panic) when young students learn so rapidly that you must rein them in at times to allow them to reflect on what they are learning. Since the studio and classroom have been my personal discovery ground over the past thirty years, it is my hope that my teaching colleagues will be intrigued as we examine issues of performance, creativity, "giftedness," and the emerging curricula that include "musical intelligence." In the field of musical performance, we so easily develop tunnel vision that draws us to "talent" conclusions at auditions and competitions. A healthy peripheral glance at the musical listeners and creators may reveal some hidden potential in our classrooms and studios. This book presents a broader scope of musical talent that seeks to unveil potential in *every* school classroom.

Metaperception

Any discussion of musical talent naturally leads to the exploration of how musicians think, create, and artistically "know." Musical thinking meshes cognitive thought with perceptive awareness of sound. Interpretive and creative decisions intertwine personal expression with this cognitive/perceptive functioning. In part I I explore how specialists across musical fields describe this internal musical process according to their individual perspectives. Gordon's idea of "audiation" describes the internal tonal imagery at the heart of music aptitude. Webster expands this concept of internal perception to one of "creative thinking in sound." The term "representation" is used often to describe artistic internal functioning. Reimer describes musical thought as "internal musical representation"; Sloboda describes the essence of musical language as an underlying "thought representation of music"; Seashore describes this internal representation of music as the "mind's ear."[1]

My search for a personal understanding of the interplay of perception, cognition, and expression in the artistic process led me beyond musical fields, seeking ways to understand how all artists "know." In the visual arts, Eisner believes that perception is at the heart of cognition.

The senses are our primary information pickup systems and provide the content through which our conceptual life takes form. . . . I believe that the representation of that life must itself employ a form of representation that is made of material available to our sensory senses of sight, touch, sound, smell, and taste. The types of meaning that we are able to construe from the forms of representation we encounter are related both to the limits and possibilities of those forms and to our ability to "read" them.[2]

"Reading" the qualitative world requires fined-tuned perceptual discrimination which Eisner describes as "connoisseurship." His fellow visual artist Arnheim shares Eisner's viewpoint that cognition equates with sensory perception. To Arnheim, visual perception equals "visual thinking."[3]

After filtering through the many terms that describe artistic internal functioning, I developed a term I believe is easy to understand and presents an artistic parallel to cognitive decision-making in academic fields. I have named this artistic thought/sensing *metaperception*. *"Metaperception" describes the cognitive/perceptual functioning of a musician or any artist while making interpretive decisions.* It is the artistic counterpart to *metacognition*, which describes the monitoring of thought while making cognitive decisions in the academics. Metacognition may be described as the process of "thinking about thinking"—mapping out ways to think in order to solve problems effectively. In the arts, metaperception may be described as "perceiving/thinking about artistic intent"—the process of filtering and manipulating sensory perceptions combined with cognitive and expressive decision-making in order to create artistic solutions.

When working on a math problem, we internally map out cognitive strategies on ways to proceed to find the correct answer. In the arts, we internally manipulate perceptions of sound, movement, color, or texture as well as thought and emotion to create an artistic statement through a particular arts medium. A musical score may display directions that tell us when to play loud, soft, speed up, or slow down. The musician must interpret the parameters of these dynamic and tempo ideas, making musical decisions through a molding of sounds and technical execution of sounds on an instrument or voice linked with personal expressive ideas. We listen, adjust, and adapt sounds and their physical production until we mesh the sound with our interpretive intent.

Metaperception is at play when a young child simply plays with sound, creating unique variations to a nursery rhyme. It is at work when a concert artist practices a passage in varying ways, seeking the sounds that will create the expressive interpretation of the performer. Metaperception ignites our musical spark, allowing us to recognize potential and aesthetically connect with performers and creators of music.

From Spark to Flame

Part I presents perspectives of talent from the viewpoints of different specialized fields across music psychology, education, performance, and gifted education. Many of the concepts that describe the sensory capacities of musical knowing in these chapters are difficult to translate into words. For that reason, I have included various "Sparkler Experiences" to help bring these abstract musical concepts to life through the personal experience of performing simple musical tasks. These tasks are easily adaptable for use in the school, studio, or home to help teachers and parents unveil aspects of musical talent. They encourage nonmusicians, parents, students, teachers, and performing musicians to experience the cognitive/perceptive functioning that is at the heart of musical talent.

Part II presents the existing status of musical talent identification, summarizes musical talent research findings from surveys and interviews across musical and gifted fields, and presents a recommended set of talent criteria and procedures for musical talent identification. Chapter 10 includes a set of Sparkler Activities highlighting each talent criterion, useful for potential talent recognition in *any* classroom or studio. The talent identification procedures in chapter 11 reflect pragmatic possibilities for gifted specialists, music educators, and parents who wish to seek out potential in schools in their community. An encapsulated *Framework for Recognizing Musical Talent*, helpful in collaborative work sessions, is included in the appendix.

Part III describes the development of talent, from birth to graduation from high school. What should we watch for as a child responds to music from the crib? How can we stimulate musical sensitivity in the preschool years when musical development is so fundamental? Information stemming from research and music education can assist parents as they guide youngsters in the early years when musical abilities first take shape. Sparkler Activities glimpse into early childhood classes across a variety of curricular philosophies, including Orff, Kódaly, Dalcroze, and other preschool programs.

Part III also traces the stages of musical training, from the first steps through the studio door to auditioning for a conservatory upon high school graduation. Musical development is presented in three stages, with reference to research findings of musical abilities at various ages, theories of musical and general cognitive development, and specific recommendations for instruction and training suitable for each developmental phase. This section examines the controversy of competitions, master teachers, and the academic-artistic tug of war that faces talented teenagers who are faced with difficult choices at a time when musical skills are most sophisticated and personalized.

The book concludes with my personal reflections as a mother, teacher, researcher, musician, program administrator, and constant explorer in search of discovering and nurturing the ever-captivating *spark*. The appendix offers resources to assist readers in their own future talent quests.

Kindling the Spark gathers stories, studies, and ideas about musical talent into one source that seeks to guide teachers, parents, and musicians in understanding this complex topic. I hope this book will inspire the reader to enjoy the aesthetic dynamic that is integral to musical performance. If the next time you encounter a musical performance by a youngster, concert artist, or street musician you tune in and listen for that *spark*, I will have succeeded.

PART I

Perspectives of Musical Talent

PERSPECTIVES

Four friends were observing the Grand Canyon for the first time—a geologist, an environmentalist, a photographer, and a poet. The geologist scientifically appraised the ancient formations of rock before him, examining and explaining fine details of this wondrous sight to his friends. The environmentalist stood close to the edge, peering into the canyon. She began a brisk dialogue with her scientific friend, pointing to different vegetation and the winding river in the canyon floor, explaining her views of the contextual changes of nature and its impact on the canyon. The photographer listened halfheartedly, busily clicking one shot after another, catching the changing light and shadow against the canyon walls. The poet listened attentively to the friendly scientific banter. She smiled while watching her photographer friend immersed in his work and sat quietly with pen and pad in hand, savoring the unique aesthetic experience. Four very different perspectives of the Grand Canyon—one analytically defined, one naturally developmental, one phenomenological, and one reflective.[1]

You observe this scene. You realize the value of each perspective of the Grand Canyon experience. You also are aware of the behavior of distinct personalities as they connect with the environment. Their views are specialized and focused to their particular interests. If you try to understand these perspectives and synthesize them with your own, you discover that you can enjoy a richer aesthetic awareness of the Grand Canyon.

With imaginative juices in high gear, visualize the concept of musical talent as that vast Grand Canyon. Part I of this book offers unique perspectives of "what talent means" from specialists across different fields. The more specialized a person becomes in a respective field, the more a perspective becomes intensely focused and defined. The scientific psychometricians convey the importance of measuring music aptitude, the sensory base of musical talent. Developmental psychologists offer ideas about the growth of talent through musical learning. Performers and teachers of performers focus on the attributes of the talented performer. You may find the parameters of "talent" stretched in our discussions of musical creativity. And exactly what makes a child musically "gifted"? The following chapters present these perspectives, recognizing the value of each and offering the opportunity to pick and choose what aligns with your personal view of musical talent.

Experiencing the Spark

We all know you can't learn to sew or play baseball by reading a book. In the same way, you really can't understand the abstract components of musical talent described in this book without personally experimenting with these ideas through some type of musical experience. Each chapter in part I offers Sparkler Experiences for *any* reader to try. As you work through each experience, reflect on the process of each musical task and how it clarifies the ideas presented in each chapter through a personal experience with music and sound.

General readers:

> The tasks are designed at a comfortable entry level. Musical terminology is explained when needed. I encourage you to give them a try and see what you discover about musical sensing and listening.

Teachers/students:

> Adapt and adjust to fit your needs as a studio or class activity. Expand further to develop each idea.

Musicians:

> Examine the process that takes place while you are engaged in each experience. The tasks will be basic. Look beneath the basics to see how abstract musical cognitive/perceptive functioning is engaged in each experience.

As you read through each chapter, you may be intrigued with new ideas. You may find yourself adamantly in disagreement with certain talent perspectives. This is good and healthy; it allows you to grow in your own personal understanding of musical talent. To keep this healthy debate alive, each chapter includes arguments for and against the discussed perspective. I have tried on different hats to present these arguments from the viewpoints of music teachers, musicians, music psychologists, or parents—whatever seemed most appropriate.

Each chapter ends with a short presentation of my own point of view, followed by questions for you to ponder and space to add your own reflections as you form your own perspective of this *spark* called musical talent

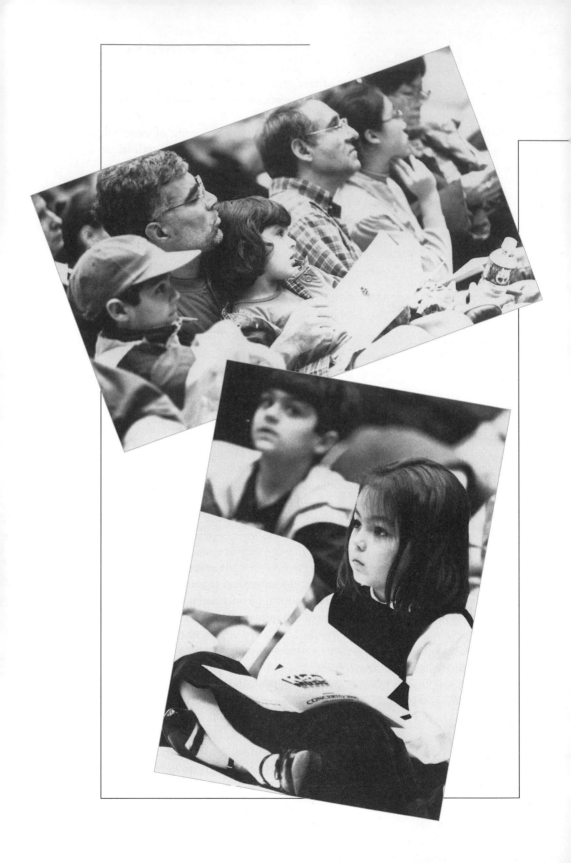

TALENT AS MUSIC APTITUDE

Hearing can be a source of . . . exquisite pleasure but it requires conscious cultivation. I have had people tell me that they had never heard the song of a wood thrush, although I knew the bell-like phrases of this bird had been ringing in their back yards every spring.
Rachel Carson, The Sense of Wonder

Several years ago, my husband called me into his studio as he was practicing for an upcoming solo violin concerto performance with the National Symphony. As I entered the room, I noticed three bows lying on the floor. Without a word, he motioned for me to be seated on the sofa. He picked up the first bow and began to play a passage of the music. He set this bow on the floor, picked up the second, and played the same passage. He repeated this process with the last bow. When he finished, he paused and looked at me. I motioned to the middle bow. He nodded in agreement. This was the bow he would use for the performance.

Musicians communicate through sound. The wordless exchange of musical ideas described here exemplifies the fine-tuned discrimination of sound that is at the heart of music aptitude. While listening to the repeated musical passage, my husband and I were both aware of the subtle qualities of sound that each bow produced as it was drawn across the strings of the violin. The first had a gutsy, robust sound; the second a melancholy, sweet quality; the third a square cleanliness. We listened, interpretively reflected on these qualities, and decided that melancholy sweetness would best match the mood of the Armenian folk tunes within the solo concerto. Words were not necessary.

Obviously, this level of musical communication is quite sophisticated. It relies on years of musical training, listening, and interpretive understanding. However, if you layer away the training and skills, we arrive at the underlying *discrimination of differences in sound*. The discrimination of sound, prior to any formal training, is where music aptitude begins.

Music exists through sound. Sound develops into music through combinations of rhythm, loudness, pitch, and the different qualities of these sounds. Music psychologists define the capacity to sense these musical components as *music aptitude*. The more discriminately one senses subtle differences in these components, the higher one's music aptitude. Music aptitude combines inherent musical capacities with listening skills that may develop without formal training or education.

Early Signs of Sound Discrimination

The perception of sound actually begins prior to birth. Prenatal research records sounds within the womb and monitors fetal responses to the sound of a mother's voice and other external stimuli. The human auditory system is functional from three to four months before birth, with fetuses beyond 28 to 30 weeks of gestation reacting to external sounds through startle responses or measured changes in heart rate.[1] The old wives' tale that playing music for the unborn child instills musical talent is actually supported by numerous studies;[2] they indicate that prenatal familiarization to certain sounds, voices, or musical sequences may contribute to the development of sensitivity to these different sound stimuli after birth. In a study by Feijoo, fetuses at 37 weeks immediately responded with movements when hearing a musical theme from *Peter and the Wolf* that had been presented to them as stimuli in the early stages of pregnancy (six–eight weeks). Interestingly, the theme was played backward as well as forward to see if reactions were any different. There was no response to the backward version—only the recognizable tune.

Hepper's study of young infants four to five days old showed their attentiveness to a musical theme from a favorite soap opera their mothers listened to daily during the last three months of their pregnancy. Numerous studies show that sound stimulation prior to birth can assist in "developing long-term preferences or general sensitivity to the type of sounds experienced."[3]

An infant's playfulness with sounds reveals the first signs of musicality. Hanuš Papoušek, a leading researcher of infants, believes this infant play helps develop artistic creativity, discovery, inventiveness, or humor in later life. Parents can stimulate this "play" by simply talking to the infant, modifying musical aspects of speech as the infant reacts, and regularly singing lullabies and nursery songs.

Mechthild Papoušek's research of infant-directed speech or "baby talk" reveals that parents across the globe intuitively use melodic contours in this preverbal communication with their infants. In fact, mother–infant dialogues display universal similarities, with Mandarin Chinese mothers using contours similar to German- or English-speaking mothers in lulling their babies to sleep or encouraging their attention. These research findings support our tendency to communicate to babies through the singsong utterances that seem so natural yet so silly at times.[4]

SPARKLER EXPERIENCE: Musical Awareness in the Nursery

Communication with an infant comes naturally. Parents or caregivers may enjoy experimenting with the following musical experiences, taking note of what sounds specifically stimulate an infant's response.

1. *Infant-directed speech or baby talk:* While rocking an infant in a quiet room, first speak in a normal way then in a light singsong quality, and finally sing a nursery rhyme or lullaby. Do you notice any change in attention and awareness as you change your mode of communication? Which mode elicits the most attentive response?

2. *Musical awareness in the crib:* Place a CD or tape player near the crib and experiment with different types of music, observing your child's interest and awareness of these sounds. Do you see a direct reaction when the music begins? Is there any reaction when you turn the music off suddenly, in the middle of a musical selection? You may enjoy noting different reactions to music that is fast versus slow, loud versus soft, high in pitch versus low, or instrumental rather than vocal. Expand beyond mood music or lullabies to include classical, jazz, opera, and pop styles.

The Measurement of Music Aptitude

The fascination of musical perception can be traced back to early Chinese theories over three thousand years old. Pythagoras's theory of pitch intervals in the sixth century B.C. led to Plato and Aristotle's discussions of the role of music in the lawful order of the Greek city-state. Augustine's description of music perception in the medieval treatise *De Musica* reflects many of the attributes of music aptitude:[5]

- The physical fact of sound
- The faculty of hearing
- The ability to imagine music without the actual sound stimulus
- The ability to remember previous musical experiences
- The ability to intellectually examine and judge musical shape and grade

The scientific analysis and measurement of human perception and discrimination of sounds began in the late 1800s, when the field of music psychology became established. The earliest publications in the field displayed fascination with aural perception and the behavioral aspects of musical talent.

In 1862, Hermann von Helmholtz published the first text in music psychology, *On the Sensations of Tone as a Physiological Basis for the Theory of Music*. It contained detailed explanations of acoustical theory and findings from his experimental work in auditory sensation. Another early theoretical music psychology text was *Wer ist musikalisch*, by Theodor Billroth (1895), which described musical talent through behavioral characteristics such as interest and musical memory, as well as specific auditory sensory capacities.

Throughout Europe, music psychologists probed the finite limits of listening through measurements of auditory perception. In Germany, Wilhelm Wundt's experiments led to measurements of the perceptual span and rates of learning. Carl Stumpf considered developing tests of musical aptitude as early as 1883 while carrying out acoustical experiments with David Popper, a celebrated cellist, and Pepito Areola, a young prodigy. In London, Francis Galton's study of hereditary genius sought a relationship between sensory discrimination and intellectual powers. His fascination with the limits of perceptive capabilities led to the invention of the Galton whistle for determining the highest audible pitch.[6]

In the United States, few can dispute the reputation of Carl Seashore as the most influential pioneer in the field of music psychology. After twenty years of experimentation, he published his *Seashore Measures of Musical Talent* in 1919. In *The Psychology of Musical Talent*, Seashore describes musical talent as a hierarchy of attributes stemming from inborn sensory capacities that function from early childhood. The basic musical capacities that constitute *music aptitude* are:

- Tonal—sense of pitch; sensitivity to melody, pitch variation, harmonies
- Dynamic—acuity of hearing and sense of loudness
- Temporal—sense of time, tempo, and rhythm
- Qualitative—sensitivity to tonal color or timbre (instrumental sounds); realization of tonal color within a harmonic context

Seashore's studies show that these basic capacities are displayed by children at an early age and that a reliable measurement of music aptitude can be made by the age of ten. After this age, Seashore contends that music aptitude becomes stabilized. Future training can enhance existing aptitude but not extend these capabilities.

> After a comparatively early age, these capacities do not vary with intelligence, with training, or with increasing age, except as the exhibition of these capacities is limited by the child's ability to understand or apply himself to the task. This fact is of utmost importance in that it makes a diagnosis of talent possible before training is begun and points to certain very definite principles of music education. We can measure these capacities reliably by the age of ten in the normal child; and this measure is likely to stand, except for the numerous vicissitudes of life which may cause deterioration. . . . It is the meaning, and not the capacity, of these forms of impression which we train and which matures with age in proportion to the degree of intelligence and emotional drive.[7]

SPARKLER EXPERIENCE: Realizing Music Aptitude

This experience focuses listening to realize the separate capacities of music aptitude. It requires repeated listening to a short musical excerpt, finetuning your ear in different ways.

Use a musical excerpt *no longer than 30 to 45 seconds*. Music that has a variety of instrumental sounds will be best for this listening exercise, but a popular song with backup can work as well. Find a quiet room and a comfortable space to relax and close your eyes as you listen for extra concentration. You will need a pencil and paper to jot down answers and ideas to the questions that follow.

1. *Tonal listening—pitch discrimination:* As you listen to the music, focus on the melody or tune you hear. Focus your listening to hear the direction of pitch movement in the opening melody—up and down.

   - Do the opening notes in the melody move up, down, or form an up-down contour?
   - Do pitches generally move stepwise or seem to jump or skip in this opening melody?
   - Which note is the highest in pitch in the opening melody? Identify by its number in the melodic sequence (fifth, seventh note) or by its word if sung.
   - Which note is the lowest in pitch in the opening melody?

   ➤

Realizing Music Aptitude (*continued*)

Often melodies have a particular pattern that is repeated. For example, *Are You Sleeping?* repeats an opening four-note pattern: $\_\,-\,^{-}\,\_\,\_\,-\,^{-}\,\_$

- Is there a melodic pattern and repetition in any melodies you hear?

If yes, sketch the pattern on your paper.

2. *Dynamic listening—volume discrimination:* This listening focus requires a basic dynamic vocabulary of terms. In musical language, the spectrum of volume reasonably includes:

pp	p	mp	mf	f	ff
pianissimo	piano	mezzo piano	mezzo forte	forte	fortissimo
very soft	soft	moderately soft	moderately loud	loud	very loud

Music that gradually gets louder shows a crescendo: <
Music that gradually gets softer shows a decrescendo: >
As you listen to the music, focus on how volume changes. Draw a *dynamic color path* using these dynamic range descriptors as you listen.

   Example: Music that begins loud, suddenly drops in volume and then grows very loud would have the following color path:

$$\begin{array}{cccc} \text{f} & \text{p} & < & \text{ff} \\ \text{loud} & \text{soft} & & \text{very loud} \end{array}$$

Listen for fine differences in volume and sketch the appropriate dynamic color path for your musical selection on paper. Dynamic levels are open to interpretive differences. There is no "right or wrong" here, merely a sense of volume range and contour.

3. *Temporal listening—tempo and rhythm discrimination:* This third listening focus requires listening for the general speed of the music and specific rhythmic patterns.

Tempo:

- Is the music very slow (*adagio*), medium speed (*moderato*), fast (*allegro*), or very fast (*presto*)?
- Does it ever change in tempo, either speeding up (*accelerando*) or slowing down (*ritardando*)? Describe where and how.

Rhythm:

- As you listen to the melody, do you hear any rhythmic pattern you can clap (not the steady beat, but rhythms within the melody)? Sketch

➤

Realizing Music Aptitude (*continued*)

these patterns figuratively, with lines, dashes, or formal rhythmic notation. Be sure to signify pauses or held notes in the rhythm in some way.

- Do you hear repeated rhythm patterns in the accompanying or backup instrumental parts that are played supporting the melody? Jot these accompanying rhythm patterns down, any way you like, to notate what you hear.

4. *Qualitative listening—timbre and harmonic discrimination:* Your previous listening experiences have prepared you for this critical listening capacity. Your listening focus will now address the different sounds of instruments, how these sounds are balanced against one another, and how sounds blend together.

- How many different instruments are playing this selection?
- Which type of instrument is playing the melody?
- What different instruments are playing the background, backup, or accompaniment?

Listen for each different instrument playing the supporting accompaniment. Can your ear follow each individual instrument part? Is one playing louder than another (musical balance)? When do all instruments play together? When are only a few instruments playing? Jot down ideas you are discovering about musical context of sound—the interplay and interweaving of multiple qualities of sound in this short musical excerpt.

In this exercise, you experienced the sensory capacities of music aptitude. Music aptitude tests measure each capacity individually. Someone with a keenly sophisticated musical ear may catch all of these musical elements in a full musical context in one listening.[9]

Seashore's belief that these capacities were largely inborn and were unaffected by training beyond the age of 10 was revolutionary and was criticized by many of his music psychologist colleagues. He did believe the capacity of tonal memory, which he called the "mind's ear," was a condition of learning that could be developed substantially through training.[8]

Music Aptitude Testing

Seashore's test battery included subtests that measured aural discrimination within each area of these sensory capacities. As a scientist, Seashore was meticulous at designing the measures to be free of bias, with significant evidence of validity and reliability. He used the sounds of tuning forks and beat-frequency oscillators rather than musical instruments to ensure that the tests were devoid of factors indigenous to music of a particular culture.

Basically, the tests required students to discriminate tones of different pitches, length, and loudness. Discrimination reached acute levels, capable of revealing fine-tuned auditory perception. For example, the tonal memory subtest consisted of fifty pairs of tonal sequences, varying in length from two to six tones. Individuals were required to identify the one tone in the second sequence that was different from the first. (A quick reference: think of someone relaying a set of two phone numbers, asking you to identify one number that is different in the second.) The pitch subtest required individuals to differentiate between pitches that ranged from 59 to 9 cents (100 cents is a semitone, or half step). This minimal pitch difference equates to a string that is a fraction of a degree out of tune on a string instrument.[10]

The Seashore tests were a landmark in the objective measurement of aural discrimination. They were revised periodically over a 20-year period and spurred both criticism and parallel interest in the development of music aptitude tests by a number of music psychologists in the United States and Europe. Basic criticism of the measures concerned the isolated, atomistic nature of measurement of musical capacities. Does this actually describe real musical functioning? Opponents argued that Seashore's studies were based on highly controlled laboratory settings rather than on field studies in the real world of music-making. The use of laboratory-controlled sound rather than musical material and instrumental sound was also criticized. James Mursell, a chief critic, contended that the tests basically measured acoustical abilities rather than musical abilities and were "much more efficient in identifying those incapable of musical achievement on a high level than in the positive diagnosis of talent or even in revealing the degree in which it exists."[11]

Over the next 30 years, the field abounded with music aptitude tests, all variations of the basic standards of measurement established by Seashore. Kwalwasser and Dykema (1930) developed tests that included achievement measures and utilized the sounds of orchestral instruments as test stimuli. Wing's *Standardized Tests of Musical Intelligence* (1939, 1969) reflected the European preference of a "Gestalt" theory of music aptitude, measuring musical understanding rather than aural recognition of isolated musical components. Bentley's *Measures of Musical Abilities* (1966) were the first designed for measuring music aptitude in young children from age

SPARKLER EXPERIENCE: Testing Your Ear

This listening activity uses ear-training performance tasks similar to those found in music aptitude tests. Obviously, the tests are rigorously constructed to have tasks that have different levels of discrimination and sounds that are controlled. This is a taste of the type of listening discrimination the test measures.

1. *Same or different:* A warm-up: recognition of short melodies that are the same or different, requires a keyboard and two people, the listener and the "tester." The tester plays a series of three notes on a keyboard, then plays a second set of three notes that are either the same or different. Begin with notes that lie close together and might create a short tune, easy to remember. Then extend to more difficult sets of tones of four or five notes that are farther apart. The listener basically identifies groups of notes as the *same* or *different.*

2. *Tonal memory:* To extend listening capabilities; modeled after Seashore's tonal memory test. Play a series of notes on a keyboard as in the warm-up exercise, then play a second series that has ONE different note. The listener must tell which note was different (first, second, third, etc.). Extend the series to four, five, then six tones.

3. *Advanced tonal memory:* Add another level of internal tonal memory to the last exercise by having the listener not only identify which note is different but also determine if this note is higher or lower than the note played in the first series.

seven to fourteen and included aural discrimination of pitches smaller than a half step, similar to Seashore. A list of tests currently in print, showing subtest contents, reliability and validity statistics, and other useful information is in the appendix.

Over the past thirty years, Edwin Gordon has taken on a major role in the development of music aptitude tests in the United States. Gordon's test batteries reflect Seashore's theory that music aptitude is developmental up to a certain age. Gordon has established the age of nine rather than Seashore's age of ten as the age when music aptitude is stabilized. After that age, he explains, training brings an increase of musical skills but only to the refinement that individual levels of stabilized musical aptitudes will allow.

Gordon's major contribution to the field of psychometrics is the development of tests capable of measuring music aptitude from kindergarten through twelfth grade. His *Primary Measures of Music Audiation (PMMA)* measure normal music aptitude in grades K–3. The test ceiling may be a bit low for the identification of young children with high aptitude. Gordon recommends the use of the *Intermediate Measures of Music Audiation (IMMA)* for the identification of musical talent in the primary grades, because it is designed to assess high music aptitude in children aged six to nine. If seeking exceptional levels of aptitude in these grades, the *Music Aptitude Profile* can be used as early as fourth grade with an extended ceiling that includes measurement through twelfth grade levels. Assessment of stabilized music aptitude for any student above fourth grade can be measured by the *Advanced Measures of Music Audiation (AMMA)* or the comprehensive *Music Aptitude Profile (MAP)*.

Figure 2.1 shows a portion of the answer sheet used in Gordon's *PMMA* and *IMMA* tests.

Gordon bases his measurement of music aptitude on the concept of "audiation." Audiation occurs "when one hears music through recall or creation (the sound not being physically present) and derives musical meaning." Seashore described this imagery as the "mind's ear" or "the musical mind

---

SPARKLER EXPERIENCE: Inner Sensing of Sound

This experience allows you to realize the sensory capacity of tonal imagery, or the ability to hear sounds internally.

1. Sing the song "Mary Had a Little Lamb" to yourself, "inside." Was the last note higher, lower, or the same as the starting note? Now sing the song out loud or pick out the melody on a keyboard. Were you correct?

2. For a more challenging tonal imagery test, sing "Happy Birthday" "inside." Was the last note higher, lower, or the same as the starting note? Check again by singing aloud or playing the tune.

3. Now it's your choice! Internally sing the first phrase of a song of your choice, again determining if the last note is lower, higher, or the same. Check with an "outside" performance. You will find that you can train your inner ear in tonal imagery through repeated exercises such as this.

FIGURE 2.1. From the pictographic answer sheet of *The Intermediate Measures of Music Audiation* (1982) by Edwin Gordon. Students are asked to circle the upper pair of faces if the second of two short melodic or rhythm patterns is the same as the first. They circle the lower pair of faces if the two patterns are different. Used with permission from GIA Publications.

at the representational level." It is how a musician makes internal decisions in music-making as well as in the perception and discrimination of sound. These descriptions of internal musical imagery actually mirror Saint Augustine's medieval description of the "ability to imagine music without the actual sound stimulus," emphasizing the ageless fascination of musical sensing.[12]

The Use of Music Aptitude Tests

With the impressive array of music aptitude tests that has been developed over the course of the twentieth century, we may naturally assume that these tests would be part of the normal procedure of determining student strengths and weakness in listening capabilities in music programs across the country. Surely they would be a normal part of musical talent identification for entry into gifted programs. However, this is not the case. This may stem from the tests themselves, the changing music educational climate, or the shift of interest in music psychology toward cognitive and developmental approaches of study beginning in the 1980s.

Studies showing the use of music aptitude testing in education and research settings were prevalent during the seventies and eighties, when these tests were actively being developed. Grashel notes 16 studies published in the *Journal of Research in Music Education* during the 1980s utilizing music aptitude testing, with Gordon's *PMMA* being used in half of these studies.[13]

The debate on the value of the tests continues in the field of music psychology. Kemp suggests that the tests are "so devoid of real musical value or meaning that they were dismissed as inappropriate for the purpose of identifying musicianship."[14] Sloboda cites several studies that show that even experienced musicians are incapable of the fine discrimination within Seashore's tests. He questions the need to test at this level of discrimination and cautions that test results should not be used as a basis of educational decisions.

> We are entitled to question the value of extremely fine discriminations below a generous minimum. Musical expertise consists in grasping the various levels of structure that exist in musical sequencing. A test of musical ability or aptitude should be demonstrably concerned with such structural skills.[15]

Even those music psychologists who see the value of objective testing in music realize problems with the tests themselves. Boyle and Radocy describe the "monster movie voice" in the Seashore tests and the requirement of three 50-minute sessions to complete Gordon's comprehensive *MAP*. True, the more comprehensive tests are long and tedious to administer. The tests concentrate on listening to isolated tones and snatches of sounds rather than the musical context one listens to as a musician. However, one may argue that the SAT consists of short verbal and mathematical problems and takes several hours to administer. It is a mainstay of academic testing in education.

The basic philosophy of music education may suggest reasons why music aptitude testing is not encouraged. School music programs strongly advocate the need to educate *all* students, regardless of talent, aptitude, or ability. Music aptitude testing may encourage limitation of instruction to those students who show strength in music aptitude scores. According to the *National Standards of Arts Education*, published by the Music Educators National Conference,

> The argument that relegates the arts to the realm of passive experience for the majority, or that says a lack of "real talent" disqualifies most people from learning to draw, to play an instrument, dance, or act, is simply wrong-headed. Clearly, students have different aptitudes and abilities in the arts, but differences are not disqualifications.[16]

The *National Standards of Arts Education* curriculum standards do recommend "special experiences designed for gifted and talented students according to their abilities and interests."[17] If schools choose to identify musically talented students, a music aptitude test may be the most sensible way to include an objective measure in the identification process.

The gifted/arts and music education literature recommends these tests as a way to provide valuable information about potential talent that may be obscured by classroom behaviors. Students with keen ears may not necessarily be adept performers. As in all identification procedures, test scores should *not* be the sole determinant of talent but should be used in conjunction with observation, performance assessment, and recommendations from a variety of sources.[18]

Once again, literature recommendations do not reflect actual practice in the field. My own analysis of data from the National Research Center for the Gifted and Talented (NRC G/T) at the University of Virginia revealed minimal use of music aptitude testing, with several locations using tests inappropriately. Further explanation of this research is in chapter 9.[19]

Often the best way to seek answers is to ask the experts. In seeking out perspectives for this book, I interviewed Edwin Gordon about the use of aptitude testing for talent identification purposes. He said:

> I have done considerable work with gifted and talented programs and have worked with individuals around the country. The thing that bothers me greatly is that they tend to look at music achievement rather than music potential. There is ample research to indicate that around 50 percent of the students in public schools with high aptitudes—those in the top 20 percent (composite scores 80 percent and above)—never participate in school music programs. The great majority of them never demonstrate any achievement whatsoever in music because they have not had the opportunity or teachers have never recognized it in them. Now, there are, of course, students with extremely low music aptitude demonstrating some achievement in music, but that is more of a cognitive skill. They can read music, they can memorize terms, or they can learn the part-writing skills of theory. The tragic thing that I see in the identification of students with high music aptitude, or music potential, is that aptitude, for all intents and purposes, is neglected. . . . Aptitude is quite different from achievement. When you are working with the identification of gifted and talented students, you have to take *both* factors into consideration.[20]

Can musical talent be described as music aptitude? To a music psychologist, the ability to sense and discriminate sound is the core element of musical talent. It is where talent begins. These elemental capacities are inherent and can be measured to unveil potential talent from the start. This measurement is one of the only ways to objectively assess musical potential prior to training, when the many variables associated with musical achievement impact accurate measurement. The music psychologist believes the "spark" begins with music aptitude.

Musical Talent as Music Aptitude:
Arguments For and Against

For: Common sense tells us that musical talent relies on the ability to sense sound with discrimination. Music aptitude is, in essence, that very discriminative ability. The scientific study of music aptitude is impressive and well documented. Therefore, use of an objective test to measure the sensory components of music aptitude equally makes sense.

- *Testing for music aptitude in private instruction:* Many private music teachers use an informal assessment of listening skills in the initial interview of a new student. Activities might include simple echo-clapping, rhythm games, and pitch matching. The administration of a short music aptitude test, appropriate to the age of the child, can give a richer profile of musical potential prior to instruction.
- *Testing for music aptitude in school music programs:* School music specialists teach large numbers of students and do not have the time to individually assess the musical potential of each student in class. Overall test results provide a musical aptitude profile of the total student body, indicating students who can profit from enrolling in music classes. Testing can also highlight students with exceptionally high aptitude, offering differentiated curricula to challenge their listening skills and musical potential. Test results may surprisingly unveil musical potential in students who do not demonstrate this talent through performance abilities in the classroom.
- *Testing for the identification of musical talent:* Formal school identification and specialized programing for students who are gifted and talented in the arts is growing steadily in the United States. Stringent guidelines for gifted identification in academic areas call for multiple procedures that include objective testing measures. If we follow similar guidelines in musical talent identification, a music aptitude test can offer the same type of objective measure as part of the identification process. Identification as early as the preschool or primary years affords the opportunity for music aptitude development prior to stabilization at age nine or ten.

Against: The arguments against using music aptitude testing as a determinant of musical talent rests with the idea of testing and the test contents rather than the concept of music aptitude as a key element of musical talent.

- *Music aptitude is greater than the sum of the tests:* The critics of Seashore believed music aptitude can not be tested through isolated listening to short, atomistic comparisons of sound. Aural discrimination or music aptitude relies on listening to a contextual mesh of sounds. Tests measure discriminatory factors, but not the real-world functioning ear of a musician.

- *Music aptitude can be determined without the tests:* Music teachers can assess the listening perception of students through musical activities rather than testing. Simple echo-singing and clapping games can highlight students who are weak or strong in basic pitch and rhythmic sensing. Activities that call for critical listening for musical elements will unveil students with a keen ear for details. Astute observation and assessment by a music specialist is the best way to identify potential musical talent.

- *Testing can be dangerous:* The idea of testing within the arts is problematic at best. The musician deals with interpretive and subjective reasoning on a daily basis. Objective testing works against the grain of this musical nature. Test results can be misused to jeopardize already threatened school music programs. School administrators may choose to eliminate music programs if a majority of students show low music aptitude. Music aptitude does not equate to music achievement; yet the fear of misreading the tests may be at the heart of their limited use. Test scores definitely raise red flags.

My view: As I synthesized ideas from the reams of resources and studies concerning music aptitude, I came away with the sense that basically everyone is in agreement about the underlying principles of music aptitude. In essence, *music aptitude is the ability to listen carefully and discriminate sounds.*

As a teacher, I have recognized the keen ear of a young child intrigued with the sound of a particular instrument playing beneath the melody in a listening lesson. I have seen children zap out computer ear training exercises, quickly tackling listening tasks similar to those found on music aptitude tests. There are those sensitive students who can aesthetically recognize and produce sounds that are round, sharp, opaque, or crystalline. All of these students show *perceptual awareness* of sound. Would they necessarily score high within the constraints of a music aptitude test?

As a musician, I understand the questions raised about the need to test for music aptitude. The real world of music-making requires discrimination of sounds within a context and structure. The ability to recognize differences in two finite pitches does not equate to the recognition of these pitches and their musical intent within a musical phrase. Rhythmic differences in isolated test examples do not equal the awareness of rhythmic pattern repetition while listening to music.

So where do I stand on the debate whether "to test or not to test"? I now assume the role of seeker of potential musical talent. The scientific development of music aptitude tests is impressive, with an array of tests available for the full gamut of grade levels and ages. It makes sense to utilize these tests as an available objective measure in school talent identification. Testing provides us with a valuable tool to uncover students with musical potential in school environments where they may not have the advantage of someone observing and guiding them through instructional tasks that highlight their keen ear. It makes sense to administer these tests prior to the age of nine, the earlier the better. As in all areas of gifted and talent identification, testing is only *one* part of the process, with observation and performance assessment completing the student talent profile. This identification process is explained fully in part II.

It is imperative that a clear explanation of exactly *what* the test measures is given and is understood by all concerned—students, administrators, teachers, and parents. Music aptitude tests measure *listening discrimination*. The tests do not determine performance capabilities, music achievement, or the strength or weakness of a school music program. The tests should not be used to eliminate students from a music program. They are useful tools to discover hidden potential listening talent.

The field of music education recognizes the need to seek out differentiated curricula for talented music students. The rationale behind talent identification is to provide curricular challenges for musically talented students, *in addition to* providing a full music curriculum for all students. Perhaps the rise in state recommendations to include the arts in talent identification and the development of successful programs for musically talented students *in conjunction with* a comprehensive school music program can satisfy those who question talent identification and testing in music education.

To me, music aptitude definitely plays a central role in musical talent. In simplest terms, the talented musician *listens carefully*.

Your view: These questions offer ways to begin reflection on ideas about music aptitude and how it relates to musical talent.

1. What is unique about the sensing of sound?
2. How is aural imagery different from visual imagery? How is it the same?
3. What are different ways, aside from testing, that might allow us to recognize a child who has a "fine-tuned" ear?
4. What are your thoughts, both positive and negative, about music aptitude testing?

5. If you were the music supervisor in a school system, would you advice music aptitude testing for the total school population? Why or why not?
6. If you were a gifted coordinator assigned to identify musical talent with music aptitude testing as your objective measure, what grade levels would you choose to target for this identification? Why?

Your reflections:

TALENT AS MUSICAL INTELLIGENCE

Intelligence is musical when its background is a storehouse of musical knowledge, a dynamo of musical interest, an outlet in musical tasks, and a warmth of musical experiences and responses. . . . The great musician, composer, conductor has the power of sustained thought, a great store of organized information, and the ability to elaborate and control their creative work at a high intellectual level.

Carl Seashore, *Psychology of Music*

Jake was enjoying his first few months of piano lessons and eager to make musical connections with all he was learning. At his last lesson, he learned the pattern of whole steps and half steps of a major scale, discovering the joy of playing his first black key in the G major scale. The teacher was hesitant to venture farther than C major and G major during that first introduction to scale structure. Jake couldn't wait to share the discovery he had made "all by himself" during his week of piano exploration.

He began his journey from the bottom C of the keyboard. He played the scale he had learned last week, jumping up five keys to G and playing that scale. Then with a wry smile, he ventured five more keys up to D, A, E, B, and so on, playing each discovered scale with imaginative fingering but accurate notes! Jake had discovered the basic scale relationship of the "circle of fifths" on his own.

Jake's curiosity and ability to find and solve a musical problem exemplifies a student who demonstrates *musical intelligence*. This term describes the process of developmental learning through music, which distinguishes it from music aptitude, which is based primarily on natural musical capacities.

The concept of musical intelligence most likely dates back to the early Chinese and Greek theories of music and most decidedly is included in the texts of Carl Seashore. The renaissance of the term can be credited to Howard Gardner, a leading cognitive psychologist at the Graduate School of Education of Harvard University, who included musical intelligence as one of seven multiple intelligences in *Frames of Mind: The Theory of Multiple Intelligences* (1983). The publication of Gardner's theory broadened the concept of intelligence from a single factor of general intelligence, or "g," to seven separate intelligences, each unique to a specific domain.

Actually, the idea of multiple intelligences is not new or novel. J. P. Guilford's *Structure of Intellect* (1959, 1967) includes over 120 different ways of knowing. Tests and curricular models based on this theory are prevalent in the field of gifted education.[1] Robert Sternberg's book *Beyond IQ: A Triarchic Theory of Human Intelligence*, published a few years after Gardner's theory, includes three basic thinking processes—*analytic, creative,* and *practical*—with the testing of this triarchic theory in development.[2]

Of these intelligence theories, Gardner's multiple intelligence (MI) theory has gained the most recognition from the general public. The attention given to the theory has allowed the idea of musical intelligence to extend to an audience well beyond the specialized field of music psychology. Through MI theory, educators, administrators, and the general public are beginning to realize that musicians have a unique way of knowing.

The MI theory originally included seven intelligences: logical-mathematical, verbal, spatial, bodily-kinesthetic, intrapersonal, interpersonal, and *musical.* An eighth, natural intelligence, has been added in recent years, with others sure to follow. Gardner's goal was to broaden the concept of intelligences beyond the logical and linguistic boundaries that are recognized and tested in education.

Gardner's theory is based on extensive studies of prodigies, gifted individuals, brain-damaged patients, savants, normal children and adults, experts in different fields, and people from different cultures. Bringing together evidence from this body of research, Gardner developed a theory that shows the existence of multiple forms of intelligence. He explains that "in ordinary life these intelligences typically work in harmony, and so their autonomy may be invisible. But when the appropriate observational lenses are donned, the peculiar nature of each intelligence emerges with sufficient (and often surprising) clarity."[3]

Musical intelligence is the earliest to emerge, as is noted in the prenatal and infant research discussed in chapter 2. Infants recognize sounds and music before they recognize the core properties of speech. The sensory components of musical intelligence mirror the components of music aptitude. Gardner acknowledges these definitive basics without expanding on their description in his chapter on musical intelligence. He presents musical intelligence through the description of musical functioning in unique ways and does not make a detailed examination of the perceptive/cognitive functioning of the intelligence.

According to Gardner, the creative process of composers includes a unique form of perceptive/cognitive functioning. Gardner's brain research accounts for localization of musical skill in the brain, with outstanding music ability possible in autistic children and with "amusia," the loss of musical ability, occurring in patients with brain damage. (The composer Ravel was struck with amusia toward the end of his life.) Musical development described in biographic studies shows clear cases of child prodigies and persons who excel in musical skill and creativity in different cultures.

Gardner also contends that musical intelligence extends beyond purely aural sensory capacities. "One central aspect of music—rhythmic organization—can exist apart from the auditory realization," allowing deaf persons an entry point to musical experiences.[4]

Years after first reading *Frames of Mind*, I had a personal experience that crystallized this idea. I was sitting in the empty, luxurious Musikverein in Vienna, Austria. On stage was Evelyn Glennie, a Scottish percussion soloist, who was touring with the National Symphony Orchestra. She was warming up, "trying out the hall" to check instruments and acoustics prior to a rehearsal and concert. It was simply Evelyn and me, in this vacant concert hall whose acoustics are one of the best in the world. I was fascinated as I observed her intricacy of movement and the subtlety of her touch awareness in handling brushes and beaters on the vast array of percussion instruments before her. She moved fluidly from one to the other, bare feet firmly on the wooden concert hall floor. I sat mesmerized by Ms. Glennie, the crystal and gold surroundings, and wondrous sounds. A few hours later, the audience was equally carried away during the concert performance. If you did not know, you would never suspect that Ms. Glennie, an amazingly talented musician, is also deaf.

Educational Research in Musical Intelligence

The Graduate School of Education at Harvard conducted years of research, through Project Zero, that focused on the cognitive process of learning and understanding, based on the concept of multiple ways of knowing. Research interest focused on the *process* of learning within and across intelligences rather than the psychometric measurement of the basic capacities within individual intelligences.

Education based on MI theory substantially transforms the traditional school curriculum and classroom environment. Rather than gathering a string of student test scores and grades as a record of achievement, students create portfolios of developing work, evaluated by their teacher and themselves. Teachers assess the performance of students engaged in problem-solving activities within an intelligence-specific domain. Classrooms become museum-like exploratory spaces, with apprentice "pods" where students of different ages work together in a topic area. The community plays a significant role in the school, with children researching their individualized projects beyond school walls and community resource people sharing their expertise with students in the classroom.

The underlying purpose of this change to an individual-centered form of education reflects the MI theory that unique ways of knowing can be realized, beyond the traditional mathematical-logical and linguistic intelligences. Gardner and David Perkins, codirectors of Project Zero, essentially are seeking an education based on rich conceptual understanding.

> Whereas short-answer tests and oral responses in classes can provide clues to student understanding, it is generally necessary to look more deeply if one desires firm evidence that understandings of significance have been obtained. For these purposes, new and unfamiliar problems, followed by open-ended clinical interviews or careful observations, provide the best way of establishing the degree of understanding that students have attained.[5]

Preschool Musical Intelligence Research

An examination of some of the procedures used in music may help clarify how musical intelligence is assessed in an MI classroom. Beginning with preschool, the music assessment procedure for Harvard's Project Spectrum research is as follows. To assess singing ability, a student and teacher meet in a one-to-one setting, and the student sings three different songs: a favorite (the student's choice), "Happy Birthday," and a song that was taught to the class several days earlier. Each child is audiotaped while singing. The teacher later assesses the first and third songs informally and evaluates the performance of "Happy Birthday" with a scoring sheet measuring pitch and note accuracy, phrase by phrase. The third song assesses a student's tonal memory of a song learned earlier.

The assessment also includes five listening activities, which include recognition of a well-known tune (Name That Tune approach), listening for errors, and some pitch-matching games using Montessori bells, which look identical but have different pitches.[6]

I am quite sure any music teacher reading this procedure would agree that it provides a comprehensive and individualized assessment of musical capabilities. The procedure requires a teacher who has knowledge of the developmental musical abilities of children of this age, whose performance ability to sing accurately in pitch is limited. The teachers also must have the listening perceptive ability to determine pitch and rhythmic accuracy themselves. These activities assess listening discrimination along with developing singing performance abilities.

SPARKLER EXPERIENCE: Assessing Preschool Musical Intelligence

This activity is similar to the preschool assessment procedure described here, basically seeing how a young child can sing in tune, listen carefully, and recognize wrong notes in a well-known tune. You will need some type of musical instrument and be able to pick out the tune "Mary Had a Little Lamb" on an available instrument. You may tape this activity if you want to assess the child's abilities more carefully, or you may simply assess informally as you share this one-on-one musical experience.

1. Begin the activity with a "pretend" birthday party, complete with a little cake and candles. Coax the child to sing "Happy Birthday" with you as you sing softly. Listen carefully to see if the child conquers the "stretched" intervals on "to you" and the big stretch on "Happy birthday dear —."

2. Have the child sing a favorite song learned from a CD, tape, TV show, or elsewhere. Again, listen for pitches that extend beyond simple steps up and down to see if the child's range is wider than five or six pitches. How many pitches seemed "out of tune" to you?

3. Ask how quickly the child can recognize a well-known tune (Name That Tune). As you play "Mary Had a Little Lamb" fairly slowly, see how many notes you play before the child recognizes the tune.

4. Now ask the child to raise a hand when there are wrong notes in the tune. Play "Mary Had a Little Lamb" several times, with a wrong note in some performances and correctly at least once. Did the child hear the wrong notes?

Students who show strong evidence of musical intelligence are taught a more difficult song. The song included in the Project Spectrum assessment book leaps an octave at the outset, shifts from major to minor and back again, and has dotted syncopated rhythms and sixteenth-eighth note patterns. Again, readers who are experienced working musically with tiny tots realize that singing "Happy Birthday" poses a pitch accuracy challenge, let alone a song with this rhythmic and tonal structure. Students who receive high assessment scores in these activities at this age clearly demonstrate high musical intelligence.

Musical Intelligence in the MI School

The MI elementary classroom emphasizes learning situations that require students to work through problem-solving activities to encourage conceptual understanding rather than rote learning of factual material. Jake's exploration of his newly learned scales exemplifies this type of discovery process of learning. Scripps and Davidson, leading researchers on musical learning in MI theory, emphasize the importance of this cognitive-developmental perspective.[7]

> The cognitive-developmental model places the highest value on the interactions of the individual within the environment. Instructional environments purposefully place the child in situations of conflict. Learning occurs with the development of problem-solving strategies required for resolving cognitive conflicts in the environment. We see the child solving musical problems through inventive means. For the cognitive-developmentalist, learning results in active change in patterns of thinking which unfold with cognitive development.[8]

A music classroom with this cognitive approach reflects an exploratory student project orientation. Rather than starting with rote learning of "Every Good Boy Deserves Fudge" and simple metric rhythm notation in grade 1, students might explore ways to create compositions and devise their own symbol system to explain them in some figural way. These *figural* representations allow students to communicate their understanding of what they hear and sing in a unique way. The *formal* representation of metric structure and score notation would follow this inventive phase of learning.

MI musical skill development encourages multiple approaches to musical learning, shifting between *production*—making music through performance, improvisation, composing; *perception*—discriminative listening; and *reflection*—thinking critically about the process of musical work. An MI music classroom would meld technical skill development on an instrument with perceptive listening for errors and details. Students would combine reading music as they play on their instruments with sightsinging and internalized realization of notes on the page. A classroom would include computers for creative composition projects. Experience in ear training and dictation of music would be commonplace. The clear emphasis is on developing a broad process of learning across different dimensions to develop richer musical understanding.

This exploratory approach to accommodate individualized MI learning is reasonable to imagine in a preschool or elementary setting. Adapting MI theory to the traditional secondary music performance class may be a bit more challenging. Harvard researchers worked with the Pittsburgh Public Schools for five years through Arts PROPEL, devising instructional strategies en-

---

SPARKLER EXPERIENCE: Inventing Your Own Music Notation

This activity reflects the exploratory learning encouraged by MI theory. As you work through the activity, reflect on *how* you are working, revising, and learning. I encourage musicians, music educators, and notation-comfortable students to take the challenge of using "free notation" rather than placing notes on a staff in this exercise. This will allow you to experience a *figural* representation of melody shape rather than the *formal* notation of a score. You will need a pencil and blank piece of paper. We begin, once again, with a familiar tune.

1. Sing "Mary Had a Little Lamb" internally at least three times. As you "listen" to internal sounds, be aware of how the melody moves up and down. Now sing the song out loud at least three times. Notate the melody in *any* way you like to show its shape. Shift from external singing to internal sensing of sound as you work through your melody mapping. You may use words, lines, dashes, graphing, whatever you want.

   When you finish, check your work by following along each mark of your notation with fingertip or pencil point as you sing or internalize sounds. Did you accurately describe the contour of the melody?

2. For a more difficult notation challenge, try singing *Happy Birthday* "inside and outside," again notating the contour of your melody as you re-sing and rework your ideas. Notice the complexity of this melody versus the first one. Does your notation of the song show the first and last note on the same pitch or on different pitches? Compare with your answer to the Sparkler Experience completed in chapter 2.

couraging musical and artistic reasoning through portfolio development, journal reflections, and different types of *domain projects*.

Domain projects emphasized student involvement in learning through rehearsal critiques, peer lessons, creative music notation, and reflective journaling. Again the curriculum emphasized learning in a weaving manner through production, perception, and reflection. Students actively took a role in realizing how to improve performance after listening to rehearsal tapes, giving lessons, and critiquing their peers and in self-assessment of their own progress on their instrument.

SPARKLER EXPERIENCE: From Figural to Formal Notation

Those comfortable with score notation may want to try this follow-up exercise as a pseudo-experiment:

From your figural mapping of "Happy Birthday," write it on a music staff in the key of C major. Rework and sing it internally *before* you play it on an instrument. After you have completed your notation, play on an instrument or a keyboard. Did you notate the song correctly and "pass the experiment?"

The Arts PROPEL curriculum assumes that "the pursuit of learning in music is worthwhile for all students, not only for those with special talent." This again reflects the basic philosophy of music education for all and again includes an inferred warning to administrators concerning "talent."[9]

Davidson and Scripp's experiments with the same types of activity as in this Sparkler Experience found that the notation of simple songs by untrained eight-year-olds looks very much like those of teenagers and adults. Notational development seems to reach a plateau around the age of seven or eight. Of interest and some concern, they also discovered that musically trained teenagers who notated what they internalized as "Happy Birthday" on a musical staff consistently wrote it incorrectly even though they sang it correctly.[10]

Musical Intelligence and Musical Talent

Jeanne Bamberger, of the Massachusetts Institute of Technology, has researched musical learning including the cognitive functioning of musically talented students, for over 20 years. Her studies show that the musical mind does not function in a linguistic or logical-mathematical way and does not follow the developmental stages of Piaget. Musical thinking requires a shift between different representations of a musical task (performing, reading a score, listening), and talented students are more adept in this cognitive/perceptive shift.

> I argue that the changing mental organizing structures that guide hearings, constructions, and descriptions at various ages and stages of musical development do not constitute a unidirectional progression in which earlier mental structures are replaced by later ones. Rather, foci of attention among relevant aspects of musical structure shift but also cumulatively build on one another. I conclude that the goal of musical development is to have access to multiple dimensions of musical structure, to be able to coordinate these dimensions, and most important, to be able to choose selectively among them, to change focus at will.[11]

Bamberger's studies show that musically talented students naturally shift from one focus to another in solving musical tasks, a process similar to the dimensional shift described in the MI theory teaching strategies. Nurturing a learning environment where students work through multiple approaches in music-making will help develop musical intelligence.

Seeking a personal viewpoint from a musician working in the field of cognitive psychology and education, I interviewed Lyle Davidson on his perspective of musical talent as observed through Project Zero research. He acknowledged the need to identify the "raw capacities and biological givens" that emanate from a young child who "shows a propensity for the material of a specific domain." He believes a music aptitude test "can target these specific subskills, but it doesn't get at all at talent. It just gets at the biological necessities."

As we discussed different personality traits, such as concentration, problem-solving skills, and the importance of reflection in learning, he suddenly remembered a vivid experience he had while doing research in China.

> So you have fifty students (age three or four) in a line, singing and dancing . . . doing songs, and essentially dances. You see that number of students in a classroom, and they are all performing the same movements. They are all singing the same songs. But you realize very quickly that there are these three that have very special qualities. It generally has to do with presence—you know what I mean? I mean, they command your attention. You *cannot* not look at them. You *cannot* not see them. It is not that they are acting out, waving their arms, or attracting attention. It's just that they have a command over the sounds, over the shaping of the whole, that is extraordinary compared with the other 47 kids.[12]

The cognitive psychologist finds fascination in examining "the spark" in the context of how a child learns in the environment rather than how components of "the spark" can be measured. The young child in China is working through the medium of music and showing "the capacity to shape meaning—to take this material, project it, shape it in a way, and create a whole statement."[13] Musical talent, to a cognitive psychologist, emanates in the *creative functioning of a student engaged in musical tasks.*

Educational Realities

Schools across the United States are developing curricula based on MI theory at a quick pace. Presumably this means that instruction for the development of musical intelligence will be included in the core curriculum of schools. This is a good thing—a time for music programs to grow and prosper, for musical talent to be recognized and nurtured. It sounds ideal.

The MI approach described in this chapter involves an intensive educational environment that draws on all aspects of musical knowing. Students learn the skills of a performer, astute listener, critic, and composer. Assessment of learning relies on teachers who can evaluate pitch accuracy, analyze creative notation of melody and rhythms, and observe subtle signs of musical perceptual understanding in the classroom. Clearly, this requires a well-trained music specialist and a substantial reorganization of the music classroom and traditional performance-oriented curriculum.

The reality of this surge to reorganize curriculum to include all of the multiple intelligences is less than ideal, especially for the intelligences functioning in artistic domains. As in any major shift in educational structuring, there are growing pains, and the proliferating "cookbook approach" curricula for the multiple intelligences do not reflect the depth of cognitive understanding at the heart of MI research.

In essence, the responsibility of teaching across all seven domains of intelligence rests on the elementary classroom teacher. Students explore activities across the intelligences, and, ideally, those who show strengths in particular intelligence areas can receive differentiated instruction to nurture these strengths. Music, drama, dance, and art are brought into the academic classroom and often integrated into academic subject areas. For schools with minimal or nonexistent music and art programs, this integrated exposure to the arts may be the sole basis of student artistic learning. More often than not, the elementary classroom teacher feels ill equipped and intimidated in teaching the arts; the result is a surface level approach that brings in artistic ideas to make academic learning "fun."

For schools fortunate enough to have a thriving music program, music specialists can assist in melding meaningful artistic experiences with academic content. This interdisciplinary approach is included in several of the music content standards in *National Standards for Arts Education*.[14] It requires extra research and planning time when music teachers are physically in the building. Most elementary music teachers travel from school to school with too many students and no extra time. If the role of music becomes only one of assisting academic subjects, the comprehensive music program suffers. Pragmatically, some substantial scheduling and organizational restructuring is needed to effectively bring an MI approach, with its musical intelligence component, into a school.

The goal of conceptual understanding across the multiple intelligences is formidable. Oversimplification of the theory has resulted in some disastrous educational misinterpretations. Careful investigation of a number of MI curricular packages and activity kits reveals that they supposedly bring "musical intelligence" into the classroom through the use of rap rhythms to help learn spelling words and playing background music as a way to relax students as they do written work or read. Music is essentially a peripheral gimmick or mood set. Neither use fosters perceptive listening or productive learning through the musical domain. In fact, students who have keen ears will have problems trying to read or do written work because they may actually be listening to that background music!

The field of gifted education, long a trying ground for new approaches to learning, has adopted MI theory in many gifted programs. MI classroom teachers are learning to recognize students who show outstanding behavior in the musical and artistic activities now included in their day-to-day curriculum. Gifted specialists are investigating ways to effectively challenge students who think and perceive artistically. Formal identification procedures for students talented in music and art are slowly emerging across the country.

The independent student approach of MI reflects the needs of musically talented students. As this educational trend grows, music programs that are securely in place can provide a comprehensive music curriculum that includes differentiated challenges for talented students. This MI trend may also convince schools to include music as a basic part of the core curriculum, which is the essential goal of music education.

Musical Talent as Musical Intelligence: Arguments For and Against

For: Any musician who has played an instrument, listened critically to music, or creatively manipulated sound through composition or improvisation realizes that there is something unique about musical "knowing." A quote by Copland puts it quite simply:

> Music may express a state of meaning for which there exists no adequate word in any language. In that case, musicians often like to say that it has only purely musical meaning. . . . What they really mean is that no appropriate word can express it, and even if it could, they do not feel the need of finding it.[15]

Musical intelligence nurtures the *understanding* of this musical meaning. What are some ways that musical intelligence positively describes the spark of musical talent?

- *Musical intelligence realizes the breadth of musical knowing:* The emphasis of learning through multiple approaches in music fosters recognition of musical talents beyond technical performance. The instructional focus on critical listening and student projects may unveil talented perceivers of sound. These students may be future critics or musicologists rather than performers.
- *Musical intelligence emanates in the process of musical learning:* So often we recognize musical talent through a performance product in an audition rather than through the observation of the process of developing musical work. The assessment process central to the MI theory evaluates how well students understand what they are hearing, performing, and creating during the revision of musical work.
- *The MI theory will recognize more students who show musical potential:* MI-oriented classrooms will have musical activities in the elementary classroom, where teachers who work with students on a daily basis can recognize students with potential talent. If schools have music specialists, these elementary teachers can be trained to assist the music specialist in seeking out these students and spearheading specialized programs for these promising students.

Against: Arguments against the concept of musical intelligence as musical talent may rest on pragmatic matters concerning implementation of the MI theory in music rather than the theoretical basis of musical intelligence.

- *The MI curricular approach is not pragmatically feasible:* The MI curriculum was developed in schools with research grant support and experts in educational research assisting with assessment and organization. The specialized training required for effective assessment and costly reorganization of existing school programs cannot be feasibly generalized. The one-on-one assessment procedures and extra time required to evaluate student tapes, portfolios, and projects is prohibitively unrealistic.
- *An MI curriculum will weaken existing music programs:* The new role of music specialist may involve assisting the academic classroom teacher

rather than providing a comprehensive, free-standing music program. Music will exist as a means of enriching academic areas rather than as a substantial part of the school curriculum. The interdisciplinary nature of the curriculum will not provide enough time to work on specific training of musical skills. This skill development is essential for all students to truly experience the perceptive/cognitive functioning within musical intelligence.

- *Musical intelligence is nothing new. Music teachers have been nurturing its development in its traditional curriculum. No need for change:* The concept of musical intelligence has essentially been around for easily over a century. Music educators and music psychologists have been developing effective curricular approaches equally long. General music classes in elementary schools present a wide spectrum of musical activities similar to those in the MI approach. It seems illogical for music students to spend their time writing in journals and looking at videotapes in a music class. Students elect to take band, orchestra, and choir because they love to perform. Let them perform and learn through the language of music.

My view: My copy of *Frames of Mind* looks rather tattered at this point, resting within my reach for easy reference. When it was first published, I eagerly read and examined the chapter on musical intelligence, seeking some solid guidance in describing "the spark." Gardner's ambiguous description of musical intelligence did not inhibit my excitement at knowing that, finally, educators would sit up and take notice of the importance of musical learning in school. Musical intelligence would be recognized and nurtured in our schools.

Interviews with researchers who were actively involved in Arts PROPEL spurred my interest further. Here was an exciting new way of approaching musical instruction that expanded individualized learning, listening perception, and creative music-making. The teachers involved in the study were excited about the engagement of students in their own learning. The instructional approach of MI coincided well with the individualized instructional approaches used in gifted education. It seemed a perfect match.

I firmly believe that musical learning for *all* students requires creative involvement in musical problem-finding and -solving. These tasks allow students to learn how to make their own musical interpretive decisions. I also believe that a performance-oriented classroom should include an opportunity for students to reflect, critique, and listen. Students who love to perform can learn the process of examining and improving their own performance abilities. The musically talented student flourishes in this type of learning environment.

As a musician and teacher of performers, I have worked in classrooms and studios with the traditional music curriculum that predominantly develops performance skills. There is no question that the experience of seeing students learn through listening and the production of sound on an instrument describes the essence of musical intelligence. An excellent teacher can mold a performing group or a private student to produce an outstanding performance. Students revel in the experience of this type of performance.

The MI approach does not take away from this performance experience but enrichens it by allowing students to become aware of the breadth of what is happening in the process of developing this performance. Students play a larger role in musical decision-making. The more a student can assess the intricacies of his or her own playing, constructively critique the musical work of peers, and internalize musical ideas from the score, the more this student understands the performance experience. Teachers who have comfortably been the "master" decision-makers in the process can learn to revel in the experience of providing a guiding scaffold for students as they create personal performance statements through this musical understanding.

The misunderstood and misguided application of the theory into practice has resulted in curricula that obviously have nothing to do with the MI theory. Every child does not need to learn map-reading using all eight intelligences. Shuffling spelling word cards is not an appropriate bodily-kinesthetic learning experience. Further development is needed of effective ways to generalize the curricular ideas from MI theory research to make possible the depth of learning the theory proposes. Artistic intelligences can be effectively integrated into the academic classroom to enrich learning, but this should not be at the cost of eliminating music or art programs. Interdisciplinary learning that links music and academic areas gives talented students rich possibilities for individualized challenge that reflects the cognitive-developmental approach to education.

The idea of talent as musical intelligence does not give us a list of descriptive components to measure. Instead it allows us to realize how potential talent can be successfully developed. *Musical intelligence nurtures musical understanding.*

Your view: You may wish to ponder the following questions and pose a few of your own.

1. How are music aptitude and musical intelligence the same? How are they different?
2. What curricular ideas developed through MI research would be feasible in performance-oriented classes and studios?

3. What was the particular cognitive/perceptive "map" you used in the process of completing the notation Sparkler Experiences in this chapter? Refer to your notation and reflect a bit—how were you thinking?
4. MI curricular approaches include "reflection" within the learning process. A musical performer is decidedly a "doer." What value (if any) does reflection play in the role of a student performer?
5. What are the positives and negatives of integrating music and the arts into the academic classroom?

Your reflections:

TALENT AS PERFORMANCE

If music be the food of love,
play on.

William Shakespeare,
Twelfth Night

The lovely student pianist was bowing graciously to an appreciative audience of music teachers from across the country. She was the junior high winner of a national competition, and her exquisite playing and careful training was apparent. Her performance was no surprise. It was polished and well prepared.

As we rustled our programs, searching for the next performer's name, the junior high cellist awkwardly stepped on stage, tried to adjust the chair and struggled with an endpin that seemed to enjoy sliding rather than sticking to the floor. After a few uncomfortable moments, she nodded to her accompanist and began to play.

This performance was a captivating surprise. From the first notes, the audience was caught up in the enthusiasm, excitement, and connection she made with her cello and the music. As she finished, with a flourished release of the bow, the audience spontaneously rose to its feet, shouting "Bravo." This young teenager, with the simple cotton dress and awkward entrance, stood transfixed. She looked around at her fellow competition winners to see them on their feet as well. She turned, bowed slightly, and gave a shy smile of appreciation.

A musician communicates through performance. The recognition of musical talent through performance makes common sense to anyone who is a musician or teacher of musicians. Music aptitude may measure musical potential, but musical talent is realized through performance. We hear it. Musi-

41

cal talent blends the inborn perceptive capacities of the individual with the physical ability to perform with personal interpretation. Quite simply, a musician or music teacher believes that you can determine talent if you just listen to the student play.

In fact, the assessment of musical talent by listening to a performance isn't quite that simple. It poses a number of problems because of its inherently subjective nature. Performance is a process as well as a product. It is phenomenological. The opening performance of the young cellist was captivating. Why? It could have been the audience's surprise at hearing a brilliant performance from a student who outwardly didn't have the trappings of a seasoned competition winner. It could have been the novelty of an unknown, flashy piece. Or it could have been the recognition of the musical talent in a young teenage musician.

When a performance captures you, when you *cannot* not notice it, you experience what I call the *dynamic of performance*. Musical performance is a phenomenological experience between the performer and listener. The musician communicates a personal interpretation through the medium of music to a listener. As the listener hears and experiences the performance, the interpretive process is shared. The mutual aesthetic experience of listener and performer creates the dynamic of performance. It is, obviously, a very subjective experience, dependent on the listener's unique tastes, listening acuity, contextual setting, and personal idea of what constitutes talent in music.

In a typical audition setting, a group of three judges sits behind a table and listens to students who perform pieces they have prepared for performance. The judges arrive at the table with predetermined personal criteria of excellence in performance and musical talent. A well-seasoned ear can quickly pick out different characteristics of a student's performance style:

- *Intellectually clean:* the meticulous student—accurate notes, technique well in hand, knowledgeable in stylistic details.
- *Musically sensitive:* the naturally expressive student—conveys a unique interpretation that intuitively shows understanding of style and mood.
- *Technically flamboyant:* the student who plays with technical proficiency and stylistic flamboyance.
- *Creatively inventive:* the creative student who can improvise showing complexity of musical understanding.[1]

All of these students communicate through different performance styles. Judges may dynamically connect with a student whose style they prefer. Which student is musically talented? Are they all musically talented? Does musical talent require all of these qualities?

The most common procedure for selecting students for specialized programs in music is through an audition setting like this. How can we identify the student with minimal formal training who shows musical potential? What criteria should be used for different performance genres such as rock, country, or jazz? How do we assess the first signs of potential talent in young children? Can we assess performance in a less threatening setting? Many questions arise when one is asked to assess talent through musical performance. Chapter 11 expands on this topic, detailing problems and providing recommendations to improve the process of performance assessment. For now, it will be useful simply to ponder these questions as the performance perspective of talent is introduced in this chapter.

Nurturing Performance Talent

A majority of performing musicians and music teachers probably agree that musical talent evolves from training and development. The basic sensory capacities are inherent, but musical talent is developmental rather than a "gift." In the nature-nurture debate over the substance of musical talent, those involved in music education or performance would pose a strong argument for the "nurturing" of talent. A student may have a high music aptitude, but the development of musical talent relies on student commitment, physical capabilities, and teacher guidance.

In the field of cognitive musical psychology, John Sloboda's scientific inquiry into the development of musical ability and performance is comparable to Seashore and Gordon's examination of music aptitude. *The Musical Mind: the Cognitive Psychology of Music* (1985) synthesizes psychological studies of musical perception with explanations of the perceptive/cognitive functioning of a musician's mind and the physical behavior of performance. Sloboda's perspective is clearly that of a performing musician, interested in the examination of *expertise* in performance and the development of musical excellence. Rather than examining what is usual or average in musical development, Sloboda seeks answers to what possibilities lie at the upper end of the spectrum.

Sloboda's cognitive-developmental approach reflects ideas similar to the studies of Davidson and Scripps in the multiple intelligences. They share the belief that talent is not an innate "gift" but develops from environmental influences and stimulation. They both focus research on the perceptive/cognitive functioning of the musical mind. Their differences lie in the population and focus of their studies. MI research examines the general population of students in a school setting. Sloboda's studies center on exceptional students and expert performers who are receiving individualized training through private instruction or specialized music schools or are professional musicians. His focus is on the cognitive/perceptive functioning of individuals whose performance is considerably above average and who show high levels of achievement.

Sloboda and his research colleagues, Michael Howe and Jane Davidson, argue that there exists a "folk psychology of talent" that believes in innately determined differences in people's capacity for musical accomplishment and in genetically programed superiority in musical abilities. This breeds an acceptance of a low general level of musical accomplishment in schools in the United States and the United Kingdom, compared to skills learned in the school's core curriculum. Their studies seek to dispel the notion that only talented students can excel in musical achievement.

> According to the folk psychology account, few people become expert musical performers because few people have the necessary talent. This folk psychology is evident in the structures and rhetoric of the music conservatories and in the beliefs of people involved in schools.[2]

In a recent survey by Davis (1994), over 75 percent of a sample of professionals in the field of education believed that composing, singing, and playing an instrument required a special gift or natural talent. Forty percent of the same sample indicated that playing chess, performing surgery, writing nonfiction, and *orchestral conducting* did not require natural talent.[3]

Sloboda and Howe conducted interview studies of 42 talented teenage musicians, discovering details of their background and musical development.[4] Their study was similar to Sosniak's interview study of 21 concert pianists.[5] Findings from these studies support the idea of environmental influence versus genetic predetermination of talent. Both studies indicated that few of the individuals showed very early signs of exceptional musical talent or prodigy characteristics. Both also showed that a majority of parents did not have a musical background. However, there was considerable parental encouragement and support throughout the musical development of the subjects in both studies. Musical talent and expertise grew developmentally from commitment, individualized instruction, and lots of practice. (Part III fully explores these studies in discussions of the different stages of talent development.)

Expertise Performance

Sloboda's studies of expertise performance provide a rich analysis of the workings of the musician's mind in the process of musical decision-making. He describes performance along two broad dimensions—technical and expressive. Technical skills are necessary for performance but result in dull, lifeless performance without expressive skills. A technical performance can be reproduced by a computer. Expressive skills give value to the performance and draw the listener to points of interest in musical structure and nuance. The student performers in our audition scenario showed different performance styles of expressivity.

Sloboda believes that musical performance has a structural basis, is rational, and has intentional expressive variations. He argues against the notion that expressive musicianship, commonly attributed to "talent," is a product of intuitive spontaneity and impossible for persons who do not naturally exhibit this quality in performance. For him, an expressive performance is a product of intentional, interpretive decision-making. It can be taught and can be done by anyone who works through the interpretive process of practice.

Through instruction, listening, and modeling, students learn how to use different physical motions, gestures, or vocal intonation to express emotion through music. Sloboda calls these gestures "ready-made templates onto which musical expression can be mapped."[6]

Each performer chooses parameters of expressive musical decisions that create a distinct performing style. This expressive variation must be large enough to be detected and interpreted by listeners at "an intellectual, aesthetic, or affective level."[7] Practice develops this performance and molds the expressive outcome. It does not "just happen" because of a musical gift.

Expert performers have acquired a large number of "templates" to work with and recognize which ones effectively communicate their musical intentions to the listener. They easily shift across musical dimensions in their interpretive decision-making. When their movements and expressive gestures become immediate through constant practice, they achieve a sense of *automaticity*.

The concept of *automaticity* derives from consistent practice of a skill that leads to a floating sensation—not really thinking of the execution of the skill. You experience this cognitive/kinesthetic phenomenon when you ride a bike or type. In music, continuous practice of a skill makes it immediate after a time. Pianists immediately fall into finger patterns; violinists bow passages without mapping them out. Kogan relates a vivid Juilliard anecdote of pianists practicing their scales while reading the newspaper.[8]

Expressive performance, when it sounds intuitive and spontaneous, has this element of automaticity. Sloboda believes expressive automaticity is present when a performer "has a large repertoire of expressive responses that can be mobilized in performance in response to specific musical structures without overt conscious deliberation."[9] Perhaps the combination of distinct performing style and automaticity is Sloboda's scientific explanation of "the spark."

Expressive Student Performance

These ideas about expert musicians are readily transferable to the interpretive process of the student performer. Young performers arrive at an audition with generalized musical knowledge of certain rules and structural patterns learned through training. Expressive decisions are molded in lessons and practice, through trial and error. The resulting expressive decisions individualize each performance.

Teachers who work through the interpretive process with students easily recognize the student who is naturally adept at creating emotional ideas through sound versus the student who must intellectually develop ideas through instruction. It may be a tiny first grader who creates the mood of a swan gliding through the stream, or a high school violinist immersed in a Paganini caprice. Talented students tend to have a natural creative musicality when making these interpretive decisions. This *creative interpretation*, I believe, creates the dynamic aesthetic of performance. The creative nature of this interpretation is discussed in the next chapter.

How does a student make interpretive decisions? A student might experiment with different dynamic scopes of a crescendo and decrescendo to show expression in a particular phrase. A subtle, gentle mood can be expressed by a narrow scope (pp < mp > pp). A more dramatic mood calls for a larger scope

---

SPARKLER EXPERIENCE: Developing an Expressive Performance

This experience works through the interpretive process of performance using a simple sound structure that includes an aesthetic entrance and exit through silence, elements of development toward a climax, and structural musical syntax. Pairing the awareness of sound with gestures that you find descriptive of these sounds mirrors the process of developing expressiveness in musical performance.

1. *Your "instruments"*: You may use hands or fingers on your lap, a table top, or other surrounding objects. A simple pencil, stick, or other found object may be used. Keep it simple. Musicians: Feel free to enjoy this exercise through improvisation on your instrument.

2. *Your sound score*: Look over the following list of sound pictures. You will move down the list, flowing one idea to the next in your performance. Think of the mood the sound picture sets and express it through your rhythmic sounds, varying volume, speed, and so on. Decide on

➤

Developing an Expressive Performance (*continued*)

effective ways to blend transitions from one picture to the next. You may include silence for dramatic effect.

Sound Collage
  Silence
  Man walking on a lonely street
  Child skipping past and around the corner
  Light rain shower
  Thunderstorm
  Light rain shower
  Child skipping in the distance
  Man walking on a lonely street
  Silence

3. *Practice:* Repeat this sequence of rhythm sounds *a minimum of eight times*. Focus on the sounds you are creating as you work. Revise and refine with each repetition. Experiment with different movements to produce different sounds (your gestural "bag of tricks"). Practice and rehearse until you feel you have created an effective sound statement. You should have the series of sounds in your collage memorized at this point. Avoid checking the book for the next sound picture in the final rehearsal stages.

4. *Performance: Close the book* and perform your sound picture sequence as if you had an audience, or try it out on an interested listener.

5. *Reflection:* Jot down several immediate reactions to the performance experience. Do you feel your interpretation was expressively "dynamic"? What did you learn about musical decision-making in the practice process? What makes musical decision-making unique?

Music Teachers: Expand this activity by having students create their own sound collages. This exercise encourages creative improvisation as well as sound manipulation using found objects. Further expansion can include computer sequencing and manipulation of sampled sounds. Instructional emphasis is on how to express a mood or picture through sound.

(pp < f > pp). Students rework musical ideas until the technical execution of tonal quality combined with dynamics matches what they feel portrays their expressive intent. This process of musical decision-making requires combined inner sensing of sounds and cognitive judgment of the effect this choice would have on a listener. The musically talented student is naturally adept at this internal decision-making, developing interpretations that show a personal connection to the music.

Expressive performance does not necessarily rely on musical training or development. Young children with potential musical talent naturally show initial signs of expressive performance through their "play" and sensitivity or awareness of sounds. They sing recognizable tunes before they are two years old and exhibit expressive rhythmic response to music.[10] A developmental psychologist may call this musical play a form of "informal practice" that develops this child's expressive performance. Parents of these youngsters would agree that these children certainly enjoy "playing" for long periods of time with their musical sounds!

Suzuki's Talent Education School

When one envisions performance talent exhibited at an early age, the name Shinichi Suzuki quickly comes to mind. Who cannot be impressed by the picture of large groups of young children with violins tucked under their chins, playing Bach, Vivaldi, and Mozart? The widely used Talent Education School method involves early training with defined practice and performance techniques.

Suzuki believes that talent is largely reliant on environmental nurturance: "talent is no accident of birth." He calls his approach "mother tongue," explaining that children are not required to have specific talent to learn their native language yet they all learn to speak this language. The answer lies in how the environment develops this "talent" from birth.

> Man is born with natural ability. A newborn child adjusts to his environment in order to live, and various abilities are acquired in the process. . . . All children skillfully reared reach a high educational level, but such rearing must start from the day of birth. Here, to my mind, lies the key to the fuller development of man's potentials and abilities.[11]

In a Suzuki perspective, the prenatal research and infant studies discussed earlier support the importance of the environmental influence on musical talent, even prior to birth. The newborn infant's awareness of a mother's voice and the recognition of the *Peter and the Wolf* theme was a result of a prenatal environment, not an "accident of birth."

To Suzuki, *talent equals ability*, and abilities can be developed. Suzuki's Talent Education School is based on the philosophy that *every* child can develop talent if given repeated exposure and stimulation. His Talent Education movement began in Matsumoto Japan in the 1940s. He published the first violin book of his instructional method after 10 years of research.

Literally hundreds of thousands of students have studied in Suzuki schools in Japan. The method spread internationally and is firmly established in the United States in strings, piano, and flute and in preschool education.[12]

The Suzuki method of instruction relies on consistent example, repetition, and refinement. Students learn music by ear and by modeled performance for a large part of their early training. Parents play a key role in instruction, attending all lessons and learning the instrument along with the child. Performance training begins as early as the child can physically handle a sized-to-fit instrument. Some Suzuki violins are as small as one-sixteenth actual size.

A typical Suzuki violin class, as described by Susan Gilli in *Preschool in the Suzuki Spirit* (1987), presents a vivid portrait of the well-structured performance training that characterizes this method. Tiny tots begin each lesson with

---

SPARKLER EXPERIENCE: Experiencing a Suzuki Musical Exercise or Game

The very first piece taught to every Suzuki student is a variation of *Twinkle Twinkle Little Star* that has the following rhythm pattern, shown in music notation and in English and syllables similar to Japanese words that are used to teach this pattern. The first lesson in a Suzuki class will work with this rhythm in many ways to prepare the student to play this rhythm on an instrument.

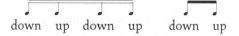

Miss- i- ssi-ppi	Hot Dog
I like cho-c'late	ice cream
ta ka ta ka	ta ka

1. Shake right hands with your child or student in this rhythm, starting with a relaxed downward gesture, and going up and down to the rhythm:

   down   up   down   up   down   up

Note that the child's arm is making movements similar to using a bow, with the appropriate right arm.

2. Transfer this same rhythm in a continuous steady flow to different rhythmic movements. Step in place in rhythm, leading continuously to clapping the rhythm, leading continuously to patting the rhythm in your lap with alternating hands.

➜

Experiencing a Suzuki Musical Exercise or Game (*continued*)

3. Now try the first Suzuki song on a piano or keyboard. The fingering is shown, and a finger shift is shown with a dotted line.

FIGURE 4.1. "Twinkle, Twinkle Little Star," with fingering for piano.

Follow these instructions to ensure appropriate physical performance:

Proper position at the piano: when the child is sitting on the piano there should be some firm cushions or phone books for them to sit on so that the tip of the elbow is at the same height as the top of the white keys when their hand is over the keys. The back should be straight, like the trunk of the tree. The arms are the branches, and the elbow of the arm should be slightly in front of the body. The child should be perching on the front half of the bench, with the back of the thigh exposed to air rather than to the bench. The feet should be supported by a box, just as an adult has support from the floor (no hanging feet in the air).

How to teach "Twinkle": The child plays groups of two black keys up and down the keyboard. Find the C by taking the child's right hand and pointing fingers 2 and 3 to the two black keys one octave above middle C. The thumb naturally falls onto the C. We use this higher "twinkle C" because it allows the arm to be free at the side of the body rather than in front of the body, where middle C is located. This promotes relaxation of the arm from the shoulder.

Taking the child's hand, support the arch of the hand with your second and third finger, letting the thumb hang loosely. Help them play the "Twinkle" rhythm, moving their arm and telling them to be like a rag doll, soft and loose. After assisting them in playing the rhythm several times, ask them when they are ready to do it on their own. Before beginning any performance, say, "ready-go" in rhythm to encourage focus, playing on command, and concentration before playing.

For a very small child, playing the rhythm only on the first C may be all that is learned at the first lesson. Students who are comfortable may also learn the G, A, G sequence of notes and fingering, always with the same physical guidance and rhythmic security. The goal of this first lesson is to teach the parent how to position the child correctly at the keyboard, teaching the first few notes of the piece, and learning how to play on command.[13]

a polite bow, tucking their violins under their arm in the appropriate manner. This important learned behavior not only acknowledges respect for the teacher but instills stage performance behavior as well. The class is chock full of movement activities done in a lively rhythm. Full body movement games loosen up the body and instill good posture from the outset. Finger-play games strengthen tiny fingers for dexterity on the instrument. Word games allow students to quickly follow crisp commands to place the violin in the proper position, stand in the correct way atop traced footprints, and maneuver the bow in different ways. Modeling, rote learning, repetition, and structured learning of concepts are basic instructional strategies of the Suzuki method.

The emphasis on listening perception and tonal memory in Suzuki violin training is dramatically described by Ronda Cole, a Suzuki violin teacher in the Washington, D.C., area who directs the Masters program in Performance and Suzuki Violin Pedagogy at the University of Maryland. After the polite bow, she begins the first violin class by playing A-440 and asks the children to sing it. Several minutes later, she asks them to remember this pitch. Over the next week, months, and years, she adds different pitches, "insisting doggedly that they have awareness of pitch in their environment, every day, many times a day." Through this defined pitch acculturation, almost all of her students acquire perfect pitch as well as relative pitch.

The philosophy of learning through listening and parental stimulation is at the heart of Suzuki training. Cole describes this philosophy in her studio:

> Children listen to the Suzuki recordings on a daily basis at home before they learn these pieces on their instrument. This gets their internal song and internal rhythm already going, so that they are searching out how to make the sounds that they hear in their heads *real* on the instrument. This definitely develops a very important kind of talent. It teaches them the talent of learning, not just the talent of playing by ear.
>
> We are also teaching the parents to teach the children at home in a manner that fosters the student process of learning to learn. We ask them to sing with their children and have expressive exchanges with them—with inflection of the voice and gestures in the hands—all of the things that later are a part of music-making.[14]

The Suzuki approach is an example of a unique teaching philosophy that emphasizes the training of instrumental performance at an early age. There are many other approaches that teach beginning performance experiences to young children that are philosophically quite different from Suzuki. The Dalcroze method lies on the other end of the spectrum, believing that early instrumental technical training impedes the mental expression of musical understanding. Students in Dalcroze classes move freely to different rhythmic pulses and pitches. They learn to improvise rather than learning through rote imitation. The Orff method uses rhythmic movement and pentatonic instruments to encourage improvisation and simple song and instrument ensembles. The Kodály method introduces hand signals to assist singing in solfége syllables. These approaches and others are described in chapter 12.

The overriding factor that separates the performance perspective of talent from the music aptitude and musical intelligence perspectives is the focus on physical performance capabilities. The judge at an audition immediately notes how well a student physically handles performance on an instrument or in voice. Sloboda's description of the cognitive functioning at work in developing an expressive performance includes gestural-technical control to a subtle degree through practice. As the preceding brief description of the Suzuki approach shows, highly structured instruction can physically prepare very young children to perform difficult musical literature. Physical skill development in musical training relies heavily on student commitment and effective practice procedures.

Commitment and Practice

Musical performance is inextricably meshed with commitment and musical achievement through practice. Seashore, the pioneer advocate of the "nature" argument, recognized the importance of commitment or "musical instinct" in the development of musical talent:

> The musician, in passing judgment upon a prospective musician, rightly says, "Give me the child with the musical instinct." By that he does not mean any one of the specific capacities we have discussed, but rather a fundamental urge, drive, or emotional dominance, craving expression from early childhood. This general trait is often feigned, fragmentary, or imaginary, but when genuine it constitutes the most certain indication of the presence of the musical mind that we have.[15]

Musicians and music teachers single out the quality of commitment as the distinguishing factor that determines which talented student will ultimately excel and achieve. Persistence in practice can overcome a student's initial deficits, handicaps, and inabilities. Marginally talented students, through diligent commitment, can actually blossom into more successful musicians than the quick-starters who have little self-discipline. Renshaw describes the typical music student at the Yehudi Menuhin school as having "a passionate commitment to music, in which the involvement is so great that music becomes an extension of the child's personality."[16]

Musicians in the studies of Sloboda and Howe and Sosniak did not display unusual musical ability at an early age, but they did show sustained interest in music from early childhood. Motivation played a stronger role than amount of practice time at the early stages of skill development. Commitment to a consistent pattern of demanding practice gained in importance as skills developed.

Recent studies by Ericsson, Krampe, and Tesch-Romer show the effectiveness of "deliberate practice" in the acquisition of expert performance:[17]

> We define deliberate practice as a highly structured activity with the explicit goal of improving some aspect of performance. In deliberate practice, the performance is carefully monitored for weaknesses and specific tasks are devised to combat them. Elite performers try to maximize the amount and outcome of their practice activities at every developmental stage.[18]

Deliberate practice is not fun and requires a great deal of self-motivation. It is quite different from recreational playing or performing with no direction toward skill development. This type of practice demands intensive levels of concentration and can be maintained for only a limited period of time. Master teachers describe the optimal level of this type of focused practice as lasting usually less than a half hour at a time.

Studies show that deliberate practice plays an essential role in the development of expertise in music, as well as chess and other domains. It takes *ten years* of intensive preparation in a particular domain to achieve an expertise level of performance. Detailed diaries of musicians at different levels of expertise indicate that expert musicians with higher levels of performance practice for about 25 hours per week, three times more than less accomplished musicians. Amateur musicians of the same age practice less than two hours per week. Ericsson, Krampe, and Tesch-Romer's study of accumulated practice by different levels of musicians over a 20-year span show that, by the age of 20, the most expert group of violinists had accumulated over 10,000 hours of deliberate practice.

The Leverhulme Project, a study of practice by Sloboda and others, showed similar results. The highest achieving group practiced 800 percent more than the lowest group by age 12. The study found that individuals who practiced as much as two hours a day achieved high levels of skill. Higher achieving students had supportive parental involvement from early childhood and had gradually attained self-motivated practice by the time they reached adolescence. Those who were in the lower achievement groups were simply told to "go and practice" by parents, without any direct involvement or interest in their musical studies.[19]

According to leading psychologists in the study of expertise in performance, parents should encourage early signs of musical interest and activity, begin formal instruction at an early age, and encourage good practice habits from the start. The establishment of defined practice skills and the development of self-disciplined practice habits play a crucial role in future success in music.

Talent as Performance: Arguments For and Against

For: Few would argue that the most prevalent display of talent in the field of music is the outstanding musician in performance. Musical talent is defined and realized by the outstanding performer. Persons who excel in conducting, composing, improvisation, and critiquing skills most likely begin their musical development through the performance of music, specializing in different areas as they realize their unique strengths in the domain.

- *The spark of musical talent is recognized most readily through performance:* The dynamic of performance is at the heart of musical talent. A performer who aesthetically connects with the audience or judging panel of an audition demonstrates what talent is all about in music. Potential talent, shy of polished technical skill development, is discernible by an experienced ear. Even at the earliest stages, a young child shows early signs of talent through singing and rhythmic activities demonstrated through performance.
- *Talent requires performance achievement and commitment:* Music aptitude testing painstakingly works to dislodge correlations to musical achievement. However, the extra-musical capacities of personal discipline and commitment play an integral part in the determination of musical talent. Disciplined, "deliberate" practice develops talent and produces expertise in performance. Performance talent is acquired through this persistent musical achievement rather than genetically received as a "gift" at birth.
- *Identifying talent through performance is pragmatic:* School music programs emphasize performance skills, from preschool musical singing and simple percussion performance to high school performing groups. Student performers who show outstanding skills can easily be recognized at different levels of development by teachers who instruct them in these school performance activities.

Against: Arguments against determining performance as talent reflect a broader concept of talent, expanding to include composition, improvisation, and listening proficiencies. Such arguments advocate the recognition of students whose technical capabilities may be limited, but demonstrate outstanding musical understanding beyond performance.

- *Musical talent lies beyond performance skills:* The confined perspective of performance limits talent recognition to those who excel in technical performance skills. Musical talent that emanates in composition and improvisation or in critiquing skills through listening will be missed and go undeveloped if schools identify only students who display talent through performance.

- *Trained talent does not mean natural talent:* The well-trained musician can be technically well choreographed to display gestural expressivity in a difficult performance by an excellent teacher. The listener is impressed, but an astute listener can recognize a carefully molded interpretation over a personally creative one. The understanding and musical reasoning that defines musical talent is lacking in this student, but the performance is impressive. The intellectual and technical achievement of training is worth recognition. However, differentiation between the well-trained student and the creative interpreter must be realized in talent identification.

- *The accumulation of practice does not produce talent. Innate talent fosters motivation to practice:* Practice without innate ability is not enough to warrant talent development. People are born with different capabilities. Those with more natural abilities to learn in a particular domain will be intrinsically motivated to practice more. Anyone who has taught can recognize persons who practice very hard and long but whose development on an instrument (or voice) will be hampered because of limited technical abilities as well as perceptive/cognitive understanding of abstract musical concepts.

- *Identification through performance is usually confined to classical orientation:* The typical audition setting is uncomfortable to a performer outside the genre of classical music. Identification of talent will miss the self-taught musicians of jazz, gospel, and rock whose musical talent will most likely go unheard because of this setting. The emphasis on the polished performance of a trained classical musician misses the talents of a student who may be exploring different instruments in performance, gaining skills as a possible future conductor, arranger, or composer. These performance skills may not take the form of outstanding skill on any one instrument, but clearly shows facility for learning a breadth of musical skills.

My view: I reflected on this chapter following a day spent behind the judge's table at a prestigious competition. I was actively seeking out signs of a spark that I might be able to compare with the performance ideas gathered from researchers and teachers in the process of writing this chapter. The young competing musicians displayed many of the expressive styles described in the chapter. Their performances were well polished. They were obviously well trained. There was no question that these students had worked deliberately in practice and had well-chosen parameters of expressive "templates" to present in performance. Rarely did technical hurdles impede their performance. Their performances showed evidence of systematic expressive devices befitting the style, with unique variety in dynamic scope. In Sloboda's analysis of expressive performance, they would pass the "expertise" test of an expressive performance.

However, only one musician drew me in to the performance from the start. Was it automaticity that made the performance seem spontaneously expressed? Was it the intense focus of the musician, knowing how to pull each musical line to a sensible conclusion? Or was it the aesthetic communication of someone perceiving, thinking, and feeling through the music? All of the judges shared the same experience from the start of the performance—an aesthetic dynamic.

Recognizing musical talent through performance may be problematic, subjective, and open to debate, but it is where this talent is aesthetically realized. The musician, from toddler to concert artist, communicates emotion through sound to the listener. When we hear a performance, do we only hear what has been developed through training, a gestural bag or tricks, or environmental influence? Or is there a unique talent that allows a student to personally interpret through sound in a creative way? There is always that one student you *cannot* not notice.

I understand the rationale of Sloboda's disdain for the "folk psychology" of talent, if this narrow view of musical capabilities contributes to the acceptance of mediocre musical development in school music programs. I decidedly support the philosophy of music educators who believe all students must learn to develop musical abilities, not just the "talented" few. I equally understand the holistic philosophy of Suzuki's method of inspiring each child to realize his or her unique "talent." However, I believe it is overly simplistic to believe that all children are musically talented. Music teachers who work with children in classrooms and studios can pinpoint the students who truly connect with musical tasks and *personally communicate through performance*. These are the students who show the spark of musical talent.

Your View: Your reactions to this chapter will depend on how closely you are involved with the performance of music, either personally or through friendship or family relationships. Some questions to get you started:

1. What are your ideas on the "nature versus nurture" debate?
2. How can we broaden the audition procedure to provide assessment of performance that includes recognition of "potential" talent? What are positives and negatives in changing the traditional audition procedure?
3. What have you learned here about expressive performance that may affect your perspective of musical talent?

4. How much of a student's talent is due to the teacher and how much to the student's own performance talents?
5. What role do you feel the extra-musical factors of commitment and practice should play in the identification of musical talent? How can this be recognized?

Your reflections:

TALENT AS CREATIVITY

Please, God, leave us this one mystery, unsolved: why man creates.
The minute that one is solved, I fear art will cease to be.

Leonard Bernstein, *Findings*

It was a few minutes past four on a Thursday, and I knew Andrew had arrived for a piano lesson. He bounded down the stairs, arrived at the piano bench with a thud, propped his dog-eared manuscript book on the piano, and looked at me with his determined "let's get started" smile—a delightfully talented young man of 15 about to share his latest composition with a welcome audience of one. He asked, "Do you know the speech from Julius Caesar, 'It must be by his death?'" I was unfamiliar with this bit of Shakespeare. He then dramatically went through the well-memorized speech, turning a bit red in the face as he shared this unfamiliar type of performance with his piano teacher. He motioned to his scribbled score, hands on the keyboard. "And this is also the speech." He then began his composition, peppering the performance with "this is fate" or "B-flat is death" to explain his motivic creative connections. The piece ended with a low B-flat repeatedly resonating as it died away (*smorzando*).

The musical creative process involves realizing sounds internally and communicating them to others in a unique way. Andrew discovered a personal way to interpret and communicate Shakespeare through the language of music. When we think of creative music-makers, we immediately envision the inspired composer, scrawling creative ideas on paper. We also recognize the jazz musician who jams through the night, improvising at will.

On a simpler plane, the young child in musical play is spontaneously creating through sound. These are the generative music-makers, creating music from scratch.

In the preceding chapter, we examined the creative-interpretive process of a musician who performs music from a written score. This deliberate decision-making process requires constant internal perceptive/cognitive manipulations (metaperception) to discover how to express a personal emotion through sound. The resulting *creative interpretation* communicates sounds that describe the expressive intent of the musician. The performer is the creative interpreter of music.

If we expand our perspective further, the person who listens perceptively and can communicate the idea of these sounds through words also shows musically creative talent. The critical listener internally processes sounds and aesthetically "translates" these sounds into a verbal interpretation. This transformation from musical to verbal domain requires musical understanding and sensitivity as well as the skills to describe sounds creatively. One may argue that the critical listener is not communicating through sound. However, this perceptive listener shares the same metaperception functioning that is at the heart of the creative process. The critic is the creative verbal interpreter of music.

The task of examining musical talent as creativity in any of these roles is a daunting one. Artists seek to leave it untouched, allowing it to remain mysterious and special. Scientists and psychologists analyze its inner workings to understand how the artistic mind functions. Psychologists examining creativity seek generalized characteristics that occur across domains. In previous chapters we have examined the sensory capacities of listening, the importance of musical understanding, and the process of developing an interpretation through musical performance. Musical creativity molds these elements into a personal musical statement. It is mysterious, intriguing, and definitive of the spark we seek.

In order to fully understand how one thinks creatively through music, we need to examine the nature of creative thinking in general. An overview of the field of creativity will explain the fundamental principles of creativity, which directly overlap into the field of musical creativity.

Creative Thinking

A creative mind thinks differently. Creative minds use *divergent* thinking to investigate many possibilities rather than *convergent* thinking to seek a single correct answer. Interest in research to find ways to measure this divergent thinking was spurred by a speech by J. P. Guilford to the American

Psychological Association in 1950. Guilford is the eminent psychologist who developed the *Structure of Intellect (SOI)* consisting of 120 different intelligences long before the idea of multiple intelligences gained popularity. Guilford described *convergent intellect* as learning about what exists; *divergent intellect* explores new territory and revises what is already known. Guilford believed that divergent thinking was measurable and challenged psychologists to seek research in the field of creativity to develop effective means of this measurement.

The key terms used in the general field of creativity to describe divergent or creative thinking stem from Guilford's *Nature of Human Intelligence* (1967). A person who thinks divergently displays:

- Fluency—the ability to think of many ideas quickly
- Flexibility—the ability to view from different perspectives
- Originality—the ability to create ideas that are unique
- Elaboration—the ability to expand and embellish existing ideas

Many other abilities are listed in various texts on creativity; however, these five descriptors are most prevalent in the literature, measurement, and curricula of creative thinking.[1]

E. Paul Torrance carried on Guilford's work and developed the *Torrance Tests of Creative Thinking* (1966), which are the most popular measures of divergent thinking. The Torrance measures have been used in over a thousand research studies, have been translated into 30 different languages, and are administered to approximately 150,000 children and adults each year. These measures are commonly used in screening procedures for gifted and talented identification. Scoring is based on *fluency* (number of responses), *flexibility* (different categories of responses), *originality* (novelty based on "statistical infrequency" norms), and *elaboration* (number of details in figural tasks).[2]

The test contains verbal and figural tasks. Verbal sections ask students to list unusual uses for a box or tin can or ask for causes or consequences of events seen in a picture. One popular activity, "Just Suppose," asks students to list what would happen if clouds had strings that hung to the ground. In drawing sections, students complete an idea suggested by an abstract sketch or construct a picture from a simple shape. One task presents students with pages of circles or parallel lines, asking them to create drawings, complete with short descriptive titles.

You may ask how a pencil and paper test can possibly measure creative thinking in music—a good question. However, this measure is used extensively in gifted and talented identification procedures, often in the specific area of musical and artistic talent identification. In fact, research has shown that general creativity testing does not have a high correlation to artistic or musical talent or creative thinking in the arts.[3] It seems obvious that the use of verbal and figurative tasks would have a low correlation to musical creative thinking; however, one would assume that visual artists would score high in the figurative drawing portion of these tests.

A recent session with some high school music and art teachers clarified why this assumption may not be so accurate. As I passed out a short section of the test to the music and art teachers, I anticipated similar degrees of fluency and originality in the written task, with the art teachers really taking off in the drawing portion of the test. I assumed pages would turn quickly as the art teachers drew one idea after another on the three pages of parallel lines in the drawing portion of the test. I was surprised to discover that most of the teachers completed only two pages in the four minutes I had allotted. As we discussed the ideas drawn, to compare for originality and flexibility, I asked if anyone had not even reached the second page. One art teacher raised her hand and offered to show her creation. On that half page of lines was an intricate drawing that described an imaginative story concerning three doors representing decisions in life, each door suitably depicting its fate through her artistic design. We were all stunned for a moment as we recognized the depth of this creative visual interpretation, and we questioned how this drawing, on a half page (points off for fluency) would "score" on this test.

A number of other tests are available for measuring general creative or divergent thinking, inspired by the measures of Guilford and Torrance. Gary Davis's book *Creativity Is Forever* presents an overview of the field of creativity with an entertaining approach and an excellent summary of available creativity measures, including specifics of reliability and validity.[4]

Torrance expanded tests into different areas as well. *Thinking Creatively in Action and Movement* (1981) is a measure for preschoolers using movement activities for students not yet able to express ideas clearly in words or drawings. Students walk or run in different ways, move imaginatively like animals, and throw paper cups into a waste basket as many ways as they can. I would encourage preschool teachers to note students whose movements are imaginative and fluidly rhythmic in this test, following up with movement in music activities to determine potential musical talent.

Torrance's book *Thinking Creatively with Sounds and Words* (1973) describes the use of sound and word stimuli to encourage original responses for both children and adults. In "Sounds and Images," the test-taker describes images inspired by four abstract sounds. Responses are scored for originality only, using statistical infrequency procedures. "Onomatopoeia and Images" presents ten image-stimulating words (zoom, boom, moan, etc.), again asking for images that are brought to mind. The "Sounds and Images" portion of this test may be helpful in identifying students who display creative talent in listening.

Aside from psychometric testing for creativity, there are many key figures who have examined the workings of the creative mind. Graham Wallas's *The Art of Thought* (1926) established the four stages of the creative process that is still used as a model for describing *how* one creates. This creative process consists of:[5]

- *Preparation:* problems are being considered. "The mess" is established, and questions are researched at the starting point of the process.
- *Incubation:* the subconscious, gestation period. The mysterious state of creation as ideas are brewing.
- *Illumination:* the "Eureka" moment of insight and creative discovery.
- *Verification:* solutions are tested, refined, and presented for approval.

Creative problem-solving models of Osborn and Parnes and, most recently, Treffinger, Isaksen, and Firestien's Creative Problem Solving Process (CPS) provide curricula for teaching creative thinking expanding on the process described by Wallas in 1926.[6] These models are used extensively in gifted education curricula.

In the field of cognitive psychology, David Perkins's book *The Mind's Best Work* (1981) attempts to dispel the notion of true discovery or mystery concerning the creative process. He believes the person who creates knows how to pattern and organize thoughts into perceptive/productive plans (schemata) while solving problems. This person truly *enjoys* originality and the pursuit of creative ideas through a process of rational decision-making. Rather than creative thoughts "bubbling up spontaneously from some ineffable inner source," Perkins believes, "creating is an intentional endeavor shaped by the person's values."[7]

Mihaly Csikszentmihalyi's idea of *flow* describes the intriguing inner workings of the mind while engaged in challenging, creative tasks. He agrees with Perkins's description of the creative person as one who relishes the *process* of creating. His theory of optimal experience describes *flow* as "the state in which people are so involved in an activity that nothing else seems to matter; the experience itself is so enjoyable that people will do it even at great cost, for the sheer sake of doing it."[8] The condition of flow requires that a person be engagingly challenged by a task.

Csikszentmihalyi's s research of talented teenagers shows that students who are talented in music and art seek out challenges while working in their art form. These students experience the state of flow when they are engaged in deliberate practice. They were "particularly enthusiastic about teachers who helped identify their strengths and structured a demanding program that led to the synthesis of a distinctive personal style." Csikszentmihalyi believes talent development is a spiral process of these engaging experiences. It is a "'path with a heart,' or the feeling of approaching a destination while enjoying the journey as an end in itself."[9]

Creative Thinking in Music

The general field of creativity has given us insight concerning the characteristics of creativity, creative thought, and the creative process. A number of music psychologists have adapted creative measures using musical tasks to assess the creative thinking of music students.

Vaughan constructed the first musical creativity test in 1971, consisting of six open-ended tasks that required improvisation, using melody bells, tom-toms, and vocal sounds. A panel of judges assessed the performance of created rhythms and melodies, and an imaginative piece describing a thunderstorm for musical fluency, rhythmic security, and ideation.[10]

Several researchers in music education developed music creativity measures exploring improvisation, composition, and creative listening. In 1976, Gorder developed the *Measures of Musical Divergent Production (MMDP)* which used four timed tasks using instruments, whistling, or singing. This secondary level measure used sketches of note heads, contours, and motives as guidelines for improvisation. Webster asked high school students to improvise progressively more difficult improvisations on a set of melody bells, ending in three variations of "Twinkle Twinkle Little Star" merged with an original improvised tune. This test also included composition and analysis tasks that required three weeks of time to develop. Scoring for both of these studies used the ideas of fluency, flexibility, originality, and elaboration, adapted to musical content.[11]

Two measures developed specifically for younger children are worth investigation by music educators and gifted specialists interested in the measurement of creative musical thinking. Both measures have been used in a number of research studies addressing musical creative thinking in young children.[12] Wang's *Measures of Creativity in Sound and Music (MCSM)* is designed for children aged three to eight and is similar in design to Torrance's preschool creativity measures. Students produce steady beats on a variety of plastic containers, create imaginative sound pictures on rhythm instruments (popcorn, giant, horse), create different ostinatos, and move to different types of music. Scores indicate musical fluency and musical imagination.

Webster's *Measure of Creative Thinking in Music (MCTM)* is designed for children aged six to ten. It consists of ten activities, including several improvisational tasks. The child first enjoys a musical question-and-answer dialogue with the tester using temple bells. Then the student uses a nerf ball on the piano and an amplified microphone to create sound pictures (frog, robot). Tasks progress in difficulty, leading to the creation of an improvisatory space story, using abstract drawings as stimuli. Each child is videotaped during this process, with scoring by a panel of judges as they review the tapes. The musical criteria for scoring the measure include:

- Musical extensiveness: the amount of clock time involved in the creative tasks
- Musical flexibility: the extent to which the musical parameters of pitch (high/low), tempo (fast/slow), and dynamics (loud/soft) were manipulated
- Musical originality: the extent to which the response is unusual or unique in musical terms and in the manner of performance
- Musical syntax: the extent to which the response is inherently logical and makes musical sense[13]

The advantage of all of these creative measures is that real-world musical tasks make up the testing procedures. Astute observation of students engaged in creative music-making is required. The problems of test administration include time needed for scheduling individual testing of children and training the observer to recognize the criteria of the measures. However, the basic musical tasks and criteria within these measures could easily be incorporated into the music classroom as part of a screening procedure for musical talent identification.

Webster believes the concept of music aptitude should be expanded beyond the convergent discrimination measured by music aptitude tests. He believes that *creative* music aptitude includes "the processes of creative thinking that begin early in life and are worthy of identification as part of our continuing effort to understand music aptitude in its fullest sense." His concept of "creative thinking in sound" goes beyond Gordon's idea of "audiation." The expressive element of creative thinking presents aural images that are more complicated and subtle in structure than those presented in current music aptitude testing.[14]

The simple observation of children in musical play can differentiate students who are engaged in creative music-making from those who are not really thinking when making sounds. In an interview, Webster elaborated on the behaviors he believes indicate creative music aptitude in young children.

> When I watch children behaviorally, it seems to me there are children who right away start "thinking in sound." You can tell by their behavior. They play something, and then they think about it, or they are imaging it. Somehow there is some link that you can almost immediately tell. There is already a shaping of sound—high/low, fast/slow, loud/soft manipulation, almost naturally as the child starts to work. There appears to be a sense of syntax after the initial gesture, a kind of refining of work. You can almost tell the child is *playing* with that idea, trying to stretch it, to manipulate it in some way. It is almost like trying to compose in a naturally improvisatory type of behavior.[15]

Webster calls for a fresh look at what lies at the heart of musical thinking and musical talent.

Reflecting on the perspectives discussed so far, one can see that there is a core concept that has been interpreted a bit differently with each perspective but basically describes the same process of internal perceptive/cognitive functioning. Gordon calls it *audiation*, with a scientific interpretation that coincides with *perceptive discrimination*. If we expand beyond discriminative tasks, we recognize that *musical intelligence* uses internal sound-sensing to solve problems across musical dimensions. Sloboda describes the mesh of perception, cognition, and emotion in expressive performance as *internal representation* of sound. Webster describes the same idea as *creative thinking in sound*. Of course, Seashore began the idea with the concept of a *musical mind*. To me the term *metaperception* describes the same internal process, and this term has the advantage of being generalized to describe artistic decision-making across the arts.

SPARKLER EXPERIENCE: Creative Thinking in Sound—*Metaperception*

The following exploration of sounds encourages you to understand the creative process and the criteria used to assess creative work in music. The tasks are similar to those found in the musical creative measures described in this chapter.

Note: This activity can be done individually or in small groups, with people working in ensemble on different found objects. The creative development of the collage in a small group will reveal those who take the lead in creative decision-making.

1. *Preparing instruments and exploring timbre:* Locate at least five "found objects" that create different types of interesting sounds (plastic and glass soda bottles, plastic containers, metal bowls, boxes, etc.) Explore and experiment with different ways to play these "instruments" until you find their individual qualities of sound or "timbres."
   - Explore at least eight different ways to play *each* object. Try different types of "drumsticks," position the object differently, and play with different dynamics and tempos. Be aware of interesting qualities of sound (timbres) you are producing.

2. *Creative improvisation:* Explore and experiment with combinations of sounds by performing on all of the found-object instruments.
   - Arrange the objects so you can easily move from one to another in a pseudo—drum set arrangement. Explore sound combinations working from one object to the next, using different dynamics, rhythms, and tempos.

→

Creative Thinking in Sound—*Metaperception* (*continued*)

3. *Creative composition:* Create a sound collage that has musical structure—beginning, middle, end. It may describe a story line, contain repeated rhythm patterns or sections, or be structured any way you like. Rework until you feel you have created a personal improvisatory statement.

4. *Creative interpretation and performance:* Perform this creation for a friend, classmate, or family member. Reflect on how you felt during the creative musical process and in your performance. Ask your audience for comments about ideas they heard through the sound collage.

5. *Assessment of your creative musical work:*

Extensiveness: How long did it take you to go through the entire creative process? Did you feel you could have spent more time in developing your ideas further? How long was the final improvisation?

Flexibility: How expressive was your musical statement, in terms of the parameters of loud/soft, fast/slow, variation in tempo or rhythmic design? Did you use a wide variety of object sounds in combination in your collage? Do you feel the overall mix of musical color of sounds indicates creative manipulation?

Originality: What was especially unique or unusual about your sound collage? Did your audience response catch these novel ideas?

Syntax: Did your audience find that the collage made musical sense? Was the idea of a musical structure, with beginning, middle, and end, clearly stated?

This musical creative thinking exercise allows you to experience a taste of the creative process of improvisation. In essence, the exercise encapsulates the ideas already discussed concerning creative thinking in a single musical experience. In the *preparation* stage, you experiment with the instruments, perceptively gathering unique sound qualities. As you explore ideas on all of the instruments, you make internal decisions based on sound manipulation both internally (*metaperceptually*) and externally (technical manipulations in performance). During this process, the more involved and focused you become, the more deeply you enter the state of *flow*. If you find a period of time that you need to stop playing and simply reflect on ideas, you may experience a brief *incubation* period. Or you may continue with intentional concentration, reflecting on different *schemata*. You may experience *illumination*, realize you suddenly "got it," and start to work at a quicker pace in developing your collage. The audience *verification* allows a musician to see if ideas are, indeed, projected to the listener. There is no greater reward than your audience being equally excited about the unique ideas you sought to communicate. Creative musical thinking is at the heart of all of the roles of the creative musician.

The Improviser

You hear strange noises from the kitchen. Clink, clank, thud-thud-thud— CRASH! Your three-year-old has discovered the drawer containing pot lids and plastic containers. As you edge your way around the corner, you find your child picking up various spoons and trying them out on this invented drum set. The cymbal crash of pot lids coming together requires a standing position finale and a bow, of course. This creative musical play shows the first signs of fascination in sound manipulation. If the child exhibits a sense of focused attention and experimenting with patterning of sounds rather than hitting things any old which way, a creative musical mind is at work.

Creative play with song, simple rhythm instruments, and rhythmic body percussion is the starting point of music education. Infants and toddlers use sounds as favorite vocal and physical playthings. Preschool and primary music education teaches students how to play simple rhythm instruments and enjoy movement to music. These rudimentary skills provide an open climate for improvisation early on in music education.

Several early childhood music curricula clearly emphasize improvisation and creative expression through music. Émile Jaques-Dalcroze's "eurythmics" encourages students to internalize rhythms through improvisatory movement to music. Students move across the floor, feeling the weight of their body as a pulse in rhythms as they move in space. Carl Orff's Schulwerk emphasizes improvisation in rhythm, movement, and instrumental ensemble. Beautifully crafted Orff instruments are used in many American schools, where children improvise in ensemble on glockenspiels, xylophones, metallophones, and hand drums. These instruments produce a wide range of timbres that allow students to explore improvisation on instruments that have no wrong notes when adjusted to the pentatonic scale. (Chapter 12 offers a complete explanation of these creative approaches to early music education.)

This type of generative play encourages divergent thinking through sound. Many ideas are available to explore, with acceptance of novel, multiple "answers" to musical problems. As children grow into more traditional musical training, the skill development of learning instruments or vocal training brings an emphasis on convergent thinking through sound. They must learn to perform the right notes, with a single correct "answer." Performance classes at the secondary level most often rely on the teacher to make the creative interpretive decisions for performance.[16] Improvisatory experiences decrease and are basically confined to jazz ensembles by high school.

In the Sparkler Experience in this chapter, the instructions suggested minimal structure and guided the task from exploration to manipulation to musical creation. If the activity had simply said "Find objects and play anything you want on them," it would be a purer test of true creative improvisation. What would be the end result? Would it be a sudden smashing away at objects, finished in a few energetic seconds? Or would you enjoy the many ways you could "play" with the sound, resulting in a similar sound collage created through your own discovery of combinations of instrument timbres and musical qualities?

The Pillsbury Foundation School provided just such a scenario of discovery for children from ages one through eight in the early 1940s. The school was more like a day care center than a normal school, with an emphasis on free exploration in musical experiences. Donald Pond, a composer, was the school's music director for eight years. His study focused on observing students naturally engaged in musical activity and examining the process and product that developed from this musical play. He observed these youngsters exploring different types of bells, xylophones, gongs, and drums with no formal instruction. He found that the timbre of a particular instrument would trigger interest in its exploration. Students used chant as well as original song, each showing different musical characteristics. The youngsters also enjoyed exploring different musical properties and rhythmic complexities. He described his role of researcher–observer as similar to "putting together a jigsaw puzzle without knowing what the completed picture was supposed to look like."[17]

Cohen used a similar technique of observation in a kindergarten setting, employing the use of a videotape behind one-way glass combined with active participation with the students. She gathered data for three years, focusing attention on several students in particular. She discovered that the experience of playing with instruments combined aural, kinesthetic, and tactile curiosity, recommending that assessment of musical work should recognize this behavior. Students would try to match their peers' musical statements on the instruments. She describes the idea of a *musical gesture* as a "musical idea that may comprise a few notes or a longer musical entity."[18] She documented these gestures and observed how students used them as patterns of musical thought while working out creative schemata. These rich observations showed that children at musical play use the same perceptive/cognitive process employed by adult improvisers and composers.

There is nothing more fascinating than observing a jazz musician jamming with colleagues, engaged in creative improvisation on a simple tune that soon vanishes amid the cascade of notes and syncopated rhythms that personalizes the performance. The performance is dynamic. Is the improvisation purely creative?

Sloboda contends that the improviser begins each performance with a preexisting blueprint or skeletal plan for the improvisation. This blueprint derives from surrounding culture, be it the jazz style of 12-bar blues or the antecedent and consequent phrases of a period in classical structure. The improviser "can rely on the given constraints of the form together with his own 'style' to give the music unity."[19] The improviser who demonstrates creative talent can fluently embellish and create beyond the past repertoire of musical ideas performed in this personal style.

Jazz styles have certain fundamental structures, with phrases repeated in given patterns in the 12-bar blues or 32-bar song. Jazz performers basically fill this structured framework with the harmonic and melodic progressions that set the musical flow from one section to the next. They learn this from listening intently to other jazz musicians and in performing with others using basic jazz harmonic progressions. The jazz performer achieves real dynamic impact when a solo improvisation brings novel ways of embellishing melodic lines, often keeping the listener on edge to see how this solo will wind its way to a comfortable return to the "tune" by the group.

Improvisation is probably the most natural way to begin to understand creative thinking in music. Young children naturally enjoy musical play. The studies and investigations of the workings of the musical mind in improvisation show a desire to create musically structured statements that communicate to others. The ideas of fluency, flexibility, elaboration, originality, and syntax give us a guiding creative vocabulary to structure observation of musical talent through improvisation.

The Composer

Andrew, my student composer, abstracted his personal interpretation of a Shakespearean speech through sound. The inspiration for this creation was a personal experience of learning the speech dramatically. The composer may be inspired by an event, a personal experience, or simply an idea from the subconscious. The composer's creative process is mysteriously intriguing. Some composers take years of development for a single composition. Others compose with immediacy. There are numerous accounts of composers' descriptions of the creative process. Each describes a similar trancelike state from which musical ideas initially emerge. This state reflects the idea of "gestation" in Wallas's description of the creative process.

Leonard Bernstein describes the gestation phenomenon as an out-of-mind state that is "on that border between twilight and the waking world."[20] Hector Berlioz describes it as "supernal ecstasy."[21] Aaron Copland agrees that germinal ideas arise from a creative state that has no rational explanation. "Inspiration may be a form of superconsciousness, or perhaps of subconsciousness—I wouldn't know; but I am sure that it is the antithesis of self-consciousness."[22]

Songwriters in rock, country, blues, and pop genres describe the same "substate" of mind in the initial process of creation. Many describe a sense of pulling or plucking ideas from the air, with spiritual inspiration. Blues guitarist Bukka White refers to "sky songs." Hank Williams simply says, "I pick up the pen and God moves it." John Lennon describes a sense of being possessed and having to get up to write immediately, "always in the middle of the bloody night when you're half awake or tired, and your critical faculties are switched off."[23]

As bits and pieces of sounds and ideas emerge, there is a delicate conscious-subconscious balancing act that allows ideas to be realized and remembered. Copland describes a type of hallucinatory state of mind in which "one half of the personality emotes and dictates while the other half listens and notates." He warns that the listening half should "look the other way, had better simulate a half attention only, for the half that dictates is easily disgruntled and avenges itself for too close inspection by fading entirely away."[24] Bernstein describes a similar challenge of remaining conscious enough to recall the ideas in this twilight zone of creation without regaining full consciousness or falling asleep. Stephen Sondheim usually writes lying down, so he can sleep easily. He writes ten minutes and sleeps for two on average.[25] Robert Schumann describes this generative mental process in detail:

> Involuntarily an idea sometimes develops itself simultaneously with the musical fancy; the eye is awake as well as the ear, and this ever-busy organ sometimes holds fast to certain outlines amid all the sounds and tones which, keeping pace with the music, form and condense into clear shapes.[26]

The compositional task of molding these ideas into musical form requires constant internalization and manipulation of musical ideas through perceptive/cognitive functioning. Metaperceptive decisions are made and revised. This is the compositional task of placing the notes heard in the head onto the paper for others to perform. It is the process that uniquely identifies the style of the composer—Mozart, Stravinsky, Sondheim, or Billy Joel.

If one could be a fly on the wall during this music-making process, one would see different ways of crafting ideas into sound. Each composer approaches the task with a different set of skills and techniques. However, all share the desire to formulate ideas through sound and communicate these sounds through music to others. It is this desire to manipulate personal ideas through sound that is fundamental to the composer. The young child who enjoys manipulating sounds shares the same desire.

SPARKLER EXPERIENCE: Exploring the Compositional Process

The difference between improvisation and composition is the requirement of some type of notation of musical ideas. If you have no music notation skills, do not dismay. Simply use creative, figurative notation of your ideas as you work. If you are a musician, confine yourself to the pentatonic structure of the exercise to allow yourself to concentrate on the process of this task. Reaching beyond this pentatonic framework may lead you into complexities not needed for the exercise.

1. *Preparation:* Find a piano or other keyboard to begin your composing. Your composition will be confined to the *black keys* of the keyboard—a pentatonic scale, which may lend an oriental flavor to your piece. Briefly explore the sound of these keys by playing melodies, two notes together, and clusters of the fist on a group of two or three black notes. Extend your exploration to the full range of the keyboard, using both hands from high to low, low to high.

2. *Initial exploration:* Now that you are comfortable physically with the parameters of your composing space, begin experimenting with combinations of ideas you like. Begin by improvising for at least *two full minutes.* By the end of this improvisation, a few bits of interesting "gestures" should be easy to repeat and remember.

3. *Notation:* Write your musical ideas on a piece of paper in any way that makes sense to you and will help you remember them. Refer to your notation as you perform each short idea. Work back and forth, from developing improvisation to notation, mapping out your ideas on paper. Use both hands, expanding your notation to show this difference in some way.

4. *Gestation:* After you feel you have made a good start in connecting several ideas, let it rest overnight. You may think about these ideas away from the keyboard but do not actively work on them for *at least one day.*

5. *Illumination:* (Thinking positively here!) As you return to your work, see how well you remember your ideas while you look over your notation. Try to develop a complete statement at this second sitting. Your musical composition should show some sense of musical syntax (beginning, middle, end), and you may use repeated sections if you like.

→

Exploring the Compositional Process (*continued*)

6. *Verification:* Perform your composition from beginning to end, adding musical ideas of dynamics and tempo to your "score" in some way. Finish the experience with a sense of completion of your creation, through notation and performance.

This Sparkler Experience can give you a personal taste of the creative compositional process. There have been many scientific attempts to be that "fly on the wall" and to examine the creative process of composers from the past to the present. An examination of the sketchbooks and manuscripts of Beethoven and Mozart reveal differences in ink, paper, and writing styles that indicate a definite break in the compositional process. They also show two very different developmental processes.

Beethoven sketched bits of ideas that often appeared in works written years later. There would be a short written idea, scratched out, followed by another that showed a few changes, leading to a completed section of a composition. From analysis of his sketchbook, Sloboda offers a view of Beethoven as a composer who had a desired harmonic framework set internally. As he worked, he would progressively try out snatches of ideas and fill in what fit this desired harmonic whole.

Mozart is well known for his immediate compositional style, writing whole compositions with minimal sketching and building of ideas. Letters to his father explained the need to write as fast as possible to try to capture the refined compositions that were in his mind and not yet notated. Ink changes in his manuscripts show complete notation of melody and bass first, with occasional vertical sections filled in at cadences. Most inner voices were completed at a later date. Sloboda contends that this initial notation allowed the composer to "fix the crucial individuating elements of the composition on paper" so it would not be lost to memory.[27] He captured the immediate ideas through the upper and lower line, filling in the harmonic texture at a later time.

Numerous research studies have attempted to capture the composer's mental state in the process of composing. This "protocol gathering" technique attempts to log the thought process of the composer as problems are worked over and solved. Studies by Bamberger and Kratus discovered different compositional strategies used by students as they worked on developing compositions. Some students used careful, planned exploration. Others worked impulsively. The amount of silence in the compositional process was also noted.[28]

Sloboda explained a self-imposed protocol in the process of writing a choral work, where he verbally described his thoughts aloud as he worked. He found that he verbalized thoughts specifically when he was trying to work through a problem. When fully engaged in metaperceptual thought, the protocol would disrupt the intensive creative "flow."[29]

Compositional talent relies on some way to maintain musical creations. Songwriters who do not read music rely on taping as they create, composing through purely aural skills. Young children may use figural representation, as one might in the Sparkler Experience in this chapter. Extensive tonal memory is a key characteristic indicating a possible future composer in a classroom.

Until recently, the recognition of compositional skills in young students has been hampered by the reliance on a certain level of musical knowledge and notational skills. Computer software that easily notates and plays back melodies played on a simple MIDI-keyboard or drawing pad has opened up the possibilities of experimenting with musical composition prior to the development of notational skills. Recent studies using these technological tools are allowing researchers to examine how students respond to musical tasks in the development of student compositions.[30] Chapter 13 examines software and instructional ideas for bringing creative thinking and composition into the music classroom and studio.

Musical talent as creativity through composition can be recognized as early as students can scrawl creative ideas from improvisation onto manila paper or zap it onto a computer screen. Bamberger, Davidson, and Scripps discovered this in their research studies of students of different ages engaged in compositional tasks, described in chapter 3. When I was asked to develop my *Explorations in Music* theory curriculum, many teachers asked why I chose to include creative composition from the very first book, when children were first learning to write noteheads on lines and spaces. The children never asked. They simply did it.

The Creative Performer

> The composer's piece is an incomplete work, but it is a perfectly definite piece carried to a perfectly definite stage. . . . Performance is the completion of a musical work, a logical continuation of the imagination, carrying the creation through from thought to physical expression.[31]

Philosopher Susan Langer describes the full creative musical experience, from composer to performer to listener. The performer continues the creative process begun by the composer. A completed composition is realized through the interpretation of a performer, communicated to a listener. The dynamic creative circle is complete and is ever changing with each performer's interpretation.

The performer has the definitive task of interpreting how the composer would want the music to sound, realizing stylistic boundaries and expressing the integrity of the music in the performance. In the preceding chapter, we discussed the element of personal choice in parameters of expressive decisions. Sloboda contends that the expert performer "has a distinct performing style that is recognizable to connoisseurs."[32] I contend that this personal performance style is apparent to most listeners when a musician of *any* age or skill level presents a *creative interpretation* in performance.

I doubt if anyone has not experienced a performance that created the dynamic connection of performer, music, and listener. What elements make up this personally creative interpretation? It may be helpful to consider views from a psychologist, a philosopher, and a composer.

Sloboda has examined the intricacies of expressive performance. Langer's philosophical writings about musical experience rest on every musician's bookshelf. Copland's literary translations of musical concepts into everyday language unveils the thoughts of a music creator. These experts share ideas about how a musician feels and how creative thinking is used in the process of performance.

Sloboda lists a number of factors that may affect a person's adeptness of expressive musical ability (or creative interpretation). (I have added italicized explanations in brackets to help clarify Sloboda's ideas.) Individuals who demonstrate expressive musical ability:[33]

- are expressive in everyday life, with cultural surroundings that encourage this expressivity.
- are knowledgeable of where expressive treatment is appropriate in the structure of the music, relying on prior experience with the particular genre of music [*musical realization of cadences, transitions, choice of phrase lengths appropriate to the structure of the music*].
- are adept at making analogical connections between a musically expressive gesture and a nonmusical idea [*playing a passage like a cascading waterfall, an elephant walking, etc.*].
- can monitor performance through practice to project expressive outcomes [*define and expand dynamic scopes to communicate intended expression to the audience*].
- experience music-generated emotional response to the expressive device rather than through extrinsic emotional factors [*connect with the intent and integrity of the music rather than personal emotional expression not related to the music*].

Langer believes "a real performance is as creative an act as composition."[34] This real performance relies on a performer's "impassioned utterance," which relies on the "contagious excitement of the artist over the vital content of the work."[35] She distinguishes between this aesthetic expression of the music and the self-expression of the performer. If a performer is expressing emotions felt at the time of performance rather than feelings linked to the intent of the music, the performance is no longer *real*. "A screaming baby gives his feeling far more release than any musician, but we don't go into a concert hall to hear a baby scream."[36] The vital aesthetic connection between the performer and the music is the key factor of a "real performance."

To Langer, the experience of music is one of "vital import, a wordlessly presented conception of what life feels like."[37] She realizes the dynamic nature of music from performer to listener and believes that the import of music is inseparable from the expressive form of the work being perceived. The performer, as creative interpreter, must realize the intent of the composer, phenomenologically experiencing the natural dynamic that derives from each performance. "The real power of music lies in the fact that it can be true to the life of feeling in a way that language cannot; for its significant forms have the ambivalence of content which words cannot have."[38]

Copland, as a composer, believes the musical interpreter is not very different from the musical creator.

> He is simply the intermediary that brings the composer's work to life—a kind of midwife to the composition. He partakes of the same dedication of purpose, the same sense of self-discovery through each performance, the same conviction that something unique is lost, possibly when his understanding of a work is lost. . . . Each time he steps out upon the concert platform we wish him luck, for he shares something of the creator's uncertain powers of projection. Thus we see that the interpretation, even though it may rightfully be thought of as an auxiliary art, does share elements of creativity with the mind that forms the work of art.[39]

If you can imagine the role of the composer, sitting in the audience listening to his or her created music being interpreted by a performer, you may wonder how the composer feels about different interpretations of his or her music. Copland believes that compositions are made to be read several ways; "otherwise a work would be said to lack richness of meaning." Each reading requires certain limits appropriate to the work. "It must have stylistic truth, which is to say it must be read within the frame of reference that is true for the composer's period and individual personality."[40]

Copland recognizes the role of the musician's personality in performance. "When a performer lacks personality we call the performance dull; when he has too much personality we complain that he obscures the piece from view. A just appreciation of the exact part played by the performer's personality in any given execution is therefore essential for precise judgment."[41]

Returning again to the question of *creative interpretation* after these discussions, we realize the difficult role of the performer in creating an interpretation that projects personal expressive ideas within the stylistic framework dictated by the musical score. Sloboda describes this subtle creative balance as "music-generated expression." To Langer, the performer shows "contagious enthusiasm" for music, which is a "vital import" of feeling. Copland describes this as "personality" balanced by the "stylistic truth" of the music.

The process of developing this interpretation through performance may, indeed, draw on past experiences that produce the "templates" Sloboda describes. I prefer to think of these as musical "schemata," as described by Perkins. Students creatively experiment with different parameters of musical expression until they discover ones that project the emotional intent or personal interpretation of the music.

Anyone who has taught or performed music has lived through this creative balance of interpretive decision-making. The student who can quickly grasp the stylistic parameters and bring unique musically expressive ideas to the lesson or the stage is a creative performer. A musician may be performing a Beethoven concerto with a major symphony orchestra or performing "The Happy Hippo" at a friendly recital of peers. The dynamic of a creative interpretation will be projected to the audience.

The Listener and Critic

The creative listener has a somewhat hidden talent. The young fellow in the back of the clarinet section of the band may be an okay performer but have a keen ear and an aesthetic fascination with the intricacies of what he is hearing. Rarely will this musical talent be realized in a school performance class setting. Even in a private studio, these students may be missed. The ear training task of isolated interval hunting and solfége work that is done in too few studios may give a clue. However, only if a student is asked to critique performances, both verbally and in written form, does this talent surface.

There is minimal research in this area, with hesitancy on the part of researchers to embrace comfortably the concept of "creative" analysis and listening. A 1974 study by Feinberg developed a model of problem-solving based on music listening, adapted from the Wallas model. Assessment was based on fluency and flexibility of thought to the context of music listening.

Feinberg's model had three sections. The first asked students to make up questions related to what they heard (emphasis on flexibility and fluency). The second provided a list of musical qualities ("aural flexibility list") checked off as they listened critically to the music. The third offered comparative listening to the same piece, asking them to choose which they liked best and to decide what was different about each. (What did the second conductor do that was different from the first?)[42]

These tasks required students to listen critically for structural, textural, and aesthetic musical elements. Opportunities were also provided to creatively interpret musical ideas through words that displayed their musical understanding and sensitivity to musical details. These tasks can reveal insightful, creative listeners.

A study by Pfiel dealt with more generative compositional content with college students. Students created a sound collage with vocal and body percussion sounds, revising it after a verbal critique. They also examined an unusual score of three instruments using simple lines on the staff corresponding to instruments played. Students were asked to imagine how it would sound and list things they did not like. Then they wrote a new piece using the same truncated notation on an open score.[43]

These tasks combined improvisation, composition, listening, and analysis in creative tasks. Students hear sounds internally and make musical judgments from this internal listening. The novel representation of sounds on the creative score required synthesis of these skills. Providing both verbal and written critique offers a wider opportunity to discover the hidden listening talents in the class.

There are a number of studies on affective responses to music that show a definite chronological development of sensitivity and artistic judgment in listening. The studies used a variety of verbal and written approaches in gathering affective responses to listening from children. Basically, children listened to short musical excerpts showing different musical styles and were asked to give their opinions or descriptions of the music. Conclusions from all of the studies established a developmental hierarchy of sensitivity to listening. Younger children were more objective and described basic tonal properties. Middle schoolers gave judgmental responses that gradually led to more balanced, reflective reasoning by high school ages. Rodriguez noted "a gradual trend for responses to become increasingly global and reflective of emotional sensitivity with age."[44] These studies recommend creative activities that encourage students to use more refined affective vocabularies to describe their feelings and understanding of musical listening experiences.[45]

Creative listening tasks in classrooms and studios can expand the vocabulary children use to describe sound as they grow musically. Nurturing critiquing and descriptive tasks through words, art work, and written text can refine this vocabulary. It is also sure to unveil creative listening talent.

Langer and Copland offer ideas about creative listening as well. Both begin with the comfortable notion that *everyone* listens and can learn to listen perceptively. Langer believes all human beings can enjoy the emotional connection with music without becoming occupied with the technical specifics of knowing musical structure or instrumental timbre. However, the power of music is greater for those who understand the details and realize how a musical end derives from these details.

Copland describes three planes of listening: *sensuous, expressive,* and *sheerly musical.* The *sensuous plane* is listening "for the sheer pleasure of the musical sound itself." We listen without thinking about what we hear. This describes background music, creating an atmosphere while we do other things. The *expressive plane* is listening for some meaning or expressive intent in the music. We are not listening for happy or sad music per se, but we are "listening" and interested in the expressive feeling we get from the music. The *sheerly musical plane* is "listening to the musical material and what happens to it." This is active listening, seeking connection with the music through conscious awareness of the musical intricacies that create the listening experience.[46]

The music critic is an active listener who has the skill of translating sound ideas into words. Students who are imaginative writers may impress you with their cleverly written ideas, indicating writing talent. However, an astute music teacher should be able to identify a student who presents novel written ideas that show understanding of the intricacies or expressive ideas of the music. Some may question the significance of recognizing students who use words to describe music as students with musical talent. A performance critique project in my own studio made me personally realize the importance of bringing this unique musical talent into focus.

I taught a young teenager in my studio for about four years who was very bright and very quiet and showed some listening skills in computer ear training. Developing his performance skills was always a challenge, but he showed musical sensitivity whenever he could technically conquer the notes. Our studio project included a year-long focus on the music of Chopin, with lots of comparative listening and in-depth performance classes. Students critiqued each other, with the goal of understanding and explaining Chopin's style through these critiques. This teenager's shy demeanor hindered recognition of this listening talent, even in a small class of musical friends. However, the written forms completed from comparative listening showed an insight into detailed listening and understanding that made quite an impact.

Students were required to listen to three different professional recordings of works they were learning, making dynamic and performance notes about each performance (using different color pencils for each performer) on a copy of their music. The instructions suggested that someone on a desert island, looking at the page, could imagine the performance from these written descriptions. Students also critiqued the recording, saying what they liked and didn't like and what they learned from listening to the piece. Most students whipped through the listening, jotting down several sentences of critique and scrawling a few notations about dynamics and pedaling on the score.

This student's score was a Technicolor picture of fine listening detail. Not only were details of pedaling, rubato effects, dynamics, and articulation noted, but mood and pictorial ideas that he imagined as he listened to the music filled each margin. One recording brought a barrage of negative comments about the dry performance that had no variation of tempo or dynamic scope.

However, under "what can I learn from this piece," he noted that practicing without using pedal and a solid sound would help him clean up articulate problems in his own performance of the piece. This one student made me realize that there are many out there we are missing—the creative listeners.

Arguments For and Against Musical Talent as Creativity

For: Descriptions of the music creators and interpreters in this chapter clearly demonstrate people and products that exemplify the very essence of the meaning of musical talent. These creative perceiver/thinkers realize sound internally and manipulate it to produce a unique, personal statement. The dynamic of this personal statement differentiates the musically talented communicator from those who simply are knowledgeable or well equipped through training.

- *Creative thinking or metaperception defines musical talent:* Creative thinking or metaperception describes the inner cognitive/perceptive process of sound manipulation and expressive interpretation that is at the core of musical talent. Scientific inquiry dissects the process objectively but sidesteps the aesthetic mesh of musician, sound, and emotion. The one-ness of this mesh defines talent in music.
- *The creative producers in any field exemplify talent and nurture fresh ideas for the future:* Persons who have lasting significance in a field usually think differently and seek ways to communicate uniquely outside the norm. Seeking out and nurturing these creative musical minds in the budding stages is a fundamental need in music education. Many musically creative students may not be enrolled in traditional performance classes at school or receiving training in private studios. Seeking ways to recognize these students and provide guidance with a bit of creative space will strengthen their musical base and broaden teaching strategies.
- *The essence of musical learning rests in the creative process and its "flow" state.* Every child in every music classroom and studio deserves to experience the challenging aesthetic experience of "flow." These creative experiences should extend beyond the elementary grades where students "play" with sounds. Individualized tasks that require creative music-making through improvisation, composition, or interpretive performance and listening are essential for all students. Providing a supportive environment for creatively talented students in music gives them "permission" to be divergent and to experiment with their novel ideas. Providing opportunities that develop interpretive decision-making in performance builds sensitive, creative interpreters.

Against: No one can safely argue *against* creativity, but one can pragmatically look at the difficulties of seeking out these creative individuals in the traditional music education setting. There is also the question about why identifying creative talent is so essential in the field of music, when only a small fraction of people in the field actually work with creative products, such as composition or improvisation.

- *Musical talent relies on the ability to perform well—period.* We can examine the intricacies of musical creation and do some fun activities with students in our studios and classrooms, but the bottom line in the field is "How well do you play?" Musically talented students seek out the challenges of performance proficiency. College auditions do not include creative problem-solving activities. They choose students who perform well. The concept of creative interpretation in performance is worth investigation; however, a student who can demonstrate outstanding performance skills through rigorous training is recognized as our outstanding musical talent. Interpretive decision-making naturally develops as the student works one-on-one with a master teacher or is part of an outstanding school performance group.
- *The addition of creative music classes where composition and improvisation are taught is not feasible in the current educational school climate.* School music programs have been downsized and often eliminated across the country. Existing music programs are pushed to the limit in personnel and scheduling. Elementary students in many states rarely see a music specialist in their schools. How can we possibly have time to teach creativity in music if we barely have time to teach basic musical skills? Administrative support for a composition class for a handful of interested students is not going to happen. The idea is wonderful, and any music educator would jump at the chance to teach this class. But a rigorous secondary music program depends heavily on quality in performance, with deadlines to meet and festivals to win to "keep our jobs."
- *Creative music talent identification is unnecessary, costly, and time prohibitive.* A good music teacher can pinpoint a creative student in the music classroom or studio. Creative music testing would be prohibitive to administer in a normal school setting. The individualized music tasks would take too much time and burden the music teacher even further. There is no need to do this type of testing in a private studio, because the student already has the opportunity to work one-on-one with the teacher. The teacher can choose to include improvisation and composition in that private setting, if so desired.

My view: Creativity lies up there with religion, politics, and love. Everyone has an opinion, and trying to clarify specifics brings controversy, debate, and misunderstanding. Some readers may wonder how performers could be considered "creative" when all they do is perform someone else's music. Musicians may wonder how anyone can question the role of creativity in the interpretive process of the performer. I am sure of raised eyebrows at the suggestion of including the critic or perspective listener in this creative discussion. (Then again, a divergent thinker seeks alternative possibilities.)

I have offered explanations here of the vocabulary and basic tenets of the field of creative research so that any reader can begin to come to terms with the question of what makes different roles in music "creative," and enter into healthy discussion and exchange with others about the issue.

I have spent the majority of my career as teacher, lecturer, and writer encouraging creative thinking in music. I suppose I have a natural bias in believing that what we observe in a talented student's behavior when engaged in musical tasks is the element of *creative thinking through sound* (*metaperception*). The recognition of musical talent requires ways to recognize this creative thinking in music—whether it is through composing, improvising, performing, or listening.

The art at the heart of music lies in the *creative process of communicating ideas and emotions through sound*, or creatively interpreting ideas to others. Improvisers and composers generatively interpret their ideas through sound. Performers and listeners interpret their expressive ideas guided by the musical score or recording. The term *creative interpretation* describes the perceptive/cognitive decision-making process in improvisation, composition, performance, or listening. I believe this term offers a better description of the process of creation shared by *all* types of music-makers than the general term *creativity*, which is most associated with improvisation or composition.

As a teacher of performers, I understand the need to develop skills of interpretive decision-making in my students. This is a complex task, seesawing between teaching students what may be appropriate within stylistic boundaries and encouraging them to have the confidence to make personal choices of their own. Talented students often experiment with unique ideas that push the edge of these boundaries. Our job is to encourage students to rework, compare, and hone their ideas to create a performance that retains the unique creativity of their interpretation along with the integrity of the composer's musical intent. The more students manipulate ideas through this metaperceptive decision-making, the more creative the interpretation becomes. A favorite quotation of mine that describes the role of any creative interpreter in music comes from Stravinsky:

> Imagination is not only the mother of caprice but the servant and handmaiden of the creative will as well. The creator's function is to sift the elements he receives from her, for human activity must impose limits upon itself. The more art is controlled, limited, worked over, the more it is free.[47]

Your view: You may find yourself challenged as you attempt to synthesize all the ideas presented so far about creativity and past scientific examinations or discussions of expressive classical performance. Prepare to leap a few reflective hurdles with these questions.

1. Do you believe a musician can develop talent and succeed in the field without being creative, as described in this chapter? Why or why not?
2. How can divergent thinking opportunities be included in performance-oriented classrooms or studios?
3. How can a student make creative decisions in expressive performance without expertise? How can a teacher guide student involvement in this interpretive decision-making?
4. Is a "creative listener" musically talented? Why or why not?
5. Develop your own definition of a "creative musician."

Your reflections:

TALENT AS GIFTEDNESS

Many children have gifts. All children have some gifts. But very few children have the good fortune to have the right background, the parents, the teachers, the opportunity, the encouragement, the love that I had.

Yehudi Menuhin, Sunday Express

Wolfgang Amadeus Mozart began composing at the age of four. He toured as a prodigy for three years before the age of ten, astounding audiences with his ability to perform on the harpsichord, voice, organ, and violin. He would compose on sight in different styles and on different instruments. He could "most accurately name from a distance any notes that may be sounded for him either singly or in chords, on the clavier or on every imaginable instrument, including bells, glasses, and clocks."[1] When his father was recovering from an illness, eight-year-old Wolfgang was not allowed to play the piano. He filled his time by composing his first symphony (K.16) for all instruments of the orchestra.

The Musical Prodigy

When we hear the word "gifted" in connection with music, the musical prodigy immediately comes to mind. The arguments of recognizing talent through performance, creative endeavors, or music aptitude tests seem incidental in comparison to the possibilities and accomplishments of the musical prodigy. There is no question that these young musicians show incredible levels of musical talent, often exhibiting musical capabilities equal to those of a highly trained adult. Mozart remains the preeminent example of the prodigy, described by his father and teacher as a "God-given miracle," knowing "in his eighth year what one would expect from a man of forty. Indeed, only he who sees him can believe it."[2]

A prodigy is a child who displays extraordinary talent at an early age. Prodigies occur most often in the field of music, exceeding the total of all other fields combined. Musical prodigies show outstanding abilities at a younger age than other prodigies, with some as young as three or four years old. The field of chess is a distant second place in number, with prodigious achievement often seen at five or six years of age. Relatively few prodigies are identified in the natural sciences, philosophy, dance, or plastic arts. Even the field of mathematics, whose young calculating wonders gain media recognition, have few true prodigies capable of original mathematical reasoning prior to their teen years.[3]

The literature offers differing opinions concerning age and prodigious talent. Feldman defines the prodigy as a child who performs at the level of a highly trained adult in a demanding field of endeavor before the age of ten. Fisher extends the age to twenty, explaining that "twenty was a more mature age, in an economic as well as a professional sense, two hundred years ago than it is today; but, on the other hand, our criteria for extraordinary achievement have risen so sharply that the score probably evens up."[4] Radford extends the idea of prodigy to include "exceptional early achievers," with a flexible cutoff age prior to 21. He also agrees that standards change, realizing that young boys commonly wrote in Greek verse in public schools one hundred years ago.[5] This is quite rare for any adult today. The idea of Mozart composing at an early age was not unusual at a time when music instruction commonly included composition and improvisation.

Biographical information of prodigies indicates an exceptional ear from a young age. Jacqueline du Pré could sing in tune before she could talk. Lorin Hollander relays that at the age of three, within four minutes of learning the letter names of notes and clefs, he called out "F-sharp" when hearing a car horn outside and "B-flat" when his father clinked a glass with a spoon. At age four, Yehudi Menuhin was given a toy violin, which he smashed to the floor because it would not "sing" the correct notes.

Three-year-old Artur Rubinstein enjoyed sitting beneath the piano while his sisters took piano lessons. He noticed that their teacher would slap their hands when they made a mistake. When his sisters practiced, he would pretend to be their teacher, slapping their hands with each wrong note that he heard. He also was adept at identifying pitches in full dissonant chords played by his piano teacher in his earliest lessons. Ten-year-old Josef Hofmann once tugged at the conductor's jacket while rehearsing a piano concerto with a major orchestra. It seems he heard an inaccurate passage in the cellos that the conductor had not noticed

Prodigies learn at a very rapid pace, usually astounding their teachers. They also relish creating and solving challenging musical problems. Nicolo Paganini stands as the violin prodigy equal to Mozart on the keyboard. His precocious technique and desire to work things out in unorthodox ways upset his earliest teachers. He could read anything at sight and continuously sought technical challenges. He wrote his first sonata at age eight and quickly began writing music too difficult for him to play so he could devise ways to conquer his self-composed technical hurdles. He claimed to have devised a magical system to enable violinists to acquire technical fluency in three years that normally would take ten. His *Twenty-four Caprices*, composed before the age of twenty, remain a supreme technical challenge to violinists today.[6]

The one element that truly defines a musical prodigy is the ability to create a performance dynamic with the audience that is captivating and, at times, overwhelming. When Ruth Slenczynska performed at age four, the audience thought she was Mozart reincarnated, playing under some kind of mysterious spell. A performance at age six actually had critics searching beneath the piano for some sign of wires or mechanisms that could produce such sounds from a young child. When young Yehudi Menuhin gave his Carnegie Hall debut, the audience would not stop cheering, with many moved to tears, until he brought his teacher on stage and finally put on his hat and coat. The composer Rossini wrote: "I have wept but three times in my life; the first, on the failure of my earliest opera; the second, when in a boat with some friends, a turkey stuffed with truffles fell overboard; and thirdly, when I heard Paganini play for the first time."[7]

In the nature-nurture argument, heredity plays a speculative role at best in determining prodigious offspring. True, there were generations of talented musicians in the Bach family—but only one Johann Sebastian. The heritage of the Strauss family in Vienna, six generations of Couperins in France, and four in the Purcell family of England cannot be ignored. Studies show that many prodigies have parents who are involved in the same or related fields. In music, parents are music teachers or performers or show an active interest in music.[8]

Environmental influences from an early age of parents and teachers (often one and the same) play a leading role in the prodigy's talent development. The parent-teacher role of Leopold Mozart is well known. We often hear of his interest in seeking financial gain by exploiting young Wolfgang and his sister Nannerl in their concert tours. He also was a devoted teacher whose music notebook was filled with marginal notations of the age and length of time it took for his son to learn certain pieces. Nannerl recalled a nightly ritual of father and son at bedtime that creates a tender picture of their relationship in musical terms. Mozart would sing a composed melody for his father, who would sing along in counterpoint. This intimate musical exchange always ended with a good night kiss.[9]

There are several prodigies whose parents discovered talents surprisingly hidden behind misdiagnosed diseases. The musical parents of Clara Wieck (who later became Clara Schumann) were distressed that their young daughter did not speak and feared that she was "dull of hearing." When she was five years old, her piano teacher father decided he would try to include her in lessons with other young children. She not only learned the piano with amazing ease but also began to speak in full sentences. Béla Bartók had a severe case of eczema from birth to age five and was misdiagnosed as having a curvature of the spine, which confined movement to lying down or standing. Full attention from a mother who tutored him at home opened up the world of music, first through drums, then the piano and composing. He returned to school at age seven, completing four grades in one year.

There is a fine line between a parent seeking to establish the disciplined practice necessary for skill development and the abusive treatment of young prodigies. The movie *Shine* depicted the childhood of Andrew Helfgott, an Australian pianist who met with mental problems as an adult stemming from the off-balance demands of a parent. Niccolo Paganini's father was an amateur violinist determined to create a prodigy through beatings, starvation, and ten hours of daily practice in a locked room. Ruth Slenczynska's father woke her at six o'clock each morning to practice in her nightgown in cold temperatures. Also a teacher, he devoted his full time to her training, demanding nine hours of practice a day, with mistakes punished by a slap across the face.

These isolated examples of horrendous childhood environments are offset by the many stories of parents who have molded their lives in support of the needs of their precocious child. The Polish parents of Artur Rubinstein, after years of searching for appropriate instruction, sought advice from Joseph Joachim, an eminent violinist living in Berlin. Joachim took the boy under his wing, with the stipulation that he not be exploited as a prodigy but gain a full musical education to maturity. The entire Menuhin family moved from the United States to Europe, with expenses underwritten by a patron, seeking to assist the musical development of Yehudi, the amazing young prodigy. Menuhin recalls the "exorbitant demands" required in raising a prodigy. "There is no doubt that I shaped my parents' lives as much as they shaped mine."[10]

So often we narrow our vision of musical prodigies to the classical genre. The same determination, talent, and diligence at a young age is part of jazz and popular music. Differences often lie in the persistence and reliance on natural, self-taught talents versus instruction from master teachers at an early age. Louis Armstrong credits a stay at the Colored Waifs Home for delinquent boys in New Orleans as the start of his musical career. During this stay he learned to play the cornet, soon becoming band leader and bugler for military calls. He left the home at 14, sporting the nickname "Satchelmouth" or "Satchmo." He spent his teenage years hauling coal for ten hours a day. After a few hours of sleep, he would play cornet on the street corner for tips until four o'clock in the morning. After a couple of hours of rest, he'd start the routine again.

Stevie Judkins, a young blind ten-year-old, was discovered playing harmonica and singing on the street corners of Detroit. The head of Motown Records heard him sing nonstop for an hour in an audition and was astounded; he renamed him "Little Stevie Wonder." At age twelve, his first single, "Fingertips," sold over a million copies.[11]

SPARKLER EXPERIENCE: A Mozart Trick of the Trade

When Leopold Mozart took his young children on tour, they often performed a kind of sideshow of outstanding musical feats to impress the audience. One featured young Mozart performing a piece with a blindfold and/or covered keyboard. The following experience teaches you how to do this Mozart trick, while realizing keyboard kinesthetic-spatial awareness. You will obviously need a piano or keyboard for this task. I encourage teachers in the studio and classroom to try this with their students.

1. *Realizing bodily-kinesthetic movement and space:* Sit at the middle of the keyboard, with the set of two black keys just above middle C lined up directly in front of you. With a flattened right hand, play these two keys. Skim over the three black keys directly to the right and play the next set of two black keys. Practice playing these two sets of black keys in a seesaw motion, keenly sensing the motion and distance of your arm with each gesture.

2. *Developing motor memory:* "Motor memory" describes the physical ease of attaining fine bodily-kinesthetic motion of the hand on the keyboard. This motor memory leads to "automaticity" through deliberate practice. After practicing your arm and hand movement from one set of two black keys to the next, try looking *directly in front of you* instead of at your hand. Keep practicing until the gesture is secure and correct. (One of the first tasks in teaching piano is to have the student keep eyes on the music while playing to help instill motor memory of movement on the keyboard.)

3. *Securing keyboard spatial awareness:* Have a friend or family member hold a book or piece of cardboard in front of you at chest level to block the view of your hand. Repeat your seesawing gesture from one

→

A Mozart Trick of the Trade (*continued*)

set of black keys to another. After you are comfortable with this movement, close your eyes and perform the spatial task.

4. *Expanding your keyboard geography:* Expand spatial leaps on the
keyboard to include the following. Each will require practice of the first
three steps, ending with a blindfolded finale.
   • Add several two-note groupings above, leaping from one to the next.
   • Use the left hand to repeat the same process down the keyboard.
   • Isolate the first note in each two black key set (C♯), playing with
   the second finger (right and left hand).
   • Perform both hands together going in contrary motion at the same
   time
   • "Olympic gold medal"—try a few two-octave leaps (skipping over
   one set).

5. *A Mozart trick for musicians:* Piano students can pretend to be Mozart
by actually covering the keyboard with a thin cloth and playing a
piece they have learned at their lessons on top of the cloth. Beginning piano pieces usually lie comfortably within a five-finger pattern with few octave leaps, so this "trick" will be easier than the
experience here.

The Development of a Musical Prodigy

Musical prodigies are drawn to music at an unusually early age. Interview
studies indicate that prodigies attentively take notice of music and accurately
sing on pitch by age two. Talent is recognized by four to five years of age,
with lessons typically beginning at ages five to seven.[12] Intensive training of
musical abilities begins quite early, as soon as parents recognize unusual
talent.

The role of the teacher in the development of prodigies is of utmost importance. Bloom and his colleagues describe a developing string of teachers.
The initial teacher offers a positive environment that inspires the joy of music.
The student then progresses to a teacher who can advance technical skills,
followed by a master teacher to develop artistry.[13] Parents of these quick
learners, realizing the need for further challenge, often seek out a master
teacher earlier in development. The high incidence of parents making major
personal sacrifices to seek out the best possible teacher shows the importance
of proper musical training.

The environmental role of parent, teacher, and child must be highly mal-leable as the prodigy grows. Teachers who seek career recognition through student accomplishments may push the child into a concert career too early. Concert managers may not consider the welfare of the child when the box office beckons. Parents have the complex role of balancing the need to offer their talented child challenging opportunities to grow musically with the equally important need to let him or her simply "be a child."

Prodigies have remarkably perceptive ears, with many (but not all) hav-ing perfect pitch from an early age. An extraordinary musical memory al-lows them to reproduce complicated music after hearing it a single time or briefly examining the score. Their retention of memorized repertoire far exceeds the norm. It is not unusual to have at least one full program of rep-ertoire and a set of concertos in memory at a given time.

Musical prodigies have the persistence and determination to achieve chal-lenging goals they set for themselves. Technical proficiency comes easily and fascinates them. Deliberate practice is an accepted daily routine, with young musicians often *choosing* to practice and perform up to six hours a day by the time they reach teen years. This is a stamina and demand for work well above the norm.

The development of musical understanding and creative interpretive abil-ity determines the prodigy who can successfully make the transition from exceptionally talented child to professional concert artist. Many have diffi-culty in this crucial transition. Young prodigies have the ability to commu-nicate through music intuitively. They never really think about how they do it—they just do it. As they reach adolescence, they begin to analyze and question their abilities.

Bamberger's studies of gifted musicians describes this stage as a "mid-life crisis." She believes it stems from cognitive changes that occur at this age. Young prodigies perform with "all-at-once imitation" that brings multiple musical dimensions under hand without analytic thought. At adolescence, there is a need to reflect, analyze, and question. The immediacy of learning is thwarted by the cognitive need to pull ideas apart for reflection and analysis.[14]

The cellist Janos Starker describes this period in a prodigy's development when you are "grown up and can no longer depend on instinct": "What happens to the bird who sings and doesn't know how it sings? That's what happens to child prodigies. They wake up and ask themselves dangerous questions about how they do it—and have no answers."[15]

Starker's adjustment to this transition lasted a mere seven months. Josef Hofman's, brought about by the Society for the Prevention of Cruelty to Children, which questioned the rigorous concert schedule of an eleven-year-old, lasted six years. Hofman found the return to the stage as a mature artist quite difficult. "You are in the shadow of your early power, and it is a heart-breaking business to climb out of it into your own light."[16] Ruth Slenczynska finally broke the bounds of her dominating father at 15; she did not return to the concert stage until her late twenties.

Ironically, the two musical prodigies who were studied extensively in research did not succeed in making a smooth transition into adulthood. Stumpf initiated the idea of testing for musical aptitude while studying Pepito Areola at the turn of the century. At 11, this prodigy was the highest-paid performer in Europe. After a decline in popularity in his late teens, he basically disappeared from the music scene. At 48 he wrote to a music magazine assuring curious historians that he was still alive, enjoying a conservatively normal musical life.

Révész's six-year study of Erwin Nyiregyházi, from age seven to thirteen, contributed comprehensive information about the musical development of a prodigy. This is the only study that analyzed prodigious musical cognitive development as well as the development of musical skills. Révész estimated Erwin's IQ as slightly above 140 when tested at age seven. At age nine, he could learn Beethoven sonatas and Bach fugues after hearing them a few times. His playing displayed impressive technique and sensitive musicality. By age 17 he had enthusiastic debuts in Berlin and New York. However, as an adult, he led a stormy existence, living as a near-vagrant without a piano for 40 years. He died in 1987, survived by the last of 10 wives.[17]

"Gifted" and "Talented"

Musical talent as "giftedness" extends beyond the rare occurrence of the child prodigy. To understand what is meant by "musically gifted" or "musically talented" or the inclusive "musically gifted and talented," a glance at how the field of music and the specialized field of gifted and talented education comes to terms with these *terms* is in order.

I have placed the words "gifted" and "talented" in quotations because these words often appear set apart in this way—as though they should be spoken with a smirk of dismay or a condescending nod. People are intrigued or upset by these terms. They elicit semantic confusion. They are labels that are misunderstood and misconstrued. Exactly what do they mean and who do they describe?

The field of gifted education has dealt with misperceptions of the terms "gifted" and "talented" for over four decades. The general public has a fluctuating love-hate relationship with the field, depending on the political climate. When the public seeks "excellence" in education, talented students are given challenging opportunities within school. When "equity" is an issue, the emphasis is on meeting the needs of the average, below average, or disadvantaged student.[18]

Few outside the field realize that, from the outset, gifted identification procedures and programs have focused on seeking and serving the *potentially talented* student as well as the student who displays outstanding performance and achievement. In the United States, gifted research primarily relies on the Jacob Javits Gifted and Talented grants of the Department of Education, which require studies to recognize and serve minority, handicapped, and underserved students. In essence, the field of gifted education emphasizes seeking effective ways to develop excellence *with* equity.

There are many models that describe the basic characteristics of giftedness or talent. One of the earliest and most recognizable is Joseph Renzulli's three-ring conception of giftedness, which interlocks three clusters of traits: *above average ability, task commitment,* and *creativity.* The overlap of all three represents an interaction that is the "necessary ingredient for creative/productive accomplishment" (fig. 6.1). Renzulli cautions that no single cluster "makes giftedness," emphasizing the need to include creativity and task commitment in addition to the recognition of cognitive abilities.

If we adapt the three-ring model to music, the gifted musician is above average in music aptitude and ability, shows commitment and self-motivation, and demonstrates creativity in musical work (creative interpretation) (fig. 6.2).

Renzulli and his wife, Sally Reis, are regarded as significant contributors to the field since the 1970s. Their many curricular models have gifted students progressively working toward more individualized problem-solving activities requiring abstract reasoning and creative production. Their models adapt and adjust to current educational trends. The original Enrichment Triad Model (1977) evolved into a Revolving Door Model (1981) involving a larger "talent pool" of students taking advantage of gifted programs. The School Wide Enrichment Model (1985) combines both models to mesh with the cooperative, flexible needs of current educational goals. The traditional models of the 1970s, which promoted advanced level instruction to the upper 3–5 percent of the school population, have evolved into a flexible system that reaches all students, offering specialized services to approximately 15 percent of the school population.[19]

A recent model by Gagné clearly differentiates "giftedness" as natural ability or aptitude from "talent" as developed ability or skill. Natural abilities (giftedness) act as the raw material, or "constituent elements," of talents. "One cannot become talented without being gifted." However, it is possible for natural abilities to remain simply as "gifts" if students do not work through the "learning, training, and practicing" stage of talent development. To Gagné, "musical talent is the demonstration of systematically developed abilities in the playing of a musical instrument at the level which places the individual among the top 10% of peers having had similar training." Gagné's Differentiated Model of Giftedness (fig. 6.3) clearly differ-

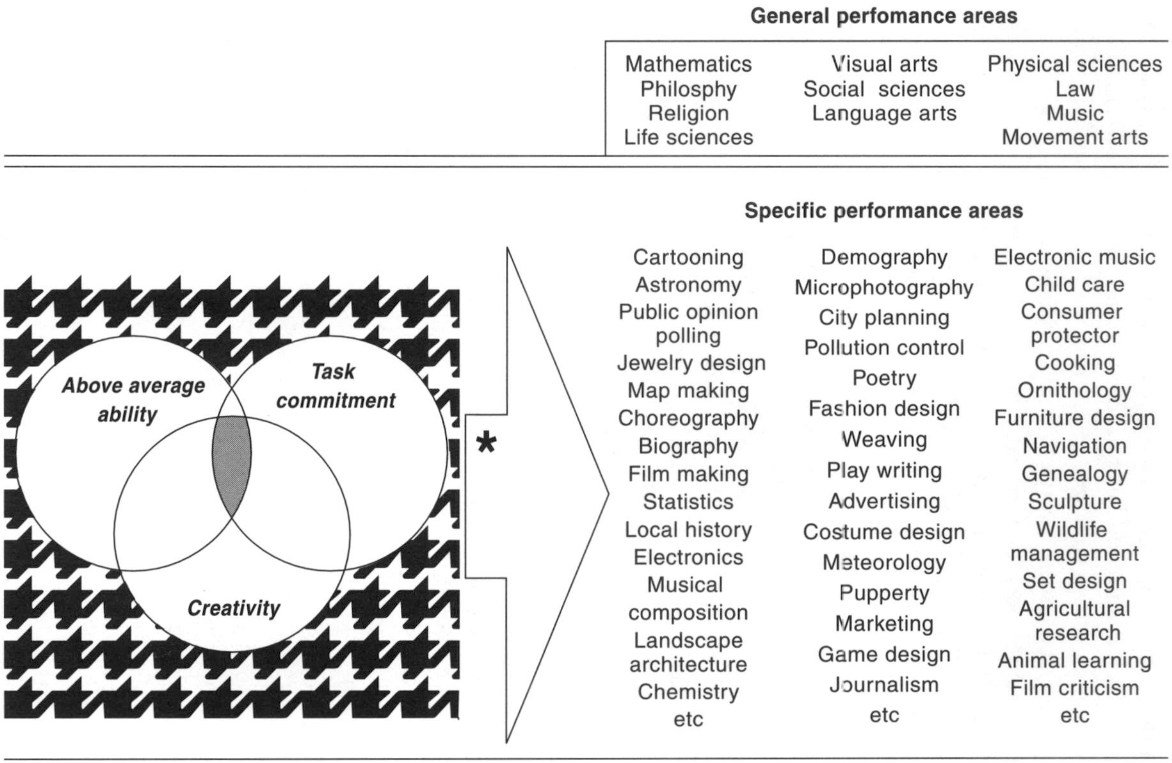

General performance areas

Mathematics	Visual arts	Physical sciences
Philosophy	Social sciences	Law
Religion	Language arts	Music
Life sciences		Movement arts

Specific performance areas

Cartooning	Demography	Electronic music
Astronomy	Microphotography	Child care
Public opinion polling	City planning	Consumer protector
Jewelry design	Pollution control	Cooking
Map making	Poetry	Ornithology
Choreography	Fashion design	Furniture design
Biography	Weaving	Navigation
Film making	Play writing	Genealogy
Statistics	Advertising	Sculpture
Local history	Costume design	Wildlife management
Electronics	Meteorology	Set design
Musical composition	Puppetry	Agricultural research
Landscape architecture	Marketing	Animal learning
Chemistry	Game design	Film criticism
etc	Journalism	etc
	etc	

Task commitment

Creativity

Above average ability

*

FIGURE 6.1. Graphic representation of Renzulli's Three-Ring Definition of Giftedness. Printed with permission from *Systems and Models for Developing Programs for the Gifted and Talented* (1986), edited by Joseph Renzulli. Creative Learning Press, Inc., PO Box 320, Mansfield Center, CT 06250. All rights reserved.

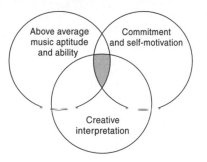

FIGURE 6.2. Three rings of musical giftedness/talent adapted from Renzulli's definition of giftedness.

entiates giftedness and talents and recognizes the catalytic influences of intrapersonal traits and environmental factors on talent development.[20]

Educators accustomed to the IQ-and-achievement-test norm of gifted identification procedures often equate "gifted" with academic and intellectual achievement while "talent" describes outstanding achievement in the arts. Often, a misguided view of "talent" lying a step below "giftedness" in importance grew from this duality, which may explain the exclusion of "talented" students in the arts from gifted identification in American schools.

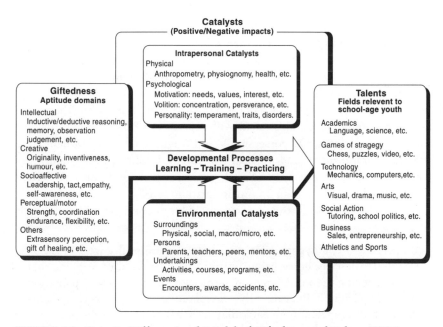

FIGURE 6.3. Gagné's Differentiated Model of Giftedness and Talent (1997).

The gifted field is making strides to include the artistic "talents" now recognized by expanded theories of intelligence. Chapter 11 describes procedures suitable for the effective identification of musically talented students.

Realizing the volatile nature of the term "gift," the field of gifted education recently made a fundamental shift in philosophy and focus. The revised definition used in the field actually omits the term altogether. "The term, 'gifted,' connotes a mature power rather than a developing ability and, therefore, is antithetic to recent research findings about children." The revised definition describes "children and youth with outstanding talent" who have the "potential for performing at remarkably high levels of accomplishment." The word "gift" has disappeared. Talent development is now the key focus of the field.[21] In celebration, I omit the bothersome quotation marks hereafter.

Musically Gifted and Talented

The field of music psychology equated musical talent with giftedness through the early research of Carl Seashore. Seashore's genetically endowed "musical talent" was actually an inherited "gift." A thorough reading of Seashore's texts show that his understanding of musical talent had a rich developmental scope; however, dissenters could not get past the notion that his concept of talent was something that did not develop past the age of nine or ten. Gordon's use of the term "music aptitude" clarified the sensory focus of what Seashore was describing as musical talent in his early tests. Colleagues were more comfortable with this term.

Researchers in expertise performance have focused on deconstructing the role of talent through systematic analysis of developmental deliberate practice. Arguments against the concept of talent may stem from experience dealing with administrators who have the misperception that only people born with musical talent or giftedness will succeed in music while those who do not naturally possess this talent will not succeed. Viewing an outstanding musical performer as possessing a "gift" ignores the role of deliberate practice, commitment, and musical training. Of course, music educators would adamantly argue against limiting music education to only the gifted and talented who score high on music aptitude tests.

Michael Howe explains this view clearly in his discussion of the childhoods of geniuses:

> If I listen to a young person playing the violin unusually well, I may be tempted to describe her as being "gifted," perhaps without realizing that by introducing the word I am drawn into agreeing with the explanation that is implicit in it, indicating that the player is not just especially competent, but competent for a particular reason, namely that she possesses a musical gift. If I begin to use the word *gifted* regularly for describing

able musicians, I may unknowingly begin to convince myself that it is good musicians' gifts that make them excellent.[22]

I personally witnessed this misconception of musical talent at a recent national seminar where I exchanged ideas with specialists in gifted education from across the country. The weekend focused on specific ways to serve the young gifted and talented student. As the only arts specialist, I brought in several talented seven-year-old musicians to perform for the conference. After their impressive performance, the audience eagerly asked the youngsters questions about how they were able to perform such difficult pieces. They were amazed to learn that these youngsters were practicing up to two hours a day at age seven. (I wasn't.) A knowledgeable colleague turned to me with an enlightened expression that showed a new understanding of artistic accomplishments and said, "They really have to work hard to be able to perform well. It just doesn't come naturally."

Research in expertise performance goes as far as compiling evidence that may even question the notion that Mozart was "gifted." Howe explains that Mozart's early performing skills were "not out of line with what would be expected in a child of that age who received intensive training and spent a considerable amount of time practicing, as Mozart undoubtedly did." His early compositions were not very remarkable, with the more substantial and original works surfacing after ten years of musical training. This falls in line with studies of expertise performance showing a required 10 years of deliberate practice in a particular domain. Even young Mozart's feats of memory coincide with the constant exposure to music he received, requiring a consistent recall of information within his specialized area of music.

Howe contends that "the suggestion that Mozart must have had an innate musical gift is unconvincing because it begs a number of questions and provides only the appearance of an explanation rather than a genuine one. A statement of that kind can never amount to more than a half-baked explanation unless it is possible to specify precisely what form such an innate gift takes, how its presence is detected, and exactly how it operates."[23]

Mozart-lovers may strongly disagree with this view. An argument against the notion that musical prodigies are a mere product of training and extensive practice is offered by Ellen Winner, a researcher in multiple intelligences who specializes in the visual arts. She believes that there is indeed such a thing as innate talent and that "giftedness cannot be entirely a product of birth," bringing in the importance of family support, education, and hard work. However, she says, "there is considerable evidence for a strong inborn, brain-based component to giftedness."

Self-motivation and commitment is a defining element of giftedness, described by Winner as a "rage to master" within a specialized domain. "The desire to work so hard at something, to practice and explore for long hours, comes from within, not without. Such intrinsic motivation typically occurs when there is a high innate ability, as long as there is sufficient parental encouragement and support. The rage to master is an ineluctable part of talent." Winner contends that gifted children differ from ordinary children in four respects:[24]

1. They learn more rapidly in the domain.
2. They are intrinsically motivated to acquire skill in the domain.
3. They make discoveries in the domain without much explicit adult scaffolding. A great deal of work is self-taught.
4. They not only make discoveries on their own, but often do things in the domain that ordinary hard workers never do—inventing new solutions, thinking, seeing, or hearing in a qualitatively different way.

The broadened conception of intelligence combined with the desire to reach a greater number of students in gifted education seems a positive development toward the future recognition and development of musical talent within public education. Knowledgeable discussions between music educators and gifted specialists to establish acceptable identification procedures will be required. Music educators need to explain the music-specific skills and listening aptitude that describes musical talent. Gifted specialists need to explain the desire to seek *potential* talent through identification and attempt to demystify the terminology of the field. It makes sense to include professional resources from the community in the discussion to help mold a program that will provide individualized instruction with private teachers and performing musicians outside the school walls.[25]

If we ease the term "gifted" out of the discussion of musical talent, we find ourselves in safer territory. Music educators and private music instructors understand talent development—it is their daily job. They realize that some students excel and require further challenges to achieve their full potential; these are musically talented students who require individualized instruction. Developing specific procedures to seek out *potentially* talented students may allow hidden listening talents to surface. If we think of musical talent as developmental, rather than inherent, misperceptions disappear.

The "Mozart Effect"

In spite of the recent acceptance of the concept of multiple forms of intelligences that include musical intelligence, there remains a gnawing need to justify musical learning in education in extra-musical terms. We should learn music because music students do better in math, or learn languages faster, or have higher self-esteem, or are less drawn to drugs and crime. Music educators share with gifted specialists the continuous adjustment mirroring the political trend of the decade. The trend in the 1990s centered on "how music can make you smarter." It began with a bit of Mozart and a small group of researchers intrigued with the connection between music and spatial-temporal reasoning.

Frances Rauscher, Gordon Shaw, and a number of associates at the University of California at Irvine had a group of college students listen to the opening 10 minutes of Mozart's Sonata for Two Pianos in D Major (K.448) prior to the administration of a test of spatial-temporal tasks. They found that students who listened to Mozart scored significantly higher than students who spent 10 minutes listening to "self-hypnosis instructions" or silence. The same team replicated the study with similar significant results using a five-day study with the same Mozart excerpt compared with listening to progressive relaxation instructions, silence, a story, minimalist music by Phillip Glass ("Music with Changing Parts"), or British-style trance music. Findings showed this unique cognitive effect caused by listening to Mozart lasted for approximately 10 to 15 minutes.[26]

The media quickly dubbed these findings the "Mozart Effect." The governor of Georgia began distributing CDs of music by Mozart to every newborn baby in the state. There was a rush for any type of classical music that would bring instant intelligence, simply by listening. The generalized exaggeration of the study's findings may bring music into classrooms, homes, and cribs, but the specifics of the study are worth investigating to understand the connection of brain functioning, music cognition, and spatial-temporal reasoning.

Rauscher and her colleagues were motivated by earlier neurological studies having to do with strengthening neural "firing patterns" in the cortical column of the cortex that allows the performance of "spatial-temporal tasks." An example of a complex spatial-temporal task is the ability to transform mental images in the absence of a physical model. A common test for this task is "paper folding and cutting" (fig. 6.4). Spatial-temporal reasoning is required for higher brain functions relevant to chess, mathematics, engineering, and *music cognition*. Leng and Shaw proposed that "exposure to music might excite the cortical firing patterns used in spatial-temporal reasoning, thereby affecting cognitive ability in tasks that share the same neural code."[27]

Rauscher work supports these ideas by suggesting that listening to music (Mozart in particular) helps to "organize temporarily, the cortical firing patterns for spatial temporal processes."[28] Improvement was uniquely confined to "spatial-temporal tasks," which involve inner imagery and not "spatial-recognition tasks," which involve the less complex ability to classify physical similarities among objects.

This popular study gave rise to similar studies with their own unique twists. In reaction to the common question "Why Mozart?" a number of studies

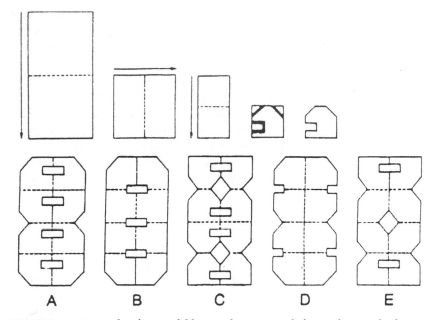

FIGURE 6.4. Example of paper folding and cutting task from *The Stanford-Binet Intelligence Scale*. The picture shows a paper before it was folded and cut (top left figure). The dotted lines and arrows represent where and in what direction the paper would be folded; the solid lines show where the paper would be cut. The students in the Raucher, Shaw, and Ky study were instructed to visualize the folds and cuts and then choose the drawing that shows how the paper would look if it were unfolded. Copyright © 1986 Riverside Publishing Company. Reproduced from sample test figures for *The Stanford-Binet Intelligence Scale*, 4th ed., by Robert L. Thorndike, Elizabeth P. Hagen, and Jerome M. Sattler, with permission of the publisher.

replicated the experiment pairing Mozart with Schubert and even Yanni, discovering that organized music, regardless of style, may enhance spatial-temporal reasoning more than repetitive music (minimalist, trance music) or silence. Numerous subsequent studies used different stimuli, including stories and music, suggesting that preference, interest, and "enjoyment arousal" may be key factors to explain improvement in test results. One study used an electroencephalaogram to record the brain activity of Mozart listeners as they took a spatial-temporal test. Rauscher extended studies to include zapping mice *in utero* with Mozart (K.488, of course) to test their navigation of a maze after birth.[29]

Ongoing studies are claiming to disprove the initial Rauscher study, noting its numerous shortcomings. These studies have used a variety of tests to measure visual-spatial functioning with different research designs, finding no resulting Mozart effect.[30]

Rauscher argues in response that researchers and the general public have misinterpreted the findings of her studies. The most common misconception is that "listening to Mozart enhances intelligence. We made no such claim. The effect is limited to spatial-temporal tasks involving mental imagery and temporal ordering."[31]

The media blitz about the listening effect has overshadowed follow-up studies that link musical study with neural facilitation. The Irvine group showed that preschool children who received eight months of music instruction on keyboards and singing scored significantly higher on spatial reasoning tasks than children who received computer lessons or no lessons after only four months of instruction. Of interest in regard to practice and commitment, these tiny three-year-olds were given the opportunity to practice their keyboards daily. These practice sessions were supervised but not enforced, yet children enjoyed practicing what they learned on a regular basis throughout the week.[32]

In addition, recent neurological research has discarded the notion of "right-brained" musicians, discovering that the process of music-making involves auditory, visual, cognitive, affective, and motor processing. Schlaug and colleagues' magnetic resonance imaging studies compared the brains of musicians and nonmusicians, seeking a biological basis for musical talent. Not only did musicians not show a right hemisphere predominance, but they actually had more pronounced left hemisphere dominance than the control group. The planum temporale of musicians with absolute pitch was enlarged on the left side, especially in those who began study before the age of seven. The study found that musical activity can enhance the growth of the brain in early childhood. Schlaug describes the brain as "plastic" during the first decade of life, recommending musical training starting at preschool levels, with active participation being more beneficial than passive listening.[33]

These studies have fired up interest in revitalizing the role of music in public education. Many schools have initiated early keyboard training at the preschool level, which enhances early musical talent development. Teachers of preschoolers will be able to recognize the first signs of musical talent before the age of five, when musically talented children normally start formal training. Early musical training in preschool will also develop listening skills in the crucial ages prior to nine, when music aptitude supposedly stabilizes.

Music, IQ, and Academics

Though strides have been made to ease the general public away from the importance of the IQ as a measurement of giftedness, the traditional label still reigns as the measurement of intelligence. Feldman cautions against the use of IQ in measuring giftedness, because it misses the prodigy as well as the savant. The prodigy in music and other fields exhibits a distinct form of giftedness showing an unusually strong talent in a single area and a powerful drive to develop it. General intelligence plays a supporting role, not a central one. The prodigy may have a high IQ but not necessarily exceptionally high. The focus of talent *within a specific area* distinguishes the prodigy from the high IQ student who is commonly labeled "gifted."[34]

An intriguing early study by Cox examined biographies of great men, determining their IQs by the activities in which they were engaged at various ages. She estimated Bach's IQ at approximately 125–40, Beethoven's at 135–40, and Mozart's at 150–55. Although these are impressive IQ ranges, taken as a group, they rated quite low in comparison to the other eminent figures in her study. Their highly focused giftedness within music also rated them as the least versatile of the group. The study's determined IQ for these distinguished composers reveals the unique problem of aligning giftedness with IQ alone.[35]

Ongoing studies have connected the study of music with reading, language skills, mathematics, general creativity, and social concerns such as self-esteem, social skills, and reduction of dropout rates. One of the most impressive findings shows that students engaged in musical instruction scored higher than the national average in both verbal and math scores on the SAT over a period of at least seven years (1987–93). The College Entrance Examination Board profiles of 95 percent of over three million students taking the SATs indicate that students studying music appreciation or performance score 19–31 points above the national average in verbal scores and 14–23 points above in math. Students who are not involved in any arts area consistently scored below the national average in both areas over the seven-year period.[36]

Pockets of schools across the country are intrigued with integrating music into the academic classroom. The Los Angeles Unified School District is integrating music into classes in physics, physical education, and math. A music-math integrated program in Florida boasts that "students who had never read a note of music were able to compose sonatas and study complex Beethoven scores by looking for recurring math-like patterns." Students who are described as "tone deaf" are composing in this class. In research at an elementary school in Salem, Massachusetts, music is used as an interdisciplinary tool in all classrooms, showing richer understanding of the patterns and structure that are the "undergirding concepts" of math and reading.[37]

The pendulum currently has a decided positive swing for music education and the possibilities of musical knowing in every classroom. Technological advances in examining the brain while engaged in music will further define the value of this musical functioning. The acceptance of multiple intelligences in growing school curricula will enhance the understanding of a separate musical intelligence. All of these factors promote the need to recognize and serve the needs of students who excel in musical knowing.

Unusual Giftedness

The Savant

The existence of giftedness in the musical savant led Gardner to the decision that musical intelligence is, indeed, a unique intelligence. The musical savant is an individual of very low intelligence whose musical accomplishments resemble those of musical prodigies at a young age. Savants often display their musical giftedness at an early age through the ability to replicate tunes after a single hearing, singing in tune at an early age, and having an exceptional tonal memory.

Savants most often occur in the domain of music, with a few interesting examples in the visual arts and in calculation in mathematics. The earlier term, "idiot savant," was changed by Treffert in 1989 to "savant syndrome" or "savant" to classify the term clearly and eliminate pejorative connotations. Musical savants are typically blind and mentally handicapped, showing autistic characteristics. Their intense interest in music usually begins young, and they are all pianists.[38]

Savant behavior displays a shallow range of emotion, which explains musical performances that are often imitative rather than expressive. Treffert's extensive review of the literature concluded that savants have a "flattened affect" emotionally, which limits performances to shallow expression and compositional efforts to patterned improvisation. Several studies have questioned these findings, showing evidence of emotional involvement with the music as verbal abilities were expanded. One study of an adult savant found that the advent of more advanced language skills also resulted in the dramatic ability to begin composing. These studies pose an intriguing link between language and music abilities in savants.[39]

Almost all of the reported musical savants have perfect pitch. Winner notes that one in twenty autistic individuals also have perfect pitch. This ability is highly present in people with Williams Syndrome and in those retarded in the areas of drawing and reasoning. She suggests the recognition of perfect pitch in special populations as a possible indication of musical ability.[40]

Blind Tom was the twenty-first child of a slave, born blind in 1849 and tagged an "idiot" from birth. When Tom was five, Colonel Bethune, his master, acquired a piano for his daughters' lessons. The young lad would sneak into the house late at night, playing with ease and accuracy the Mozart pieces he had heard through the window. Bethune began exhibiting Blind Tom at the age of eight, with much success and wide acclaim of his extraordinary musical abilities. Among his feats was the ability to play two tunes simultaneously on the piano while singing a third. On one occasion, an opera composer was called to the stage to play a piece he had just composed. Tom listened attentively, then sat and played the piece perfectly, including the same performance style of the composer. He would improvise, play his own compositions, and even perform recitations in Greek, Latin, and German. Exaggerated accounts put his repertoire at five thousand musical works by the end of his life.[41]

An intensive study of Noel Patterson, an autistic savant in Britain, contributes new information explaining the underlying nature of savant abilities. Rather than a rote auditory memory, his ability involved the memory of tonal structures and relationships. He remembered a piece based on traditional harmonic structures more easily than an atonal modern piece. When matched with a professional musician, both had equal difficulty memorizing the atonal piece, but Patterson memorized the traditional piece more accurately than the professional musician. This internalization of the structure and acquired "templates" of traditional Western music allowed him to improvise within this style with ease.[42]

Miller's four-year study describes this savant ability as a sense of "musical syntax," where ease of memory depends on structural aspects of music. Savants remember music with harmonic structure more easily than isolated melodies. The choice of the piano as an instrument by the savant supports this structural need—placing music within a spatial organization of keys, similar to a musical alphabet. "Like a child whose language expression and comprehension reflects the rules of syntax, so does the musical savant's performance show musical syntax rule use. In neither case is conscious knowledge of the system of rules necessary."[43]

Well-documented cases of musical savants show evidence of *extended* absolute pitch, in which the ability is extended over the whole scale and is independent of the instrument used. This is extraordinary, when realizing that in the general population this ability shows up in less than one in 10,000.

When five severely retarded music savant adults were paired with young music students with several years of training, the savants far outperformed the young musicians in musical competence and inventiveness. Each was asked to complete a tune, improvise an accompaniment, invent a melody and accompaniment, and improvise in a jazz style. Researchers concluded that these findings indicate the existence of a musical intelligence that is at least partly independent of general intelligence.[44]

Williams Syndrome

There is a unique chromosomal disorder called Williams syndrome (WS) that is a form of mild to moderate retardation, characterized by a pixie-like facial appearance, an assortment of physical motor difficulties, and heart problems. People with Williams syndrome also have an exceptional tonal memory, relative to perfect pitch, a strong rhythmic sense, and a genuine "passion for music." These persons have an unusual sensitivity to sound called *hyperacusis*, present in 95 percent of persons with the syndrome. Beluggi, a major researcher in the field, describes the account of a parent whose child repeatedly asked for vacuum cleaners for Christmas, now owning eighteen. The child can name the models by the sound of their motors.[45]

J. C. P. Williams identified the syndrome in 1961 after examining a number of children who shared similar medical problems and cognitive impairments. The syndrome is estimated to occur in one in 20,000 people. The link between unusual musical ability and Williams syndrome was made in 1993, resulting in growing interest from neurological and educational researchers.

Neurological studies show that the brain of WS individuals is smaller than normal. However, the part of the brain that is shown to be enlarged in professional musicians with perfect pitch (planum temporale) actually makes up a higher proportion of the brain in WS individuals. These persons have a high degree of rhythmic engagement, or "rhythmicity," often offering creative answers rather than mimicked repetition in echo-clapping experiments. Preliminary research shows audiation abilities at the level of "relatively preserved language," again suggesting a connection between musical abilities and the unusually enhanced language abilities found in WS individuals—another intriguing language-music link.[46]

There are accounts of WS individuals who can retain the lyrics and melodies of songs heard years earlier and the ability to learn asymmetrical rhythms easily while playing a drum. They compose and improvise with great facility, can learn to sing in foreign languages with perfect accents, and all lack stage fright. One WS woman lacked the spatial aptitude to truly understand placements of notes on the staff but had a repertoire of over two thousand songs in over 24 different languages. Students with Williams syndrome require specialized teaching strategies to work with muscular and spatial difficulties and learn more quickly and easily through modeling and rote learning.[47]

Ongoing research is trying to solve the mystery of why these individuals display high language skills and musical ability when they have limited cognitive capabilities. This research claims that "the types of behaviors we report form strong evidence for the notion that musical ability is independent of, and uncorrelated (to a large degree) with, overall cognitive functioning."[48] This research may unlock the mystery of the musical mind. From the amazing abilities of the prodigy to the intriguing capabilities of the savant and individuals with Williams Syndrome, the breadth of musical talent lies within the realm of musical "giftedness."

Musical Talent As Giftedness:
Arguments For and Against

For: Common sense tells us that children are born with different innate abilities. From birth, environment plays a major role in the development of these abilities. Parents may devote hours of attention in guiding young children to learn music, clearly demonstrated in the Suzuki teaching philosophy. All of these children will acquire *some* measure of musical ability. However, a handful of these children will acquire amazing ability in an amazingly short period of time. Parents will guide, perhaps, but the "rage to master" and achieve comes from within the child. These are musically gifted children.

- *Giftedness describes extraordinary talent—in any field:* Imagine calling Einstein a "talented" mathematician. It simply doesn't fit. His eminence in the scientific field is called genius. Are Mozart, Bach, or Beethoven musical geniuses? The term is suitable to describe their eminence in the domain of music. These composers were included in numerous studies of genius. When these figures were children, were they called geniuses, or were they deemed "gifted?" It seems a fitting term to describe extraordinary abilities at an early age. Why are we so afraid of excellence and extraordinary ability? If we create a realistic continuum of abilities in *any* field, it might include the following terms in the following order: below average, average, above average, talented, very talented, gifted, genius,
  potentially
  talented
  (developmental possibilities).
- *Musical giftedness should not be watered down to fit everyone:* The idea that all children are gifted in music doesn't make sense. Even Menuhin's statement at the beginning of this chapter hints at differing degrees of "gifts." All children *are* capable of learning music and acquiring musical ability. This makes sense and is the reason why music education should be part of the basic curriculum of *every* child. Howe's fear of overusing the term *gifted* to describe every "able musician" is not too far from the truth. The terms *gifted* or *talented* often go hand-in-hand with *any* child who is involved in music.

  Do we describe a student who is achieving "average" or "able" work in math or science as a gifted student? Is an "above average" football player going to be chosen for the all-star team? We shake our heads and smile. No way. In music, however, many people equate *any* participation in a performing group in a high school with musical talent. Many others equate *any* child who is enrolled in private music instruction as "talented" or "gifted." These children are involved in musical activities because they like music and find interest in participation. These students have musical abilities that would probably come close to a bell curve if measured. Why are we satisfied with accepting *any* ability as musical talent?
- *Musical giftedness or talent should be identified:* Schools are quick to point to the number of students enrolled in gifted and talented programs

or advanced placement classes at the high school level. These students are displayed as models of the excellence of the school's instruction. They are individually identified by gifted specialists, with this code of excellence in their school records.

Outstanding students in the arts have not been commonly recognized through gifted and talented identification. Now is the time for the gifted field to address this oversight. We should take advantage of the political-educational pendulum that is paying attention to music and its potential. Musically talented students should be identified with the same rigor given to students in academic areas. This identification should seek out potentially talented students as well as those demonstrating outstanding talent. Providing challenges to develop talent for these students will raise the level of the music program as a whole.

Against: The idea of musical giftedness gives a misleading picture of what talent development is all about. The term carries the unrealistic view of musical talent simply arriving at birth. Environmental exposure, parental support, and the proper musical training create musical talent—not a "gift." It would be difficult to dispute the fact that people are born with different abilities. This should not be an excuse to downplay the importance of real commitment in the development of talent. The term *giftedness* creates that image.

- *The term "giftedness" should be eliminated:* There is no more damaging term to use in music than "giftedness." Even the term "talent" is problematic, stemming from the Seashore use of the term. If discussions among music educators, gifted specialists, and independent music teachers can center on how to develop talent, we can speak a common language. Musicians and music teachers have personally experienced the process of musical talent development. They recognize that students who excel have talent. It is simply a matter of brainstorming on the most appropriate way to identify talent and potential talent for their particular school environment.
- *Giftedness and talent should not be singled out for special attention:* There is a very real danger that the process of identifying talent will give school administrators the golden opportunity to cut back the school music program to include only "gifted" students. The strength of a music program depends on the strength of the performing groups. Students love being in the band, choir, or orchestra. Talented students may be section leaders or be featured as soloists. They are given individualized performance opportunities. It's what they want as musicians. Formal identification may be more dangerous than helpful for the music program.
- *Music's link to intelligence poses problems for music education:* Now that "musical intelligence" has gained recognition, there are a lot of mis-

guided connections that impede musical talent development in schools. The interdisciplinary courses that feature "tone deaf" math students becoming instant composers use gimmicks rather than substantial musical knowledge. The focus on using music as a means to an end in academic areas sounds intriguing but can be disastrous for the music program. The worst case scenario is that schools that use music as a peripheral gimmick in academic classes will believe that this sufficiently includes music in the curriculum. The best case scenario is that music teachers and academic teachers develop innovative courses that fascinate students and effectively integrate learning. The music teacher's new interdisciplinary role is added to an overload of classes and may eliminate a performance class, where students gain the necessary skills to develop into musicians.

My View: There is a classic Far Side cartoon of an elephant on stage sitting at the piano. He is looking out at the audience in dismay. Above his head the balloon reads, "What am I doing here? I can't play this thing I'm a flutist, for crying out loud!"[49] That cartoon exemplifies how I felt as a musician of many years entering the field of gifted education. I was hearing "educationalese" I had never heard before. As I broadened my perspective, I tried to understand how one observes artistic knowing from outside the domain. Then I would switch roles to learn what an artist must do to translate *into words* what music-makers do in their nonverbal language of music.

Translation of terminology is a key factor in this dual role. In the academic literature the word "performance" means any type of behavior other than a pencil and paper test. To musicians this word is much more specific. In the gifted field, identification procedures seek to unveil and develop potential talent. In music, talent identification is understood as audition and outstanding performance. When I communicate to gifted specialists, I use a different language from that of my sessions with arts teachers. I have come to appreciate the impact a simple term such as "gifted" can elicit in a conversation. I often feel like whispering it, as our grandparents used to do when they mentioned "cancer." ("Gift" is, after all, a four-letter word!)

The intriguing studies that are finding hidden powers in music may help explain the perceptive/cognitive functioning of metaperception to those outside artistic fields. The endeavors that share "neural codes" in the brain are chess, mathematics, engineering, and music cognition. The spatial-temporal reasoning that describes this brain function is the ability to *transform a mental image* in the absence of a physical model. A chess player must visualize future moves of his opponent, with prodigies projecting possible moves to the end of the game and remembering past games in totality. The engineer visualizes how the manipulation of shapes, objects, or working parts will function as a whole. Math images are more abstract in visualization. Music imagery is sound, which is equally abstract because, like math, it is not an "object" that can be visualized. Sound occurs over time—is temporal—and requires an inner aural sense. Musicians do not normally visualize the score, though composers may. The more we examine how sensory perception (listening to Mozart) plays a vital role in cognition, the more we can learn about artistic ways of knowing.

Your View: You are now in a position to come to terms with the description of musical talent from your unique perspective. These questions bring the final "gifted" perspective into the mix, so you can synthesize and reflect a bit before heading into part two, where theoretical perspectives meet real-world conditions and opinions.

1. Why do you believe there is so much tension when the word "gifted" enters the discussion of musical talent?
2. There is adamant argument against "giftedness" as an innate ability. Why do you think this is so, and where do you stand in this debate?
3. What are some realistic ways musical talent can be recognized and fostered in your local school system?
4. What are the repercussions, both positive and negative, in widening the margin of gifted identification to 15 percent rather than the traditional 3–5 percent who demonstrate outstanding abilities?
5. What is your perspective of musical talent?

Your reflections:

REFLECTIONS

The Grand Canyon scene from chapter one seems a distant memory now that we have examined the perspectives of musical talent from experts across different fields. A synthesis of the ideas gleaned from these opening chapters can be embodied once again in that scene and those four friends.

The scientific examiner searches beneath the surface for answers. He analyzes the inner core, piece by piece. The psychometricians who systematically refine the measurement of the capacities of music aptitude believe in analyzing the sensory core of musical talent. From this scientific perspective, we learn that the talented musician *listens carefully* and can *discriminate differences in sound*. Music aptitude describes the basic capacities that provide this keen discrimination. *A musically talented person is fine-tuned in awareness and differentiation of pitch, rhythm, dynamics, and timbre.*

Our environmental observer searches for answers revealed in surrounding influences and changes over the course of time. She is more concerned with examining how the ongoing flux and flow transforms the whole. The developmental psychologists who examine music intelligence agree that music aptitude is the sensory base of musical talent. However, there is much more to consider and explore. How do these sensory capacities function while engaged in real musical tasks? What tasks can instill metaperceptive functioning as the child develops? From the perspective of the cognitive developmental psychologist, we learn that *musical intelligence is a perceptive/ cognitive unique way of knowing. The musically talented student develops musical intelligence by solving challenging musical problems that inventively work across the dimensions of performance, composing, improvisation, listening, and critiquing musical work.*

Our photographer captures the scene through an artistic eye, ever searching for a personal way to interpret this experience to others through his art form. Many hours are spent in the darkroom working through this creative process. With persistence, time, and focus, that personal visual statement will emerge. The performer realizes musical talent through the same artistic process, with the same persistence, focus, and hours of practice. Through the perspective of the performer and the teacher of performers, we have learned that *the talented performer has internal motivation and commitment to achieve through music.* Family support and musical training play an essential role in the development of performance. *The performance of a talented musician often creates an aesthetic dynamic because it communicates a personal interpretation to the audience.*

Where do the ideas for a poem come from? Our poet has notated a personal interpretation of her experience at the rim of the canyon. The poem does not describe the scientific core or the history of the terrain. In a personal style that transforms the experience internally, she interprets her view through a poem. Where do the ideas for a composition or an improvisation come from? Generative music makers share moments of semiconscious inspiration that internalize experiences through sound. Creative musicians seek divergent ways of expressing themselves to others. The creatively talented performer must sift through stylistic boundaries to develop a creative interpretation in performance. The creative listener must translate an interpretation of sound into words. *The creatively talented musician discovers unique ways to communicate a personal interpretation through music to others.*

The four friends may all be "gifted" or have some talent in their individual fields. This vicarious observation did not include criteria that would guide us in this recognition of talent. The perspective of giftedness highlights the problems that derive from terminology, labels, and misconceptions. Examination of the characteristics of prodigies and savants gives us a glimpse of the possibilities and mysteries that are part of musical talent. The talent descriptors of creativity, music aptitude, performance, and musical intelligence emanate in these children. These are exceptional talents that are easily recognizable and fascinating to study and teach.

What of the many children whose talents are not so obviously prodigious but lie in wait of recognition in our classrooms? Children with potential talent need opportunities to allow it to grow and blossom. The educational climate seems ripe for an active dialogue across music and gifted fields to seek ways to nurture this potential as well as to challenge students who truly excel in music. Understanding the different perspectives of the people sitting around the table may prove profitable in these future dialogues.

PART II

Recognizing Musical Talent

PERSPECTIVES OF
TALENT IDENTIFICATION

*American public education does not recognize that if a man is
callous, indifferent, and impotent in his abilities to see when he looks,
and to hear when he listens, he is just as deficient in the development
of his God-given human potentialities as he would be if he could not
read or write.*
> William Schuman, "The Performing Arts in the Curriculum"

In part I the discussion of talent began with a poetic scene and ended with
reflective after-thoughts, befitting the theoretical nature of the subject. The
quest to recognize the spark of potential talent in young children brings us
into the very real world of the school classroom. Suppose it is your task to
observe student behavior in a third grade elementary music class and identify students who show evidence of potential talent. Your attention is drawn
to the following students:

Student A is playing a melody from her music book on a xylophone. She
decides to elaborate by creating a "variation." Excited, she busily starts
notating and revising her ideas on manuscript paper.
Observation Notes: Musical training is evident. Performs with ease. Shows
curiosity, creativity in musical tasks. An outstanding student.

Student B is sitting in a listening center with headphones on, totally absorbed in the activity of circling patterns he hears. He taps his pencil as he
listens, quickly working through the ear-training exercise. A quick check
shows that his answers are correct.

Observation Notes: Fine-tuned listening. Quite perceptive and quick in complex listening tasks. He is rather shy in group activities.

Student C volunteers to sing and act out a solo in a cowboy song. He performs with confidence, singing in tune and with expression, obviously enjoying himself. His performance is met with spontaneous applause.
Observation Notes: Quite a showman. Comfortable in front of an audience. Clear, clean vocal quality and intonation. Performs with personal flair. Shows leadership skills in group activities. Energy plus enthusiasm.

Student D works with a number of Orff instruments, simply "fooling around" with sounds and rhythms. Each repetition shows a bit more development of an imaginative improvisation, which she describes as a "summer storm."
Observation Notes: Sensitive awareness of mood in music. Syncopated rhythms used in improvisation—retained well by ear. Adept at learning by ear. Not comfortable working with notation.

You recognize students who display characteristics of talent in different ways. Student A is solving problems across musical dimensions, showing signs of talent as musical intelligence. Student B is the keen listener and would do well in a music aptitude test. Student C is the natural performer. Student D is the aesthetic creator of music. Effective identification of potential talent should address this full breadth of musical behavior.

Now adjust this hypothetical scenario along the following continuum of possibilities, reflecting on outcomes:

- You are one of three observers, all knowledgeable in music and gifted education.
- You unobtrusively observe the class for several weeks.
- You are the music teacher in the classroom, identifying potential talent.
- You are an elementary classroom teacher, with no formal music training, identifying potential musical talent.
- You are not there. Talent identification does not include the arts.
- There is no music program in the school.

This mental exercise extends the possibilities and problems that arise in the identification of musically talented students. The last few options present the worst case scenarios. Unfortunately, these conditions are a reality in over half of the schools in the United States. The National Coalition for Music Education reports that 55 percent of the nation's schools are either unserved by music education or served on a part-time basis.[1] Effective procedures for talent identification in music will require flexibility to pragmatically adapt to this continuum of possibilities.

Rationale for Talent Identification

Formal school recognition of musical talent rests on the educational necessity for this identification. Why should we recognize these children? We can argue this question from many philosophical and educational standpoints. Federal legislation can play a decided role in prompting an answer with action. In 1972, the Marland Report included a definition of gifted and talented children that included the identification of talent in the visual and performing arts. The 1970s were decidedly within the "excellence" pendulum swing, giving rise to the establishment of gifted programs across the country. At this point, music aptitude tests were in their second stage, with specialized tests emerging to include primary level students.

The arts were one of six areas that required identification "by professionally qualified persons" and "differentiated educational programs and/or services beyond those normally provided by the regular school program." The definition of gifted and talented children from this report states:

> Children capable of high performance include those with demonstrated achievement and/or potential ability in any of the following areas, singly or in combination:
>
> 1. general intellectual ability
> 2. specific academic aptitude
> 3. creative or productive thinking
> 4. leadership ability
> 5. visual and performing arts ability
> 6. psychomotor ability
>
> It can be assumed that utilization of these criteria for identification of the gifted and talented will encompass a minimum of 3 to 5 percent of the school population. (Public Law 91-230)[2]

This definition was revised in 1978, eliminating "psychomotor abilities" for economic rather than philosophical reasons. Athletic programs, which had healthy school budgets, were draining funds that were specifically designed for gifted programs. Establishing this definition within federal legislation expanded the concept of giftedness beyond the academics to include nonverbal and performance skills. It also included the desire to seek out *potential* talent in these areas.

The *National Report on Identification* (1982) stood behind this comprehensive definition. Renzulli, the developer of the three-ring definition of giftedness, argued that it did not include nonintellective factors such as task commitment.[3] Some identification erroneously considered each category as a separate entity to identify, posing misconceptions similar to those in multiple intelligence curricula today. These talents and abilities interweave and are not isolated or mutually exclusive.

Over the next 20 years, the expanded nature of this definition was not reflected in gifted identification procedures. Predominant identification procedures still relied on IQ and achievement test scores and grades. Artistic talent identification was largely ignored. A 1987 survey of large cities in ten north-central states (population over 50,000) found no provision for musical talent within their gifted programs. Nationally, only four states required visual and performing arts identification. Multiple research studies and panel reports urged that measures go beyond academic achievement, but there was a large gap between the theory professed by the gifted field, and the practice at hand.[4]

As the pendulum began to swing toward educational equity in the 1990s, a new definition was in order. In 1993, the current definition of "outstanding talent" was established in *National Excellence: A Case for Developing America's Talent*, notably replacing the term "gifted" with "outstanding talent":

Children and youth with outstanding talent perform or show the potential for performing at remarkably high levels of accomplishment when compared with others of their age, experience, or environment.

These children and youth exhibit high performance capability in intellectual, creative, and/or artistic areas, possess an unusual leadership capacity, or excel in specific academic fields. They require services or activities not ordinarily provided by schools.

Outstanding talents are present in children and youth from all cultural groups, across all economic strata, and in all areas of human endeavor. (Public Law 100-297-4003)[5]

Riding on the coattails of this document came the publication of the *National Standards for Arts Education* (1994), which established content and achievement standards at all grade levels in music, theater, dance, and visual arts. This document and accompanying arts-specific curriculum guides were developed by the Consortium of National Arts Education Associations. The music curriculum guide specifically includes differentiation for talented music students: "Special experiences are designed for musically gifted and talented students according to their abilities and interests."[6]

These combined documents established national interest in setting standards and recognizing outstanding performance and achievement. Coupled with these formal educational publications was a growing interest in musical talent from professionals across the fields of music and gifted education. In 1990, the *Music Educators Journal* devoted a special focus issue to gifted and talented students.

The private sector of music instruction held national conferences that included sessions on musical giftedness. The *American Music Teacher* published several articles on the topic as well. The Division of Visual and Performing Arts was formally established within the National Association for Gifted Children. Teachers in the private and public sectors of education were posing questions and raising issues about talent in music and the arts [7]

The Identification Process

The process for identifying students who are academically gifted and talented has been well established for decades. The procedure is multifaceted so as to secure the establishment of a broad talent profile for each student. Initial identification includes nominations and observation ratings by teachers, parents, and peers and even self-nomination. Student grades and test scores on achievement and IQ tests are then examined, followed by assessment of creativity through testing or observation of work while engaged in creative problem-solving activities within class.

In music, an identification procedure can use a similar approach for gathering data from multiple sources to establish a student talent profile. Observation of students engaged in musical tasks, combined with specific musical performance assessment, is a logical stage of the process. The optional use of music aptitude or music creativity testing is also possible.

There are minimal resources currently available to assist gifted and talented (GT) coordinators or music administrators seeking formal identification of musical talent in their schools. School systems interested in identification usually rely on locally developed forms. A glance at forms used in the gifted field that include reference to music or artistic talent characteristics can serve as a basic starting reference point.

The most common observational rating scales used in GT identification are the *Scales for Rating the Behavior of Characteristics of Superior Students (SRBCSS)*. This instrument includes a set of 10 rating scales designed to obtain teacher estimates of student behavior in various areas, including art, music, drama, and communication. The Musical Characteristic Rating Scale from the *SRBCSS* includes seven characteristics of musical behavior (fig. 8.1). Three reflect student *interest* in musical activities (1, 4, 5). Music-specific characteristics include perceptual discrimination (two items), tonal memory/sense of pitch (one item), and a rhythmic pulse (one item). The scales have recently been revised from their 1976 edition, basically expanding the number of weighted ratings from four to six.[8]

A study by the National Research Center on the Gifted and Talented found that giftedness in the visual and performing arts was measured primarily by

Student's Name (or Asssigned Code No.) _____

Musical Characteristics

The student . . .	Never	Very Rarely	Rarely	Occasionally	Frequently	Always
1. shows a sustained interest in music—seeks out opportunities to hear and create music.	☐	☐	☐	☐	☐	☐
2. perceives fine differences in musical tone (pitch, loudness, timbre, duration).	☐	☐	☐	☐	☐	☐
3. easily remembers melodies and can produce them accurately.	☐	☐	☐	☐	☐	☐
4. eagerly participates in musical activities.	☐	☐	☐	☐	☐	☐
5. plays a musical instrument (or indicates a strong desire to).	☐	☐	☐	☐	☐	☐
6. is sensitive to the rhythm of music; responds to changes in the tempo of music through body movements.	☐	☐	☐	☐	☐	☐
7. is aware of and can identify a variety of sounds heard at a given moment—is sensitive to "background" noises, to chords that accompany a melody, to the different sounds of singers or instrumentalists in a performance.	☐	☐	☐	☐	☐	☐
Add Column Total:	☐	☐	☐	☐	☐	☐
Multiply by Weight:	1	2	3	4	5	6
Add Weighted Column Totals:	☐ +	☐ +	☐ +	☐ +	☐ +	☐

Scale Total: ☐

FIGURE 8.1. The Musical Characteristics Scale from the *SRBCSS*. Reprinted with permission from *Scales for Rating the Behavioral Characteristics of Superior Students* (1976, rev. 1997), by Joseph Renzulli, Linda Smith, Alan White, Carolyn Callahan, and Robert Hartman. Creative Learning Press, Inc., PO Box 320, Mansfield Center, CT. All rights reserved.

this rating scale. GT coordinators have long been familiar with this set of scales, so their use in music identification is not surprising.[9]

The gifted and music education literature include a number of unpublished rating scales and checklists of musical talent characteristics; however, none of these instruments indicate research-based development and provide scant information for use.[10] The *Khatena-Morse Multitalent Perception Inventory* offers a self-perception measure designed to identify talent in art, music, leadership, and creativity. Multitalent is defined as "versatility of accomplishment" in these four areas. Inventories provide useful biographical information and clues of interest in different areas. However, they are generalized in purpose rather than arts or music specific.[11] A valid instrument for musical talent identification requires music-specific criteria deemed pertinent to talent by music and gifted specialists.

Musical Performance Assessment

Your observation of the third grade music class assessed the youngsters' behavior while engaged in musical performance tasks. At the elementary level, this type of assessment may use rating scales or checklists completed by classroom teachers and/or music specialists. This may be followed by more individualized performance activities, depending on the level of screening needed. As performance is individualized and brought into an audition setting, it may be assessed by one or more outside specialists. The literature recommends that this individualized performance be judged by artist/teachers who have expertise in recognizing potential as well as demonstrated talent. These judges also must be aware of the inclusive nature of the identification process, which is quite different from the exclusive assessment of performance at a competition.

Forms used for musical performance assessment vary widely, from categorized rating scales to a blank page designed for a written critique. Any music teacher or musician who has had the experience of adjudicating at a festival, competition, or audition has personally witnessed the array of possibilities.

Boyle and Radocy's *Measurement and Evaluation of Musical Experiences* suggests the development of forms that include rating scales that measure the judges' opinion of what they are hearing (fig. 8.2). They also recommend assessment that provides a balanced approach of overall effect and specific aspects of performance, "where the particular performance aspects function as guidance, but not necessarily as specific categories to be quantified."[12] This type of format is common in the area of musical performance, where a written critique returned to the teacher and student provides valuable feedback. Often criteria are checked or circled for attention, with emphasis on large amounts

INSTRUMENTAL

Student name _____   Instrument _____

Judge's name _____   Composer/work _____

Governor's School for the Arts Adjudication Form

Accuracy of pitch/intonation

Most pitches inaccurate	Some pitches are missed, usually the more difficult	Most pitches are accurate

Accuracy of rhythm

Most rhythms inaccurate	Some pitches are missed, usually the more difficult	Most pitches are accurate

Tone production

Thin, pinched, not properly supported	Some good tone, inconsistent	Full, pleasant sound

Observation of score markings

Minimal markings are observed	Some markings are performed	All markings are accurately performed

Proper musical interpretation

Very little interpretation observed	Some musical interpretation	Extremely musical interpretation

Scales

Scales frequently wrong	Some mistakes in scale performance	Scales performed accurately

Sight reading

Sight reading frequently wrong	Sight mistakes in sigh reading performance	Sight reading performed perfectly

Judge's recommendation

_____ Recommend highly   _____ Recommend   _____ Don't recommend

FIGURE 8.2. An audition form that uses a Likert scale for performance assessment. Used with permission from the Kentucky Governor's School for the Arts.

of white space on the page to write comments concerning the performance. Judging forms used in the national level competitions of the Music Teachers National Association are simply blank pages, with a few general criteria included in the brief introductory statement at the top of the page.

My own personal experience behind judging tables can attest to the disdain colleagues have for any sort of numbers on the page. Assigning objective quantitative ratings during the subjective experience of performance seems like an oxymoronic task. How can a college jury session assign a numeric grade for the performance of a Beethoven sonata? Is the performance of that Bach Prelude and Fugue an 88 or a 92? It seems so inappropriate. However a few words that describe essential performance criteria provide ways to assess specific elements that explain the rationale behind the 88 (final grade B+) or 92 (final grade A). If the student sees, for example, that notes and rhythm were accurate (A) but stylistically the performance was inappropriate (B–), more specific information is being provided to explain the final grade.

In identification, criteria on audition forms may include performance-specific elements as well as behavioral elements. After all, performance is a phenomenological product/process. Quantitative input that includes essential criteria that are visually easy to use will be most effective for judging. A form with enough space for a healthy critique may reveal reactions to a student's involvement with the music, a student's creative play with certain interpretive choices, and other behavioral observations that go beyond rating tone, dynamics, and rhythmic accuracy.

Figures 8.3 and 8.4 are examples of forms that show the dual type of format recommended by Boyle and Radocy. One (fig. 8.3) quantifies musical elements; the other (fig. 8.4) provides criteria to circle, check, or write a plus or minus.[13]

Figure 8.5 shows a form used in an audition for gifted identification.[14] This form features a small space for comments, with quantified rating of performance specifics taking most of the page. A glance at the difference in these assessment forms indicates ample space for qualitative written comments in the field of music performance versus an emphasis on quantitative data in the field of gifted education with minimal space for comments. Ratings clearly quantify the immediate performance. Although quantitative data affords ease in comparison between student ratings (scores!), qualitative comments can offer valuable personal comments about the observed potential of the student. The two lines squeezed in at the bottom of the form do not allow enough room for substantive personal comments.

The Musical Identification Tally Sheet used by ArtsConnection uses a unique form to assess musical behavior and performance.[15] Figure 8.6 shows a six-grid portion of this multiple grid tally sheet. Each grid contains abbreviated criteria, with individual student names written in the bottom blank portion of each box. The small box in the lower right corner receives an overall rating of 1–3 by observers for selection to the program. Arts specialists and classroom teachers assess behavior and performance in a specialized music class over a five- to seven-week period. The specialists both teach and observe in these classes of approximately 30 students. As in most performance assessment procedures, discussion follows these individual evaluations. The assessment procedure requires training for all involved.

In part I of this book we discussed the subjective dynamic of performance. Researchers in the field of music recognize the impact of this dynamic on the reliability of performance assessment. Boyle and Radocy explain the specifics of this subjectivity:

Literature:

Accuracy
Notes
Rhythm
Rests
Fingering
Dynamics
Slurs, etc.
Memory

Technique
Touches
Tone quality
Clarity
Velocity
Balance between hands
Pedal
Physical approach
   fingers
   hand
   arm
   posture, etc.

Interpretation
Style of
   piece
   period
Phrasing
Tempo
Sensitivity
Touch variety
Sound colors

Artistic maturity
Other comments
Etc.

Judge's signature: _____ Rating: _____

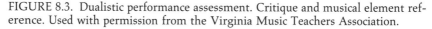

A+ = Superior   A = Excellent   A– = Very good   B = Good   C = Fair

FIGURE 8.3. Dualistic performance assessment. Critique and musical element reference. Used with permission from the Virginia Music Teachers Association.

The measurement of musical performance is inherently subjective. Music consists of sequential aural sensations; any judgment of a musical performance is based on those sensations as they are processed by the judge's brain. While many listeners may agree regarding particular judgments, especially if they involve "right" notes, decisions involving correct tempi, phrasing nuances, execution of ornamentation, and tone quality are the decisions of individuals functioning as subjects; hence, the decisions are subjective.[16]

The difficulty of reliable agreement among judges is a constant challenge in performance assessment. The judges panel of the Arts Talent Search Program (ARTS), which assesses thousands of videotapes, uses a unique method

Contemporary

Title ———————————————— Composer ————————————————————

Points in each category:
5 = superior   4 = excellent   3 = very good   2 = good   1 = fair

Performance skills   ——————————

    artistry
    poise, stage deportment
    memory
    projection

Technique   ——————————

    accuracy
    rhythm
    clarity, legato, staccato
    dynamics
    control of articulation
    tonal contrast, balance
    dexterity, smooth transitions
    management of the instrument
    hand position
    pedaling

Interpretation   ——————————

    phrasing, slurs
    tempo
    mood
    tone color
    rubato
    ornaments
    registration

General comments & overall performance   ——————————

                                    Total for contemporary place ——————————

FIGURE 8.4. Dualistic performance assessment. Critique and quantified musical elements. Used with permission from the Maryland Music Teachers Association.

of "calibration" to establish suitable criteria and procedures. The full range of submitted tapes are reviewed and rated, and discrepancies in ratings are discussed. The review proceeds until relatively little disagreement exists, improving the interjudge reliability through this process.[17]

Mills found that nonspecialists and specialists had similar assessment results when using generalized behavioral constructs rather than music-specific criteria. However, she used bipolar statements (performance was muddy/clean; dynamics were appropriate/inappropriate), resulting data is limited to extreme positive or negative ratings. Elliot found that professional judges showed disparity of judgement and poor reliability, compared with student peer and self-assessments when listening to taped perfor-

Music Audition Sheet

Name _____ Instrument(s) _____

Level 1 _____ Piece _____

Each student should be judged according
to his/her level of attainment _____
_____

Circle the appropriate number (0 = low, 5 = high)

1. Tone, quality and intonation   0 1 2 3 4 5

2. Fluency and dexterity   0 1 2 3 4 5

3. Rhythm and tempo   0 1 2 3 4 5

4. Phrasing and tonal shading   0 1 2 3 4 5

5. Articulation (diction for voice, pedal for
   piano   0 1 2 3 4 5

6. Dynamics   0 1 2 3 4 5

7. Overall interpretation   0 1 2 3 4 5

8. Poise   0 1 2 3 4 5

9. Choice of piece (according to level)   0 1 2 3 4 5

10. Scales   0 1 2 3 4 5

11. Sight reading   0 1 2 3 4 5

    Total points (total musical effect)

Comments (i.e., potential, basic musicality, creativity, imagination):

_____

_____

Acceptable for program at highest level _____

Acceptable for program _____

Not acceptable for program _____

Adjudicated by _____

Date _____

FIGURE 8.5. Music audition form for a gifted program using quantified musical elements with a short critique. Used with permission from the Center for Creative Youth at Wesleyan University, Middletown, CT.

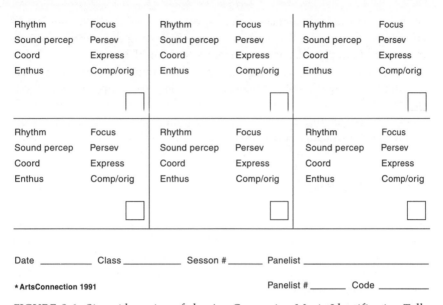

FIGURE 8.6. Six-grid portion of the ArtsConnection Music Identification Tally Sheet. Used with permission from ArtsConnection, 120 West 46th Street, New York, NY 10036.

mances. Levinson calls this disparity of judgment "perspective relativity of evaluation of performance" (PREP). He argues that performance can be evaluated by a number of legitimately different perspectives, with assessment depending on context of performance and the different ends that performance serves.[18]

This assessment research realizes the constant problem of subjectivity in judging and poses possibilities of expanding perspectives beyond the music

---

I ask you once again to engage in a bit of visualization. Place yourself in an imagined position as judge entering a high school music room, about to listen to a series of students who have been nominated for gifted identification by their music teachers. You are handed a clipboard with forms neatly stacked beneath the metal clip. Which of the forms shown in this section would be most comfortable to use in this situation? Which would provide the type of information you feel is necessary and effective in musical talent identification? What adaptations need to be made? These are decisions that need to be addressed by gifted and music coordinators *prior* to the judge's entry into that high school music room.

specialist to include student assessments. Why not include the student's self-critique in the process? During an interview following the audition, adjudicators could simply ask for the student's opinion of the performance or a reflective written critique. This simple addition can provide information regarding the student's self-confidence, particular goals in performance, critiquing skills, and maturity of musical vocabulary and understanding. It would be eye-opening to see how peers would assess the different performances of the students in that third grade music class.

Musical Talent Research

Much of the research discussed in part I shied away from specifying talent characteristics or ways to identify musical talent. Several were intent on its destruction. Over the past decade, several significant research studies that have explored aspects of talent development across fields have uncovered some recurring descriptors of talent worth our attention.

Bloom asked outstanding adults in the fields of music, art, athletics, mathematics, and science to recall and describe influencing factors in their talent development. In this volume, Sosniak describes the stages of development in the lives of 21 concert pianists, making clear the importance of family support, early training, and the marked stages of instruction with different teachers. The role of school education was minimal in this development. Although the concert pianists were not prodigies, they had early signs of talent and the routine of practice instilled from an early age. Their craving for technical improvement and challenging musical opportunities mirror Winner's "rage to master."

Bloom concluded that talented individuals across all fields have some general qualities. They all *learn rapidly and well*, especially at the intermediate stage of development. This is often a talent descriptor that teachers use to screen for advanced instruction. Music students all show *sensitivity to sound* and *good pitch discrimination*—the essentials of high music aptitude. The general qualities that are present in all talent fields are:[19]

- Strong interest and emotional commitment to a particular talent field
- Desire to reach a high level of attainment in the talent field
- Willingness to put in the great amounts of time and effort needed to reach very high levels of achievement in the talent field.

Csikszentmihalyi, Rathunde, and Whalen's study of two hundred talented teenagers across the fields of athletics, art, music, science, and math contributed the perception of talent as a social construction, dependent on positive values in the particular context in which a person lives. "Potential talent cannot be realized unless it is embedded in a cultural domain and unless it is socially nurtured until it is recognized as a genuine contribution by a field and permitted to unfold."[20]

According to these researchers, talent is developmental rather than an "all-or-nothing phenomenon." It is psychologically complex, with contextual factors impacting its development. Talent is nurtured through the acquisition of *information* or knowledge about a domain; *motivation* provided by the family and persons in a specialized field; and *discipline* created by a set of habits allowing long-term concentrated study that results in superior performance. By the teenage years, talented students in all of these domains need to develop a set of *metaskills* that allow them to work with intense concentration and curiosity in the solitary cultivation of their talents. These skills provide intrinsic rewards to self-motivated, goal-driven talented teens.

These authors' concluding summary of factors associated with talent development includes:[21]

1. Skills that are considered useful in one's culture
2. Personality traits conducive to concentration (achievement, endurance) as well as to being open to experience (awareness, sentience, understanding)
3. Learned habits conducive to cultivating talent
4. Conservative sexual attitudes, and awareness of the conflict between productive work and peer relations
5. Families that provide both support and challenge
6. Teachers who are supportive and model enjoyable involvement in the field
7. Goals that seek both expressive and instrumental rewards
8. Optimal experiences of *flow* when engaged in one's talent area

Sloboda and Howe's interview study specifically focused on musical talent (aspects of this study were discussed in Part I). The study targeted 42 talented teenagers enrolled in a specialized music school, interviewing them about their early childhood, influences in their lives, and their school environment prior to the specialized music school. Their findings were similar to Bloom's in regard to parental support and the lack of convincing evidence of exceptional talent emerging at an early age. Students began training at ages six to nine, with practice normally one hour or less in the first few years of training. This study revealed the same personal initiative to learn, with students realizing a sense of pride in having an ability that was unique among their peers. This uniqueness often was an obstacle to their social acceptance as teenagers prior to specialized schooling.[22]

These interview studies establish the importance of family and teacher support in talent development. They all show the talent profile of a highly committed individual who perseveres toward self-initiated goals. This characteristic *flow* or *rage to master* intensifies Renzulli's idea of *task commitment*.

Several research studies have investigated perceptions of musical talent or giftedness from teachers and students of different ages. Logsdon found that elementary and college music teachers, when presented with a questionnaire on musical giftedness, significantly chose "foil items" of erroneous stereotypes of giftedness rather than the traits he had included in a theoretical model of musical giftedness.[23] Persson's "phenomenological concept" of musical talent showed that the characteristics of music aptitude were of minimal importance in the opinion of college musicians, accounting for 13 percent of all entries on a list of student-initiated talent descriptors. Nonmusic characteristics of *personality* accounted for a majority of the responses (39 percent). Many interpersonal and intrapersonal traits were listed as prerequisites of musical achievement. Creative involvement with music, interpretively or generatively, accounted for 16 percent. These findings again support the importance of including nonmusical behavioral characteristics in musical talent identification.[24]

Teaching Observations of Musical Talent

We have learned that the private music teacher plays a major role in talent development through interview studies and glimpses into the lives of musical prodigies. Teachers who work with these students in their studios on a daily basis have observed talent behavior one-on-one. Several articles in the *American Music Teacher* present a talent profile that begins with the ability to *learn quickly* and show a great deal of facility or *physical ease* on the instrument. This physical ease and the basic aural skills of pitch and rhythmic discrimination are acknowledged as innate. The role of private instructor is to teach practice habits and ways to solve musical problems in this practice. Skill preparation is the primary task of the teacher, building the "technical equipment needed to express musical ideas." *Self-motivation* and *commitment* are key indicators of the unusually talented student. These characteristics are the "optimal distinguishing elements as to who will most greatly excel and achieve among the numerous gifted people in the world."[25]

Uszler cautions that the normal audition process identifies talent "after the fact." Results may recognize the "overprepared or externally indoctrinated student" as the talented student, dismissing the potentially talented student who is uncomfortable in a formal performance setting. Music aptitude testing and tasks that require student self-initiative while working with music will help uncover these hidden talents. Most of the literature across educational fields shared this need to seek out students who may have potential talent not yet noticeable in performance ability.[26]

The music and gifted education literature describes musical talent as a mixture of music-specific capabilities and personality or achievement factors. The aural discrimination skills of music aptitude seem to be a given starting point, specifically mentioning the *ability to discriminate pitch and rhythm* and the *inner sensing of sound*. These discrimination factors are coupled with music-specific characteristics of *tonal memory* (can remember songs and melodies) and *aesthetic sensitivity* (aware of mood or character of the music).

Creativity is a characteristic that raises controversy or confusion as a factor of musical talent. It is most often linked with composition and improvisation as a creative product. In the private studio, it is a relative term, dependent on the originality of the musician's personality. Uszler uniquely links creativity with interpretation. "Autonomy and divergence are characteristic of the arts; exploratory discovery may lead to unique performing interpretations as well as to original composition."[27]

A small handful of researchers are studying talent identification and development in the field of gifted/arts. Oreck and Baum's research through ArtsConnection focused on seeking ways to identify talent in music and dance in several inner-city schools in New York City. They sought procedures and criteria that would highlight potential artistic talent of students whose academic achievement was marginal. They were well aware of the problems of considering achievement and prior training as factors in talent identification in the children they were observing. The approach of a written music aptitude test seemed questionable for these students as well.

The musical talent criteria developed through their Talent Beyond Words research were categorized into three areas: *skills, motivation,* and *creativity*. An encapsulated outline of the criteria includes:

Skills
- Rhythm
- Perception of sound
- Coordination

Motivation
- Enthusiasm
- Ability to Focus
- Perseverance

Creativity
- Expressiveness
- Composition and improvisation

These criteria reflect a more arts-specific focus than those found in the gifted literature. For example, commitment and motivation are highly generalized terms; however, a child who is fully focused, enthusiastic, and persevering in tasks is easy to recognize. The term *creativity*, as I mentioned earlier, ranks with love, politics, and religion in its wide range of meanings to different people. The two subcategories of creativity used here clearly show interpretive creativity alongside generative musical creativity. The performance tasks meld dance and music, requiring observation of "coordination" in the identification procedures.[28]

A synthesis of talent characteristics from the literature, research, and the perspectives discussed in part I shows some very prevalent commonalities, basic talent descriptors that have become old friends at this point because they reappear with each perspective. Subcategories and added characteristics may be established through research that will come, but these factors are comfortable starting points for any discussion of musical talent identification. The following list presents the basic characteristics of musical talent:

Musical Talent Criteria:
Music aptitude
- Sense of rhythm and its discrimination
- Sense of pitch and its discrimination
- Perceptual awareness of and sensitivity to sound

Other
- Physical ease and natural facility in performance
- Dynamic of expressive performance
- Creative interpretation in composition, improvisation, performance, and critique
- Commitment and self-motivation

Chapter 9 presents research I conducted that defines these criteria and offers recommendations from experts in the gifted/music fields. Some readers may choose to skip this research summary and proceed to chapters 10 and 11, where I fully explain the "spark" and procedures for its recognition.

Questions for discussion:

1. In the third grade classroom scenario at the beginning of this chapter, what behaviors would be most comfortable for classroom teachers to recognize as potential musical talent? What behaviors would require observation by music teachers or specialists?
2. What are some reasons that might account for the lack of talent identification procedures in the arts over the years?

3. Compare the two definitions of "gifted and talented" students. Do you believe the 1993 definition works for or against the inclusion of music and the arts in school gifted and talented identification? Why?

4. Examine the *SRBCSS* characteristics of music talent. From your developed perspective of musical talent, what characteristics would you delete, edit, or add? How would you word these potential talent characteristics?

5. If you were designing a form to be used in an audition for a high school gifted program, what format would you choose? Sketch your ideas on paper to show how it would visually fit on the page.

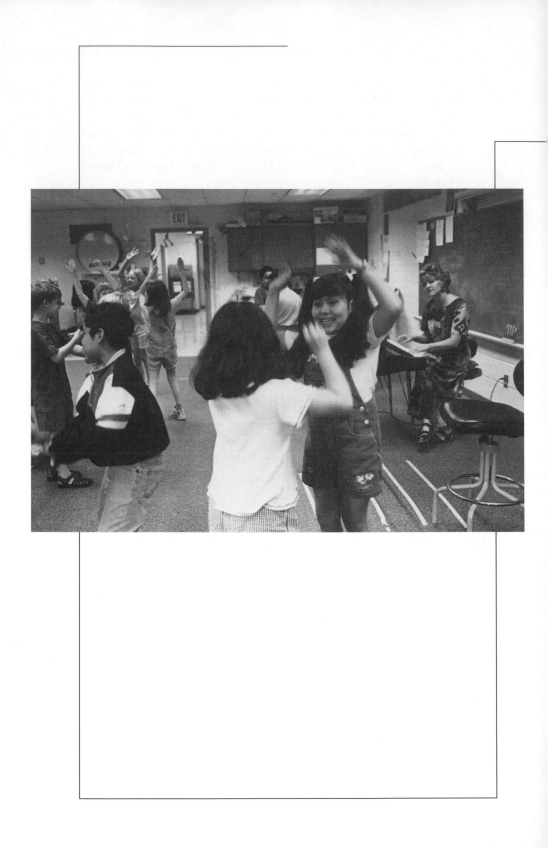

THE QUEST

The real voyage of discovery consists not in seeking new landscapes, but in having new eyes.

Marcel Proust

A point has been reached in this discussion of musical talent and its identification where some concrete questions must be answered. We have examined perspectives of talent across fields and synthesized a simple set of musical talent criteria. Will teachers and musicians agree that these criteria are valid indicators of talent in students they teach on a daily basis? What must be added to define this criteria further? We recognize the need to identify talented students in music; however, we have yet to find an effective procedure to carry out this identification. What is the best way to unveil potential as well as demonstrated talent in a variety of school settings? The research discussed in this chapter sought to answer these pressing questions.

This personal quest began with an analysis of data from the National Research Center on the Gifted and Talented (NRC G/T) at the University of Virginia, augmented by data from different specialized schools. This analysis provided a look at the status quo of what criteria and procedures were currently being used in schools across the country. A survey containing criteria and procedures drawn from this analysis was sent to musicians, teachers, researchers, and specialists across the music and gifted fields in over 15 states. My goal was to see which criteria were deemed "absolutely essential" by people who work with talented music students. In addition, what procedures are currently being used and what types of activities will effectively reveal musical talent? The survey also sought opinions about what performance criteria were important to consider on assessment forms. Quantitative results created a list of criteria and procedures that showed their degree of importance according to the mean of the survey rating scales.

Numbers on paper provide quantitative results. However, discussions with experts across the music and gifted fields could allow clarification of ideas, substantive qualitative input, and brainstorming of possible procedures for identification that all seem invaluable for answering questions concerning musical talent. Therefore, this research concluded with a set of interviews of experts across the music and gifted fields of education, research, performance, and psychology to gather this vital information. In addition, a group interview of teachers, administrators, and musicians offered the opportunity to glean ideas from the type of group that realistically would meet to discuss identification in a local school system. These qualitative findings brought the numbers of the surveys to life—with some clear-cut congruences and some surprising discrepancies.[1]

The Status Quo—Background Analysis

The first startling realization from the background analysis was the scarcity of identification procedures that included musical talent. Of the 1,200 identification folders in the NRC G/T, only *14* contained identification information concerning music or the arts. Additional mailings allowed this number to grow to 92 documents, sent from 48 different locations.[2]

Analysis revealed that most school systems devise their own forms and checklists for identification purposes, with few including adequate assessment tools in the arts. Locally devised forms tend to be loosely constructed, often containing criteria that mismatch the musical constructs they are supposed to identify. Audition forms display an array of possibilities, from categorized checklists, rating scales, and scoring sheets to open critique forms. This mix of formats stems from their diversity of use, from elementary music identification to entry auditions of specialized music schools.

Testing is a problematic issue as well. Fewer than a third of the schools included any form of musical testing, with minimal testing specifically in the area of music aptitude. Musical creativity and achievement were tested in three locations using locally developed measures, with a single site using *Thinking Creatively with Sounds and Images*, the test discussed in part I that assesses aural perception and creativity. Almost half of the locations inappropriately used IQ and achievement tests as screening procedures in the arts. Students in the arts are clearly limited or neglected if identification requires an IQ cutoff score.

The predominant method of performance assessment is the audition of individualized performance. Performance activities range from assigned tasks of singing, clapping, or listening on elementary identification forms to the audition of prepared musical performance for entry to specialized arts schools and summer arts programs.

The content analysis of different talent criteria in these forms showed that the four most prevalent behavioral characteristics describe *general* rather than *music-specific* behavior. The characteristics of *interest* (74 percent), *confidence* (70 percent), and *commitment* (67 percent) occur more often than the perceptual discrimination factors of music aptitude (52 percent). This reflects the talent research findings discussed in chapter 8 and supports the self-motivation talent traits of Renzulli and Winner. Accuracy of performance is decidedly important, with rhythmic and pitch accuracy prevalent on 90–95 percent of the forms. Criteria of creative behavior and creative interpretation in performance appear in 55–66 percent of these forms. A complete list of prevalent criteria resulting from this analysis is found in table 9.1.

Conclusions from the NRC G/T analysis show that music identification is sparse, with an array of instruments and procedures that fit local needs but do not use research-based criteria. Talent criteria include motivational fac-

TABLE 9.1. Content analysis results: Talent criteria items found in over 50 percent of the instruments

Frequency of criterion item on forms, number of forms containing item, and % this represents of total analyzed instruments

Identification Instruments:		*Total = 27*	
Behavioral Characteristics	Freq.	No. inst.	% of tot.
Shows sustained interest in musical activities	37	20	74
Shows confidence in performance	24	19	70
Shows commitment in arts area	27	18	67
Is highly creative	30	18	66
Responds discriminately to rhythm, melody, harmony	16	14	52
Audition Forms:		*Total = 41*	
Music Performance Descriptors	Freq.	No. inst.	% of tot.
Pitch accuracy	52	39	95
Rhythmic accuracy	44	37	90
Detailed articulation/bowing	30	25	61
Tonal color	26	23	56
Appropriate tempo	26	23	56
Creativity in interpretation	23	21	51

tors as well as capacities of music aptitude and creative interpretation. Performance assessment largely rests on the traditional audition setting, with talent identification resting predominantly on accuracy of performance.

A Survey of Talent Characteristics and Procedures

A survey containing several rating scales developed from the background analysis was completed by a purposeful sampling of 134 teachers and specialists who work with talented music students in various capacities and in different teaching environments.[3] A list of prevalent talent characteristics and performance assessment criteria from the background analysis were rated on a scale from 1 (of no importance) to 5 (absolutely essential). (These rating scales are included in the appendix).

SPARKLER EXPERIENCE:
Your Opinion of Talent Characteristics and Performance Criteria

Before reading the results of the survey, I encourage you to experience it by completing the rating scales in the appendix. You may enjoy comparing your ratings with those of teachers and musicians from the survey. You do not have to be involved in teaching or performing to have opinions about musical talent and performance. If you are actively involved in music, you may discover that your personal perspectives are quite different from those of your musical colleagues.

The results of the musical talent potential characteristic scale (table 9.2) again show that motivational factors of *sustained interest* and *self-discipline* are considered more important than music-specific behaviors of music aptitude. Aesthetic-creative aspects of talent appear mid to low (8 and 12) on the complete list of 17 items. Notable is the low importance given to academic giftedness in determining musical talent, reinforcing the inappropriate use of IQ and achievement testing for the purpose of musical talent identification.

In the results from the performance rating scale (table 9.3), not surprisingly, *rhythmic and note accuracy* head the list with exceedingly high means (4.73, 4.65). *Rhythmic pulse, dynamic contrasts,* and *technical fluency* all received ratings above 4.00 (important). Noteworthy is the element of *originality,* at the bottom of the list, with creative interpretation not far above.

The survey asked teachers and specialists working in schools to note identification procedures currently in use. The live audition and student interview were the most prevalent procedures for musical talent identification

TABLE 9.2. Results of the assessment of musical potential scale

Behavioral Characteristics	Group Mean
†1. *Shows a sustained interest in music and performing*	4.35
2. *Is self-disciplined*	4.26
*†3. *Responds discriminately to rhythm, melody, harmony*	4.23
*†4. *Can perceive fine differences in musical tone (pitch, loudness, timbre)*	4.17
5. Shows commitment in arts area	3.87
6. Is self critical; sets high standards	3.82
7. Can sing in tune well	3.81
8. Shows sensitivity to aesthetic elements of music (mood, style)	3.82
†9. Remembers and reproduces melodies with ease and accuracy	3.75
10. Can express emotions through sound or music	3.71
*11. Has a high degree of tonal memory	3.68
12. Is highly creative	3.56
13. Shows confidence in performing	3.55
14. Enjoys moving to rhythms and music	3.44
15. Evokes emotional responses from audience	3.31
*†16. Can identify a variety of sounds heard at a given moment	3.29
17. Is gifted in academic areas	2.92

Italics indicate characteristics considered important (4.00) to absolutely essential (5.00).
*indicates components of music aptitude
†indicates musical characteristics found in the *SRBCSS*.

(63 percent), with a number of schools including the availability of audio or videotaped auditions. Twelve locations included *parent* interviews along with student interviews, an intriguing addition that may provide information regarding family support and encouragement. Testing information revealed the use of music aptitude tests in only four locations and again included the misuse of tests for creativity, general aptitude, and achievement for musical talent identification.

The survey also asked respondents to check activities that might be useful for talent identification, circling those they felt were inadequate for this purpose. Table 9.4 shows the results of this checklist. Italicized performance tasks checked by over 50 percent of the respondents reflect the basic audition-oriented performance tasks and discriminatory skills of music aptitude. Noteworthy are the items with an asterisk near the bottom of the list that pertain to creative and aesthetic musical tasks. These were circled as "inadequate for musical talent identification" on 11–20 percent of the surveys.

Research surveys confirm the issues raised in part I. The emphasis of motivational factors in musical talent development is a recurring theme in every perspective, literature across fields, and the content analysis of identi-

TABLE 9.3. Results of the assessment of musical performance scale

Performance Descriptors	Group Mean
1. *Pitch note accuracy*	4.73
2. *Rhythmic accuracy*	4.65
3. *Steady rhythmic pulse*	4.41
4. *Dynamic contrasts*	4.02
5. *Technical fluency*	4.02
6. Appropriate tempo	3.96
7. Sensitivity to mood	3.96
8. Tonal color	3.76
9. Detailed articulation/bowing	3.72
10. Creativity in interpretation	3.68
11. Stylistic awareness	3.68
12. Confident memory	3.55
13. Poised stage presence	3.48
14. Originality	3.04

Italics indicate performance descriptors that were considered important (4.00) to absolutely essential (5.00).

fication instruments. The high ratings of *sustained interest, commitment,* and *self-discipline* reinforce the need to recognize this behavior in talent identification. The very high ratings of *pitch and note accuracy* mirror their prevalence on instruments in the background analysis. This comes as no surprise. The audition remains as the mainstay of musical performance assessment. Testing plays a minimal role in identification procedures, with evidence of the misuse of generalized aptitude and achievement testing for artistic talent identification.

The role of creative musical tasks and creative interpretation in the identification of musically talented students is not well covered in the existing literature or considered highly important by survey results. The student who has "originality" and enjoys "creating new sounds" clearly will not be identified as someone with potential musical talent according to this survey. These survey results show the need to revise and refine available tools of talent assessment to incorporate this key area of musical ability.

Personal Talent Perspectives: The Interviews

Part I of this book developed perspectives of talent from various research and professional viewpoints. My interviews with persons who work across music and gifted fields confirm basic criteria clearly recognizable as talent descrip-

TABLE 9.4. Results of the performance assessment procedure checklist: Musical behavior/performance activities used for performance assessment

Musical Behavior/Performance Activities	Activity Used by:	% of Total
1. *Performance of prepared piece*	97	78
2. *Sightsinging/sightreading*	76	61
3. *Match pitches*	70	56
4. *Listen for differences in pitch*	67	54
5. Technique performance (scales, arpeggios, etc.)	61	49
6. Etude or technical study	61	49
7. Echo-clap rhythms	54	44
8. Sing a familiar song	50	40
9. Listen for differences in rhythm	50	40
10. Sightread and clap rhythms	49	39
*11. Respond creatively to listening	29	24
*12. Improvise	28	23
*13. Describe mood, style, color from listening	22	18
14. Recognize texture, timbre in listening	19	15
*15. Create new sounds	17	14

Total respondents = 124. Italics indicate activities used for music performance assessment by over 50 percent of the respondents.
Asterisks indicate tasks circled as "inadequate for musical talent identification" in 11–20% of the surveys.

tors and suggest additional procedures for discovering potential not yet realized. These discussions also clarify the role of creativity and creative interpretation in this talent profile.

Interviewees included people who work with young subjects through research, teach students in the classroom or private studio, guide talented secondary students involved in specialized gifted/arts programs, and help disadvantaged students shine through the arts. The group interview offered a chance to see what can happen if we open the school doors and talk to professional musicians and private teachers in the community. (Information regarding the interviewees is located in the appendix; their initials are used for reference to quoted material in this section.) Views were shared across the basic areas of talent that emerged through the study: perceptual awareness and discrimination, creative interpretation, metaperception, performance, and motivation.[4]

Perceptual Awareness and Discrimination

In simplest terms, we recognize the perceptual awareness and discrimination at the heart of music aptitude and musical intelligence when a child *lis-*

tens carefully and *is aware of sound*. This child is intently drawn to sounds and music and after listening experiences may ask discriminative questions about sounds heard.

According to interviewees, rhythm is more naturally a part of potential talent than pitch. Simply put, "without rhythm, it's nothing." Echoes of Czikszentmihalyi's notion of cultural acceptance and social nurturing grew from discussions of a current generation where "people don't sing anymore. . . . We live in an age that is basically more rhythmic than melodic." (SS)

We normally think of rhythmic response to music as keeping the beat through clapping or stepping. In interview after interview, this sense was described as a natural bodily awareness that is more fluid in nature, moving "in weight and flow." "It has to be an internal thing—to have a sense of music in their body . . . their gestures are not stiff, but fluid." (EG)

> I think in many talented children a rhythmic response is like a totally bodily response. Somehow you sense that the whole body is participating in the perception of the rhythm. It is not that the child is jigging around or dancing . . . you are aware that the rhythmic response is deeply internalized. (MU)

Without exception, any discussion concerning the idea of matching pitches or singing in tune concluded that this ability is useful to observe in the identification process but should not be a screening-out factor for potential talent. This clearly contradicted survey findings, which rated this procedure at the top of the list.

"Raw skills that are part of talent can be learned to a large extent, so they are not really good indicators of talent in a bigger sense. . . . Someone who has a good ear . . . will often not go as far as someone who doesn't have a good ear but learns how to listen." (SS) One professional musician felt his own perfect pitch was sometimes a detriment because he must continually adjust what he hears when pianos that are out of tune or recordings have pitches that vary from his inner sense. (WH)

Creative Interpretation

The most decisive factor in determining potential musical talent in children, according to respondents in *every* interview, rested on criteria that were related to a child's creative and expressive involvement in musical activities. Students would extend, manipulate, and generally "play" with musical ideas. These students show an eagerness to express themselves through music, either through a natural spontaneity of turning a phrase in a tune or improvising a rhythmic pattern in a call-and-response activity. They show a natural ability to "think in sound," to "shape and project musical meaning," and to be fully involved in "communicating personal intentions" through music. This perceptual/cognitive process describes metaperception.

How do children "play" with sounds? A young child might sing, "Oh we're going to Grandma's house" while in the back seat of a car or march around the room as a one-child band of instrumental imitations. Children may take a musical idea and extend or transform it in different ways, similar to physically manipulating playdough. They sing a phrase over and over, "stomping around the room and putting words to it—nonsense syllables. These kids play with language, adapting and changing until it is completely different. They do the same with music" (YC).

> A child's imagination begins in the first years of life, and some children create sound structures inside and try to make them happen before they have had any training. Children who have that ability, the creative way to do that, have something of a gift or capacity we should know about, and we should build upon as teachers. Children who may not have this natural capacity can be educated to think more creatively by just explaining how to think this way and encouraging them to do it. (PW)

Can formal training be a detriment to creative interpretation? Several teachers described the challenge of maintaining a balance with talented students who thrive for excellence in performance.

> You have a 15-year-old clarinetist alone in this room. It would never occur to this clarinet player to just kick this music stand over and just blow into his instrument for the fun of it. Well, I think that's a real shame. . . . The way these musicians are trained—if they don't have that page in front of them and those notes in front of them, they assume there is nothing to play. I just think that sort of puts a limitation on a young musician's imagination. (DT)

> With practically everyone, the more they're on the piece, the better they play it. But with the talented student, very often that's not the case. Because very often that freshness of inspiration is better in the early stages before it's polished. Then by the time it's polished, and every nit-picky thing's down there, they've sort of lost the inspiration. So I think that's really the challenge of working with talented students. (SS)

The idea of talent as creative interpretation through response to listening is a controversial issue. The criteria is valuable to include if it helps identify students who may not demonstrate talent through performance skill. However, these students may be those who are more readily creative in general. Unique words and creative ideas might offer clues to personal involvement with the music—or they might be the product of a student "who simply enjoys responding in unique and individual ways" (MU).

Metaperception

The interviews with experts in various fields offered a chance to explore the idea of that "spark" we intuitively notice in a child's performance. Can we put this into words? Often this spark of potential talent is realized through the initial impression of a child's attentive and physical demeanor. We see a child's focused involvement in the manipulation of musical sound or experience an aesthetic connection with a performer's creative musical interpretation. The student is inwardly sensing sound, remembering it, molding it, and communicating it to an audience. When a student shows signs of metaperceptive involvement, we experience that spark.

Often in interviews, there would be a pause, and then a reflective description of an experience where a child seemed to show "an added dimension . . . of someone who is thinking by himself, who is testing out other possibilities, who is problem-solving." (MU) Talented students seem to have a "riveting personality." "Everyone has their chosen style, but a talented person has a quality that is larger than everyday" (SS).

> These children exhibit a genuine eagerness to express themselves. . . . I watch their eyes and see what they are looking at, because I think talent, in the early stages, manifests itself in a kind of a sixth sense that some kids have that *this* is a picture of *this*. You can tell by how they are looking whether they are doing that. (SS)

Dynamic of Performance

What criteria can assess potential talent in a student's musical abilities? What role does the aesthetic dynamic play in this identification? Performance tasks that combine listening with musical performance highlight music aptitude or musical intelligence. The more students work across multiple dimensions in musical work, the clearer the observation of talent. Basics include abilities to sustain a beat, repeat and extend rhythmic ideas, and respond to small differences in tempo or metric pulse. The ability to sing exactly in tune or match pitch is not essential, but the ability to remember melodies and repeat phrases within reasonable pitch is important to assess in musical performance.

Coordination and fine motor skills are criteria that are useful to observe but not precursors of musical talent. Fine motor skills are essential for certain instruments, especially those that require early training, such as the violin or piano. Further discussion concluded that this was instrument specific and a kinesthetic intelligence that may correlate to talent. "You can be coordinated, but that's not going to make you musical. If you are coordinated and you move with grace, then you could be rhythmical" (EG).

The criteria of poise and confidence in performance are considered developmental through training. More apt is the recognition of performance that is *comfortable* and *natural*. Rehearsal or classroom settings provide a more comfortable environment for this performance assessment. "Some kids and some of us adults will do a whole lot better in rehearsal than in performance. The belief that, because music is a performing art, we should already be comfortable with the performance aspect, and if we're not then there is something wrong with us, or we don't have that kind of potential, is one of those unspoken prejudices that we have in the assessment of performing arts" (BO).

One factor that can lead to a false perspective of musical talent is technique. Anyone listening to young children who have mastered technical tasks are impressed by their physical talents on the instrument. Often well-trained students will present an "overpolished performance," based on special effects and exaggerated gestures, that seems to convey emotional involvement. These experts pry into the particulars of this beguiling physical talent:

> We often misjudge young performers who have mastered certain physical skills and rote activities that culminate in what is deemed a musical performance. In many instances, such technically facile children (this is especially true in very young children) are performing without listening to what they play. You can tell when a piece is almost always played in exactly the same way no matter what's the place, what's the room, what's the instrument, what's the time of day, who is in the audience. . . . It sounds pretty much the same. There is a robotic quality. . . . Granted, the "robot" is playing very well, but without a personal connection to the sounds. (MU)

The dynamic of performance requires students to work through music metaperceptively and communicate their personal ideas to others through musical performance. Does it take the astute ear of a musician to recognize this potential talent? Lyle Davidson, whose experience observing a young child in China I mentioned in part I, noted that after that experience, he was curious if the classroom teacher would be able to notice the "presence" that vividly struck him. "Afterwards you talk to the teacher, with the translators help, and you realize that the teacher has also found those two children. And you realize, aha, we are looking at the same thing, and we are doing this without any preparation. Those are the primitive measures" (LD).

Commitment and Self-Motivation

There is overwhelming agreement that motivation factors should be included in talent identification criteria. These behaviors are essential if students are to succeed in musical studies. The idea of "sustained interest," rated highly in prior analysis, was bothersome in interviews. The idea of self-motivation while engaged in musical tasks seemed more appropriate for the purpose of identification. "A student who is *motivated* by music is clearly different from a student who is *interested* in music" (EG). Further, some populations of students, such as inner-city students, have difficulty sustaining interest in anything over an extended time period.

Terms such as *focus, enthusiasm,* and *perseverance* center on a student's direct involvement with musical activities rather than general interest over a period of time. The idea of "self-discipline" is equally inappropriate. "High-energy kids" in arts programs can often have behavior problems in regular classes. Words like "self-discipline" have a behavioral connotation that impedes teacher nominations for these students.

Commitment is considered a fundamental requirement for musical work. A student who sets high standards and goals shows talent, but this quality may be learned through instruction. A clue to commitment is observation of a student's preference for complexity and detail, with obvious patterning and organization of thought in musical work.

Terminology is a critical hurdle to overcome to clarify motivational factors of musical talent. Words such as *persistence, perseverance,* and *internal motivation* are comfortable. The idea of an artistic focus, be it for five minutes, or even one minute, is easily recognizable and reflects a student working metaperceptively in musical tasks.

Finally, the recognition of self and peer critique highlights students who are listening carefully as they perform as well as being astute in critiquing others. This type of understanding requires verbal translation beyond the performance domain. These are the "hidden talents" discussed in part I. "Sometimes a student will write very penetrating critiques but not be able to play very well. That's important. I think that's an index of a kind of musical capacity that would otherwise not be revealed" (LD).

> What's fascinating is to watch those cases where the reflective process is really leading performance, and guiding the performance. It's one thing that symmetry between performing ability and reflective ability is maintained. It is another when the performing is affected by and becomes closer to the reflective ability. It's very exciting when that starts to happen. That's really counterintuitive. (LD)

Identification Procedures

It was thoroughly refreshing to have the opportunity to brainstorm ideas with individuals across the music and gifted fields about ideas concerning identification that were fresh in approach, realistic in implementation, and directly linked to the assessment of the criteria developed in our dialogues.

An effective identification procedure should include data from multiple sources, extend to different types of musical genres, and include musical talents that are not performance based. Nominations from church choir directors, private music teachers, and other community sources can augment the lists from school teachers and specialists. Identification that includes jazz, folk, and music of different ethnic cultures expands the musical talent profile.

There is no question that parental support and guidance is vital for musical talent development. Most felt that a parent interview is unrealistic, believing that a biographical or interest inventory can best serve identification purposes.

Testing continues to be an issue that generates mixed views. Musicians acknowledge the existence of music aptitude tests but resist recommending their use in identification. Most agree that tests should not be used as the sole determiner of musical talent. An interview with test developer Edwin Gordon revealed the importance of choosing the correct level of testing to measure high music aptitude. He believes having a profile of the music aptitude of each child prior to musical instruction facilitates designing instruction to nurture aptitude strengths and improve weaknesses. "One of the things I would do if I had enough musically gifted children—I would administer the *PMMA* and *IMMA*. Then, once I found a group that was exceptional, I would administer the *MAP*" (EG).

A small-group setting (5 to 10 students) is quite workable for performance assessment in an elementary identification process. If students with minimal performance experience were placed in a threatening individualized audition setting, they may not demonstrate their true performance capabilities. Asking a young child to sing alone in an audition-like setting "is a terrorizing experience, and kids, if they don't sing a lot of songs, then they're not going to do it"(BO).

Recommended observation procedures at the elementary level may vary depending on the presence of a music specialist in the school. More than one observer is recommended, with at least one being a musician or private teacher from the community. Training should be led by someone who has expertise in the observation of potential as well as developed musical talent.

The presence of observers in a classroom often brings out "too shy" or "acting out" behavior or other "kid behavior in relation to authority figures" (SS). One possible solution may be videotaping small group activities as a way to observe students. With videotaping so prevalent in today's schools, a camera in a strategic musical learning center can easily be made to blend into the woodwork and enable observation of students working with music in a natural classroom setting. This strategy alleviates the disruption of scheduling observations in a busy school day.

With multiple observers, there is always the danger of a dominating personality manipulating decisions. This may be alleviated through more speci-
ficity on the assessment instrument and less reliance on selection resting on
consensus through discussion. If videotapes are used, each observer can sub-
mit separate reports, which can be collated and compared.

Observation can include assessment of improving musical behavior/per-
formance over a period of time. Rating scales can be developed that include
multiple ratings of observed behavior. A behavioral checklist may include
music aptitude capacities combined with a series of questions describing how
a child grows, behaves, talks, or draws about music. This combined checklist
and biographical inventory could be devised for each person observing the
child, including parents.

The instruments used for observation should combine quantitative measures of behaviors and abilities with a critiqued assessment of musical be-
havior/performance. A blank piece of paper is not acceptable, and certain
quantitative data should be required for statistical purposes.

Musical Activities Highlighting Potential Talent

What activities can highlight potential talent and be adapted for use in a
general classroom? The simplest suggested activities are call and response
of rhythms and melodies from teacher to student, providing opportunities
for the creative extension of ideas. These melodies can be simple words,
stemming from topics being covered in class that day. Students who offer
rhythmic patterns to words or melody tidbits to fit the topic of the day may
be the student an elementary teacher will easily spot as a potentially creative musician.

Behaviors indicative of talent in a basic classroom include readily picking
out a tune on an available instrument or singing and searching for the correct chords to push on the autoharp. Teachers can watch for the student who
simply sings or hums spontaneously and moves fluidly. "All children sing,
but talented children sing a little more confidently, move a little more to
music. They express their sensitivity to sound in those ways" (SS).

Improvisation was an area of discussion that elicited ideas regarding teaching and observing creative musical work. Creative skills should be a "perva-
sive part of how we teach music" (PW). The terms "improvisation and composition" are intimidating to classroom teachers and even to some music
teachers. Terms such as *manipulate, experiment,* or *explore* encourage creative musical experiences without the intimidation.

> What you are really focusing on is just freedom. The kids just play some-
> thing. . . . You are just sensing . . . just seeing the child's approach to the
> instrument . . . how they are going at it. They are connected in some

way to the rhythm that is being played. Are they putting in some variation? Are they listening to what they are playing? (BO)

The role of the computer and synthesizer open up vast creative possibilities for the manipulation of musical sounds. Suggested creative projects include small-group activities using an electronic keyboard loaded with sequenced bass sounds. Students can improvise within certain parameters (all
black keys or all white keys). With a multitude of combinations sequenced
in and earphones in place, this activity could be done in any classroom.

The use of journals is a way to monitor reflective ideas and unveil possible
potential missed in performance. A rehearsal critique allows students to assess their own performance. Peer lessons encourage students to verbalize
musical ideas to others. Lyle Davidson, researcher involved in Arts PRO-
PEL, comments:

> I've seen beginners give lessons to more advanced players, and it pro-
> vided an occasion of drawing out a richer vocabulary and a richer set of
> reference points for the beginning student. Hearing things in a differ-
> ent way realizes a lot about performance, from listening to and critiqu-
> ing a better performance. (LD)

These interviews suggested a talent identification process that reaches a
bit farther in scope than the process described in the literature or found in
the analyzed instruments. The use of music aptitude testing needs further
discussion and possible research to confirm its effectiveness in a comprehensive identification process. The interviews contributed observation recommendations that work in a natural classroom setting and activities that can
be included in a comprehensive music curriculum. Most important, these
procedures and activities reflect the criteria that are valid indicators of potential musical talent.

Conclusions of the Study

This study attempted to answer some essential questions concerning musical talent identification. A synthesis of talent criteria was established that
reaches beyond the aural discrimination capacities of music aptitude to
include motivational factors, performance abilities, and the recognition of
creative elements of talent. Discussions developed terminology that is
comfortable for those working with talented music students in schools and
studios.

Fresh approaches to musical talent identification include widening the
spectrum of talent genre and extending nominations beyond school walls.
Observations can seek out hidden potential through comfortable performance

settings within the classroom and activities that include listening and creative musical tasks. Music identification activities are adaptable for general classroom use and provide novel ideas that include the use of computers, videotaped activities, and student critique. Musical talent identification can easily be done in any school through collaborative efforts with music specialists in the school or the community.

There are still some unresolved issues to address in future research efforts concerning musical talent identification. Testing for music aptitude or music creativity allows an objective measure to be included in identification. Should this be included as an accepted part of musical talent identification? The development of observation techniques for recognizing potential talent needs to address effective settings, training, and observation personnel. A renewed approach to audition settings may find ways to include student critique and creative tasks in this talent assessment.

Perhaps the most intriguing issue is the role of creativity and creative interpretation as an indicator of potential talent. If the study had concluded with the quantitative survey, results would show that procedures that highlight creative experience through music are "inadequate for talent identification." To the experts, teachers, and specialists, creative interpretation was the defining ingredient of potential talent. Further study of how students creatively make metaperceptive decisions while engaged in generative or interpretive musical tasks will unveil further understanding of creative interpretation. Gifted curricula emphasize the process of solving creative problems. The development of programs for talented music students based on similar curricular guidelines will offer students these opportunities.

The next two chapters describe the criteria and recommended procedures for musical talent identification derived from this study. Chapter 10 includes Sparkler curricular activities that highlight potential talent in each talent criterion. Observational rating scales reflecting these criteria are found in chapter 11.

The *Framework for Recognizing Musical Talent*, located in the appendix, presents a summary of research, criteria, identification procedures, and recommended activities in an expanded outline form. This framework can serve as a reference for future collaborative sessions of those who are seeking to develop effective musical talent identification in schools in any community.

Questions for Discussion:

1. What role do you feel creativity and creative interpretation plays in the identification of musical talent?
2. A rural school system has no music teachers and wants to seek out students who show potential talent at the elementary level. What are some procedures that would work for this situation?

3. Interviews discussed the observation of students who show a "spark" of talent through their performance or creative musical work. How would you describe this "spark"?
4. What are the positive and negative aspects of the traditional audition for the identification of musical talent at the secondary level?
5. Of the issues raised in the conclusion of this chapter, which do you feel is most important to pursue and why? What could be added?

THE SPARK

Underpinnings of Musical Talent

spark (n.): A particle capable of being kindled or developed.
Merriam Webster Dictionary

The musical spark that I have discussed in theoretical terms, sought through research, and personally reflected on now requires simple definition. What are the basic underpinnings of musical talent that we can recognize, "kindle," and develop? If we take away the technical intricacies of musical training, a set of talent criteria emerge that describe how one musically "knows" and the behaviors that develop this musical "knowing." These musical underpinnings are *the ability to be keenly aware of sounds, to inwardly sense and manipulate these sounds, and to communicate them to others through personal interpretation.* These are the simple basics, from kindergarten to the Van Cliburn Competition. Take away the technical trappings, and there you have it.

This chapter puts ideas gathered from earlier chapters into a simplified musical talent framework that can be used as a cohesive reference for musical talent identification. Each criterion is explained, with talent indicators and procedures to trigger this recognition. The criteria that describe the basic underpinning of musical talent consist of:

- Musical awareness and discrimination
  perceptual awareness of sound
  rhythmic sense
  sense of pitch
- Creative Interpretation
  metaperception

- Dynamic of performance
- Motivation and commitment

To support active use of this chapter as a way to recognize musical talent, Sparkler Activities that highlight each talent criterion are offered throughout the chapter. Asterisks (*) indicate key talent behaviors, and there are follow-up activities to expand opportunities for identification.

Musical Awareness and Discrimination

Musical "knowing" begins with the ability to listen. Musical awareness describes the perceptive sensitivity to sounds. Musical discrimination is the sensing of differences in sounds. These inherent sensory capacities are described as *music aptitude* by music psychologists and *music intelligence* by cognitive developmental psychologists. The capacity to sense musical components of rhythm, loudness, pitch, and the tonal quality of sounds may be psychometrically measured through the administration of a music aptitude test. These capacities can also be assessed through activities that focus on aural perception, rhythmic movement, and tonal memory of melodies or songs. Musical awareness and discrimination consists of three basic sensory components— the *perceptual awareness of sound, a rhythmic sense,* and *a sense of pitch.*

Perceptual Awareness of Sound

The musically talented person is keenly aware of sounds, both musical and environmental. This person will listen with focused concentration, showing an inward sensing of these sounds. This is someone who will listen intensely to the exclusion of all else and stop what he or she is doing because the sound is so fascinating. For example, an adult may suddenly be drawn to the sound of a radio in the next room and tune out nearby conversations. A young child may continually ask "What is that sound? Where does it come from?"

The inner sensing of sound allows this person to remember melodies and rhythms, which he or she can repeat through singing or performing. In rote learning of a song, a talented child will easily pick up the tune after hearing it only once or twice. A fine-tuned listening teenager may be frustrated when directions are repeated two and three times in class when he heard them loud and clear the first time.

Most people can recognize some differences in sounds, but the musically talented person is keenly aware of the slightest differences in melodies, rhythms, speed, and the tonal qualities of sounds. Listening to music or the environment floods us with a multitude of sounds at once. The musically talented person can isolate and identify individual sounds or musical components within this complex context. The young child may discover that the clarinet is playing the melody in a symphony or recognize a specific synthesizer sound in a rock tune. An adult may actually listen carefully for details in the music in a crowded elevator.

Talent Indicators—Perceptual Awareness and Discrimination:
  Look for someone who "tunes in" when listening.

The person who is perceptually aware of sound:

- is keenly aware of musical and environmental sounds
- listens with focused concentration
- can sense sound inwardly and remember it
- can hear slight differences in sounds, melodies, and rhythms
- can isolate and identify individual sounds or musical ideas in a complex musical or sound context

Rhythmic Sense

The musically talented person instinctively responds to rhythm. This response is manifest in a flowing sense of the rhythmic pulse. This person can easily maintain a steady pulse when performing and creatively extend rhythmic ideas. Most children can easily clap to the beat of the music. A talented child may move to the beat in fluid gestures while clapping. When enjoying a question-and-answer rhythm game, this child may demonstrate inventive rhythmic ideas rather than a simple repetition.

A rhythmic person will recognize and react to slight changes in the tempo (speed) and meter (sense of 2-, 3-, 4-beat patterns) of the music. This internal rhythmic sense allows this person to remember rhythms and discriminate subtle differences when listening to rhythms. When moving to music, this person will instinctively change movements as the tempo speeds up or slows down. She will realize a change from a march (4 beats) to a waltz (3 beats) through clapping or simply tapping a foot.

Talent Indicators—Rhythmic Sense:
  Look for someone who instinctively "feels" a rhythmic pulse.

The person with a fine rhythmic sense:

- physically responds to rhythm in a fluid manner
- can feel and maintain a steady pulse in performance
- can internally discriminate differences in rhythms
- recognizes and adjusts to slight changes in tempo or meter
- can repeat and creatively extend rhythmic ideas

Sense of Pitch

The musically talented person hears pitches moving up or down in melodies and can remember this melodic shape. This person can repeat these melodies and creatively extend them. If given the opportunity to explore an instrument, this person enjoys picking out a tune by transferring the inner sense of pitch onto an instrument. Anyone who plays "by ear" and enjoys improvising a bit with the tunes has a strong sense of pitch.

The ability to match pitches and sing in tune is often used as a determining factor for identification of this sense of pitch. Although helpful to consider, this singing task should not be used as a sole indicator or excluding factor of this talent capacity. Anyone who has had the experience of being put on the spot to sing alone with others listening realizes the awkwardness of this situation. Instrumentalists with strong senses of pitch may not necessarily be strong singers.

Talent Indicators—Sense of Pitch:
Look for someone who enjoys exploring tunes.

A person who has a fine sense of pitch:

- can internally discriminate differences in pitch
- can remember melodies and repeat them
- can repeat and creatively extend melodic ideas
- can pick out tunes on an available instrument

How to Recognize Musical Awareness and Discrimination

We recognize musical awareness and discrimination when students are involved in perceptive listening tasks or in listening and performance activities. School talent identification can include music aptitude testing if an objective psychometric measure of listening perception and discrimination is desired.

Music aptitude tests are available for various grade levels or ages. Students listen to short melodic and rhythmic patterns that are the same or different in pitch, louder or softer, or played by different instruments. Scores reflect perceptual strengths and weaknesses, creating a music aptitude profile based on perceptive listening. Proper use of testing for music aptitude should reflect the age of the student and allow for a high enough test ceiling to project high music aptitudes.[1] (Refer to the appendix for specific content, age specifications, and statistical information about music aptitude tests.)

Assessment of these perceptual capacities can also be accomplished by observing students involved in listening and performance activities. Listening activities that ask students to "fine-tune" their ears for details will draw out students with a keen awareness of sound. Students with a strong rhythmic sense will volunteer to lead echo-clapping games and enjoy creating interesting answers to call-and-response rhythm games. Students who discover the correct chords to push on an autoharp or pick out a simple tune on an available keyboard show a strong sense of pitch. The use of Orff or percussion instruments in improvisation and song accompaniments can highlight students with a strong sense of rhythm and pitch.

Opportunities for students to critique their own performance or the performance of peers or professionals will often uncover students who have a keen ear. These perceptive listeners may not be the outstanding performers because of physical limitations or lack of training. This listening talent is often overlooked in normal identification procedures.

Sparkler Activities

Musical Awareness and Discrimination

The following Sparkler Activities, when done in small groups or individually, highlight musical awareness and discrimination. The activities are simple and adaptable to the needs of classroom teachers, studio teachers, or parents. Each activity includes a brief description, sample questions to guide the activity, and a suggested follow-up activity. An asterisk (*) indicates key musical talent behaviors for each talent characteristic.

1. MUSICAL MICROSCOPE: *Listening for specific musical elements in compositions.*

Select a CD, tape, or recording that has a strong metric pulse (two-, three-, or four-beat pattern is best). Choose music that has a clear-cut melody that is repeated and has definite differences in dynamics (loud and soft). Play a short excerpt of the music (no longer than one minute) *four times* while the listeners move as suggested here. This layered approach to listening focuses on different musical elements with each repetition. These listening elements are: (1) metric pulse; (2) rhythmic pattern of the melody; (3) dynamics; (4) tonal memory and sense of pitch. You may replay the music to allow extra listening for different musical elements.

Some suggested music:

- Mozart, *German Dances* (take your pick): short with repeated melodies, clear-cut dynamics
- Mozart, *Eine Kleine Nachtmusik* (any movement): strong metric pulse, melodies are easy to remember

- Haydn *Surprise Symphony* (second movement—*Andante*): recognizable melody, colorful dynamics

Questions to guide the activity:

1. Metric pulse: Can you clap or pat your legs to the beat of the music, showing strong beats? Do you find a pattern of two, three, four, five, or six beats in the music? Can you move to the music showing this pattern?
2. Rhythm pattern: Can you clap the rhythm of the melody? Can you repeat this rhythm when the music is turned off? Can you clap the rhythm of the melody while stepping the steady beat (complex rhythm/coordination task)?
3. Dynamics: Where is the loudest point in the music? Where is the softest? Raise your hand when you hear the loudest part, put your finger to your lips when you hear the softest. (Try this one with eyes closed.)
4. Tonal memory, sense of pitch: Can you sing the melody along with the music? Can you sing this melody once the music is turned off? What instruments are playing the melody?

Perceptual awareness of sound; sense of rhythm and pitch: Recognize the person who naturally feels the rhythmic pulse of the music with a flowing physical sense. Look carefully for the person who can conquer the complex rhythm/coordination task in item 2. Notice who easily repeats rhythms and melodies after the music is turned off. Recognize the person who can hear the loudest and softest points first and can isolate specific instrumental sounds.

FOLLOW-UP: *Perceptual discrimination:* Listen to another musical excerpt, discriminating listening for (1) instruments that play the melody; (2) instruments that play the background music (accompaniment); (3) comparison of dynamics of these instruments; (4) rhythm patterns played by the melody and accompaniment.[2]

2. SOUNDS IN A DAY: *Listening for subtle environmental sounds.*

Enjoy creating a journal of sounds that you hear every day. The listener will make notes in a small notebook that is kept in a nearby pocket for a full day. A portable cassette player may also be used for recording interesting sounds discovered. Describing sounds through words is difficult. What is important is the type of interesting sounds discovered simply by paying attention to them.

Questions to guide the activity:

- What kind of sound does a squirrel make? A mourning dove? Can you discover the sounds of other animals and birds that visit your yard?
- What noises do you hear in the house every day? Which is the loudest? Which is the softest?

- What sounds do you hear when you sit quietly with eyes closed for two minutes?
- What does it sound like when a marble is dropped into a metal bowl? a cup? a coffee can? What other sounds can the marble make?

Perceptual awareness of sound: Recognize the person who discovers obscure or unusual sounds. Also take note of an extended list of discovered sounds. The person who has taken time to describe the sound carefully or imitate it vocally shows a curiosity and interest in sounds.

FOLLOW-UP: When taking a walk, traveling in a car, or sitting in a classroom, spontaneously call out "Listen up"—everyone must then be quiet and focus listening for a full minute. Ask what was heard and note interesting answers.

3. MUSICAL QUESTIONS AND ANSWERS: *Call-and-response rhythms and improvisation.*

Echo-clapping is a basic music activity from early childhood on up. Body percussion adds the sounds of stamping, snapping fingers, patting legs, or other movements for sound variety and coordination development. The leader (teacher, parent, or child) claps a rhythm that is repeated by the group or "follower."

Call and response extends echo-clapping to include creative "answers" using rhythms. The activity begins with simple repetition of rhythms, leading to a rhythmic question-and-answer approach. Encouraging longer rhythm answers leads to more complex improvised responses. The FOLLOW-UP uses percussion instruments or Orff melodic instruments (set in a pentatonic scale) to encourage extended improvisation.

A. Echo Game: The leader claps the rhythm of a simple sentence while chanting the words. The leader progresses from simple rhythms to more complex while using different body percussion sounds. A child or group echoes the words and rhythms. Then everyone "thinks" the rhythm of the words inside as they clap or do body rhythms.

With words—   rhythm clapping with words "inside":

Example: "I like ice cream"

"I like cho-c'late cake"

"I like huckleberry pie"

"I like potato chips and french fries"

B. Call and Response: The leader rhythmically chants a musical question using any words that will encourage a creative response from the "answerer." Begin with questions that have easy answers and extend to encourage creative musical answers.

NOTE: The game can be done in a circle, with everyone doing a simple repeated rhythm movement (stamp, clap, stamp, clap) to keep a four-beat rhythm pattern.

Examples: (suggested rhythms)

"What is your name?"   "My name is————"

"What's your favorite food?"   "I like ————"

C. The leader now works with rhythms alone, clapping or doing body percussion with an improvised rhythm, answered by a creative response by individual students. Longer "answers" highlight students with imaginative rhythmic ideas.

Sense of rhythm: Recognize students who naturally fall into a rhythmic "feel" in their responses. Answers that show syncopation, unusual use of silence, or shaping of sound are definite talent indicators.

FOLLOW-UP: *Sense of pitch:* Extend call and response to include simple melody questions and answers, always keeping a steady beat. *Improvisation:* Use percussion or Orff instruments to do musical questions and answers, encouraging extended answers for improvisatory play.

Creative Interpretation

The musically talented person creatively interprets sound or music, communicating a uniquely personal musical performance or product. This creative interpretation may be a spontaneous manipulation of sounds, a carefully refined performance, or a musical composition. It may also be evident in an insightful critique of a musical performance or an interpretive impression in direct response to listening.

The development of a creative interpretation involves the inner sensing and manipulation of sound combined with personal expression. This *metaperception* can be applied to any art form. It describes the visual artist reflectively examining a work in progress, the dancer's inward realization of movement and space, and the actor's internal emotional development of a character.

The musically creative person enjoys extending, manipulating, and experimenting with sounds. Most children enjoy briefly "playing" with sounds. The creative young child will discover a collection of sounds *at length* when given a group of percussion instruments to play with. A creative adult musician may play for hours in a jazz jam session.

The creative performer is eager to express interpretive ideas through music and shows a personal involvement in the music when performing. There is an obvious metaperceptive process at work when engaged in practice or refining musical work. When on stage, in front of the class, or singing for Mom and Dad, this performer is totally engaged in the musical performance.

The musically creative person is aesthetically sensitive to the mood of music in listening as well as in performance. She enjoys revising and reworking ideas and shows insight in self-assessment of work as well as the critiquing of the musical performance of others. These critiques require the ability to translate qualities of sound into words, either verbally or in written form. Recognition of this critiquing talent requires the ability to discriminate between critiques that demonstrate sensitivity to musical qualities and those that simply demonstrate skill in verbal or written talents.

A creative child enjoys expressing unique ideas. The creative listener will express unique ideas that pinpoint specifics within the music. A youngster may create a colorful story describing music heard, explaining the storyline as the music plays. A teenager may suggest to a peer, "Can you make that descending run sound like a dripping icicle?"

Talent Indicators—Creative Interpretation:
  Look for someone who enjoys expressing personal ideas through music or the manipulation of sounds.

The person who creatively interprets:

- enjoys extending, manipulating, and experimenting with sound
- may spontaneously sing and move to music
- is sensitive to the mood of music heard and performed
- is eager to express ideas through music
- enjoys shaping and refining musical ideas
- works metaperceptively in revising musical work
- shows a sense of personal involvement in performance

How to Recognize Creative Interpretation

We recognize creative interpretation when we observe persons in the process of working creatively through music. This may take the form of free creation through simple call-and-response extensions or rhythmic or tonal improvisation. A person who draws your attention by "personalizing" these musical statements shows strength in interpretive creativity. This personal statement may be a young child's rhythmic response that keeps going and going, showing enjoyment of syncopation or a variety of sounds. It may be someone who sits at the piano and doodles, improvising or creating a composition that has a mood and obvious expression.

Creative interpretation is noticeable when students are in the process of making musical decisions while practicing or revising musical work. A young child may "play" with tunes by singing instead of talking or repeat nursery rhymes in different ways. This child is fascinated with the sound of words and plays with them by repeating them in a singsong manner.

At a more sophisticated level, a person working metaperceptively will practice by repeating musical work, with each repetition showing an obvious manipulation of sound derived from inner musical thought. Repetitive drills display obvious improvement both technically and musically rather than simply going through the motions. When this student refines work in performance, the expressive musicality is communicated to the audience. This student will catch the attention of the audience, even if technical limitations may mar the performance. Judges' comments may note a "musical student" reflecting the personal communication or *dynamic* created through the performance.

Finally, we recognize creative interpretation when students listen and respond to music. The student who describes mood or pictures that show depth in connection to aesthetic qualities in the music is interpretively creative. Note students who choose to write about musically interpretive ideas in their journals. Take note of the keen ear of a student who is critiquing peers or a recording and includes comments on ways to improve musical qualities and expression of the piece.

There are several measures available that assess creative thinking in music, which may prove useful for school talent identification of metaperceptive skills and creative interpretation. These measures are available from their authors and described in chapter 5.[3]

Activities that highlight creative interpretation begin with simple call-and-response exercises that include creative extensions (MUSICAL QUESTIONS AND ANSWERS). Any type of improvisation between verses of songs with body percussion, rhythm instruments, or Orff instruments will easily highlight someone who enjoys this freedom of expression. Listen for rhythms or melodies that are unique, use of silence, or directional changes that are out of the ordinary.

The use of computers, MIDI keyboards, and synthesizers opens up unlimited opportunities to unveil students who are musically creative but may not demonstrate this talent through performance. Refer to chapter 13 for specific use of computers in talent development, seeking software that encourages creative exploration of sounds. Look for students who are captivated with creating new sounds, are sequencing sounds that produce unique musical products, and show focused concentration while working on sound projects on the computer.

Problem-solving activities that require students to work through music afford an excellent opportunity to see students working creatively in musical decision-making. In the academics, the problem-solving process teaches students to solve a problem that may have a definite answer (a mathematical equation), or a problem that requires a creative solution (designing a playground for the school). Students learn to brainstorm ideas on paper, do research to gather more information, map out ideas to solve the problem, implement the solution, and seek acceptance.[4]

In the arts, problems often need to be formulated before they can be solved (problem-finding). The "problems" are motivated by aesthetic needs. How can I make this Bach minuet sound like a baroque dance? What kind of sound will portray a mood of serenity? This is a terrific chord progression—what can I do with it? The process requires a form of nonverbal brainstorming by playing with different sound choices metaperceptively. Allowing students ample time to experiment and "find and solve" problems through music will definitely highlight students with talent in interpretive creativity.

Sparkler Activities

Creative Interpretation

1. SOUND STORIES: *Creating a sound composition from found objects.*

   A. Gather a group of found objects that produce different interesting sounds. (Teachers can ask students to bring in objects that make interesting sounds. Parents and children can go on a scavenger hunt for "musical" objects at home.) Each person plays their "instrument," producing at least *five* different sounds. Encourage sounds that are both loud and soft and have interesting tonal colors.

   B. Small groups are formed (no more than five to a group), with students choosing who to work with by deciding which sounds would be interesting to combine with their own. Each group develops a sound story that *only uses the sounds of their objects*. This will require problem-solving to decide on the story line, experiment with different sounds, and rehearse the proper sequence of sounds and refinement of dynamics, tempo, and silences.

   C. Groups perform the sound stories. After the performance, other students guess what is happening in the story. Students realize there are no "correct" answers, because sounds are being interpreted differently by each person in the audience. (At home, parents can develop the story with their child with a performance for siblings, friends, or spouse.)

Questions to guide the activity:

- How many different ways can you produce sound on your object? What do these sounds remind you of?
- What happens when you play your "instrument" faster? Slower? Louder? Softer?
- To create a sound story, you must link sounds together that will tell a story to the listener. Which object that you heard will help tell a story with your object?
- Make sure each group begins work by listening to the sound of everyone's object again. What ideas can you develop from these sounds? Everyone shares these ideas and brainstorms to develop their story line.
- How does your story clearly show a beginning, a middle, and an end? What variety of sounds did you use to tell your story?
- Did you allow enough rehearsal time to develop the story? Did you go through the final version at least five times?

*Recognize students who discover a number of different sounds from their object, and are absorbed in the manipulation of these sounds at different tempos and dynamic levels. Student leaders will naturally emerge in any group activity. Seek out students who may be contributing creative ideas and are conscientious in rehearsal but may not necessarily be leading the group.

FOLLOW-UP: *Individual* sound stories will definitely highlight students with talent in creative interpretation. These students will be organizing sounds, developing a story sequence, and performing on a number of "instruments" alone—quite a challenge. Students can also add sound effects to a story they have written. These sounds can describe actions, moods, or even characters—giving ample opportunity to see creative work through music, combined with verbal skills.

2. SOUND PAINTING: *Improvisation using tonal color and different tempi and dynamics.*

A. This activity asks students to interpret colors they see through sounds they play. Gather some color sample cards from a local paint store or cut out pieces of colored paper or fabric swatches. Students can use Orff instruments, a piano keyboard, synthesizer, percussion instruments, or other available instruments in combinations suitable for their interpretations.

B. Each student (or small group) should have from four to five colors to interpret. Color papers or fabric swatches are placed in front of the instruments so they can look at them as they play the instruments.

Allow three to five minutes for them to experiment with musical ideas. Students should revise and rework through rehearsal before they present their "sound paintings" in performance.

C. The performance will allow students to play instruments in any order and repeated in any way they like to portray their sound painting. If the piece is performed by a group, one person may be the "painter" who points to the colors as the group performs.

D. Allow time after the performance for students to explain their musical decisions, and for audience response and critique.

Questions to guide this activity:

- Look at each color carefully and imagine a sound that would describe it. Which instrument will you use? What range (high, medium, low)? What dynamic level (loud, soft)? What tempo (fast, medium, slow)?
- As you work through your piece, decide how you want to blend from one color to the next. How will this change your musical sounds?
- Did you allow time to really "hear" each color? Did you have any silence in your music? (White, perhaps?)
- To guide critique: What color was the brightest? What was the darkest? Why? When was the music fast? What color did this depict? What was good about this performance? How could the musical colors have been clearer to the audience?

*Recognize the person who creates intriguing sounds and can communicate colorful ideas through sound to the audience. If the activity is done in small groups, seek out students who are contributing creative ideas that link sound with color. Students who are not comfortable with musical creativity will have some difficulty with this activity.

FOLLOW-UP: A more challenging activity asks students to do the same type of color-sound interpretation looking at abstract paintings. This is an excellent starting point for discussions about elements of color, shape, form, and rhythm in both art and music. Observe students who make connections easily and are obviously engaged in the activity.

3. MUSICAL KALEIDOSCOPE:[5] *Responding to music through art, written work.*

A. Select a musical composition or excerpt that is instrumental and no longer than two minutes in length. Each listener has a large piece of drawing paper, four crayons of different colors, and a blank piece of unlined paper and a pencil. Ask them to choose crayon colors that are dark, bright, bold, and delicate.

B. All listeners close their eyes as they listen to the music the first time. When the music is finished, they open their eyes and select a crayon that is suitable for the opening of the music.

C. The music is played again, with everyone freely drawing designs as the music plays—changing crayons as they sense changes in mood and musical color. Students should not try to depict a picture or figurative drawing but naturally move crayons on the paper as they listen and respond to the music.

D. When the music is finished, students look at the picture they have drawn. They decide on a single word that fits the mood of the colors and sounds they have experienced. They place that word in the middle of the blank white paper and draw a circle around it.

E. This word is the central theme for "clustering" ideas that evolve from it. Words that quickly come to mind are connected with lines and circles leading to more ideas and words so that the page becomes a web of free thinking ideas derived from the central theme. (Optional: a third performance of music during this clustering.)

F. A poem, short story, or additional art work is developed from this webbing of ideas.

*Recognize students who spontaneously change colors and design as the music changes. Look for interesting emergence of ideas in the clustering exercise. Finished written work or art work should be assessed for interpretive connections rather than writing and art skills. This activity will highlight students who are aesthetically sensitive to music.

FOLLOW-UP: Play another excerpt that has a definite mood (dramatic, tranquil, playful). Use the same listening activity of drawing with crayons and clustering. Have students break into small groups and share their individual central cluster words and ideas. The group brainstorms to discover similarities, developing movement and dramatization that fits the music. Each group works with their own tape recorder, rehearsing with the music toward a class performance. Critiques following the performance unveil aesthetic listeners and students who seek further refinement of interpretation.

The Dynamic of Performance

A musician communicates through performance. The elements of music aptitude, metaperception, and creative interpretation shape this performance. This performance may be an expressive improvisation during music class or a polished performance displaying hours of diligent practice. Both commu nicate a musical statement to the listener. Both can communicate musical talent through the *dynamic of performance.*

The dynamic of performance realizes musical performance as a process/product. Because musical performance is a temporal art form, the product is itself a process. The musician communicates an interpretation through this performance process to the listener. The listener hears the performance, sharing in the interpretive process. The mutual aesthetic experience of listener and performer creates the dynamic of performance. This performance dynamic is pivotal in recognizing the "spark" of talent. This dynamic is also subjective in nature, which increases the complexity of the identification of musical talent.

The musically talented person shows a natural, physical ease in rhythmic movement, singing, and performing on an instrument. The student communicates a personal interpretation by showing metaperceptive focus in performance. The performance shows evidence of student awareness of sound, sense of rhythm and pitch, and emotional involvement in the music. In essence, the person communicates the criteria of musical talent to the listener through performance.

Talent Indicators—Dynamic of Performance:
Recognize a person who is personally involved when performing.

The person who shows musical talent through musical performance:

- shows a natural, physical ease in rhythmic movement or performance
- performs with a fluid sense of rhythmic pulse
- is eager to express emotion through performance or interpretive response to music
- shows evidence of listening and shaping interpretive ideas while performing
- communicates interpretive sensitivity in performance

How to Recognize Talent through Performance

We recognize talent in musical performance by observing persons involved in the process of music-making. Effective assessment requires observation of a continuum of performances, watching development, improvement, and refinement in action. The more the person is involved in making decisions during the process, the greater the opportunity to unveil musical talent. This performance may be the sound "play" of a simple tune by a child sitting alone on the living room floor or the practice, rehearsal, and final performance of a soloist for a competitive performance.

Any opportunity for peers to work together in making musical decisions is ideal for observing performance talents. Peer lessons, critiquing sessions, and rehearsals encourage an atmosphere where persons feel free to express personal ideas and to experiment with musical decisions. The music studio and classroom generally are teacher directed, with students responding to musical decisions made by the teacher. Teachers are encouraged to guide the beginning of these classes, then distance themselves physically to observe the group for evidence of potential performance talent. Videotaping these sessions is helpful to allow identification by a number of observers.

The recognition of talent through improvised performance relies on observation of students in the process of developing an improvisation. If a number of young students are improvising on Orff or percussion instruments, notice the student who reaches a bit farther in flexibility of rhythms and melodies. A student who remembers and repeats ideas with a bit of variety in this improvisation shows strength in creative performance abilities. If given time alone to experiment, this student will develop an improvisation with a sense of musical syntax—a beginning, a developed idea, and an ending.

The audition setting that is the norm for acceptance to specialized music programs favors students with outstanding training, achievement, and performance experience. This atmosphere is threatening to most students and does not always foster the best performance from the student. Students with potential musical talent with minimal training are either dismissed or never show up to audition. Administrators in the position of identifying talent at this type of audition must realize *all* of the criteria of potential musical talent and not let identification or acceptance depend solely on the musical product/result of achievement and training. Refer to chapter 11 for ideas that extend the audition setting to include more effective observation of potential talent through problem-solving activities.

Students who keep a practice journal, setting their own personal weekly goals, will be more personally involved in improving their own performance. The process of improving performance fosters recognition of potential talent. The performance portfolio described in chapter 14 will expand on this idea. Students who view and critique rehearsals are more apt to improve performance as a group and individually. Motivation to achieve and musical performance are inextricably linked in talent development, whether brief or extended over time.

Sparkler Activities

Dynamic of Performance

1. DEVELOPED IMPROVISATION: *Developing and improving performance.*

   A. Each person experiments with four percussion instruments with the task of developing an improvisation for performance. The improvisation can range in length from 30 seconds to longer than one minute, depending on the age or the person involved in the activity.

B. Allow at least *five minutes* for development of the improvisation. A basic structure is helpful for framing the improvisation (ABA, rondo form; ABACA, coda).

C. Each person works with the instruments alone and may map out general ideas on paper if desired. The paper is a mapping guideline to assist in remembering ideas—*not* for the notation of a composition. Improvisation development will rely on repetition of ideas, and memory of these ideas.

D. After the appropriate time needed for development, each person performs the developed improvisation.

*Recognize persons who are totally absorbed in work while developing the improvisation. Notice complexity of musical ideas, evidence of tonal memory of ideas, revision, and refinement of work. The final performance/product should not be the sole assessment of performance talent.

2. PEER REHEARSAL: *Critiquing and improving group performance* (for use in a music classroom).

A. Videotape the performance of a piece during a class session. At the outset of the next class, play the videotape, asking students to write a critique of what they observe about the performance. Guide this critique by having them observe specific musical elements as well as giving an overall opinion of the performance.

Questions to guide the critique:

- How was the balance of melody and accompaniment or backup?
- How was the tempo and rhythm in the performance?
- What were the scope of dynamics? Did they reflect what is written in the music?
- What did you like about the performance?
- What specific things need improvement? How can we improve these areas?

B. Choose a student conductor to begin the rehearsal. The group performs again with this student conductor, who works with group ideas through the rehearsal, adding personal input and seeking further suggestions from the performing group. Several students can take the role of conductor during the course of a class session. Teacher involvement should remain at a minimum.

*Recognize skill in critiquing the performance tape for improvement suggestions and awareness of musical detail. Note input from students during student-conducted sessions for possible critiquing talent.

3. PEER LESSONS: *Critiquing and improving individual performance* (for performance classes and private instruction).

Note: This activity will work best with students who have had musical training. Anyone involved in music remembers the first time they taught and how much they learned in the process. Describing musical performance in words requires critical translation between musical and verbal domains. Students who develop this translation learn to communicate musical ideas to others and clarify their musical understanding in the process.

> A. Students work in pairs, taking turns being the "teacher." The student performs a piece that has been assigned. The student "teacher" begins with positive comments about the performance, then recommends specific suggestions for improvement. Peer lessons should include drill of sections to see if working in partners can help find a solution to performance problems.

Guidelines for students prior to the peer lessons:

- The student begins by playing all of the prepared piece.
- The "teacher" always begins with positive points of this performance.
- Be specific in what needs improvement, and go over trouble spots at least four times to find ways to improve performance.
- Allow an additional performance at the end, with comments relating to improvements made in the performance.

*Notice "teachers" who can verbalize musical ideas and are quick to locate and find solutions to problem spots.

FOLLOW-UP: Development of a duet or ensemble with students learning and rehearsing a piece on their own. Observe the process of learning from scratch, and note what problems they can solve together. Also note what critiquing development is needed for them to identify unnoticed problem spots.

Commitment and Self-Motivation

The musically talented person displays a number of behavioral characteristics that are not music specific but are motivational factors that play a vital part in the development of musical talent. These factors describe the overall working style of the musically talented person. They include focus in concentration, persistence, perseverance, an independent working style, and self-motivation.

The musically talented person can focus intently while engaged in musical tasks and often can concentrate over extended periods of time in musical practice. The musician who is engrossed in work in the practice room may not realize how much time is passing. This person will physically jump when someone enters the room and breaks this focused concentration on a musical task.

Musical practice requires persistence and perseverance to conquer physical drills and musically reshape interpretive ideas. When people ask a musician "How long do you practice?" they are usually surprised at the length of time needed for serious study. Talented students will work at a musical problem until it is solved—they just won't quit until it is conquered. This is true of both students who use specific practice techniques learned from lessons and the self-taught musician, who will extensively doodle around until conquering a tune by ear or developing harmonies and improvisations extending this tune.

The musically talented person is comfortable working independently in music and knows how to organize tasks. The temperament of being able to work alone on concentrated tasks is the norm for a musician. This student enjoys complexity and attention to detail and may show a natural awareness of patterns in music.

This self-critical person sets high standards when assessing his or her own work and critiquing the musical work of others. The fast-paced energy and accelerated learning of the musically talented person contributes to setting personal challenges that often exceed what teachers may expect. This person will rarely be satisfied with a performance and will seek to refine the work for further polish. The keen ear of the musically talented student catches details in the performance of others, with pertinent recommendations for improvement.

Commitment and self-motivation are factors that directly impact musical success. The talented student who does not have this personal conviction may not achieve as much as the above average student who shows outstanding dedication to musical work.

Talent Indicators—Commitment and Self-Motivation:
Look for the person who works through music with diligence and drive.

The person who shows commitment and self-motivation in musical work:

- focuses intently while engaged in musical tasks
- can concentrate for extended periods of time during practice
- shows persistence and perseverance in musical tasks
- enjoys working independently in musical tasks
- refines and critiques musical work of self and others
- sets high standards

How to Recognize Talent through Commitment and Self-Motivation

The simplest way to recognize a person's commitment to music is by assigning a challenging musical task and seeing how the person meets this challenge. If the goal is met, and perhaps exceeded beyond expectations, it shows internal motivation to achieve and improve. The internally motivated student will usually set self-made challenging goals.

The music student who enjoys practicing or working alone in musical tasks is clearly self-motivated in music. The young child who chooses to play with simple percussion instruments, sings to himself, and continually listens to children's songs on recordings is one to watch. The beginner at lessons who dutifully practices assigned pieces (with parental guidance and encouragement) and then extends practice with some creative playing, discovering tunes, or sightplaying additional music "just for fun" is a motivated student.

In the music classroom, the talented student is intrigued by musical challenges. If a small group is given the task of developing an accompaniment to a song, this student may either take charge in organizing tasks or will be persistent in repeated practice for improvement. However, group dynamics may mask the quiet, diligent, dedicated student. Assignment of individual projects or musical tasks will decidedly unveil this motivated student.

Internal motivation is a behavioral characteristic that can be developed through effective teaching strategies. Early training that develops successful practice techniques, goal-oriented learning, and repertoire that allows a bit of a challenge nurtures discipline and self-motivation. As the student gains confidence in guiding his or her own practice and improvement, self-motivation blossoms.

Sparkler Activities

Commitment and Self-Motivation

1. PRACTICE PLUS: *Self-monitoring goal-oriented practice and improvement* (for performance classes and private instruction).

Students and teachers mutually develop a practice book that includes assignments and various ways to monitor practice and provide student input and assessment. This structured, student-monitored approach to practice will encourage discipline and self-motivation. It also gives the teacher a look at what occurs at home.

  A. Students choose weekly and long-term goals to achieve in musical training. These goals are listed in their practice book, with several boxes to check to show progress. Teachers can see how students can assess their own improvement, and students have a "say" in checking off goals they feel they have conquered.

B. Students keep track of the amount of practice spent on each assigned piece or technical assignment rather than using a simple check mark. This will easily identify student interests and encourage structured practice. Students will realize how much time it takes for adequate practice on different assignments.

C. Open space for student comments on the page encourages questions and student assessment of goals (example: I completed my goal in only one day!).

*Recognize the student who achieves goals easily and seeks more difficult levels of accomplishment. Notice diligence in recording practice times and additional notes made concerning practice by the student.

2. INTRIGUING EXTRAS: *Extending musical work beyond what is assigned or suggested* (for music classes, performance classes, and private instruction).

Assign a musical task that has an appealing "bonus" attached. See which students take these extra challenges. Possible intriguing extras:

A. Listening assignment: After writing a critique or general impression, students can create a poem or art piece interpreting the mood of the music.

B. Theory assignment: Students compose a simple four- to eight-measure piece using theory concepts learned in the lesson.

C. Performance assignment: Students earn extra points for "bonus" pieces learned further ahead in a method book or additional solo literature. *Note:* A talented beginning student may attempt to finish the entire book in a short span of time.

D. Performance assignment: Create technique or performance "Olympics" that consist of challenging goals chosen by the student. Students decide on adequate levels of accomplishment for bronze, silver, and gold—with gold a decided reach for the student. This can be an amazing motivator.

	Bronze	Silver	Gold
Examples: Number of memorized pieces	5	10	15
Learning scales	Major	Harmonic Minor	Melodic Minor
Scale facility, metronome:	88	96	100

*Recognize the student who thoroughly enjoys these "extras," relishing each challenge.

3. STUDENT "TEACHING": *Developing teaching materials for peers.*

When students are given the opportunity to develop their own exercises, pieces, or written theory work, they learn "how they learn" and "how music works." Each creation requires lots of repetition, reworking, and refinement to put ideas on paper that peers can use—ideal conditions to boost self-motivation.

   A. Students individually choose the opening rhythm pattern of a song they know and create a different melody using the same rhythm. Peers learn this new melody and try to backtrack to recognize the rhythm of the original song.

   B. Theme and Variations: Use the opening melody of the song learned in class as the theme. Each student creates a "variation" to this melody. (This can be done through improvisation or notation).

   C. Students create a set of technical exercises similar to those being learned—with a personal twist. (They will be most likely more challenging than those assigned.)

Putting It All Together

The musical underpinnings described in this chapter represent an attempt to unravel a few layers of the enigma that surrounds the topic of musical talent. So often, when musical talent is discussed, there is a sense of tension and intimidation on the part of those who are not musically trained or well versed in the terminology of the musical world. Among musicians the topic is bound to produce a debate and strong subjective opinions. The factors of proper training, age, a good ear versus note-reading ability, creative improvisation versus prepared performance, aptitude versus achievement, ad infinitum, add layer upon layer of complexity to the subject at hand. I hope this chapter has simplified the topic for those outside of the musical field and has presented a basic framework acceptable for those within music for future discussions of musical talent identification. Specific procedures for this identification are discussed in the next chapter.

The criteria in this identification framework simplify the idea of musical talent to a basic spark that is not a function of age, musical training, achievement, or general intelligence. The spark of musical talent consists of the perceptive sensory capacities of music, the metaperceptive ability to internally make musical decisions, and the ability to communicate personal musical ideas through performance. The motivating factors of commitment and drive in musical work are important behavioral characteristics that directly affect musical talent development.

Questions for discussion:

1. What are some activities that can help parents determine perceptual awareness in their preschool-age child?
2. What additional activities could reveal a student's sense of pitch in a classroom?
3. Echo-clapping, chanting, and call-and-response activities are normal procedures in primary and elementary education. What should these activities include to help observe creative interpretation?
4. The performance Sparkler Activities in this chapter focused on student monitoring of performance and rehearsal. Do you agree or disagree with this teaching approach? Why?
5. One of the major functions of a music teacher is to teach practice habits and instill commitment in young musicians. What are effective teaching strategies that can do this?

UNVEILING THE SPARK

If a man has a talent and cannot use it, he has failed. If he has a talent and uses only half of it, he has partly failed. If he has a talent and learns somehow to use the whole of it, he has gloriously succeeded, and won a satisfaction and triumph few men ever know.
Thomas Wolfe, *The Web and the Rock*

Once again returning to that third grade class of music-makers and donning the role of observer, we now recognize the breadth of musical talent we seek, and have a taste of activities that can highlight different aspects of this talent. It is now necessary to know why we are there, what happened prior to our arrival, and what happens next. We are ready to look at the overall process required to recognize musical talent in a school setting and the programing that will serve the needs of these identified students.

The rationale behind including musical talent in gifted identification rests on the renewed interest in musical ways of knowing or "musical intelligence" and the broadened philosophy and definition of "outstanding talent" recently embraced in the field of gifted education. Music-related neurological research has drawn interest from the media and general public, which also helps swing the educational pendulum toward the recognition of musical talent as a viable educational necessity.

First and foremost, administrators must realize that talent identification is an *extension* of an existing music program, not a replacement. *All* children should learn music as a basic part of their education. As discussed earlier, identification is *not* for the purpose of choosing students for a music program. Its purpose is to provide more challenging and individualized instruction for students who have the potential to develop talents beyond what is provided by the normal school curriculum.

Effective procedures for talent recognition require solid understanding of the criteria of potential talent, observation of students in the process of music-making, and multiple stages reflecting local gifted/music program needs. Gifted specialists, who have traditionally relied on the quantitative assurance of test scores for identification, should broaden their scope to include the assessment of musical performance and listening behavior. They should also understand the process of metaperceptive learning in the arts. Music educators, who have traditionally relied on performance-driven assessment as the sole means of talent recognition, must seek ways to include talents beyond performance and consider the option of music aptitude testing in this identification. The scrutiny of details in the process across these fields will nurture a collaborative team that can develop programs to serve the needs of musically talented students.

The gifted field has been in the identification business for many decades. Although procedures vary considerably, there are some basic ways most students are assessed in the recognition of outstanding talent in academic fields. The following outline presents this procedure on the left, with suggestions for effective adaption for the recognition of potential talent in music on the right.

Basic Procedures for Talent Recognition:

GIFTED/TALENT	MUSICAL TALENT
Nomination Procedures:	*Nomination Procedures:*
Observational checklists and rating scales	Checklists and rating scales should contain valid criteria in *music* based on research and gifted/arts literature. Avoid generalized arts rating scales.
Observation by classroom teacher	Augment classroom observation with observation by music specialists and artist/teachers in the community who have expertise in recognizing potential musical talent.
Nomination from multiple sources (teacher, peer, self, parent)	Musical activities often extend or initially begin outside of school. Include data concerning student abilities from home and community resources.
Encourage identification of underserved populations	Recognize multiple talent areas and genre within music, emphasizing recognition of underserved populations.

Identification procedures at fixed grade levels	Potential musical talent can emerge at various grade levels, depending on physical development. Recognition of musical talent in the primary grades will secure long-range development.
Achievement: Grades	*Achievement/Performance:* Assessment of student behavior and performance in the process of developing musical work.
IQ, achievement testing	Avoid the use of standardized testing of intelligence or achievement. The administration of a music aptitude test can provide an objective measure to include in the procedure. This testing *should not* be used as the sole determination of talent.
Creativity: Testing (Torrance tests)	*Creativity:* Avoid the use of generalized creativity testing. Seek out measures or procedures for assessing *musical* creativity.
Performance assessment of creative problem-solving	Assessment of behavior/performance recognizing the factor of *creative interpretation* in generative and interpretive performance and listening.

Starting Points

The recognition of musical talent relies on the careful eye and perceptive ear of the preschool or elementary classroom teacher as well as the music specialist in a school. Research in music psychology, music aptitude testing, and neurological studies advise early training and development prior to the age of nine, with many sources encouraging development as early as preschool. Preschool activities that include singing, listening, and movement provide excellent opportunities to observe musical potential.

The preschool teacher who loves music will naturally share this love with children. The simple use of an autoharp, preschool percussion instruments, and a CD player brings the possibility of "sparkler activities" that can highlight early signs of rhythmic and pitch sensing as well as perceptual awareness of sound. Rather than shying away from the prospect of recognizing music potential at this tender age, we should seize the opportunity to guide students and their parents in providing additional musical enrichment for toddlers who clearly show signs of the spark.

Elementary schools fortunate enough to have a rigorous music program provide general music instruction in classes lasting from a half hour to fifty minutes once a week. Unfortunately, many schools offer music classes less often, with others having no music specialist at all. Music specialists are more likely to recognize potential talent than classroom teachers, simply because they are musically trained and can assess normal versus out-standing behaviors in musical work. Music teachers assigned to the same school(s) over a number of years can see children grow and musical talents develop along with this physical growth. However, they work with hundreds of children each week, posing a scheduling dilemma for individualized observation.

It is ill advised to leave the classroom teacher out of the loop in this recognition process because of lack of musical training. These teachers can be strong allies in the search simply because they see a single class of children all day, every day. With lots of encouragement and a bit of training, the general classroom teacher can periodically use "sparkler activities," similar to those in chapter 10, that align with a GT identification procedure. This brings music into the general classroom for all students and provides a perspective that may catch the listener or shy student whose overall behavior this teacher knows well. Ideally, this recognition task will spur ongoing musical activities that nurture musical thinking within the general classroom.

Step 1 is to engage students in musical activities similar to the Sparkler Activities in chapter 10, noting the outstanding students (see asterisks) carefully at the conclusion of each activity. The teacher can simply notate names or student initials on a designated "sparkler notepad" set aside for these musical activities. Names are added to this notepad as activities highlighting each different talent area are completed. This talent curriculum approach allows observation of students in the process of music-making over time in a normal classroom setting. It also encourages recognition of students who may show strength in a single area of talent corresponding to a particular activity's focus.

This first step in talent recognition is fairly easy to introduce into any elementary classroom or music classroom. The activities are accessible to all students and quite simple to teach. Teachers focus attention on the specific talent area of each sparkler activity and learn how to recognize the basic musical behaviors of potential talent through the process. At this point, there are names under categorized criteria with some added personal teacher notes. The next step individualizes ratings for each student on the list across all of the potential talent criteria.

The use of generalized "arts" rating scales is not recommended because they generically link the arts as one. Musical talent is quite different from artistic talent. A dancer is not an actor. Effective observation instruments for musical talent identification require valid criteria and should be easy to use for music specialists, classroom teachers, and community music resources. Criteria should reflect the observation of the full breadth of potential talent in musical behavior and performance.

My observational rating scale, *Indicators of Potential Talent in Music* (fig. 11.1), reflects the criteria developed from the research summarized in chapter 9 and is designed for use by a wide range of observers. The scale encapsulates the criteria presented in chapter 10, summarizing talent indicators in simple terms on a single page, using the reverse side for a page of comments.[1]

The rating scale is divided into three sections: *aptitude and ability, creative interpretation*, and *commitment*. These three divisions are similar to the three rings of Renzulli's giftedness model—above average ability, creativity, and task commitment. Gifted coordinators should immediately see this connection, and music teachers can understand this categorization of music criteria as well. These talent indicators extend beyond performance and include motivational factors that encourage talent development. The items with an asterisk may be omitted for use with young children.

The *Aptitude and Ability* talent indicators recognize:
1. A sense of pitch and tonal memory
2. Rhythmic sense and pulse
3. Perceptual awareness and discrimination
4. Perceptual awareness and discrimination
5. Natural performance ability

The *Creative Interpretation* talent indicators recognize:
6. Generative improvisation and composition
7. Aesthetic awareness through listening
8. Expressive involvement through performance

The *Commitment* talent indicators recognize:
9. Perseverance, concentration, and internal motivation
10. Refinement and critiquing of musical work

Parents and the students themselves can offer valuable biographical information to augment the initial talent profile. The parent/student *Musical Interest Form* (fig. 11.2) is useful for this purpose. The parent rating scale is parallel to the school's rating scale and is adapted to the home environment. Items 1–5 indicate aptitude and abilities; items 6–8 reflect criteria of creative interpretation; items 9–10 show interest in musical tasks and focused con-

Indicators of Potential Talent in Music

Observation Rating Scale

Student Name _____ Age _____ Grade _____

School _____ Type of Class: _____

Person completing form _____ Title: _____

You have known student _____ years _____ months Date: _____

Please indicate how often the student listed above has shown the following behaviors by circling the appropriate number.

1	2	3	4
seldom or never	occasionally	frequently	almost always

Aptitude and Ability

1. Can remember and repeat melodies and rhythms.   1 2 3 4
2. Keeps a steady pulse and responds to subtle changes   1 2 3 4
   in rhythm and tempo of music.
3. Can hear small differences in melodies, rhythms,   1 2 3 4
   and sounds.
*4. Can differentiate individual sounds in context: identifies   1 2 3 4
   patterns, melodies, instruments in a musical composition
   or specific environmental sounds.
5. Performs with accuracy and ease.   1 2 3 4

Creative Interpretation

6. Enjoys experimenting with sounds: making up songs and   1 2 3 4
   manipulating melodies and rhythms.
*7. Is aware of slight changes in mood, loudness or softness,   1 2 3 4
   and sounds of different instruments in music.
8. Performs and reacts to music with personal expression: 1 2 3 4
   shows intensity and involvement with the music.

Commitment

9. Shows perseverance in musical activities: works with   1 2 3 4
   focused concentration, energy, and internal motivation.
10. Strives to refine musical ideas: sets high goals,   1 2 3 4
   constructively critiques musical work of others and self.

Please use the back of this form for further comments describing specific strengths or weaknesses of this student that would be helpful in determining the potential talent of this student in the area of music.

FIGURE 11.1. Observation rating form—*Indicators of Potential Talent in Music.* © 1995. Joanne Haroutounian.

centration. The language is suitable for parents, with talent indicators describing behaviors observed in simple musical activities independent of musical training. Biographical information from both parent and student provides a glimpse of the child's musical activities outside of school. This valuable data can help determine individualized musical interests.

Tests and Measurement

Gifted education often requires some form of objective testing in its talent identification procedures. In prior chapters I have repeatedly explained the problems of such testing. Gifted specialists and administrators should *not* use general creativity tests, aptitude and IQ tests, or academic achievement tests as measures for the identification of musically talented students. This cannot be emphasized enough. Research shows that these scores are not suitable for identification in the arts, with setting threshold scores possibly excluding potentially talented students in music.

Music aptitude testing is a viable option for use in musical talent identification. However, administrators should not misconstrue interpretation of music aptitude tests as measurements of music achievement, basic knowledge of theory, or a way to evaluate the effectiveness of a music program. The sole purpose of these tests is to measure individual strengths and weaknesses in listening skills.

The administration of appropriate levels of music aptitude tests to a general population of students offers valuable objective measurement of the basic sensory capacities inherent to musical talent. These tests may unveil potential talent of students who have a fine-tuned ear but do not exhibit talent through musical performance. Testing students in kindergarten or first grade offers early recognition and opportunities for talent development of students with high music aptitude. The following list summarizes important points to consider in reference to music aptitude testing and talent identification:

- Testing should be used in conjunction with the observation of musical behavior and performance. It *should not* be the sole determinant of talent recognition.
- The appropriate music aptitude test should be determined by the age or grade of the students, with a high enough ceiling to recognize high music aptitude for this age or grade level. (Refer to the appendix for test information.)
- School administrators and gifted coordinators should understand that music aptitude tests measure aural discrimination—not musical achievement or abilities.

The use of music creativity measures is still in the exploratory stages. Use of the music measures of Webster or Wang and the initial use of Torrance's

Musical Interest Form

Parent/Student Information

Student Name _____ Age _____ Grade _____
School _____ Teacher: _____
Parent /Guardian _____ Phone: _____
Address _____
City _____ Zip _____

Part A is completed by the parent or guardian: Part B is completed by the student.

Part A

Parent or guardian: We want to learn what your child is doing outside of school, and what types of musical activities or interests you have observed at home. Please circle the number that you feel most closely represents how often you observe your child in the following activities

1	2	3	4
seldom or never	occasionally	frequently	almost always

My child:

1. Remembers and sings tunes from television, radio, records, tapes and so on   1   2   3   4
2. Responds to the rhythm of music he hears by moving, clapping and so on   1   2   3   4
3. Is particularly sensitive to sounds of all kinds, music and everyday sounds   1   2   3   4
4. Notices small details within a musical selection or in environmental sounds   1   2   3   4
5. Enjoys performing for family and friends, and performs with ease.   1   2   3   4
6. Enjoys creating or experimenting with tunes, rhythms, or sounds   1   2   3   4
7. Is aware of slight changes in mood, loudness or softness, and sounds of different instruments in music   1   2   3   4
8. Sings, moves or reacts to music with expression   1   2   3   4
9. Shows focused concentration when listening or reacting to music   1   2   3   4
10. Enjoys reworking musical ideas   1   2   3   4

Describe musical activities your child enjoys outside of school, including church choir, music lessons, family activities and so on.

_____
_____
_____
_____

Please offer your own evaluation of your child's musical interests and abilities.

_____

_____

_____

_____

Additional comments that may be helpful for us to know about your child.

_____

_____

_____

Part B

To be completed by student. Please answer the following questions.

1. Do you play an instrument? ☐ yes ☐ no
   Name of instrument(s): _____ Years played _____
   Do you ☐ take private lessons? Teacher: _____
           ☐ take group lessons?   Teacher: _____
           ☐ take lessons at school? ☐ teach yourself?

2. Do you sing in a choir? ☐ yes ☐ no Where? _____

3. Do you play in a band/orchestra? ☐ yes ☐ no Where? _____

4. List three of your favorite songs, records or tapes.

_____

_____

5. What musical activities do you like? _____

_____

_____

6. Describe what you like best about musical things you do. _____

_____

7. What other interests do you have? _____

_____

_____

8. What else would you like us to know about you? _____

_____

_____

_____

FIGURE 11.2. *Musical Interest Form*—nomination form for parent/student information. © 1995. Joanne Haroutounian.

Thinking Creatively in Action and Movement or *Thinking Creatively with Sounds and Words* may assist teachers in unveiling creative thinking through musical contexts.[2] The use of observers who have some expertise in creative musical talent is advisable in any of these formal testing procedures.

Gifted programs seeking additional objective test data may include a music achievement test above certain grade levels. Up to this point I have avoided including achievement in identification procedures because I have been targeting the identification of students prior to musical training. If identification procedures begin at grade 3 or higher, achievement tests can be quite helpful in determining the level and extent of programming needed for talented students. These tests also will determine the quality of prior instruction, as well as the needs of future instruction.

The *Music Achievement Test (MAT)*, developed by Richard Colwell, offers a battery of four tests that have been reviewed as "the best, most comprehensive, and most widely used standardized achievement test battery in music currently available."[3] These tests measure:

1. Pitch, interval, and meter discrimination
2. Major-minor, tonal center, and auditory-visual score discrimination
3. Tonal memory, melody, pitch, and instrument recognition
4. Musical style, auditory-visual score discrimination, and chord and cadence recognition

Edwin Gordon offers the *Iowa Tests of Music Literacy*, which measure tonal and rhythmic concepts across six levels of difficulty.[4] These tests can be used from fourth grade on and measure aural perception, reading recognition, and notational understanding within each of these concepts. Reviews of this test battery claim that "by concentrating exclusively on perceptual and notational skills, and by providing a multi-level battery, Gordon has created the finest tests available for grades 4–12 of these fundamental and important abilities."[5] If music achievement tests are included as part of the identification procedure, gifted/music specialists must assess whether a comprehensive measure or a more specialized measure is desirable.

There are several measures available that offer the quantitative assessment of performing abilities of young singers and instrumentalists in grades 5 and above. The *Belwin-Mills Singing Achievement Test* is a short 10-minute performance test that measures sight-singing skills of students in grades 5 and above. The *Watkins-Farnum Performance Scale* is a standardized achievement scale for all band instruments. The *Farnum String Scale* measures performance levels of string instruments. These scales are designed to identify the present level of performance for the purpose of assessing student progress. Reviews of these tests caution their findings, again due to the variability in judges' evaluations of quality in performance. As in any performance assessment measure, subjectivity influences these "objective" assessment measures.[6]

Performance Assessment Procedures

As already discussed, the assessment of musical performance is a necessary ingredient in talent recognition. I have examined the subjective nature of this assessment as well as the personal difficulty facing the individual performer in an audition setting. We also must realize that there are two different types of assessment needs in musical talent identification. Preschool to elementary age procedures primarily pinpoint potentially talented students observed in classroom musical activities, prior to individualized training. Secondary-level assessment screens students for specialized music programs or performing arts schools. This level of assessment recognizes talented students who demonstrate personal musical achievement and commitment.

Elementary Performance Assessment

The observation of the third grade classroom at the beginning of part II, assessing musical behavior through listening, movement, and performance, was the first stage of identification, where we are seeking signs of talent in a normal classroom setting. Let's back up and view this task with a bit more focus. Observing a room full of students engaged in musical activities for identification purposes is quite a challenge, even to someone with a well-trained eye and ear. Classroom teachers may find the task quite daunting.

Narrowing the field facilitates observation and allows more individualized experiences for the children. A creative project or performance "rehearsal" that involves a small group of children working together to rework and refine ideas in performance will unveil potential talent in a comfortable setting. Individual students who choose to try creative improvisation or sing a solo line in classroom musical activities naturally show a desire to perform. Teachers or outside observers can take this opportunity to recognize their musical abilities.

Outside observers in a classroom pose the problems of students either acting up or "clamming up." Anyone who has experienced an observer entering the room has witnessed this very "audition-like" situation. Isolating students in a single room performing specialized tasks with a strange adult watching and scrawling notes will equally hinder natural performance ease.

Several ideas that emerged from my research interviews are worth investigating to try to solve this outside observer dilemma. Videotaping a corner of the room where individualized projects are underway may be an intriguing way to gather examples of student behavior in the process of musical decision-making with no adult interaction. Tapes can be viewed individually, with rating of criteria and qualitative comments. Any problems of rater interaction are eliminated in this assessment procedure.

The idea of a "talent team" is a comprehensive approach to identification. A team of experts train school music and classroom teachers in observational techniques and guides them through sparkler-type activities. They oversee observation, guiding teachers in effective assessment procedures. Multistaged procedures may include challenging small group activities for initially identified students if further screening is needed for the local program. This team can also suggest effective ways to differentiate curricula for identified students. After the team leaves, teachers trained in the process can comfortably continue musical talent recognition and development in the future.

Effective observation of musical behavior and performance in the preschool through elementary grades requires:

- Observation of students in small groups (five to eight)
- Musical tasks that extend beyond performance, to include listening and creative exploration
- Musical tasks that involve reworking and refining musical work

Persons involved in the observation of this behavior/performance should:

- understand the purpose and process of potential talent identification
- have some training in observational techniques
- observe more than once, assessing improvement in musical work
- include classroom and/or school music teachers, assisted by community musicians or private teachers

Secondary Performance Assessment

Secondary-level performance assessment relies predominantly on the traditional audition setting. These audition procedures screen secondary students for specialized music programs or performing arts schools. Auditions occur at a specified time, and students arrive with one or more prepared pieces to perform. Certain schools or programs may also require a variety of repertoire, sightreading, and some technical scale work. These auditions mirror a tradition set in place as early as musical organizations needed to selectively assess musicians' abilities.

Adjudicators at this level seek students who show outstanding abilities in performance, which essentially depends on training and achievement. Unveiling students with potential talent beyond skilled performance will require understanding of this potential at auditions. In addition, procedures that reach beyond this audition format may include process-oriented tasks, listening, and creative possibilities. Student interviews or feedback following an audition can provide valuable information regarding self-assessment and commitment.

Administrators seeking students to attend performing arts schools and Governors' School programs realize that their pool of potential students come from a variety of musical backgrounds. Interviewees from Governors' School programs emphasized the latitude used in auditions to recognize promising students with minimal formal training. For example, one student did not sightread well but performed a solo brilliantly at the audition—a borderline choice for the program. When judges interviewed the student, they discovered that he had never had private lessons, which gave them the latitude to include this student. "This student displayed significant potential over and above what he might have achieved with private instruction."[7] The student interview brought this significant information to light.

Auditions for the New Orleans Center for Creative Arts (NOCCA), a specialized high school and career training center for talented students, emphasize "basic talent and interest rather than prior experience." Recognizing the limitations of training within a public school setting, they offer a preparatory program to allow students to reach the required entry level of the school. The school sets entrance criteria at a level such that, after three years of NOCCA training, students can be ready for a career in that art form.[8]

Interlochen Arts Academy, one of the oldest private residential arts high schools in the country, takes a progressive policy in admission, often taking a chance on a promising student. "If a strict academic standard (or arts measurement) had to be unfailingly applied, the enrollment would be a bit lumpy and many deserving students would not have a chance to show what they can do." The Academy feels self-motivation is one of the most important attributes to recognize. "Talent helps, but desire is essential."[9]

Professionals in the field of music and the arts realize that there is a calico quilt of student abilities at the secondary level. How can we effectively unveil the potential talent of students who are uncomfortable in any audition setting? The many students who are not in the high school band or choir but spend every waking hour creating music on electric guitars or drums in their basement immediately come to mind. We can seek a comfortable niche for these students and provide musical guidance and possible mentorship with professional musicians in the jazz or rock field. An "open mike" night at a high school may draw these students out, with a supportive crowd and a few attentive music teachers listening with open ears and minds in the audience.

Reaching beyond the audition can take the form of an added process-oriented activity that shows student decision-making in creative listening or refining of musical work. Observation of a small group of students engaged in a problem-solving activity that involves listening to and creating music will reveal students who show strength in musical decision-making. These students may not necessarily be technically adept in performance. Watching students rehearse an ensemble piece in a reading session allows a look at students making musical decisions without adult supervision. There is nothing more rewarding than seeing that timid violist in the high school orchestra suddenly emerge as a leading decision-maker when given a chance in a string quartet setting away from a dominating teacher.

When I was director of the Summer Enrichment Program in the Arts of the University of Virginia, we experimented with an extended form of audition. The program worked across the arts, with students collaborating in creative projects during the four-week session. The audition process required a half day of attendance by secondary level students. The process included:

- A small group problem-solving activity that required listening and development of a creative performance based on this listening. This activity had written directions and no teacher guidance or assistance. The process of the development of this performance was observed by three professional performer/teachers.
- Small group creative activities that revealed critiquing as well as creative performance in a supportive setting
- Individualized audition and interview

The professional performers and teachers who served as adjudicator/observers were intrigued by this unusual approach to the audition. The small group creative sessions were designed to ease students into creative exploration with peers. During that single day there were a handful of students who came alive during the creative group activities yet showed minimal confidence in performance skills in the audition. The adjudicator/observers were amazed at what they would have overlooked if the activities beyond the audition were excluded from the process. Interestingly, these few students were the leaders in the summer session, creating inventive collaborative arts performances and products. An extension of an audition to include similar process-oriented observed activities may be worth exploring in secondary level assessment procedures.[10]

Gifted Programs in Music

Now that students are formally identified, schools must service the needs of these students. In gifted education, the term *differentiated curriculum* refers to a curriculum that reaches beyond the normal school curriculum and is individualized to meet the needs of talented students. Teachers are encouraged to expand existing curricula to include activities that add breadth and depth to learning for *all* students, with challenging incentives for talented students. Part III describes the specifics of curriculum differentiation.

Differentiation for a young talented student may include more individualized learning opportunities in school through private lessons, theory training, or early entry into the band or orchestra (normally starting in upper elementary grades). Schools can link these students with arts organizations, teachers, or mentors who can provide learning opportunities in the community. Parents should inquire about differentiated services offered in music at their school.

Gifted "pull-out programs" give groups of talented students the opportunity to work together during a scheduled time frame in school on creative problem-solving activities that nurture thinking skills. In music, these programs can include composition and theory as well as creative listening opportunities that present challenging projects beyond what may be taught in the normal music or general classroom. These classes afford students the opportunity to work with peers who are excited about challenging work within their shared interest area. Unfortunately, these types of in-school programs are diminishing across the country because of objections to their supposed "elitist" nature and the disruption caused by students leaving classrooms.

Differentiation in curriculum at the secondary level may include classes in music theory or literature at the Advanced Placement level, specialized performance classes, or the option of independent study, which gives students free rein to organize a comprehensive curriculum according to their interests. A performance-oriented independent study may include private instruction or professional mentorships, a full solo recital, chamber music experience, teaching, or serving others through performance skills. Additional ideas may include independent study of Advanced Placement theory and interdisciplinary projects merging music and science, math, languages, English, or history. These experiences extend opportunities beyond the performance-oriented offerings of most secondary schools and provide talented students with the challenge of merging their talents with individual interests. These options are often available to students but may not be emphasized because of limited scheduling and personnel. Students and parents may seek assistance in organizing an independent study through the school guidance counselor. An independent study normally takes three to six months of advanced preparation.

The Apprentice Program in Arlington County, Virginia, is an example of a secondary level arts/gifted program that offers differentiated opportunities to students and utilizes community resources. Students carefully keep track of hours of arts experience outside of school and receive academic credit for the program. The program provides the flexibility that is vitally needed for secondary level students involved in the arts. Students in grades 10–12 have the opportunity to work in ensembles, participate in master classes and rehearsals at the Kennedy Center in Washington, D.C., and receive specialized training from area artists. They perform in an annual public recital and appear on cable TV for the community. Students periodically meet for seminars in interrelated arts where they discuss individual experiences in the program. This type of program can be placed in any school, differentiating learning through community arts resources.[11]

Enrichment programs offered on Saturdays, in the summer, or after school are alternatives to in-school services. The option of opening these classes to any interested student rather than identified students allows entry by students who may have growing potential in music. These classes serve as another avenue to identify students with potential talent who may not emerge within the school music program. Each local school system can organize suitable curricular offerings for these programs that can include interdisciplinary work as well as challenging music-specific content.

The South Carolina Governor's School for the Arts offers a unique example of this type of program through Saturday arts workshops for administrators, teachers, and prospective talented arts students in rural areas around the state. Professional artist-educators work with individuals at all levels in promoting arts education, and there is an increase in the number of students from rural areas who may be accepted into the state's Governor's School program.[12]

Governor's School programs are summer programs or year-long secondary programs that lie under the umbrella of gifted education at the state level. Students are nominated for these programs by their high school arts teachers and usually have several levels of audition before the final selection is made for attendance. There are a number of Governor's School programs in different states specifically developed for students talented in the arts.[13] These programs offer intensive study within arts disciplines, with some including interdisciplinary collaborative work across arts areas. Summer Governor's School programs normally have four-week to five-week sessions for juniors and seniors in high school and are residentially held on a college campus.

The unique contribution that Governors' Schools give to musically talented students is the experience of working collaboratively with students in other arts areas, often developing inter-arts creative projects or exploring interdisciplinary work with talented peers. Talented teenagers in the arts are immersed in their particular artforms. These summer programs provide a chance to realize how their peers learn in other arts areas, allow them to experiment with ideas beyond their specialized field, and feel comfortable taking risks—a basic tenet of all gifted programs.

Specialized training outside of school may also include private instruction by independent music teachers in the community or preparatory level programs connected with colleges, universities, and conservatories. Use of these outside resources depends on the ability of families to pay for private or specialized lessons for talent development.

Specialized Music and Performing Arts Schools

For many students, attendance at a specialized school for music or the performing arts allows more opportunities for in-depth music education and talent differentiation. These schools range from arts-focused magnet schools at the elementary level to early acceptance into a music conservatory.

Magnet schools in the arts are spreading in urban and suburban communities across the country in response to the current popularity of specialized or theme-based schools. Elementary magnet schools emphasize artistic integration in academic areas and offer more intensive arts training at these crucial developmental years. At the secondary level, students may attend classes at an arts magnet school for half a day, while working on academic work in their regular high school.

The New Orleans Center for the Creative Arts is an example of a high school arts training program that works in conjunction with the public school system. Students attend a half day of intensive arts instruction at the center, then attend their regular high school for the rest of the day. Students receive their high school diploma from their regular school, earning a minimum of three units of credit per year from the NOCCA.[14]

Specialized arts academies or high schools for the performing arts offer a full academic program paired with intensive training in different arts areas. The Duke Ellington School of the Arts in Washington, D.C., offers students a full academic and artistic curriculum that includes the performing and visual arts offerings plus literary/media arts and museum studies. Ellington focuses on creating a supportive environment for inner-city youth, training them in the discipline that is required for artistic training. They boast an acceptance level to college of over 90 percent, a dropout rate of less than 1 percent, and virtually no problems with violence.[15]

Many conservatories and colleges offer precollegiate training for outstanding students on weekends. Probably the most prestigious is the Juilliard Pre-College Division, which offers private lessons, solfége, theory, orchestra, choir, and chamber music in its curriculum. The program is open to students of all ages, with entrance criteria decidedly geared to the highly talented student seeking a performance career. The average age at admission is 12–15 years old, with a few noted string "tinies" who start as early as age seven.[16]

Conservatories and colleges of music are realizing the changing fabric of the musical culture in the United States and shaping programs to reach out to students who normally would not be able to take advantage of classical music instruction. They are also aware of the dwindling talent pool caused by the deterioration of school music programs across the country. The Juilliard School has instituted the Music Advancement Program (MAP) as an outreach program. Teachers audition promising young students from different New York City neighborhoods. These students take studio lessons and ensembles on Saturdays from the MAP faculty for a period of two years.[17]

Chapter 14 discusses the role of specialized schools and programs in the development of talent. The appendix offers a listing of addresses and phone numbers for resources concerning gifted programs in general, magnet schools, Governors' Schools, and the NETWORK resource of over four hundred schools and programs specializing in the visual and performing arts.

MUSICLINK

Part II has laid the groundwork for musical talent identification by providing a rationale for this identification, research-based talent criteria and procedures that can assist in unveiling this talent, and some examples of effective gifted programs in music. My personal experience of developing the MUSICLINK program from these ideas allowed idealistic expectations to meet the pragmatic needs of seeking and developing potential musical talent in today's educational climate.

The conception and development of this unique program originated with several sentences that jumped out at me from the gifted literature. "The task of programming, a delicate issue in many academic programs, is much easier in music; all we need to do is to match the student with a private teacher and leave the two of them to their own devices."[18] This "Eureka" moment put the idea for MUSICLINK into place.

The literature abounds with assertions of the importance of seeking individualized training beyond the school environment for students showing potential talent in music. Linking a young promising student with a private teacher early on nurtures musical development from the start. Every private teacher I know would jump at the chance to teach an eager, talented young student. If this student could not afford lessons, a scholarship could surely be arranged. There is always room for that *one* student who really wants to learn and shows that spark of potential.

Gifted programing in music, to me, serves two essential purposes. The first seeks recognition of student who show potential talent, offering them opportunities to fully develop this talent. The second, equally important, purpose is to provide challenging opportunities for outstanding music students who have demonstrated commitment to advanced musical study.

The MUSICLINK program serves both of these purposes. The budding student is serviced through LessonLink; the blossoming artist through StudyLink. The LessonLink program provides scholarship lessons for private instruction for potentially talented students who may not be able to afford lessons and have been identified by their school music or classroom teacher. StudyLink recognizes the advanced music student at the secondary level through independent study that links private instruction with the school.

Over the course of the past decade, the program has spread to the national level, linked with the Music Teachers National Association and expanded into the MUSICLINK Foundation. As national coordinator, and Foundation director, I have learned how a simple idea—linking one teacher plus one school plus one student—can easily be applied in a variety of communities and school settings. I have also learned that the myths and misunderstandings about musical talent abound in every corner of the country. Offering lessons to economically disadvantaged students is one thing, but recognizing their potential talent is another. Allowing students the opportunity for mentorship in academic programs is a feather in the cap of the gifted program. Extending that option to musically talented students poses the territorial problem of competing with the existing music program.

The hurdles overcome in helping a program grow and adapt to each community are rewarded when I hear students who have been part of the LessonLink program display their musical skills in a recital, proud to have been recognized for their talent. We measure long-term success when a LessonLink student can develop into a StudyLink student.

The program offers the opportunity to study the effects of long-term private instruction for economically disadvantaged students. We have found that successful continuation of musical studies relies on family support, with one parent taking the responsibility of transportation to lessons (often a difficulty with these families) and monitoring practice at home. Profiles of these developing musicians show students whose musical interests are broad and who are actively participating in school music programs along with private instruction. During the crucial teenage transitional period, the students who continue music through high school show they have established personal commitment to their music and socially enjoy musical activities in school.

These students do not fit the normal profile of the talented students whose families can afford to sacrifice time and money to develop their musical training. Often teachers, parents, and students must adapt and adjust schedules around providing transportation in order to secure ongoing instruction. Cultural and language barriers often impede the initial stages of lessons. However, the volunteer teachers who take part in the program realize how valuable these lessons are to the children.

The constant flow of letters and calls give personal portraits of these children and their families. One eager first grader played a simple piece learned at his first lesson in a school assembly. Another came home in tears when she couldn't practice at school because the piano room was locked. One father, upon receiving a piano through the program for his home, quickly refinished it as a showpiece in their living room (the donated piano had been a bright shade of green!). He knew that music provided a way for his children to enjoy being home rather than in the streets.

Students in StudyLink (there is no financial need requirement in this program) have designed impressive independent studies in performance as well as interdisciplinary work combining music with Spanish and even calculus. A student included a paper that described the similarities between the secondary dominant in music and the antiderivative in calculus so teachers in both fields could understand this connection.

MUSICLINK's LessonLink program is unique among many other outreach programs that offer music instruction to disadvantaged students because it begins with the *recognition of potential talent*. This recognition stands as a motivating influence as students continue lessons. Many colleagues ask why we should include this talent recognition in the program. I easily point to the students who have been taking over six years of private lessons through the program and are now receiving recognition through Governor's School or gifted/arts acceptance at the high school level. Their self-image as musicians was fostered through early recognition of their potential talent.

Now that the program has grown in numbers, we have discovered some interesting statistical findings derived from use of the *Indicators of Potential Talent in Music* rating scale used for nomination to the LessonLink program. The process asks music teachers in the schools, classroom teachers (if there are no music teachers), and parents to complete the talent indicator rating forms shown in this chapter (fig. 11.1, 11.2). After six months of private instruction, the independent music teachers complete the same form. There are interesting similarities and differences in these ratings (fig. 11.3).

Findings show that school music specialists rate students the highest in most categories with an overall mean of 3.61. Independent music teachers have an overall mean of 3.40, followed by ratings by classroom teachers (3.37). Parents not only show the most conservative overall mean (3.20), but their ratings are significantly lower than school music specialists in six characteristics.[19]

These statistical findings show that parents are critically aware of their child's behavior in relation to musical talent and their input may prove valuable in developing a comprehensive student talent profile. Comments on the Music Interest Forms reveal that students are actively engaged in church activities, enjoy experimenting with instruments with family members, and pick out tunes or make up their own at home, just for fun. Parents note that they became aware of their child's interest in music through spontaneous singing from a young age.[20]

Ratings of the specific talent characteristics on the scale showed that the basic capacities of music aptitude (tonal memory and rhythmic pulse) received notably high ratings (3.54–3.56). The characteristic with the lowest group mean was creative experimentation (3.19). Characteristics that described aspects of creative interpretation in performance (expressive performance, 3.40) or in reaction to music (aesthetic sensitivity, 3.49) were notably higher.

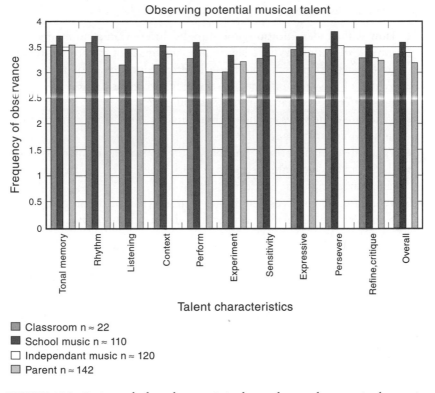

FIGURE 11.3. Ratings of talent characteristics by teachers and parents in the nomination of students for the MUSICLINK program.

Again it is apparent that the components of music aptitude remain as basic observable indicators of talent. Again, it appears that creative experimentation is not often observed, with higher observance of creative interpretation through performance or reaction to music. The term *creative interpretation* may prove helpful in realizing the breadth of observable creative talents.

My personal experience through MUSICLINK has strengthened my belief in seeking out students who show potential musical talent in every classroom. The students in this program are not necessarily the "wunderkind" prodigies discussed in chapter 6. Many may be described as "above average" in Renzulli's terms. However, the recognition of their enthusiasm and abilities at an early age afforded them the opportunity to develop their musical potential. These are students who would ordinarily never pass through studio doors for private instruction. With a bit of cooperative effort, I believe schools can easily put an identification process in place that can unveil *every* student who shows that musical spark of talent.

Questions for discussion:

1. How will an identification procedure be different in a rural versus an inner-city setting? What adaptions can you make of the procedures described in this chapter to suit these different educational environments?
2. Which of the recommended observation strategies do you feel is the most effective? What are other possibilities?
3. What are some ways a band or choir director can differentiate curriculum in the performance classroom?
4. What are some ideas for "pull-out" programs at the elementary level that would include interdisciplinary work combining music with an academic area or another artform?
5. What are the positives and negatives in specialized training at a high school for the performing arts or half-day magnet program?

PART III

Developing Musical Talent

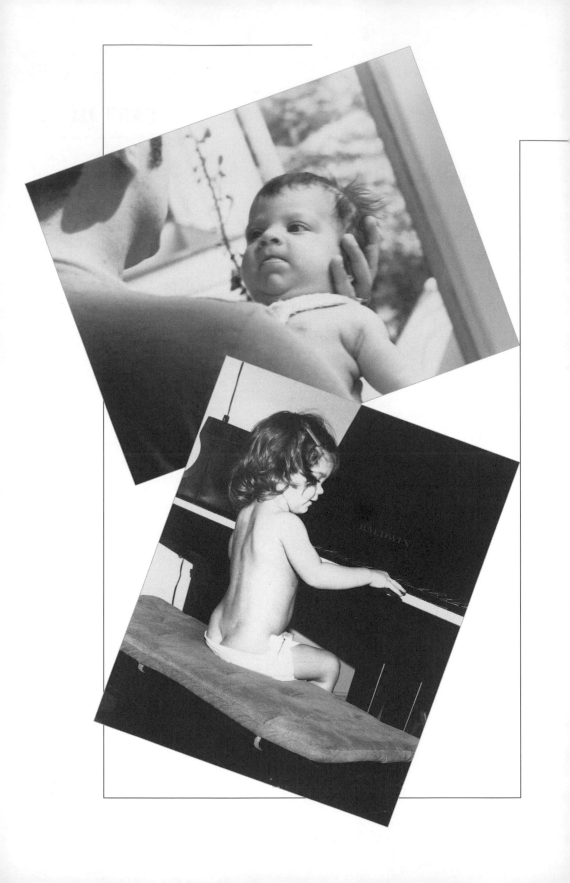

KINDLING THE SPARK

Early Development

Hush little baby don't say a word
Papa's gonna buy you a mockingbird
If that mockingbird don't sing
Papa's gonna buy you a diamond ring

Anonymous folk song

A lullaby winds its way through the intimate confines of the nursery, as a restless baby is soothed to sleep. The rhythm and rocking chair synchronize a pulse as a mother sings softly to her child. The baby listens to the gentle flow of the melody, which drifts into a hum that vibrates against the sleeping child's tiny head. A few short years later, Mom smiles as she looks in to her three-year-old's room. Her daughter is nestled in the same rocking chair, singing a rather lopsided version of the same lullaby, gently stroking a rag doll wrapped in a frayed old baby blanket.

Children listen before they are born. They are aware of their mother's heartbeat and the different environmental sounds that filter into the cozy womb. They are surrounded by the low-pitched pulsating sounds of their mother's cardiovascular system at work. Studies show that pregnant singers find their babies much quieter when they are singing. Instrumentalists report the opposite effect, with lots of internal activity when they are performing. Even before birth, a child recognizes the sound of a mother's voice and responds to music or familiar sounds.[1]

Musical Development—Prenatal to Age Five

Prenatal studies abound that can measure the movements and startle reflexes of these yet-to-be-born listeners. Loud, sudden noises (above 100 db) cause the fetal heart to beat faster and an immediate startle response. One experiment zapped 15 seconds of a Bach organ prelude (at 100 db) through headphones nestled close to a mother's abdomen. Not surprisingly, the fetal heart rate accelerated within five seconds of this musical stimulation.[2]

Once a baby is born, the effects of these prenatal sounds still have an influence on behavior. Studies of newborns by Salk in the 1960s resulted in the popularity of crib devices that play the sound of an adult heartbeat to soothe babies to sleep. Other studies show the same soothing effect for seven-day-old neonates listening to taped sounds of intrauterine background noises.[3]

From birth, the mother's voice is distinguished from other women's voices and recognized more readily than the father's voice—again stemming from prenatal listening experiences. Studies note that young infants suck away in excitement when hearing a story that their mothers had read aloud prior to birth but are relatively inactive when hearing an unfamiliar story. Similar preference reactions occurred to familiar prenatal lullabies versus new songs sung after birth. The "mother tongue" philosophy of Suzuki is reflected in these studies as well, showing that infants just a few days old can discriminate between the language of their mother and another language. Perceptual discrimination is already recognizable, within the first month of life.[4]

Parents speak to their infants slowly, with a high-pitched voice and broad pitch fluctuation—the "infant-directed" speech discussed in chapter 2. Words have elongated vowels, with more repetitious phrasing and rhythmic regularity. This style of speech creates a heightened affective response, which Stern calls "affect attunement" in *The Interpersonal World of the Infant*. Parents create an "inner-relatedness" with their child by matching the pitch and quality of their voice with the observed behavior of the infant.[5] Infants naturally prefer this type of speech to normal adult-directed speech. Rising contours capture their attention, falling contours help soothe them, and bell-shaped contours get their attention and relay an expression of approval. When parents sing a lullaby with a gentle tone of voice, slow tempo, and the falling contours of narrow-ranged melodies, they meld infant-directed speech into music. The infant's ability to perceive pitch, contour, range, and tempo in speech naturally generalizes to musical sounds.[6]

Discrimination of specific musical sounds is apparent from around five months of age. Infants can discriminate between familiar versus novel melodic contours, sensing how the melody moves up and down in direction.

Rhythmic pattern discrimination is evident, with some studies finding that infants can detect changes in transposed melodies as slight as a semitone or half step.[7]

Infants also have a tendency to group rhythms or pitches heard (XXX–OOO). They do not notice a pause between patterns (XXX—OOO), but a pause within a pattern (XX—XOOO) catches their attention. Awareness of pitch was put to the infant test, with one study actually training three- to six-month-old babies to match a single pitch played on a pitch pipe, having them "practice" for 40 days.[8]

In the 1970s, Moog conducted a large cross-sectional study of listening perception with five hundred children of varying ages from three months to five years; this study is a major resource on the early stages of musical development. These young subjects listened to a comprehensive set of tests consisting of nursery songs, words spoken in rhythm, rhythm patterns, consonant and dissonant instrumental music, and nonmusical sounds (vacuum cleaner and traffic). Moog found that six-month-old infants would stop and turn toward the music but not the tapes with sound or rhythms. Babies showed attentiveness for a few seconds as they listened to the music, then they would smile at their mothers. They were attracted to the quality of what Moog called "sensuously beautiful sound." By nine months, they noticeably swayed or bounced to musical sounds, turning away with displeasure from the tapes of rhythms and noises.[9]

Infants are not only listening but learning to communicate through sound, with signs of musicality emerging in the very first months of life. Babies create melodic "cooing" sounds when two to three months old, followed by exploratory vocal play at four to six months. Mechthild Papoušek, a specialist in the stimulation of musical learning from infancy, describes this vocal play as "a favorite, inexhaustible toy available even in the parent's absence." Infants are motivated to "reproduce sounds discovered by chance and to repeat and modify their vocal products with overt signs of effort, eagerness, and joy."[10] They are simply having fun with sounds. This vocal play reaches its peak at around six months and may be stimulated through "intuitive parenting," where parents communicate with the infant by echoing these sounds, creating a preverbal musical conversation.

Creative vocal play develops into repetitive babbling (seven–eleven months), leading to canonic babbling, repeating ma-ma-ma-ma or da-da-da-da (nine–thirteen months), and a "one-word" stage (twelve–eighteen months). This babbling of speech and music grows together, with children often singing babbling songs before saying their first words. Language and music mutually develop as a child reaches one year of age. The many anecdotes of prodigies being able to sing before they can speak may not necessarily be signals of precocity but of an "intuitive parent" who stimulated an infant with music and vocal interplay in the first months of life.[11]

SPARKLER EXPERIENCE: Infant Musical Stimulation

These practices of musical stimulation by parents or caregivers allow infants and adults to communicate intimately through musical sounds, nurturing personal musical expression.

A. When speaking to your child, use "infant-directed" speech, a rising and falling singsong vocal quality. Note infant responses to different inflections in your voice.

B. Hold your baby face to face. Model and encourage vocal play by matching and communicating through imitative "play" of sounds.

C. Use kinesthetic rhythmic pattern play by gently shaking your baby's feet or hands while chanting or singing. Physically stroke, tap, pat, and tickle to the beat or rhythm pattern. If you nod or shake your head while singing or vocally playing, you model a rhythmic pulse visually for the baby.

D. Play simple games with dynamics and pitch, using tactile stimulation. A favorite is the tickling game of fingers crawling up the tummy to tickle the chin. Use a crescendo (gradually get louder) in your voice as you rise in pitch reaching the chin, and a decrescendo (gradually get softer) as the hand crawls back away.

E. Above all—*sing*! Lullabies, rock tunes, arias, spontaneous, silly songs—anything will do, the more the better. "Dancing" with your infant while singing doubles the fun and the stimulation.

After their first birthday, youngsters begin to discover how to play with a single syllable, first babbling with this sound in various pitches and soon developing simple melodic contours—shaped bits of melodies that move up and down. They are not trying to imitate songs but rather have refined their vocal play to a type of interval play.

By 18 months, children spontaneously sing with more stability to pitch than the sliding contours of earlier song babbling. Initial melodic contours are usually narrow in range—no greater than a third—and normally move from high to low. The favorite descending *minor third* chanting interval ("Rain, rain, go away,") soon leads to the added fourth ("Come again *some other day*"). In normal musical development, these ranges stretch to the range of a fifth and sixth after the second birthday, using leaps and steps in their shaping. Prior to the age of two, singing still plays with contours of sound, with growing parameters, but is not organized into a sense of scale structure.

Around the age of two and a half, children learn to imitate parts of songs they hear. They begin by extracting a single word or two, or parts of words, that are brought into their comfortable contour range and repeated over and over. At first, these words will not necessarily imitate the pitches or rhythms of the song but are "borrowed" to play with in their imaginative songs. For example, "pat a cake" or "oink oink" from simple children's songs become sound "toys" to play with.

A Project Zero longitudinal study of nine youngsters over the course of five years describes a four-step process in which children fill in the gaps between comfortably established ranges during the first five years of life. Rather than thinking of key structure or fixed pitches, children establish a *contour scheme*— an up-and-down figurative melody shape in different levels of mental organization. Each contour scheme has a specific range (third, fourth, fifth, sixth), melodic direction (high to low, up and down), and stability of pitch from one to another (sliding versus clear changes). As the range increases in scope, melodic direction shows more variety and pitch becomes more stabilized, with normal children in the study using scale structures before their sixth birthday.[12]

A longitudinal study of four preschool children by McKernon arrived at similar conclusions. Children "glissed" pitches together until around 18 months of age. At this age, there were recognizable notes and some words from learned songs in place. These children began to approximate the melodic contour of learned songs after two years.[13]

When do children really sing *songs*, with rhythms and pitches similar to those heard? Moog found that 76 percent of the children he studied could sing at least one line of a song, more or less correctly, by the age of four. By five, half of the children could sing the whole song correctly, with a few "squeezed" intervals. The six-year-old time frame seems to be a reliable target age for singing with stabilized pitch.[14] There is wide agreement by preschool music educators that the imaginative songs of preschoolers should not be corrected by parents who hear notes a bit "off key." This childlike tonality should be allowed to grow in its own way. Encouraging this type of musical exploration nurtures creatively thinking through music.

Ries's study of 48 young children discovered singing ability developing at a much earlier age when studying spontaneous singing. Her study showed that babies spontaneously sing in an expressive manner, with style, articulation, and vocal quality. She suggests a developmental sequence of pitch or melody by 7 months, articulation (separation of sounds) at 11 months, and very simple rhythms by 19 months, when words are added. Learned songs develop more slowly. Children at two and a half could sing spontaneous songs with definite tonality, much earlier than the majority of studies noted earlier. Ries observed these children in their homes, where music was an im-

portant part of the family life. This may account for the atypical early development of these musical abilities. Were these children "talented," or did
these abilities grow from their supportive surroundings?[15]

When does a child clap a steady beat and show rhythmic movement to
music? The bobbing and swaying of the eight-month-old infant in response
to music develops into the ability to match the movements of others by the
age of two or two and a half. Bentley's study of young children for the development of his music aptitude test discovered that children naturally "coa-
lesce" rhythmically to the dominant rhythmic figure established in groups
of children at play. When children sing loud they will sometimes speed up
the tempo and get slower when they sing softer. By age three, children can
make broad distinctions between fast and slow, but the ability to maintain a
steady pulse to music is not established until even beyond six years old.[16]

We discussed the 1940 studies of the Pillsbury Foundation School in part
I. Young children from age one and a half to eight played in a school well
equipped with an array of instruments chosen for their "simplicity, variety,
intrinsic worth, and adaptability to the purposes of the children." A set of
studies in the 1970s replicated this setting, providing instruments such as
Chinese tom-toms and a variety of Orff instruments for the children's creative experimentation. At first, children headed for the noisiest instruments,
playing with uncontrolled gestures. As their play continued, they would
concentrate on different timbres and dynamics first, then create pitches. These
tiny improvisers enjoyed producing sounds from anything and everything
around them, seeking sounds that pleased them. "Music is, for young children, primarily the discovery of sound." At 18 months, children gravitated
toward the sounds of bells, whistles, and clocks. Four-year-olds enjoyed experimenting with notes on a piano.[17]

Environmental musical stimulation during the preschool years is a key
factor in the development of potential talent. Moog discovered that between
the ages of three and four, children who came from homes where music was
played and listened to on a daily basis showed a clear advantage in his testing. This is the age when children are snatching words, contours, and phrases
of songs they hear and developing them through imaginative play. A home
with the sound of music from a CD or radio or a parent singing or playing
an instrument establishes music as a part of everyday life for a child. Interplay through singing games establishes the joy of musical sharing between
the parent and child. This type of stimulating environment nurtures musical talent at this age.

One of the children in the Project Zero longitudinal study was a talented
young girl whose home life clearly influenced her rapid musical development
in preschool years. Both parents were musicians, teaching private lessons in
the home. They naturally stimulated her participation in musical activities
on a daily basis. As soon as she could talk, they taught her the musical solfége

syllables (do, re, mi, fa, so, la, ti, do). By the age of two she was singing children's songs with adult-like pitch and rhythmic confidence. At four she studied cello, then piano and composition. Her vocal talents landed her the lead role of "Annie" in a local production at the age of 10.

She and her father enjoyed a singing game in which he would begin a phrase and she would "answer" by singing its ending. They would take turns providing musical contours that she might creatively end on an unusual note, just for a creative twist and a shared smile. This type of singing game became intuitive to the parent and child, probably progressing from earlier vocal play when she was an infant.[18] One is reminded of a similar game played by a young boy and his father at bedtime—the young Amadeus with Leopold Mozart.

A brief summary of the normal development of musical abilities from prenatal to age five is as follows:

Musical Abilities—Prenatal to Age Five

- *Prenatal discrimination*
  mother's voice
  certain environmental sounds
  music that is played repeatedly
- *Perceptual discrimination and abilities, 0–5 months*
  mother's voice, spoken and sung
  melodic contour shapes, individual pitch
  rhythmic patterns
  cooing (2–3 months)
- *Perceptual discrimination and abilities, 6 months–1 year*
  vocal play (4–7 months)
  repetitive babbling (7–11 months)
  canonic babbling (9–13 months)
  bobbing and moving in response to music (6–8 months)
  turning head toward music, showing expression and attentiveness
    (6 months)
- *Perceptual discrimination and abilities, 1–6 years*
  one-word babbling (12–18 months)
  spontaneous singing and chanting (18 months)
  interest in creating sounds with instruments—bells, whistles
    (18 months)
  imitating parts of songs—single word repetitions (2½)
  matching movements of others in response to music (2½)
  interest in playing notes on the piano (4)
  beginning of preschool music lessons or classes (3–6)
  singing songs relatively in pitch and structure (5–6)
  clapping a steady beat (6 and after)

This concise guide is synthesized from numerous studies by music psychologists and developmental psychologists who have critically observed and recorded early musical behavior. Biographical studies have shown that precocious musical behavior is not always present in early childhood. However, parents do notice an affinity to music and stimulate this interest at an early age, with lessons normally beginning between ages five and seven. Parents who notice their child singing songs fairly well in pitch with a full octave range before the age of five should take notice.

The years before school are golden years for establishing music as a normal way of expressing joy and play for young children. Music played in the home is the first step. Active parental involvement is an all-important second step. Family outings to concerts that appeal to children is a decided third step. Many community orchestras offer special "toddler" concerts where children may even enjoy an instrument "petting zoo," where musicians socially interact with the children. These experiences can make lasting impressions on a youngster of this age.

When my daughter was a toddler of three, she had already experienced a home environment similar to that of the young child in the Project Zero study. She began piano lessons at three, and we regularly played singing games, which she shared with her stuffed animals as well (responding in their "voices"). Opera is not normal fare for this age, but I ventured to take her to a rehearsal of *The Bartered Bride*. When the rehearsal ran over time, the orchestra was free to leave and the rehearsal pianist took over to end the rehearsal. Rather than carrying a sleeping toddler out of the auditorium, we had to remain until the end of the rehearsal so she could see the bear dance and hear all of the musical story. She grew to be quite talented in music through piano, cello, dance, and voice, perhaps inspired by these early musical experiences. To parents of youngsters who are fascinated with musical sounds, a short venture into a concert hall may bring similar lasting reactions.

Early Childhood to Elementary Music Instruction

The last few decades have seen a notable rise in the availability of preschool music instruction, through classes or private lessons. Leading European systems of musical education have filtered into early childhood and elementary curricula in music programs in the United States. There is an array of possibilities for parents seeking musical instruction for young children. Instruction can begin as early as birth, with programs that feature parent/child experiences in small groups guided by a trained teacher. Early instrumental instruction is offered through Suzuki training, several organized early keyboard programs, or private lessons and/or group classes provided by an independent teacher. Simply walk into a well-equipped music store and you will see a vast assortment of new materials specifically geared to the pre-school age student, especially in piano.

Parents may be unfamiliar with the philosophies, teacher training, or curricular offerings of these different approaches to early musical development. Music educators in elementary schools who work with children who are directly "graduating" from these programs may appreciate a glance at the skills these programs develop. Performing musicians and private instructors may be intrigued by the curricula of Orff, Kodály, and Dalcroze. An overview follows of different types of early childhood and elementary programs, showing the possibilities of musical talent development extending from birth through age 10.

Early Childhood Music Programs

Early childhood music programs are based on curricula that encourage development of the basic skills of singing, movement, creativity, and rhythmic play that reflect the musical abilities of young children. The following summary of a selected group of preschool programs lists for each a resource for further information; student ages; and teacher training specifics. Each overview also includes a sample Sparkler Activity reflecting teaching techniques used in the program, to give a sense of activities that are typically included in early childhood curricula.[19]

Kindermusik International

Kindermusik originated in West Germany in the 1960s, based on the Musicklasche Früherziehung music curriculum. Daniel Pratt initially developed the program in the United States in the 1970s. Renamed Kindermusik International in 1993, the program is now owned by Music Resources International and extends to 20 different countries.

The program's curriculum emphasizes the sequential development of musical abilities through speaking, singing, and moving. The classes use simple percussion instruments and include musical games involving the whole body, finger play, and group interaction. Parents or caregivers play an integral role in the program, actively participating in the early level classes and extending activities to the home. As children grow, parents arrive at the end of class to observe what needs to be done at home. Kindermusik offers instruments and other materials for home use.

Resource:
Kindermusik International
Box 26575
Greensboro, NC 27415
800-628-5687
www.kindermusik.com

Age: Birth to age seven

The program offers four levels, reflecting the needs of each age:

Kindermusik Village	For newborns to one-year-olds, with parent or caregiver
Kindermusik: Our Time	For ages one to three with parent or caregiver
Growing with Kindermusik	For ages three to five, with children alone, 15 minutes with parent
Kindermusik for the Young Child	For ages four through seven; 30-minute class, no parent; 15 minutes with parent
The Young Child	For ages four to seven; 60 to 75-minute class, no parent; 10 minutes with parent

Teacher Requirements: Individuals with an interest or background in music education receive training through the Kindermusik Institute. After training, educators become licensed to teach the program. Additional professional seminars are offered for ongoing training development opportunities.

SPARKLER ACTIVITY: "I Love You"

This activity is from the *Kindermusik Village* program, presenting vocal play, movement, and singing to parents connecting with their infants.

The teacher asks parents to stand, holding their babies and moving freely to the song "Skinnamarink" as it is played on the Kindermusik CD. The song includes the recurring phrase "I love you." Each time the phrase occurs, parents stop moving and sing "I love you" as they look at their baby face to face. As they become familiar with the simple song, they hold the baby in different positions, always calling attention to the slow, three-note phrase "I love you." Babies might be lying down, with arms "dancing" to the music, stopping on the phrase. Parents can provide a gentle bounce on the lap with each beat of the music, again stopping for "I love you." Additional reinforcement of eye contact and attentiveness to this phrase is done by crawling alongside the baby, dancing alongside an early walker, or waving a scarf near the baby for each "I love you."

Parents reinforce the "I love you" phrase in face-to-face vocal play through babbling, using these words. Engaging facial expression and long pauses are encouraged to stimulate infant response. Parents are encouraged to vary their vocal play by using a high speaking voice, whispering, singing, using slow/fast speech or smooth/short enunciation.

Skinnamarink

FIGURE 12.1. "Skinnamarink" from the Kindermusik Village Curriculum. Used by permission of Kindermusik International, Inc., Greensboro, NC © 1999.

Musikgarten

Musikgarten is a relatively new early childhood program, established in 1997 by Lorna Lutz Heyge and Audrey Sillick. The model is also patterned after the German Musicklasche Früherziehung. Musikgarten is a flexible curriculum that includes interactive musical experiences between child and parent. Small group classes include movement, finger games, songs, stories, listening activities, and the use of simple percussion instruments.

Resource:
  Musikgarten
  P.O. Box 10846

Greensboro, NC 27404-0846
800-216-6864
musgarten@aol.com
www.musikgarten.org

Ages: Birth to age seven

The program has four different offerings:

Family Music	From birth to age three, with parent or caregiver
The Cycle of Seasons	From ages two and a half to four and a half
The Music Makers	From ages four to
God's Children Sing	From ages one and a half to 5—faith and spiritual content

Teacher Requirements: Training workshops of 15 hours per course for teacher certification. Workshops are open to anyone who has rhythmic sense and a strong sense of pitch.

SPARKLER ACTIVITY: Finger Play: "Ten Wiggly Fingers"

Finger play is a common activity for early childhood that encourages imaginative expression as well as the development of small muscle coordination. The following example of finger play is an activity in the *Cycle of Seasons* curriculum. The teacher holds hands up and wiggles fingers, while speaking the verse slowly and expressively, moving according to the text. The verse is repeated, modeling motions for children and encouraging them to join in.

> *Ten Wiggly Fingers*
> by J. Burge
>
> Ten wiggly fingers
> Wiggle from side to side
> Ten wiggly fingers
> Going for a ride.
> Ten wiggly fingers
> Wiggle up and down
> Ten wiggly fingers
> Riding down to town.
>
> Ten wiggly fingers
> Wiggle round and round
> Ten wiggly fingers
> Don't make a single sound.

→

Finger Play: "Ten Wiggly Fingers" (*continued*)

Ten wiggly fingers
Playing hide and seek
Ten wiggly fingers
Now they're gone! Don't peek.

From Lorna Heyge and Audrey Sillick, *The Cycle of Seasons A Musical Celebration of the Year for Young Children* © 1994 Musikgarten/Music Matters. Used by permission.

Music Together

Music Together began at the Center for Music and Young Children in Princeton, New Jersey, in 1987, developed by Kenneth K. Guilmartin and Lili M. Levinowitz. The program offers parent-child interactive experiences through singing, movement, and the use of simple rhythm instruments. The program fosters the idea of mixed ages within the same class, nurturing sibling experiences with parents in a single class setting, instead of separating by age. The program emphasizes the parent as a music-making model. Parents receive a publication, *Music and Your Child: A Guide for Parents and Caregivers*, along with an audiotape and songbook of the materials taught in the curriculum. The child's musical development is monitored through a Music Development Observation Record.

Resource:
   Music Together
   66 Witherspoon St.
   Princeton, NJ 08542
   800-728-2692 ext. 13
   www.MusicTogether.com

Ages: Birth to age four. Classes are mixed age grouping, with parents. An infant class (birth to eight months) is available, as well as a class for three- to four-year-olds who have had at least three semesters of experience with the program. Because the program is a parent-child program, parents are integrally participating in all classes.

Teacher Requirements: An introductory one-day class is available to any interested parent, teacher, or musician. Advanced three- to four-day sessions following this introduction provide teacher training for the program. Ongoing workshops are available for additional professional development in the program.

SPARKLER ACTIVITY: Dance Around Together

This parent-and-child activity involves singing and dancing and is appropriate for mixed age preschool children. The song comes from the *"Triangle" Song Collection*, a book of songs, chants, and play-along music developed for the program.

The teacher says "Let's do some dancing!" with a clear "Stand up" gesture. The teacher grabs the hand of a nearby child and demonstrates how to dance in a circle for parents to follow. The teacher encourages everyone to "dance with your mom or dad or friend." Additional motions to the song include jumping, running, picking up younger children while dancing, and pat-a-cake-style clapping with partners while listening and singing to the music.

These are just a few examples of many preschool music programs available to nurture musical development in young children. All develop the basic skills of movement, rhythm, listening, word and finger play, and singing. All emphasize the role of the parent sharing the joy of music with their child. Parents seeking a worthwhile preschool program should examine training, curricular design, and the breadth of musical experiences offered for their child.

Dance Around Together

Traditional, arranged and adapted by
K. Guilmartin and L. Levinowitz

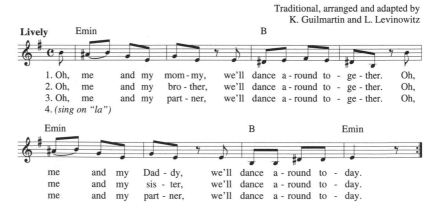

1. Oh, me and my mom-my, we'll dance a-round to - ge - ther. Oh,
2. Oh, me and my bro - ther, we'll dance a-round to - ge - ther. Oh,
3. Oh, me and my part - ner, we'll dance a-round to - ge - ther. Oh,
4. *(sing on "la")*

me and my Dad - dy, we'll dance a - round to - day.
me and my sis - ter, we'll dance a - round to - day.
me and my part - ner, we'll dance a - round to - day.

FIGURE 12.2. "Dance Around Together," from the *"Triangle" Song Collection* (2000), by Lili Levinowitz, and Kenneth K. Guilmartin. Used with permission from Music Together, Princeton, NJ.

Early Instrumental Instruction

We have discussed how preschoolers as young as three years old can delight in the discovery of the violin or piano through Suzuki training. There are a number of programs that specifically introduce preschoolers to the keyboard. These programs offer a variety of group activities that include singing, listening, ear training, improvisation, ensemble performance, and composition. The Yamaha Music Education System, widely developed in Japan, was introduced to the United States in 1964. It includes group instruction for students from age 4 to 10, leading to comprehensive musical training that includes composition and improvisatory skills. A Canadian program that is spreading in the United States, called Music for Young Children, offers introductory exploration of the keyboard for three- to nine-year-olds, with parental participation reinforcing concepts at home between classes. Its unique involvement of composition at each level resulted in a festival with over 11,000 entries in 1999.[20]

There has been a dramatic increase in the publication of materials for preschool keyboard instruction since 1995. Many independent music teachers are including preschool keyboard instruction in their studios, often in groups or in a combination of short private lessons plus group lessons. Studios may include computer music games in this instruction. If a young child is fascinated by the sounds of a keyboard or piano, parents can informally explore musical ideas with materials available at music stores to see if more formal instruction might be beneficial to their child during these tender years. Preschool keyboard instruction essentially acquaints the child with the instrument and explores musical games to instill interest and develop coordination and listening skills.

Elementary Music Education

American music education has adapted aspects of the methods developed by Orff and Kodály in school music curricula across the country. The movement and music curriculum of Dalcroze is often included in preschool and elementary classes as well. The positive result is a comprehensive curriculum that includes the content that has long been established in music education (American and international folk songs) taught through the use of hand signals, rhythmic movement, and accompanying ostinatos. In order to compare these methods, the same musical content ("Rain, Rain, Go Away") is used in each Sparkler Activity, highlighting the different teaching strategies used in each method.

Dalcroze

Émile Jaques-Dalcroze was a professor of music in Geneva, Switzerland, who developed a music curriculum based on whole-body responses through movement to stimulate awareness of pulse, musical shape, and sound. The idea of this development grew from his dismay in working with students trained in the conventional conservatory music education, whose performance habits were mechanical, lacking understanding of the theoretical concepts at the heart of musical learning. The curriculum is based on *eurythmics*, or rhythmic movement (translated as "good rhythm"). The philosophy of Dalcroze is that children should realize rhythms, pitches, and sounds through improvisatory response before the formal instruction of instrumental skills.

Eurythmics differs from dance because dance is an art form that essentially develops dance technique, with music serving as a means of learning how to dance. Eurythmics utilizes movement in order to learn *music*. As early as 1898, Dalcroze established the idea of "muscular sense," or bodily-kinesthetic intelligence:

> I am beginning to think of a musical education in which the body would play the role of intermediary between sound and thought, so becoming an expressive instrument. Bodily movement is an experience felt by a sixth sense, the muscular sense. This consists of the relationship between the dynamics of movement and the position of the body in space, between the duration of movement and its extent, between the preparation of movement and its performance. This muscular sense must be capable of being grasped by the intellect, and since it demands the collaboration of all the muscles, voluntary and involuntary, its rhythmic education needs movement of the whole body.[21]

Dalcroze instruction involves parents in activities up to the age of four, with pupil-parent engagement part of the creative nature of instruction. Dalcroze instruction does not require formal practice between classes. However, encouraging similar movement to music listened to at home (by parent and child) instills the philosophy further.

Resource:
Dalcroze Society of America
www.dalcrozeusa.org

Age: Two years to adult

Teacher Requirements: Bachelor's degree, preferably in music. The program requires 60 hours of pretraining and up to 180 hours of training at a college or university. There are three levels of certification: the Dalcroze Certificate authorizes its holder to teach children and beginning adults. The License (180 hours of training) authorizes the teaching of advanced work at graduate and conservatory levels. The Diploma, available only from the Dalcroze Institute in Geneva, authorizes its holder to confer certification.

> **SPARKLER ACTIVITY: Eurythmic Movement to "Rain Rain Go Away"**
>
> A teacher sits at a piano and says "step to my beat" as children move across the room to improvised piano music, moving to a strong downbeat with a dip in the step, rising on tiptoe on beats 2, 3, and 4. Once students seem comfortable moving to this metric feel, the teacher brings in the simple tune "Rain Rain Go Away" into the improvisation. When the teacher says "Show me the raindrops," students use hand gestures while moving to interpret this idea rhythmically while they continue moving to the beat.
>
> The rhythm of the words may be put into the feet alone, with a dip on "Rain" and quick tiptoe steps on "rain go away, come again another day," elongating the phrase length. The teacher has the class continue their rhythmic movement, removing the piano accompaniment and having them internalize the song while moving to its pulse and rhythmic pattern. Further internalization may include standing still, "hearing" the first phrase of the song ("Rain, rain, go away"), and tiptoeing the second ("come again another day").

Carl Orff

Carl Orff was an eminent Bavarian composer and a remarkable music educator who developed a unique philosophy that "treated rhythm and melody as elemental forces, as germ-cells, out of which all music grows."[22] The Orff curriculum begins with rhythmic structure growing from speech patterns, chants, and body percussion (clapping, stamping, snapping, and "patchen"— slapping legs or body with hands), which combines coordination with rhythmic skill development.

The melodies in Orff's *Schulwerk* are based on modal sounds, beginning with the pentatonic scale in book 1. These first songs are based on the simple descending minor third, with an added fourth, the earliest comfortable intervals used by young children.

Orff instruments provide a full spectrum of timbres and ranges, with xylophones, glockenspiels, and "metallophones" as the basic melodic instruments. When played together, their timbres create a beautiful mesh of different tonal colors. These instruments have removable bars that allow students to play only the notes needed (no mistakes!) and provide easy access to the pentatonic scale, which allows free reign to improvisation while singing. Children easily get accustomed to removing all Fs and Bs on their instruments, creating the pentatonic scale of C–D–E–G–A–C. Finger cymbals, wood blocks, and a fretted cello are also scored in the *Schulwerk*. Orff hand drums and tympani add rich timbre to rhythmic work.

The Orff curriculum emphasizes ensemble performance, using various ostinatos (short repeating rhythmic or melodic figures) as an accompaniment to singing and improvising on instruments. Movement with hand drums provides eurhythm-type experiences that describe musical form as well as rhythmic structure. Songs and rhythmic work contain many canons (similar to rounds) to instill independence plus complexity of sounds in ensemble.

Orff believes the primary purpose of music education is

> the development of a child's creative faculty which manifests itself in the ability to improvise. . . . Speaking and singing, poetry and music, music and movement, playing and dancing are not yet separated in the world of children. They are essentially one and indivisible, all governed by the play-instinct which is a prime mover in the development of art and ritual.[23]

Resource:

American Orff Schulwerk Association
Box 391089
Cleveland, OH 44139
440-543-5366

Age: Age three to adult. Activities from the Orff curriculum are integrated into existing music programs, from preschool through elementary levels. Preschool activities normally are limited to improvised movement, creative musical story-telling, and kinesthetic skill development. Ensemble instrumental work usually begins in the elementary grades.

Teacher Requirements: Three levels of certification, with 60 contact hours (three graduate credits) per level. Level 1: training in the basic pedagogy of book 1, use of pentatonic scale in instruction; level 2: extended training to modal theory, books 2–4 ; level 3: training and apprentice teacher to qualify as a master teacher to train others in Orff pedagogy.

SPARKLER ACTIVITY: "Rain, Rain Go Away"

This activity is based on a song from book 1 of *Music for Children*, using Orff teaching techniques. These activities are suitable for primary grades. First graders who can handle the integrated activities easily would show signs of potential talent

Teaching the song, with stamp-clap ostinato: The teacher sings the nursery song "Rain Rain Go Away" in short snatches, with children echoing back.

→

"Rain, Rain Go Away" (*continued*)

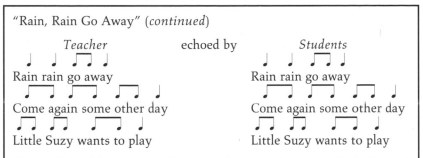

The teacher adds a clap on the strong beats as she sings ("Rain," "go," "Come," "other," etc.), with children adding claps as they sing. Between strong beats, the hands are turned upright and out to show a beat. This prepares children for the same gesture used for rests when using mallets on the Orff instruments. This echo and model approach is a fundamental teaching technique in Orff.

When this is comfortable, the teacher adds a stamp and clap ostinato on each beat, echoed by the children:

| Rain | rain | go a- way | Come a-gain some other | day. |
| Stamp | clap | stamp clap | Stamp clap stamp | clap |

As children get familiar with singing the entire song at once, a variety of rhythmic ostinatos may be used, depending on the age of the children. The ostinatos in the *Orff Schulwerk* version of this song are written on a rhythmic two-line staff. They indicate three different rhythm parts accompanying the simple song. This type of multirhythmic activity would be challenging for first graders.

Teaching the song with Orff instruments: The teacher molds rhythmic ostinato movements to those used in accompaniments to the song. The clap-rest-clap-rest ostinato can become a C–G chord ostinato, played with two mallets on different instruments. All bars except C and G will be removed from the instrument so there will be no mistakes. Children will bring mallets up and out to show the beat of the rests. The stamp-clap ostinato may be replaced by a melodic G–E ostinato that reinforces the pitches of the song. Again, children only see G and E bars and play these with one mallet. A triangle can be added, played at the start of each phrase ("rain," "come"). An imaginative introduction and coda (ending) can be added (pitter-patter with chanting minor third–triangle "solo" at the end).

Zoltán Kodály

Zoltán Kodály was a Hungarian composer, musicologist, educator, and philosopher who personally transformed Hungarian schools through his con-

FIGURE 12.3. Excerpt from "Rain, Rain Go Away," in Carl Orff, *Music for Children*, vol. 1, English adaptation by Doreen Hall and Arnold Walter. © 1956 by Schott Musik International. © Renewed. All rights reserved. Used by permission of European American Music Distributors Corporation, sole U.S. and Canadian agent for Schott Musik International.

cepts of music education. These concepts quickly spread throughout Europe and were absorbed into American schools through the work of Mary Helen Richards in the 1960s. During the 1960s, when America was seeking a method that would provide musical literacy in the schools, Kodály's structured, developmental approach to sightreading, ear training, and rhythmic training seemed ideal for that purpose.

Kodály believed music education was based on singing and the internalization of sound. His curriculum began with traditional folk songs that lie within the comfortable pentatonic range of a fourth, with descending melodies of a minor third. He borrowed the idea of a system of a moveable "do" from Guido d'Arezzo's eleventh-century vocal solfége and the idea of hand signals for these solfége syllables from John Curwen, an Englishman who devised these visual signals in 1862. The Kodály method uses these borrowed techniques, combined with the developmental structure of a curriculum based on folk melodies.

The Kodály method has children verbalize rhythms through the use of syllables rather than numbered beats or beat divisions. Rhythmic notation does away with the note heads, allowing a kind of rhythmic shorthand in notating rhythms on paper (fig. 12.4).[24]

The hand signals show the different scale levels, rising higher with the signals from the bottom "do" to the top "do." Children can immediately see the rising scale as they sing it, visualizing "so" dropping down to "mi" through these visual aids (fig. 12.5).

Standard notation	Syllables	Rhythm symbols
♩	ta		
♫	ti-ti	⊓
𝅗𝅥	ta-ah	𝅗𝅥
o	ta-ah-ah-ah	o
♬♬	ti-ri-ti-ri	⊓⊓

FIGURE 12.4. Kodály rhythm syllables and symbols.

Resource:
   Organization of American Kodály Education
   Sharon Summers, Director
   PO Box 9804
   Fargo, ND 58106
   701-235-0366
   oakemail@corpcomm.net
   www.oake.org

Ages: Preschool programs may borrow a few of the rhythmic ideas from the Kodály approach, but it is primarily a curriculum for the elementary grades, K–6.

Teacher Requirements: Most teachers seeking Kodály training have a music education degree. The specialization for Kodály instruction in music education takes three summers of training, which consists of 225 contact hours. Training includes pedagogy, movement, and the basic gesture and vocal techniques of the method. Instrumental training in recorder and dulcimer is also given.

This brief look at the different programs available to young children shows the careful attention music educators have given to curriculum that nurtures early signs of musical potential. Music educators realize the importance of beginning musical learning at these tender years, when ears are curious about new sounds, bodies love to wiggle and move to music, and voices are eager to sing the simple songs that comfortably fit into their developing vocal range. So many parents ask, "When should my child begin music lessons?" These group activities are an excellent starting point for any future musical training.

Questions for discussion:

  1. What research mentioned in this chapter intrigued you because of its focus or findings? What are some additional ideas we should pursue

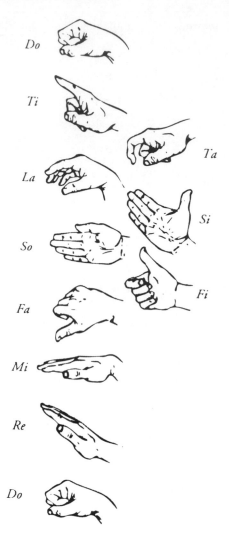

FIGURE 12.5. Kodály hand signals. From P. Tacka and M. Houlahan (1995), *Sound Thinking: Developing Musical Literacy*. Vol. 1. Used with permission from Boosey and Hawkes. All rights reserved.

in relation to research of infants, young children, musical perception, and creativity?

2. Name five characteristics that may indicate potential musical talent in a child prior to the age of four.

3. What are the core elements of the curriculum of early childhood music programs? What types of activities can highlight potential talent in these core elements?

SPARKLER ACTIVITY: "Rain Rain Go Away"

1. *Learning the song with hand signals:* The teacher begins by humming the song to see if children recognize the tune. All sing the song together. The teacher feeds in the hand signals while singing, with the children observing how the notes fit each hand gesture. The teacher shifts to the syllables "so," "mi," and "la," echo singing with the children until they can successfully copy these gestures. Discussion of which is the higher note may follow to instill the visual, aural, and internal understanding of the song.

2. *Adding rhythmic notation of the song:* This song uses the very first rhythm syllables learned in Kodály—"ta" for a quarter note, written as a line; and "ti-ti" for two eighth notes, written as two lines joined at the top. It is assumed for this activity that children have learned these symbols.

   Children sing the song again, clapping every note they sing to show its rhythmic pattern. This leads into humming the song and clapping, and finally internalizing the song and clapping its rhythm. The teacher and children clap the first phrase ("Rain rain go away"). Children offer to write this rhythm on the board in stick notation. The second phrase follows. Another child may add "s," "m," and "l" below the stick rhythms to show the "notation" of the full song. For a finale performance, children clap and sing while a leader points to the rhythm.

4. What are the similarities and differences among the curricula of Dalcroze, Orff, and Kodály? What adaptations do you feel are needed to align with American music education?
5. What are the positives and negatives of beginning formal music instruction for children in the preschool years?

FROM SPARK TO FLAME

Nurturing Musical Talent

*From the very beginning of his education, the child should experience
the joy of discovery.*

Alfred North Whitehead

The minute you open the studio door and make eye contact with the eager
child on the front steps, you are hooked. There is something about this child
that captures your attention. This child has potential talent. You know even before
you have heard a note of music. Seasoned teachers have this intuitive feeling and
can sense the energy and enthusiasm of these youngsters. They may be quiet and
shy, yet their eyes give them away. You are eager to check out your "hunch." After
a few minutes of musical tasks in the studio, with parents sizing up the teacher-
pupil possibilities, you realize you were correct. So let's get started!

Anyone who has taken music lessons remembers that very first lesson, when
books are slick and new and every maneuver learned on the instrument is
an adventure. The talented youngster literally takes off full speed ahead in
this adventure. The journey can be exciting and rewarding, if the match of
teacher and student "clicks." In previous chapters we have described the
importance of training in the lives of young, talented children, but we have
not examined *how* this training nurtures talent.

In this chapter I attempt to answer some important questions concerning
training and talent development. What must we know about musical learning to match training with student reasoning abilities at different ages? Where
do we begin? How can we keep a talented student comfortably challenged in
the studio or classroom? This chapter will answer some of the basic ques-

tions regarding musical learning, beginning private instruction, the private studio, suitable curriculum for the young talented student, and creative opportunities that will nurture a young musician.

Stages of Musical Learning

When last we left our creative preschooler, lots of imaginative singing was taking place, with a growing sense of tonality to the "real" songs in the culture. By the age of four, the entire song is imitated. At five or six, a young singer has emerged who is comfortably learning new songs by rote. The next few years are critical in the development of musical talent. Understanding the cognitive and musical development of children at this age will help gauge musical expectations.

Any discussion of child psychology must begin with Jean Piaget (1898–1980), a Swiss biologist who founded the theory of *genetic epistemology*. Since then this theory has served as the major reference of the cognitive development of children in the fields of child psychology, education, and formal logic. Musical psychologists have disputed, adapted, and adjusted Piaget's theory to explain the development of musical functioning.[1]

Piaget's theory says that children's cognitive development logically grows through four stages from birth to age 11. In each stage, they think or behave in certain ways (*schemata*). They learn to organize (*assimilate*) new experiences, or *schemes*, and adapt to the surrounding environment (*accommodation*). As they reach a level of balance or *equilibrium*, they progress to the next cognitive level. The theory contends that children must systematically proceed from one level to the next, eventually developing the cognitive functioning of an adult after age 11.

The first stage of Piaget's theory is *sensori-motor*, lasting from birth to the age of two. At this stage in music, the child enters the world with primitive reflexes and learns to voluntarily bounce to the beat, enjoy vocal play, and spontaneously sing. Logically, during this stage a child will develop the cognitive ability to realize that a toy that is out of sight still exists.

The *preoperational* stage, from ages two to seven, is the illogical stage of symbolic play. Musical youngsters are using words as vocal toys in imaginative songs. They slowly develop a comfortable range as they assimilate songs from their environment and adapt them to "squeeze" into these ranges. By the age of seven, they are beginning to find a stabilized tune in their singing.

Preoperational children, when seeing identical amounts of water poured into two differently shaped containers, will say there is more water in one container than the other. At this stage, judgments are intuitive and ego centered and deal with one problem at a time. The combination of concepts such as dynamics (loud/soft) and pitch (high/low) in music is difficult to understand at this stage.[2]

The longest and most controversial stage in Piaget's theory is the *concrete operational* stage, which occurs between the ages of seven and eleven. During this stage a child acquires *conservation* abilities. The child will assimilate the understanding that there is the same amount of water poured into differently shaped containers. In music, this cognitive reasoning allows the understanding of transposition of melodies (same melodies in different keys) or inversion of chords (same notes juxtapositioned differently).[3] The acquisition of conservation abilities coincides with the musical development of basic skills learned in school or individualized instruction. An understanding of the ages at which children comfortably conserve musical concepts helps in the development of appropriate curricula to match musical abilities. Talented students are likely to acquire these abilities earlier and faster.

Shuter-Dyson and Gabriel note a number of research studies attempting to locate ages where children are able to conserve specific higher-level musical concepts. One study worked with concepts of transposition of themes (playing themes an octave higher or lower), ornamentation (adding ideas to the melody), augmentation/diminution (shortening or lengthening the theme), changing the theme rhythmically, and other more difficult "deformations" of the theme.[4] Another worked with complex conservation tasks such as inversion, retrograde, and retrograde-inversion of a melody (playing it intervallically "upside down," backward, and combining these concepts) using resonator bells. Findings aligned with Piaget's theory, with 12- to 14-year-olds able to understand these concepts more readily than 5- to 10-year-olds.[5]

Piaget's final stage of development is called *formal operations*; from age eleven, the child is mentally becoming an adult and able to combine various groups of mental operations. The young adolescent can now reason deductively and scientifically test this reasoning. In music, students are capable of interpretive reasoning and are sensitive to stylistic nuances in performance.

Hargreaves proposes a descriptive model of musical development similar to Piaget's theory, consisting of five age-related stages. The crucial beginning years of formal instruction arrive when the mind must shift from figural, single concept dimensions to multidimensional concepts leading to the "rules" that govern metric, formal musical knowing.[6]

Stage	Age	Musical Perceptive/Cognitive Functions
1. Sensorimotor	0–2 years	Similar to Piaget, babbling stage
2. Figural	2–5 years	Figural, single dimension, pitch, contour
3. Schematic	5–8 years	Figural to metric, more than one dimension. Conservation of musical properties
4. Rule systems	8–15 years	Formal-metric, analytic recognition of intervals, key stability
5. Professional	15+	Metacognitive, reflective

Piaget's idea of a stepwise process of cognitive thought in the arts is debated by a number of psychologists. They argue that rather than this ladder-like logical process of growth, the arts develop through greater perceptual awareness. Sloboda believes that "musical awareness between the ages of five and ten seems to reflect a general intellectual change from enactive competence, which is displayed within the bounds of specific and directed activities, to a reflective awareness of the structures and principles which underlie such competence."[7] In simple terms, children of 10 begin to analyze and reflect on the patterns and characteristics that are within the songs that were simply *sung* when they were five.

The idea of the song being known first *enactively* and then with more awareness or metaperceptive reasoning reflects Jerome Bruner's educational theory of a "spiral curriculum." Questioning the stepwise development theory of Piaget, Bruner believes that children can be taught skills in some form at any age. As they develop and master these skills, they refine them at repeatedly higher levels. A musician will bring to mind scales and arpeggios that are taught during the first year and are ever-present as skills develop and advance.[8]

Gardner also believes that Piaget's theory as inapplicable to language, music, or plastic arts because Piaget's cognitive operations do not apply to artistic activity and aesthetic reasoning. Piaget's stages coincide more with scientific and mathematical cognitive development.

> I question the central claim of developmental psychology: that most children pass through a set of stages, culminating in the attainment of formal operational thought at the time of early adolescence. Instead, I conclude that most of us remain, with respect to most domains, at the level of a five-year-old thinker.[9]

In *The Arts and Human Development*, Gardner describes the existence of three systems that exist from birth:

Making—acts or actions
Perceiving—discriminations or distinctions
Feeling—affects

Gardner's *symbol system* relies on the *domain-specific* development of skills. Artistic development is "a process wherein the three initially discrete systems gradually begin to influence each other, with interaction eventually becoming so dominant that each system inevitably involves the other one."[10] In musical development, these systems translate into psychomotor or skill development (making), perceptual listening skills (perceiving), and affective responses to music (feeling).

Actually, Piaget did realize that often a young child would appear "more gifted" than an older child in artistic fields. This occurrence clearly did not correspond to his developmental theory, and he cautioned educators to take note of the need to develop these artistic capabilities.

It is much more difficult to establish stages of development in the case of artistic tendencies than it is in that of other mental functions. . . . Without an appropriate art education which will succeed in cultivating these means of expression and in encouraging these first manifestations of aesthetic creation, the actions of adults and the restraints of school and family life have the effect in most cases of checking or thwarting such tendencies instead of enriching them.[11]

Talented students in any field lie askew to structured development and decidedly learn "outside the lines" of the normal curriculum. In music, they are the children whose capabilities are the exceptions to Piaget's stages, and they may spiral quickly through developmental cycles of learning. Talent development requires attention to environmental influences and instructional strategies responding to the needs of these exceptional students.

Bloom's *Developing Talent in Young People*, cited in earlier chapters, offers a rich biographic perspective of influences that guided the talent development of leading achievers in the fields of sports, math, science, music, and art. The study found that the development of talent consists of three basic phases of learning and requires long-term commitment to a specific field.

The first phase of talent development is one of *play and romance*, with "enormous encouragement of interest and involvement, stimulation, freedom to explore, and immediate rewards."[12] The first private teacher and the family play primary roles in the nurturing environment of this initial phase. The second phase is one of *precision and discipline*, where the dominant goals are skill, technique, and accuracy. During the third phase, the advancing student develops *individuality and insight*, generalizing and integrating concepts and recognizing that the chosen field will play a significant role in the future. These three phases closely reflect Whitehead's phases of longitudinal development of learning (romance, precision, generalization), established in 1929.[13]

If we synthesize and simplify all of these theories of development, we discover a fairly similar continuum of musical capabilities. Differences lie in the delineation of stages or spiraled learning. The young child begins musical discovery at the playful, enactive stage where learning derives from the immediacy of performing and "doing" musical tasks. As musical skills develop, the child begins to hear more, to see more, and to perform with a higher level of aesthetic subtlety and musical understanding. The child now seeks precision and discipline in this performance. Advancing students work to individualize expressive interpretations and analytically understand the structure of the music they are learning. The private teacher's goal is to develop skills so a child can musically communicate the personal ideas that are metaperceptively understandable at each stage of this learning continuum. Talented students developing at an accelerated pace require instruction that entices them with musical challenges from the first lesson.

Beginning Private Instruction

A flashback to the young child on the front steps of the teacher's studio brings us to the question of how the parents found the teacher, what will happen in the opening interview, and what can be expected in the first year of lessons and beyond. The child may be arriving after several months or years in pre-school classes that have developed fundamental musical skills. Or the child may be arriving at that front door at age three or four, seeking advice from this teacher on possible early instruction because parents see noticeable musical potential at an early age.

Parents of talented children seek ways to nurture the natural curiosity and interest of their children but are cautious about starting formal instruction too soon. How do parents know when to begin private instruction for their child? The following guidelines may provide parents with a few answers to this important question.

Guidelines for Beginning Private Music Instruction:

1. *The child must show a strong interest in the lessons.* A child who continually uses music as a playtime activity, singing, moving, possibly trying to pick out a tune on an available instrument, is a prime candidate for lessons. If lessons are the choice of the parent, with minimal interest by the young child, these lessons will probably be unsuccessful and an unpleasant experience for the child.

   Parent Observation: Watch your child during musical play. Is there obvious careful thought and persistent repetition in this behavior? Is your child using coordinated movements and individualized finger gestures in instrumental play?

2. *The child must have developed the physical coordination and capability to play the instrument.* If children begin an instrument before they are physically able to play it, the experience is frustrating. No one wants a negative start to music lessons. Small muscle coordination requires independence of the fingers and the ability to do several things at once. The most common instruments for early musical training are violin and piano. Seek out a possible informal session with a private teacher to see if the child is ready for lessons.

Parent Observation: If you seek piano lessons, observe how your child "plays" on a keyboard. Children usually use the pointer finger approach, picking out tunes with one finger. This does not show finger independence. If a child can independently play each finger, one after another, 1(thumb)–2–3–4–5–4–3–2–1, without holding all five "squished" onto the key at once, there is independence of fingers. Within a few months, lessons will require children to "skip" fingers, 1–3–5–3–1 in both hands, and play a two- or three-note chord (135) together. This is a quick check of piano fundamental skills for a beginner. A piano teacher may be able to work a child slowly through these fundamentals, but a child who already has these small motor skills will be more comfortably set for lessons.

3. *The child and parent must realize that music lessons require practice.* At this point in the book, the aspect of practice has been established as essential in musical talent development. In the first few months of lessons, the teacher helps the child develop effective practice habits. When lessons begin, parents should seek guidance from the private teacher in ways to provide positive monitoring of practice at home. The role of consistent practice is an essential part of private instruction. The amount of practice time required depends on the teacher's studio and the length of the child's lesson.

   Parent Observation: Prior to lessons, encourage your child to "practice" some of the creative things you observe in musical play. Your child might like to prepare a "recital" of these child creations for stuffed animals and parents or caregivers in the home audience. This will require some preparation and working out of musical ideas that you can observe for attention span and interest in musical work.

Machover and Uszler's *Sound Choices: Guiding Your Child's Musical Experiences* offers a wonderfully comprehensive reference for parents, guiding them through all stages of musical development, with pointers on choosing a teacher, choosing an instrument, assisting in practice, and a wealth of books, recordings, and software resources. They suggest that lessons begin as early as first grade for the normal child, recommending starting the summer prior to the beginning of school so that the child will acquire a routine of practice before the onset of school schedules.

Choosing a Teacher

The first music teacher establishes the basic love of music in the child. This initial teacher does not necessarily need the credentials of a master teacher but does need to have had the experience of working with young children to instill a commitment to the enjoyment of working and achieving through music. The biographic studies of talented musicians confirm these qualities, describing these teachers as "very kindly, and very nice" and "enormously patient." These talented youngsters looked forward to lessons each week, where instruction was informal and personal, always reflecting warmth and affection.[14]

A recent study of 257 young musicians compared the perceptions of teachers by a full range of students, from those who dropped out of music to those who became successful musicians. Results showed that positive "personal" characteristics of this first teacher were significantly different for those who were successful and those who dropped out of lessons. At the earliest stage of instruction, the teacher's personal relationship with the child is more important than the "professional" skills of performance. Musically successful students rated their first teacher high in qualities of being friendly (chatty, relaxed, and encouraging). Professional performance qualities gain in importance as the child reaches the intermediate stage of talent development.[15]

Machover and Uszler describe the characteristics of the early teacher specifically for musically talented children:

> The early teacher needs to be supportive and motivating, as well as qualified and reasonably demanding. The child's instincts need to be given some latitude in order that talent not be forced in one direction or the other. Public performing should generally be informal and competition downplayed.[16]

Pairing a quick, eager student with a teacher who follows a specific path of repertoire with no skips, leaps, or sidesteps simply will not work. A teacher who believes music above all should be "fun" may be lax in establishing the fundamental technical work that is essential for musical training. The task master that demands only technical regimen for the first six months, with no child-friendly repertoire provides an experience that decidedly makes music "not fun." Parents of potentially talented students must seek the correct balance of a teacher who is nurturing in character but knowledgeable in establishing musical fundamentals from the start.

Although there are over 100,000 independent music teachers in the United States, locating a suitable teacher for a talented youngster may require a bit of research.[17] The independent music profession relies on word-of-mouth recommendations from parents of current students. Teachers who are members of a professional music organization may be on a list of nationally certified teachers or may actively participate in local professional music teaching activities. If a young child is clearly demonstrating outstanding levels of talent, a call to a local university, college, or professional music teachers organization may be useful in locating a teacher who works with exceptional young musicians. A list of national music organizations that can provide useful information for locating music schools and professional independent teachers is in the appendix.

The First Lessons

The child on the front steps now enters the private teacher's home or studio for the initial interview and "audition" to assess the child's readiness for private instruction. An informal interview provides the opportunity to observe the successful mesh of teacher and student personalities while engaged in musical activities. Realizing the importance of this "first teacher" in a child's musical life, parents may wish to seek an interview with several different teachers for comparison.

Teachers can take this opportunity to observe the student's musical behavior while engaged in a variety of simple musical activities. This informal teacher-student musical "play" provides an excellent way to observe potential talent if these musical tasks include progressive levels of difficulty. The following set of activities can assist private teachers in assessing potential talent in their prospective student. Each activity begins with simple tasks, growing more complex in stages across the basic criteria of talent. Teachers may adapt or adjust activities as needed to align with their personal teaching style. An asterisk (*) indicates the point where the task is difficult for a normal beginner (age six to seven). Children who can continue tasks past this point may have potential talent.

SPARKLER ACTIVITY: "Getting to Know You"

1. *Criteria: Sense of rhythm, perceptual awareness*

   Rhythm echo and response: To loosen up the atmosphere, the teacher can start with an echo rhythm game, using words at first, leading to rhythm echoes and clap/response "conversations." The teacher can begin with clapping, progressing to combinations of stamp (S), clap (C), patchen—tapping legs (P), and snapping fingers (SN). Adapt if the child can not yet snap fingers—a complex small motor feat.

   A. *Echoes*—teacher first, then student. Some ideas to get started:

Teacher	Student	Rhythm
How are you?	How are you?	♩ ♩ ♩.
		C C C
I'm feeling just fine	I'm feeling just fine	♩ ♫ ♩ ♩
		S C C S C
What a lovely day	etc.	♫ ♩ ♫ ♩ ♩
		P P P P C
Let's play a game		♩ ♫. ♩
		S P P C

   →

"Getting to Know You" (*continued*)

This is so much fun, I love it!   S S   P P   C C   S N   S N   ✳

So glad you're here   S   P P   C C S N   ✳
     with me.
     And so on.

    B. *Echoes—words echoed by rhythms:* The teacher will say these words, or others, and the student will show the rhythm of the words with their choice of body percussion sounds (C, P, S, SN).

    C. *Clap and response:* The teacher will begin body percussion rhythms with simple rhythms, asking the student to answer with different rhythms. At first, the child will use the same metric feel (four beats). Listen for "answers" that show differences and syncopation. Reverse roles, asking the student to ask the questions—you provide answers, extending beyond four beats. *Reverse roles again, with the teacher asking rhythm questions, encouraging the student to extend answers as creatively as he or she wants.

Note: You may also use echo-clapping Sparkler Activities from chapter 10.

*Teachers who wish to assess how quickly the child can learn rhythmic notation may use my *Rhythm Antics*, which presents basic rhythms in exercises using the metronome in a Kodály-type structure that is easy to learn quickly. Observe the student's ability to keep with the metronome beat and adeptness in learning how to read notated rhythms in the exercises.[18]

2. *Criteria: Perceptual awareness and dynamic discrimination, sense of pulse*
   Moving and listening to music:

    A. Improvise on your instrument in 4/4, having the child move around the room showing the downbeat pulse by bending legs and moving arms. Look for fluidity of movement and a sense of pulse. Switch from 4/4 to 3/4 and back again to see if the child can easily adjust in movement.

    B. Change dynamics in your playing, asking the child to show big gestures when the music is loud and small gestures when it is soft. Begin in 4/4 and exaggerate dynamic levels. Gradually bring dynamic levels closer together. *Combine dynamic contrasts and metric shifts.

→

"Getting to Know You" (*continued*)

3. *Criteria: Perceptual discrimination—sense of pitch*

   Tonal memory: Using the same rhythm phrases as earlier, sing simple melodies, always beginning with *so, la*, and *mi* of the scale—the natural chant range of children. Children answer by singing these same pitches. Extend to the full octave to see if the child can stay relatively in pitch.

       Example: How are you?
                   s   s   m

       I'm feeling just fine
       s   l   l   s   m

       What a lovely day
       s   s m   m d (low *do*)

       This is so much fun, I love it!
       ✳s s l   s   s   m d d (low, then octave above)

Note: You may also use the Sparkler Activities in chapter 10 that work with the sense of pitch.

4. *Criteria: Creative interpretation*

   A musical story: Use a keyboard or various percussion instruments arranged in front of the child. The child may be more at ease playing only the black notes on the keyboard. Make up a short story, with pauses for sound effects. The child will listen to the story and fill in the sounds that describe the mood you set. For example: "Once upon a time, there was a BIG elephant (*pause*) and a teeny-tiny mouse (*pause*) who were best friends. They decided to go on a trip to space (*pause*) in a rocket ship (*pause*)." Reverse roles, making the sound effects for the child's story. *Encourage the child to do both the story and the sounds.

5. *Creative listening:* Have a tape player, paper, and crayons available in another room. Prepare a short taped excerpt of instrumental music (no longer one minute) that is colorful and immediately creates a mood—no songs with words. Ask the child to first listen to the music with eyes closed. Rewind and have the child draw whatever he or she wants while listening to the music again. The child may continue to draw after the music stops.

   This "alone" time allows adults to chat in the studio while the child does the listening activity. Parents may ask questions about the studio, and the teacher can feel free to discuss observed capabilities without the child being in the room. The child then shares the musical picture and story that was created from the listening experience. *If this sharing allows parents and the teacher to listen to the music as the

                                        →

> child explains the drawing, it will encourage the child to show specific connections between the drawing and the listening—"This bird is when you hear the flutes—here!" Or if instruments' names are not known—(sound of trumpets) "That's the bright sun!"
>
> These activities may be expanded to include any of the Sparkler Activities from this book that appeal to the private teacher. Emphasis in this first teacher-student musical exchange is on a sense of communicating through sound and thinking while engaged in creative musical tasks.

The Private Studio

The first year of lessons establishes the basic habits of a musician in the child's life. A musician practices, solves problems in the music, performs for others, and begins to develop technical skills necessary to advance on the instrument. The first music teacher provides the key role in establishing this musical foundation. The learning environment for this development depends largely on the opportunities available at the private studio of this first music teacher.

There is about as much variety in the philosophy and offerings of independent music studios as there are private music teachers. It is the nature of the profession, which doubly shows the importance of making the right match with a talented student. Private instruction may be taken in the home of an independent teacher, in a separate studio setting, or in a community music school. Some teachers may have group or partner lessons offered for young children, others may combine private and group instruction, and many offer additional computer-MIDI labs.

What are some studio offerings that can enhance talent development from the start?

- *A studio that has a variety of age and developmental levels* will provide peer dynamics as well as older role models for the child. A teacher who provides instruction from beginning through advanced levels is familiar with the span of developmental learning. A teacher with this breadth of experience is more likely to recognize a young student's need to enjoy a faster pace, adapting repertoire and technical needs accordingly.
- *A studio that offers a combination of private instruction plus performance and/or theory classes* encourages short-term performance and theory goals. Students enjoy comfortable peer performance opportunities, with options of critique and listening skill development. Theory work expands musical learning beyond repertoire and technique.
- *A studio that includes multiple performance experiences*, from informal classes to periodic recitals, provides assessment of student progress

and a sense of studio accountability. Astute listening from year to year shows how students are progressing in the studio and provides a real-world formal recital experience for all students.

- *A studio that includes activities offered by professional music organizations* offers assessment of performance, theory work, or technical progress by outside judges. These experiences foster student motivation to attain self-determined goals in activities that have structured progressive levels.
- *A studio that includes theory, improvisation, composition, and creative and critical listening activities* nurtures a talented student's ability to work across musical dimensions. These activities enhance metaperceptive decision-making and provide the tools for creating music themselves. Many modern studios offer computer lab time for ear training and theory drill. A lab that includes music software that encourages students to play with sounds, compose, sequence, and notate enhances musical learning beyond drill and practice.

The Talented Beginner

The young talented student requires stimulation and a comfortable challenge in learning. The environment of positive encouragement, with goal-oriented rewards, and stimulation from home nurture this budding talent. Talented young musicians are quick learners, requiring a constant check by the teacher to ensure understanding and accuracy beneath the flow of notes that speed by in those first few years of training. Sosniak's young pianists knew they were different from their peers at school, feeling "special" because they were able to do "something that was all mine."[19] The more parents can nurture the idea of music as a unique way to be "special," the more the child can think of himself or herself as a musician.

Musical training does require "work," with proper practice to progress on the instrument. We have discussed the evidence of the need for at least 10 years of deliberate practice to achieve expertise in different fields. Studies show there is a marked difference in development between children whose parents are interested in their child's practice to those who simply say "Go and practice."[20]

This commitment to practice begins in the first year of training. There is no sure way to make practice fun for young children, but there are some pointers that can guide parents in securing a positive practice setting.

- Practice should be in a quiet space where the child can work without disturbance. Very young children will need guided supervision by parents. Teachers of young children often have parents observe lessons and advise parents on ways to assist practice.

- Monitoring practice for consistency establishes long-lasting habits. When the child personally fills in practice rosters with checks, stickers, and so on to show completion of work, their is immediate self-assessment of work done and a type of minireward for this work. Parents can add creative incentives to augment those prescribed by the teacher—but avoid overdoing extrinsic rewards. (A week of solid practice should not equal a new doll or expensive toy.)
- Practice requires a type of piggy-backing of skill-developing goals. In order to achieve the goal of playing through a piece correctly, smaller subgoals may need correction first. Goal 1 may be to repeat a problem measure five times or until it is always correct. This allows the child to listen, remember, and develop technical placement for this problem. Goal 2 may be to count out loud through the piece to get the rhythm right. Goal 3 may be a single line done correctly several times. These simple subgoals work toward solving the overall goal of playing through the whole piece correctly.[21]

  Young children normally simply play through, mistakes and all. Learning how to practice with subgoals establishes good habits from the start. Talented children will often speed through learning, skimming over this type of practice. Astute teachers will be sure there are a few especially challenging pieces that will definitely *require* this type of practice for talented students.
- Periodic informal performances of the child for an interested parent will inspire goal-oriented work. The parent or caregiver who asks for a child to play their favorite pieces will discover the child's preferences and afford them an attentive, appreciative audience.

What are some behavioral characteristics of beginning students who show potential talent? The following list combines ideas from gifted education with musical attributes gathered from literature and experience.[22] These characteristics can be observed in the form of positive as well as negative behaviors.

Characteristics of the Musically Talented Student:

Positive	Negative
High motivation and drive	Dislikes routine and drill
Learns rapidly, remarkable memory	Omits detail in the score
Enjoys a challenge	Sets unrealistic goals
Is self-critical, evaluative	Gets frustrated easily
Concentrates intensely	Resists interruption
Shows persistence in tasks	May be stubborn, uncooperative
Is alert, observant, shows curiosity	Impatient with technical drill
Is emotionally sensitive	Has difficulty accepting criticism
Enjoys experimenting and creating	May not follow directions

Anyone who has worked with young, talented students will agree that they love to play fast. They are fascinated with their new-found abilities, and their high energy often takes over. They crave learning new pieces—*many* of them. They may skim over details and play sloppily, which is surprising for students with such adept ears. These behaviors fall in line with the initial "romance" phase of capturing the fun and excitement of the experience without worrying about precision and details.

The sense of fun and exploration can work successfully in molding effective learning for these students. The metronome easily becomes a wonderful toy in the hands of children who learn to set their own tempo at practice and mark off progress as pieces are repeated correctly at one tempo, steadily rising to higher metronome markings. They will still aim for the fastest possible tempo but have systematically guided practice to achieve their goal.

Years ago a little tyke of seven came to a lesson in my studio with metronome numbers scrawled in every space of the margin of an early level exercise. She smiled as she whizzed through those few measures at MM 208 (the highest level of the pendulum style). Her zeal in metronome practice and fascination with technical goals gradually developed into amazing scale facility by her teenage years.

Teachers working with these young students can take the opportunity to encourage exploration of repertoire by having the students prepare "bonus pieces" that they can prepare beyond the lesson requirements. Teachers can give points or stickers for pieces that show accuracy of notes, rhythm, dynamics, and so on in these pieces. Students may enjoy the challenge of self-initiative and reward for accurate work they taught themselves. These are just a few examples of how lessons can be "differentiated" for talented students in a private studio.

Differentiated Curriculum

A curriculum is a "course of study," according to Webster. To those who study the development of curriculum, it includes what one learns (content), how one learns (process), and the result of this learning (product). Expanding further, one can include the "hidden curriculum" of context, describing the effects of learning from the immediate environment and individual factors that impact learning.[23]

We have discussed *differentiation* as a way of expanding the curriculum to meet the needs of the talented student. This differentiation basically extends learning through added depth, breadth, acceleration, and variety. The gifted field offers models of differentiation suitable for academic areas that create a matrix of possibilities for use in the school classroom.[24] In order to adapt these ideas to the private studio, we first need to examine how they work in schools. Although approaches differ in visual maps for teachers to organize curriculum, the gifted literature shares the following basic modifications for differentiation:

Differentiated Curriculum Modifications in Gifted Education:

- Content
  is concept based, presenting broad based themes
  uses abstract themes that are transferable across disciplines
  is complex by number, diversity, and relationships
  includes a variety of ideas and materials
- Process
  develops higher-level thinking skills of critical and creative thinking
  emphasizes open-ended tasks, exploration and discovery of ideas
  is fast-paced and varied in approach
- Product
  results in "real" products that reveal new ideas
  uses new techniques, materials, forms
  encourages development of self-understanding
  is assessed by peers and student as well as teacher

The gifted education field applies these basic modifications to any academic area, emphasizing the development of thinking skills to assist students in solving problems creatively in the process of developing "real" products of their own. Tomlinson cites an example of a kindergarten project on the broad-based theme of "neighborhoods and communities." These youngsters researched, designed, and built a model of a portion of their town, with students learning to measure and construct blank buildings that later developed into a tiny representation of their town, kindergarten style. The process also included interviews with people who worked in the buildings the students were designing to help them learn about the roles people play in their community. Students created a "real" model of their town that required research, critical analysis, and creative artistic construction. The creative project allowed all of the students a much richer understanding of "neighborhood" than what would have been learned through a text on the subject. Gifted students completed the more complex tasks of measurement and construction and contributed individual ideas that added complexity and detail to the project.[25]

How can these ideas possibly be adapted to music instruction, especially in a music studio with one-on-one instruction, where the goal is acquiring performance and listening skills? A logical starting point is an overview of the curricular ideas from instrumental instruction or the field of *pedagogy*.

Music Pedagogy

The field of music pedagogy has a long tradition of establishing individualized teaching approaches based on the acquired learning of teaching strategies from past master teachers in print or through personal experience in performance training. There is a wealth of pedagogical texts written by master teachers dating back centuries, presenting strategies to acquire technical expertise and aesthetic subtleties at the advanced level. There is a direct lineage of master teachers and their students, who become the next generation of master teacher, all creating a tradition for that individual "method," which is transformed with each generational shift.

The development of curriculum in the private studio relies on a bit of common sense and practical experience. Teachers organize curricular *content* by combining elementary method books, music repertoire, and materials adapted to the needs of individual students. One hour in a well-stocked music store will quickly reveal the breadth of materials available for the beginning student. Experienced independent teachers know how to mix and match available methods and repertoire to fit the learning styles and pace of their students. Talented students require content that extends beyond the habitual adherence to the primary and elementary method books that is often the norm at beginning levels.

The curricular *process* in pedagogy follows the path of skill development toward performance, with individual teaching strategies reflecting ideas from performance training, teaching workshops, professional conferences, and experience. There are a number of pedagogy texts that provide guidance in the scope and sequence of repertoire and technique and offer practical suggestions that deal with the business of a private studio. Several include helpful teaching guides and curricular planning ideas.[26]

Process-oriented texts written by master teachers fall into three general categories—*physical, interpretive,* and *performance preparation*. The majority of these texts offer detailed descriptions of teaching strategies related to solving physical problems of tone, touch, breathing, fingering, bowing, and other technical details of performance. Interpretive teaching recommendations include appropriate stylistic performance, phrasing, and dynamic-aesthetic details. Practical teaching suggestions deal with practice plans and procedures, memorization, and alleviation of performance anxiety. The vast majority address teaching and performing at the advanced level.[27]

There are few pedagogy books that address the teacher-student dynamic of learning in the teaching process. Most authors reflect anecdotally on their personal teaching strategies. Some examples from the field of piano pedagogy include Eloise Ristad's psychological slant to teaching, which is described in personal anecdotes filled with accounts of creative strategies used in workshops. Seymour Bernstein emphasizes the psychological significance of practice in life through adult or advanced student case studies. Stewart Gordon's reflections on the art of teaching include suggestions for working with the extremely gifted student. "The best way to serve the gifted student is to offer the most exacting challenges and the highest level of teaching within us. What may have to be adjusted, rather, is the rate at which we proceed."[28]

The scarcity of specific books on the *process* of the curriculum may stem from acceptance of the traditional approach of teacher-directed learning that has long been the mainstay of private instruction. If you enter a private studio, you are most likely to see a combination of a teacher modeling a performance and guiding students through their own performance through verbal directions and corrections. Differentiating this curriculum requires a bit of extension in all directions to encourage multiple dimensions of learning during the crucial early years.

Differentiated Curriculum in the Private Studio

Rarely do we see a more perfect environmental setting for developing individualized learning than a private music studio. One-on-one instruction may last a number of years with the same teacher, leading to an intimate knowledge of a student's interests and learning style. The sensitive teacher can adjust teaching approaches, repertoire, and pacing to match the needs of the student. There is no ceiling to acceleration and no confined curricular demands limiting a teacher's creative endeavors. Differentiation requires the private teacher to take risks in extending the studio's curriculum to explore new musical territories, to experiment with tactics that bring the student to the fore in decision-making, and recognize the value of expanding the scope of learning beyond performance.

Over 30 years of experience working in various capacities in music and the arts tells me that teachers who work in the arts are not prone to dutifully complete lesson plans. For that reason, I have chosen to present the idea of differentiation as simply as possible, relying on a basic mapping guideline that will help teachers brainstorm ideas on ways to stretch their curriculum in depth, breadth, pacing, and creativity. The *differentiation map* in figure 13.1 shows the basic components of a curriculum in the central box. Arrows indicate ways this curriculum can be stretched to include opportunities of depth, breadth, pacing, and creativity (appropriately extending to the "right brain"). The thick arrows indicate a challenging stretch of curriculum for the regular students in the studio. The narrow arrows represent extended opportunities for talented students.

This simple brainstorming outline can be used at all different levels of curricular planning and across the components of content, process, and prod-

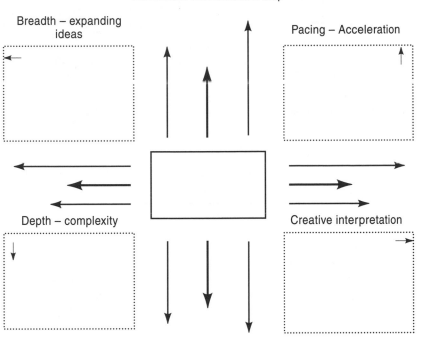

FIGURE 13.1. A map of curriculum differentiation in the arts.

uct. For example, the map in figure 13.2 places *content* in the central box. The dotted "brainstorming boxes" show different examples of ways this content can be stretched in all directions. Private teachers differentiate repertoire for students, stretching the capabilities of talented students through more accelerated materials (↑). Often these students will receive more differentiated depth (↓) in technical skills needed for touch and tonal detail in this repertoire. The arrow to the left indicates ways to expand beyond repertoire, as well as posing the opportunity to explore interdisciplinary connections. The arrow to the right includes content that encourages student exploration and interpretive creativity.

The acceleration brainstorm box introduces the idea of "curriculum compacting." This strategy is used in gifted education to allow students in the academics to work quickly through materials they readily understand.[29] For a talented beginner, this may begin with the idea of student-initiated "bonus pieces" presented earlier, leading to rapid completion of several levels of method books in a few months. "Quantity and quality" refers to the importance of giving these quick learners enough challenging content so that practice time is used efficiently throughout the week. The meaningful quality of

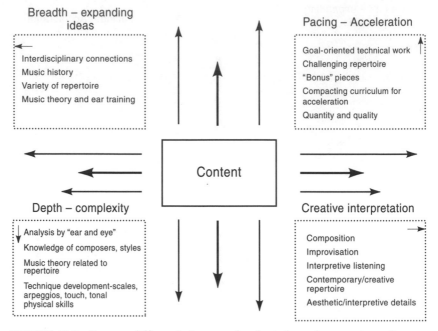

FIGURE 13.2. Content differentiation map for the independent music studio.

this content will secure student interest and a higher level of metaperceptive functioning.

The idea of differentiating the *process* of musical learning in the studio requires an emphasis on a sideways stretch to include student-centered learning (←) and the artistic perceptive/cognitive skills that are the components of musical talent (→). Private teachers should readily understand the depth (↓) and acceleration (↑)ideas shown on the process map in figure 13.3.

We return to the recognizable components of musical talent, now structured as a set of thinking/perceptive skills or "ways of knowing" for use in curriculum planning to encourage talent development. They are given the name *Artistic Ways of Knowing* because they are generalizable across the performing arts.[30]

Artistic Ways of Knowing:

- Perceptual discrimination—"fine tuned" perception
- Metaperception—cognitive/perceptual process of making interpretive decisions
- Creative interpretation—exploring, reworking, refining artistic (musical) ideas

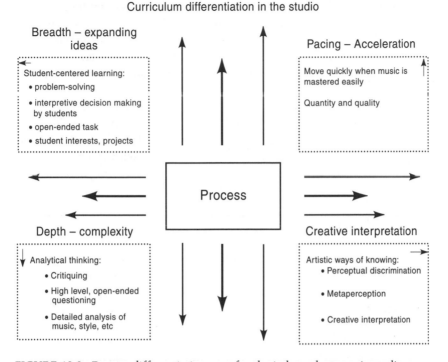

Curriculum differentiation in the studio

Breadth – expanding ideas

Student-centered learning:
- problem-solving
- interpretive decision making by students
- open-ended task
- student interests, projects

Pacing – Acceleration

Move quickly when music is mastered easily

Quantity and quality

Process

Depth – complexity

Analytical thinking:
- Critiquing
- High level, open-ended questioning
- Detailed analysis of music, style, etc

Creative interpretation

Artistic ways of knowing:
- Perceptual discrimination
- Metaperception
- Creative interpretation

FIGURE 13.3. Process differentiation map for the independent music studio.

- Dynamic of performance—communication of a creative interpretation to others
- Critiquing—perceptive evaluation and assessment

The process differentiation map shows these artistic thinking skills in the brainstorming box reaching toward the aesthetic-creative right. Feeding these perceptive/cognitive skills into the studio teaching process, adapted to different types of teaching strategies, will decidedly develop creative interpretation and potential musical talent.

The left brainstorming box of student-centered learning includes instruction that addresses student interests and input. In student-centered learning, the teacher serves as knowledgeable facilitator, allowing students to share ideas freely as they mutually work through the process of solving musical problems and making interpretive decisions. It requires a delicate balance of interchange between the teacher and student. Certain areas of physical-technical skill development require teacher expertise to guide instruction. However, open-ended questioning allows the student to know how and why these skills are being done and how they can be practiced.

One strategy asks students to "think aloud," verbally describing the specifics of a musical task. Students explain details in the score of a new piece before sightreading it or explain the purpose of an exercise before playing it. Students retrospectively critique themselves immediately after a brief performance task. This strategy draws deliberate attention to the learning process and emphasizes the child's awareness of metaperceptive skills.[31]

A pedagogical study by Mackworth-Young discovered that pupil-centered lessons, where pupils' thoughts and feelings are the primary consideration in lessons, resulted in "greater enjoyment, increased interest, positive attitudes, motivation and progress." She experimented with teacher-directed, pupil-directed, and pupil-centered strategies in lessons with three elementary students. Although there was variability in each child's learning style, she found that pupil-centered lessons were the most successful."[32]

This teaching process is more time intensive than teacher-directed learning. Competition-oriented teachers can effectively choreograph talented youngsters through repetitive physical drill to produce the "overpolished and special effects" performances that are impressive, especially at young ages. Taking the time to bring the child into the decision-making process requires a challenging shift in this teaching approach. However, teachers will discover that these students adjust more easily during the adolescent "midlife crisis" because instruction, from the start, allowed them to understand and actively participate in musical decisions. True rewards arrive when these teachers realize the joy of mutually discussing musical options at an advanced aesthetic level by teenage years.

The product performance map in figure 13.4 recognizes the creative musical product as well as musical performance as a studio goal in the curriculum. In performance the addition of critique and student assessment adds depth ($\downarrow$) to the curriculum. Expanding the breadth of performance experiences ($\leftarrow$) allows students the opportunity to explore different musical genres and share music with others through chamber ensembles. Creative studio projects ($\rightarrow$) include student compositions and performances that reflect the "real" product similar to the end result of gifted projects in school.

A final recital in a studio can evolve into a "recital project," based on student-centered projects that incorporate repertoire, composition, research, and interdisciplinary connections.[33] This may simply be a "recital story," where young students work together to create a story line and brief compositions (traveling or walking music) that thematically link pieces (animals, journey in space, etc.) they have learned.

One creative studio had students performing a full range of American contemporary pieces, researching the composers of the pieces they were performing. An added "real" feature included email contacts and student interviews with living American composers, and a guest visit from a composer to discuss the creative process with students.[34] A personal creative

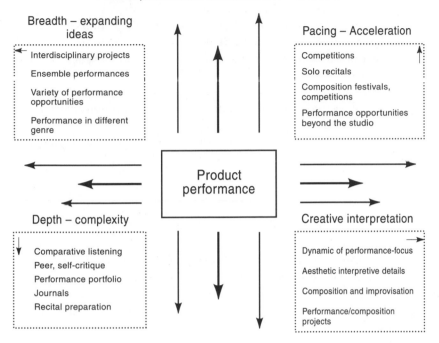

FIGURE 13.4. Product/performance differentiation map for the independent music studio.

project from my studio included a group of seven youngsters learning the works of Satie. They brainstormed their opinions of his style, describing it as peculiar and not making any sense. As a result, they created a book of their own compositions in the style of Satie entitled *A Seven Piece Puzzle*, described in a preface as "little pieces that don't seem to fit together with the right picture."[35] The possibilities for creative projects combining studio thematic goals and student ideas is limitless.

The use of these differentiation maps to brainstorm curricular ideas in the studio can work a number of ways. Teachers can place a broad-based theme for the year in the central box, brainstorming on ways this will stretch the scope of learning for all of the students in the studio. Placing an individual student's name in the central box can spur ideas on ways to stretch repertoire, technical regimen, teaching approaches, and final performance/products for the child. Sharing this brainstorming activity with the student emphasizes student-centered curriculum planning, with the student choosing stretched possibilities that will most likely exceed teacher expectations. The blank differentiation map in the appendix can be duplicated for this curriculum planning.

Creative Play

The first years of musical study begin at an age when children have explored imaginative singing and possible preschool musical experiences where creative play molds the curriculum. Creative improvisation and composition can be a natural extension of early instrumental training. The child who learns notation on a musical score and plays these sounds on an instrument can easily reverse these new-found skills through creative play on an instrument.

Early lessons can provide niches of time for the teacher and student to create musical stories as in the "Getting to Know You" activity in this chapter. These activities can allow children to create musical stories with no words—simply the explored sounds of the instrument—expanding in scope beyond the few notes learned in their simple repertoire. Practice can include a "play-time" break to allow imaginative play at home to create these musical ideas.

Students can enjoy figuratively mapping ideas they hear in music even before notational skills are learned. Studies show that preschool children describe sounds first through scribbles (not associated with music in any systematic way), which develop to "enactive line-drawings" showing the metric pulse of the music, leading to melodic line drawings indicating the rise and fall of the melody. Children with higher music aptitude produce more descriptive invented notations even at these young ages. Prenotational composition activities that let students draw what they are hearing, in their own way, encourage budding metaperceptive understanding of sound shapes.[36]

Technology has provided innovative ways for youngsters to ease these imaginative ideas onto a musical score. Through the use of a MIDI keyboard connected to a simple notation software package, a young child can play notes on the keyboard that will appear on the screen in their proper place on the staff. Rhythm alignment in notation, originally a bothersome problem because of the need for superaccuracy of performance, continually improves with each new software release.

Many studios offer extended time before or after lessons for work in a specially designed music computer lab. Most schools are well equipped with computers, with some computer centers located in school libraries. School music programs seeking ways to differentiate curriculum may choose to equip these computers with music software, providing opportunities for students to compose while working in the library or in the general classroom or in special projects during music class.

The ease of notating anything played on the MIDI keyboard also has the drawback of students not recognizing the intricacies of placing those notes properly on the staff themselves. Again, the importance of learning to work across dimensions is to be emphasized for young talented students. Composition is a valuable tool for developing musical understanding of different dimensions in the early years of instruction.

When children improvise, they *play* and *listen* to what they play (two dimensions). When they try to figuratively *write what they hear*, they must create a way to understand that *this* (what I play) means *this* (my musical mapping of this sound) (dimension 3). This can be done simply through rhythmic stick notation, adding letter names under each note, reinforcing the knowledge of notational skills learned at this level.

Working with small sections, the student learns how to *write the notes on the correct places on the musical staff* (dimension 4). This process reinforces understanding of rhythms and notes and clarifies how these notes arrive on that page of music in the first place. From this student draft, the transcription onto a MIDI keyboard (dimension 5) and into the computer creates a professional-looking final product to share with parents and grandparents and keep for posterity. This single improvisation-composition task allows a young child to apply understanding across five musical dimensions.[37]

Every year the software industry offers several dozen new software packages suitable for music education. Many teachers are familiar with software packages that teach basic note-learning and ear training drills. Publishers of music series often offer computer software that corresponds with pieces learned at lessons. MIDI sequencing options even offer accompaniments to simple elementary pieces that help students keep a steady pulse. In addition, there is an ever-growing collection of interactive CD-ROM programs about composers, musical compositions, and instruments available for all ages to explore. Multimedia packages "edutain" young children by bringing musical concepts into game-like learning. Parents and teachers need to carefully evaluate richness of content, student interactive work, and scoring possibilities for assessment of progress.

The software listed here is categorized to show its use in creative problem-solving and musical creativity. Children who enjoy playing at the computer will benefit from the experience of software that encourages musical creativity. (This software has been available for a number of years; if any of these are not still available, it can be used as a reference to locate other software that provides the same types of experience for developing music students.)

Notation: These programs write music on a staff that is played into the computer on a MIDI keyboard or is positioned on the staff using a mouse.

- Overture 2 (Cakewalk)
- Music Time Deluxe (Passport)
- Encore (Passport)

Exploration of sounds and sound shapes: These programs use creative approaches to music-making, creative problem-solving, and sound manipulation.

- Making Music (Morton Subotnick, Voyager-Learning Technologies)
- Making More Music (Morton Subotnick, Voyager-Learning Technologies)
- Music Ace I and II (Harmonic Vision) (A music literacy program that includes a creative "doodle pad")
- The Juilliard Musical Adventure (Theatrix Interactive)
- Developing Musical Intuitions (Oxford University Press)

Sequencing sounds: These programs allow students to create mixtures of instrumental sounds in combination, creating an orchestra or combo in the computer.

- Musicshop 2.02 (Opcode)
- Home Studio (Cakewalk)

Improvisation: These programs provide selective backups for use with a MIDI. Students improvise while listening to different styles of accompaniment. They also learn how to compose from this improvisation.

- Band in a Box (PG Music)
- Mega Rock Rap & Roll (Silver Burdett Ginn)

The first phase of musical training creates the identity of being a musician and provides a positive experience with music through the relationship of the teacher, parents, and child. During these first developmental years, the teacher guides the training to equip the student with musical essentials and a variety of learning that will inspire creative work across musical dimensions. If this instruction includes differentiation in curriculum, musical learning will stretch the possibilities of all students and encourage challenge in all directions for talented students. The talented student acquires the perceptive/cognitive skills that will nurture the musical reasoning needed for the middle and advanced stages of development.

Questions for discussion:

1. What are some complex musical tasks that children are expected to understand in the first two years of training (ages six to eight) that might be described as "conservation tasks"?
2. What are some additional guidelines you can recommend to parents to help them decide the best time to begin private instruction for their child?

3. What are some ways the profession of independent music teaching can improve communication to the public concerning the location and qualification of teachers?
4. What are some additional activities that can highlight potential talent at the initial interview?
5. Discuss the positive and negative aspects of differentiated curriculum in the private studio. How does it affect traditional teaching strategies?

THE FLAME

Teenage Years

A lot of the most gifted children with the most artistic talent are teenagers, and somehow the thing that they do best in life—that the good Lord seems to have equipped them to do most naturally—is systematically excluded from their education because it conflicts with the assumption that everybody has to do certain things at a certain age.

Mark Schubart

Close to a dozen years have gone by and we find ourselves seated on folding chairs enjoying the final recital of a private studio of talented piano students. Each year there are a few new eager faces as the younger students deftly work through pieces that seem very complex for such little fingers to play so quickly. We notice the students who have been seasoned through training, now in those tenuous intermediate years. Their intense desire for precision shows maturing musical ideas, but often arrives at awkward adolescence when being on stage has an added gravity of meaning.

We search for the advanced teenagers—those students we have seen truly blossom through the long process of talent development. Numbers have dwindled in this studio. One has decided to move out of state and is now studying at a conservatory. Another has decided to concentrate efforts on the oboe, begun in elementary school band, with time restraints easing piano lessons out of her schedule. Academic and parental pressures have caused last year's shining star, a junior seeking an Ivy League college education, to quit as well. There remains one teenager who ends the program with a flourish, receiving many hugs from young admirers and awards galore following the program. This is our tiny, eager student from the front steps. A senior, having completed a full twelve years of instruction with many competitions and solo recitals under his belt, he bids farewell to this comfortable, nurturing studio. He enters college as a math major.

Many private teachers, parents, and music students may recognize this scene as a very realistic portrayal of possibilities in musical talent development. The first years of training are "romance," with parents aglow when hearing their talented youngster perform with such confidence and flair. The middle years consist of flux and flow, a phase when students search for the "whys" and "hows" beneath the notes that were so easily played in prior years. Musical training now presents persistent challenges. Late-starters may speed into these years with determination. Others may begin a second instrument or composition classes to broaden musical experiences. The simple beginnings of talent development acquire added complications during these middle years of training.

Phase 3 arrives in the high school years, when talented students have reached a level of repertoire that demands a great deal of practice and in-depth instruction. Advanced students truly crave time to practice and work through music at an abstract level. Parents who were so proud of their promising child now see a teenager who may seek music as a career. This was not anticipated and is not always a welcome choice for parents. There are many talented teenagers who leave music in high school because of academic demands. Private teachers see these talents, aflame with promise, extinguished prior to the closure they could achieve if lessons continued through high school years. This chapter examines the developing musician and the problems that arise in the crucial time from adolescence through teenage high school years.[1]

Private Study in the Middle Years

Somewhere between the age of 10 and 13, young talented musicians begin to crave accuracy. The notes that whizzed by, just for fun, now are bothersome if they are not clean and precise. During this phase of development, students are intent on musical details, notice flaws in their playing, and seek out knowledgeable criticism from peers and teachers. Lessons change in character, with more emphasis on technical skills to acquire the aural and physical vocabulary necessary to interpret with more maturity through the instrument. Competitions and judged events provide valuable assessment from outside ears and a sense of accomplishment through performance.

This middle stage of development often calls for a change of private studio, depending on the experience and scope of the beginning teacher's studio. Several studies show that a series of transitions and learning environments is common for talented students. Parents and students seek teachers with more musical expertise and challenging student expectations. Many initial teachers encourage this change of studio, recognizing this need for more demanding instruction.[2]

Lessons now involve a combination of detailed technical regimen and depth of musical discussion and understanding. For the most part, teachers are at the helm in deciding what musical problems to work on. They guide students in which paths to follow to solve problems, with varying degrees of student-centered/teacher-directed approaches. Sosniak describes this teacher-student relationship:

> Although the teachers set the direction for the students, the pianists were expected to take an active role in solving technical problems and thinking about musical issues. . . . There was a reciprocal respect between the teachers and the students. The teachers found themselves working with students who could, perhaps, become fine musicians, youngsters with reasonable ability and an intense involvement (fostered earlier) with music. The students found themselves with teachers who were dedicated to music and who appreciated ability and commitment.[3]

One of the concert pianists looks back:

> We talked about when this composer lived, and what kinds of things were going on. Cultural attachments and the like in the other arts. What this represented, what this went along with, or what was parallel to this. Significance on the very spiritual level. Very detailed. Very intense.[4]

Often these teachers were role models to emulate, with students' musical interests spurred on by the personal attributes these teachers possessed. A talented adolescent describes her teacher as "a brilliant teacher . . . a great player as well. . . . I really look up to her. I'd like to have a lifestyle like her, she does solo work and percussion work and ensemble work, teaching, she's got everything."[5]

Practice

Talent development in the middle years relies heavily on the student's commitment to practice, bolstered by the parent's encouragement of musical studies. Without this combined support and growing work ethic, music lessons may end. This is the critical period when the young talented musician, who learned quickly and easily in the first few years of lessons, must acquire the self-discipline required for more advanced musical development. Music is no longer fun and games but a subject that requires systematic work, often on tedious technical tasks. Informal practice gives way to formal or "deliberate" practice. In interviews with winners of a national competition, after a decade, these young adults looked back at this transitional period as a time when parents needed to prod and push, as well as establish scheduling of musical priorities in a growing adolescent school and social calendar.[6]

Each teacher establishes a personal set of strategies that assist students in solving musical problems through practice. Effective use of these strategies equates to deliberate practice.

To return to the role of fly on the wall, we observe a student in the process of deliberate practice. The adolescent pianist takes out the score of a sonata and visually looks over notes written by her teacher on the first few pages. She adjusts the metronome to the tempo they had established together as a good "practice tempo" and plays through the opening exposition section with the metronome. She turns off the metronome and begins to work on an isolated problem spot she encountered in the run-through. She plays one small section (two to four measures) each hand alone a number of times. She begins at a slow tempo, marking fingering changes needed in a sixteenth-note passage. She tries these fingerings in different dotted rhythms to get physically comfortable with them. Once individual hands are comfortable with this passage, she tries them together, first slowly, then with rhythmic variety. She realizes the passage falls into a pattern of broken triads, which she plays hands together as blocked chords, saying the key of each out loud as she plays them. Once comfortable with this passage played hands together, she augments the written dynamics to see if she can play it louder than intended, to ensure solid placement and confidence, then easing back to the desired dynamic level. She tries it out with the metronome, beginning four notches slower than the practice tempo and moving up notch by notch until she reaches the weekly metronome goal. Once secure, she adds measures just before and after this spot, to work on continuity through the problem area.

This student tried just a few practice strategies commonly used for technical problem-solving. The run-through allowed her to assess her current abilities and find problems. Isolation of small sections is the golden rule of practice. Her use of each hand alone practice, varieties of rhythms, blocking of chords, and exaggerated dynamics are some of the strategies Berr describes as "transformational practice techniques." These techniques add, subtract, or substitute elements from the original.[7] They allow the student to manipulate physical coordination until it can comfortably match musical intentions. As you read through the procedure, can you determine the length of time it would take to deliberately practice these few measures? This is the type of practice expected in the intermediate stage of talent development.

As I was writing this chapter, the local music teacher association held an essay contest for music students on the topic of "What My Practice Means to Me." One adolescent described her piano as a "good listener" that could tell more about herself than she could. She finds herself "drawn to the piano" as "an emotional release." A teenage clarinetist realizes that she is "disciplined in an activity that I enjoy and have made a regular part of my life." She recognizes the value of working through frustration and not quitting—a lesson that is transferable to other aspects of life. "This fairly simple lesson is hard to learn, but I have been fortunate to learn it early in life."[8] To these young musicians, practice has become a vital part of their daily life and emotional growth.

There are many texts describing an array of practice strategies, including memorizing and practicing away from the instrument to nurture meta-perceptive understanding of the music. Some texts assist teachers and students in the monitoring of practice through student self-assessment and journaling. Acquiring the "metaskills" of deliberate practice strategies at this time instills the self-discipline needed to succeed in the advanced stage of talent development.[9]

My Performance Portfolio is a practice tool that encourages students to self-assess their own developing performances and determine practice strategies to improve these performances. This type of self-evaluation and written critique reveals students who are perceptive listeners and critics. It also engages students in developing their own strategies for practice.

The Performance Portfolio critique forms were developed in a pedagogy group project working with teachers and students from a number of private studios. They offer two levels of student critique. The open form in Figure 14.1a is designed for the beginning performer-listener, with teachers focusing listening on a single musical concept and specific problematic spots to listen for in the assigned piece. Figure 14.1b shows a student's completed form after listening to four progressive performances of the same piece. After listening to the tape of their performance of the piece, students first write "constructive comments" (always starting with a positive remark), then rate their performance numerically. Although teachers are reluctant to assign numbers to performances, students seem to love this activity, as witnessed by several scores of 3.75 as an overall average arriving on forms used in studios who were part of the pedagogy project.[10]

The Performance Portfolio form in figure 14.2 includes specific musical elements, with blank spaces available for student or teacher additions. This form is designed for students who have been introduced to all of the different musical elements. The back of the form is divided into four sections asking students to give constructive comments and map out a practice plan for improvement. Final comments offer students the opportunity to listen to all performances, evaluating their overall improvement. As students enter more extended repertoire, they may make notes directly on their score as they listen to their performance.

Use of this form over a three-year period in my studio of students who were in the intermediate to advanced levels of instruction resulted in a de-

PERFORMANCE CRITIQUE FORM

Listening Focus Form

Evaluator: _____

Directions:

Use this form to judge your own taped performances of a composition you are learning. Place the date of the performance in the appropriate box. As you listen, jot down sentences that describe the performance you hear at the bottom and on reverse side of the form. Always include GOOD things about the performance, as well as specific things that need improvement. After you have listened to the performance, place numbers that match the level of performance for the listening taks written below.

Use the following scale to judge the performance:

1	2	3	4	5
Insecure	Needs Work	Average	Almost there	Polished

COMPOSITION: _____ COMPOSER: _____

LISTENING FOCUS: _____

	1	2	3	4
Dates of performances:				
Listen for:				
1. _____				
2. _____				
3. _____				
4. _____				
5. _____				

1. Strong points in my performance:

Things that need work:

My practice plan to improvement:

2. Strong points in my performance:

Things that need work:

My practice plan to improvement:

---

3. Strong points in my performance:

Things that need work:

My practice plan to improvement:

---

4. Strong points in my performance:

Things that need work:

My practice plan to improvement:

FINAL EVALUATION: What improvements do you hear in your playing through these performances?

FIGURE 14.1a. Listening focus critique forms from the Performance Portfolio. © 1994. Fig. 14.1b shows an example of teacher-assigned listening tasks and student assessment of four performances.

PERFORMANCE CRITIQUE FORM

Listening Focus Form

Evaluator: _____

Directions:

Use this form to judge your own taped performances of a composition you are learning. Place the date of the performance in the appropriate box. As you listen, jot down sentences that describe the performance you hear at the bottom and on reverse side of the form. Always include GOOD things about the performance, as well as specific things that need improvement. After you have listened to the performance, place numbers that match the level of performance for the listening taks written below.

Use the following scale to judge the performance:

1	2	3	4	5
Insecure	Needs Work	Average	Almost there	Polished

COMPOSITION: _Musette in D_   COMPOSER: _Bach_

LISTENING FOCUS: _Rhythm and Tempo_

	1	2	3	4
Dates of performances:	9/10	9/17	9/24	10/3
Listen for:				
1. Steady beat between m 2-3, 7-8	1	3	4	5
2. Even ♩ ♩ ♩	3	4	5	5
3. Keep tempo in middle section	2	3	3	4
4. Steady beat and tempo m. 17-20	1	2	3	4
5. Basic steady beat + tempo overall	2	3	4	4

1. Strong points in my performance:

Most ♪♩♩ were OK

Things that need work:

Rhythm! m2-3 have a big space. Middle is sloppy!

My practice plan to improvement:

Use metronome and play line 1 + 2 5 times
Drill middle section

2. Strong points in my performance: Better than last time. Really got ♩♩♩ good.

Things that need work:

Middle part - especially page 19, line 2

My practice plan to improvement:

Drill again. Metronome for trouble spot - middle

3. Strong points in my performance:

I got jumps! Staying in tempo pretty good.

Things that need work:

Trouble spot at end of middle part

My practice plan to improvement:

5 times met. middle

4. Strong points in my performance: Great job!

Things that need work:

My practice plan to improvement:

FINAL EVALUATION: What improvements do you hear in your playing through these performances?

FIGURE 14.1b.

PERFORMANCE CRITIQUE FORM

Musical Concept Form

Evaluator: _____

Use this form to judge your own taped performances of a composition you are learning. Place the date of the performance in the appropriate box. As you listen, jot down sentences that describe the performance you hear on the reverse side of the form. Constructive comments include strengths about the performance, as well as specific things that need improvement. After you have listened to the performance, place numbers that match the level of performance in each of the musical concept areas listed. You may add additional concepts or listening tasks on the open lines provided under each category.

Use the following scale to evaluate your performance:

1	2	3	4	5
Insecure	Needs Work	Average	Almost there	Polished

COMPOSITION: _____ COMPOSER: _____

	Performance Dates:	1	2	3	4
RHYTHM & TEMPO:	Accurate rhythm				
_____	Appropriate tempo				
_____	Consistent tempo				
MELODY:	Well balanced				
_____	Well shaped phrasing				
_____	Suitable tone quality				
TECHNIQUE:	Accurate notes				
_____	Precise articulation				
_____	Cleanliness				
MUSICALITY:	Observed dynamics				
_____	Showed mucical poise				
_____	Portrayed mood of music				
MEMORY:	Securely learned				
OVERALL PERFORMANCE:					

FIGURE 14.2. Music concept critique form from the Performance Portfolio. © 1994.

cided improvement in peer critiques, both verbal and written. At the end of three years, students were critiquing so well in classes that part of the final studio recital featured pieces learned by students guided only through peer critique, with no teacher intervention or instruction. It was quite rewarding seeing these teenagers nod and applaud for their successful peer-students.

Practice during this transitional middle period of development requires a setting in the home that is conducive to this type of concentrated musical work. Positive comments, understanding of frustrations, and a step back from physical presence in the practice room will help guide growing self-discipline and commitment.

There is no question that parents play a key role in establishing a specific practice schedule for the young child. The middle phase, from sixth to eighth grade, finds the rebellious adolescent balking at parental interference in dictating practice requirements. An open discussion with teacher, child, and parent can develop a schedule the *student* feels will attain the specific goals required for lessons and performances. A student who has established a self-imposed habit of practice by the ninth grade will be sure to maintain practice through the difficult high school years. If parents are still coaxing and arguing for practice at this age, it is doubtful that lessons will continue through high school.

Performance and Competition

Performance experiences during this stage emphasize assessment of technical proficiency and growing musical understanding. These performances provide goals that reward the perseverance of practice. Talented musicians, guided by their teachers, seek out opportunities for critiques from knowledgeable judges, through competitive events at various levels. Recitals beyond the studio level and school musical activities offer more venues for performance experience during these years. A progressive stepwise process helps students gain confidence in performance. Students perform the same repertoire within a studio class, a studio recital, a local recital, a local competition—toward a larger competition.

The role of competition in talent development is always a subject of controversy. Is this experience healthy or detrimental to the development of talent? Is it necessary for success in music? The interviewed winners of the MTNA competition all noted that the value of competition does not depend on winning but on the intensity of preparation, personal achievement of a goal, and the musical growth derived from the experience. Sosniak reported similar reactions to the involvement in competitions at this age, with musicians walking away from a competition realizing what needs to be worked on to improve a performance as well as some notable recognition for taking part in the competition.[11]

In *No Contest*, Kohn cites over a hundred studies that show that competition does not equate to success or superior performance. "Superior performance not only does not *require* competition; it usually seems to require its absence." Greater achievement and performance in school classrooms grew from cooperative work in small groups, dealing with complex problem-solving. Although competition can appeal to students and make teaching easier, "it circumvents rather than solves pedagogical problems."[12] The win/lose parameters of competition may appeal to certain students, but it does not necessarily develop the emotional sensitivity that defines musical talent.

Competitions also can bring the outside pressures of parents and teachers, whose career images or personal expectations seek that first-place spot for the child. At this age, students are seeking insight into more depth of musical understanding, and the teacher has a demanding role in this process. A competition focus may narrow study to repertoire requirements that will impress judges. Exploration of a breadth of repertoire choices may be limited when competitions are a high priority at this stage of development.

Uszler describes the talented student's typical "diet of difficult pieces" that are impressive for competition, neglecting the comprehensive exploration of shorter works of varied composers to strengthen understanding of different compositional styles. She compares this approach to flying from one major city to the next by jet rather than visiting small towns, walking down country lanes, and "smelling the proverbial roses."[13]

Paul Pollei, artistic director of the Gina Bachauer International Piano Competition, surprisingly shares this view of competition at this developmental stage. He cautions teachers on the dangers of creating a competition-oriented studio environment:

> Some parents and teachers are so obsessed with the goal of winning that it becomes a singular activity of the studio and family to train products who will participate and, they hope, win the next competition. Teachers accept students and plan curricula accordingly, with one goal in mind—entering students in the next competition. By so doing, the students . . . are submitted to a battery of inquisition, testing, and psychological nervousness which may reak havoc . . . for the students on a permanent basis.[14]

More than any time in the development of talent, this tenuous stage of personal and musical development brings the psychological concerns of young musicians being greatly influenced by dominating influences of parent and teacher. Scott McBride Smith, the director of the International Institute for Young Musicians, has witnessed young outstanding performers and the problems arising from the dynamic with parents and teachers at this age.

What we think of as a prodigy in our world today . . . it's a kind of force feeding in a way. . . . He doesn't really have a life. He just has a schedule. Parents don't give their children any space—I notice it as a nationwide phenomenon. So many of these kids, in a way, have a double personality. They have a personality for adults, and they have a kind of rebellious, knotty personality that expresses itself when your back is turned. A lot of their vitality and creativity goes into maintaining that double personality, but if you know the families and you know the mothers, you see why they have to do it, and you probably would too. . . . How is that going to stack up in his playing? They need a little space when they're growing up. They need to make a few errors on their own. It's OK to fail sometimes. Well, many parents don't like that. I think those things are necessary to develop your own voice, or your own desire to express yourself in your playing.[15]

The "midlife crisis" of the prodigy arrives at this stage as well. By the age of 10 to 12 the prodigy is well into advanced literature, learned primarily through quick technical response and enactive performance talents. Bamberger explains this crisis as one in which "performers undergo significant changes in their internal representation of musical structure itself." The all-at-once imitation that functions well for a child performer now meets up with an adolescent need to differentiate musical dimensions and "develop means for coordinating these now separate musical dimensions and their underlying representations."[16]

This transitional shift extends to most talented students at this age who are beginning to understand metaperceptive decision-making in music. Prior to this age, these youngsters were making these decisions intuitively, without reflecting on them. Pulling them apart and taking a look at them requires reflective analysis and a bit of growing time for this adjustment.

Many young talented students are already performing extensively in concert as well as competition at this age. Others are just getting excited about their arrival at the level of challenging repertoire. And still others have never acquired private formal instruction but have used these years as a time to explore creative musical ideas through genres outside a structured classical development.

Jenny Boyd has compiled findings of 75 interviews with leading songwriters and musicians across jazz, rock, and pop fields. These biographical sketches of talent development show children arriving at adolescence with a sense of musical understanding derived from environmental musical influences around them, a self-initiative to learn about these sounds, and the commitment to teach themselves and seek guidance from adults who are either performers or family members.

Boyd found that 95 percent of initial interest in music came from family influence. Many grandfathers, uncles, or parents gave those first guitar lessons to young, eager children. Musical interests grew through experience in gospel choirs, listening to many recordings, and live performances of jazz groups. Often relatives or friends shared music and gave informal lessons that nurtured these creative musicians to reach performance levels good enough to play publicly by teenage years.

B. B. King's first three chords were taught by his parish preacher. At 12, Eric Clapton's mother gave him money to buy a guitar, which he learned from a family friend who squeezed in lessons after closing hours in the back room of his liquor store. Sinead O'Connor's childhood was filled with Irish ballads performed by parents steeped in Dublin's musical heritage. She recalls: "From a young age I understood songs could get over very strong emotions." At 12, she began writing songs as she walked along to school. Many of these creative artists briefly sought formal music lessons to learn to read music, having primarily begun in an aural tradition of musical training. By adolescence they were comfortable performing, and most were encouraged by parents as well. These artists from different backgrounds and genres shared similar needs with the talented students who have studied formally, often acquiring self-initiated strategies to solve musical problems in their practice.[17]

Characteristics of this middle period of training in the development of musical talent are:

- Desire for accuracy and precision in performance
- Acquisition of more refined practice techniques
- Development of technical proficiency
- Instruction orientation in technique and musical understanding
- Cognitive shift of musical thinking—from enactive to metaperceptive analysis and understanding
- Interest in performing opportunities that include judged competitive settings
- Delicate psychological balance of teacher, parent, and student in relation to practice, competition, and performance

Differentiated Curriculum in Music Education

The young child who has ventured through years of private instruction has also received music education in school. The possibilities available to promising students in school will help set the stage for the advanced level of talent development. The quality and comprehensiveness of this education relies largely on the local priorities of music in the school's curriculum. The range of possibilities is quite dramatic.

If an elementary school has no music teacher, the result will be peripheral learning of music depending on the capabilities and interests of classroom teachers. Bresler's ethnographic study found that the quality of music instruction in these circumstances is marginalized to its "dispensable role as entertainment."[18] An elementary school with no music specialist will negatively impact the basic instruction of band and string instruments, traditionally begun in fourth or fifth grade. This scenario does not fare well for *any* child's development of essential musical skills, let alone the child who shows potential talent.

A healthy music education program has music specialists in every elementary school, offering classes more than once a week. Instruction in band and string instruments begins in elementary grades, extending through high school with different levels of performance groups offering acceleration for talented students. Middle school classes in general music for all students lead to high school electives of music theory, music history, and specialized performance groups such as madrigal, show choir, or jazz band. Ideal situations may include classes in advanced placement level theory or composition and music technology. Most states offer an infrastructure of performance recognition for outstanding students through district, regional, and statewide performance groups, with participation based on audition or teacher nomination. This comprehensive music curriculum provides a wealth of opportunities for all students, with appropriate differentiation for talented students within easy reach.

A majority of schools more readily realize a somewhat middle ground in musical offerings in the curriculum. General music classes at the elementary level may meet weekly or biweekly, with instrumental instruction beginning at the elementary level and filtering through secondary programs as electives. Enrollment and curricular restrictions may hamper classes beyond performance at the secondary level. Differentiation for musically talented students would not normally be part of this curriculum.

The philosophy of music education believes in the essential need for all students to learn and understand music. The literature often regards *all* students who select performance classes as musically talented. Recent discussions and debates in the field concern themselves with extending curricular offerings beyond performance, primarily based on educating the general school population in the appreciation and critical judgment of music. Reimer cautions that academic approaches to the subject should not exclude "the immediacy of musical involvement . . . through focused study including listening, performing, improvising, and composing as essential ingredients."[19] In defining how music should be "basic," Fowler explains:

> In music, particularly in the high school, all that concentration on skill development for the select students in band and chorus has been recognized for what it so often is—not an education in the musical heritage but a perfecting of performance. Our educational practices in the arts have betrayed us. In music, the goal has not been education through per-

formance so much as performance as an end in itself. The goal has not been to teach all students their musical heritage but rather to teach production to the talented. We have been remarkably effective at achieving the latter and outrageously negligent at providing the former.[20]

In 1994, this philosophical discussion bore fruit in the publication of *National Standards for Arts Education*, which established a need for "quality and accountability" in curricular development. The nine content standards reach beyond performance to include improvisation, composition, analyzation, evaluation, history, and interdisciplinary connections. This breadth of curricular choice invites differentiation for all students, with ample room for challenges for talented students. The curriculum guide states the need to serve gifted and talented students. This publication is used continuously as a reference in music education publications and conferences to encourage the use of these standards in school curriculum.

If we pair this publication with the revised inclusive definition of talent and multiple intelligence curricula in gifted education, we arrive at an opportune time for differentiating curriculum for the musically talented student within school. This requires some cooperative planning between music teachers and gifted specialists. Gifted specialists can explain strategies and individual differentiation needs of students who can excel beyond the normal curriculum in music. Music teachers can design a curriculum that incorporates the national standards in this differentiation.

The differentiation maps presented in chapter 13 for the private studio can also be used effectively for the music educator. The basic parameters of depth, breadth, acceleration, and creativity remain the same, with ideas in brainstorming boxes now reflecting classroom activities.

The content differentiation map in figure 14.3 includes all nine national content standards, appropriately placed in brainstorming boxes. The breadth—expanding ideas box (←) includes interdisciplinary connections (content standard 8), encouraging students to creatively combine music with other disciplines. Combining study of music and its historical significance (content standard 9) will challenge students who show musicological interests. Further differentiation can include independent studies where students develop interdisciplinary or historical curricula themselves, seeking research and mentorship opportunities beyond school.

The acceleration brainstorm box (↑) once again includes the idea of "curriculum compacting." This gifted strategy, designed for the secondary level, allows students who can easily grasp the material to move ahead at their own pace, designing individualized projects beyond the curriculum to keep them challenged. This reaches a giant step beyond the solo performance experiences or all-state opportunities that normally recognize talented students in the music program. Exceptional students design a challenging curriculum according to

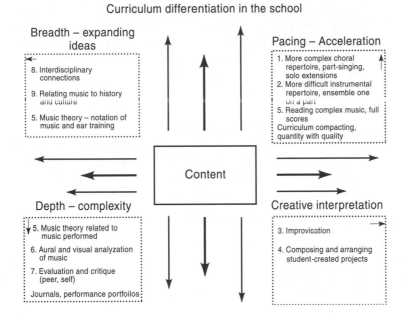

FIGURE 14.3. Content differentiation map for school music programs.

their interests, working jointly with the school music program, private teacher, or a nearby college. A challenging curricular project or class may include a performance project or solo recital, ensemble work, teaching, community service, interdisciplinary connections, or a creative product.

Curriculum compacting need not be limited to secondary levels. A creative elementary general music teacher devised an intriguing way to allow students to excel at their own pace, similar to curriculum compacting, in a third grade recorder class. She created multiple levels of recorder music, from "novice" to "master." Each recorder packet included songs from their music class, themes from classical music, analysis of concepts, and pages for students to compose their own pieces. Students moved from one level to the next at their own pace, with assessment of performance, composition, and improvisation required to pass each level. As students advanced, the bustling atmosphere of peer lessons and assessment created student-centered learning that took on added meaning in classes where most students were learning English as a second language. Students who quickly excelled to the "master" level often took on the role of teacher for the entire class and enjoyed more complex compositional tasks using the computer. This teacher noted that students were often more critical of performance in their peer assessments than she was, nurturing critical listening at grade 3.[21]

The process differentiation map in figure 14.4 includes the same artistic ways of knowing on the creative-aesthetic side (→), emphasizing the need to address metaperceptive functioning by developing the skills for students to make musical decisions. The music education literature recognizes the need to change the traditional role of teacher as decision-maker in the performance classroom.[22] Incorporating these artistic "thinking skills" into any music classroom through student-centered activities will encourage students to develop their own creative interpretations.

Student-centered teaching strategies (←) of "musical problem-solving" develop student's skills in critical and creative thinking and mirror strategies used in gifted education. Musical problem-solving requires an atmosphere that encourages student/teacher discussion, experimentation of ideas in small groups, and assessment of progress from students and teacher.[23] Questioning that encourages interpretive experimentation develops metaperception in this problem-solving process.

DeLorenzo's study of sixth graders involved in problem-solving in a group composition project revealed that students who were highly involved in the process explored and organized sounds according to expressive qualities. Their

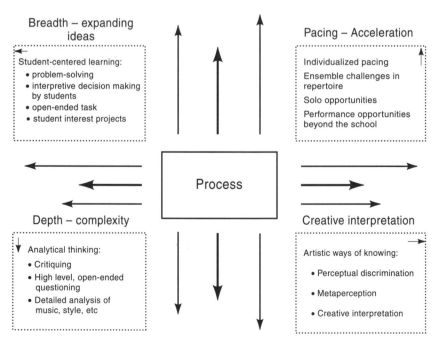

FIGURE 14.4. Process differentiation map for school music programs.

choices were based on metaperceptive structuring of the problem rather than on teacher-provided choices for the assignment. In contrast, "uninvolved" students rarely based their decisions on musical concerns.[24]

Elliott's description of the process of making "musical judgments in action" through musical problem-solving clearly reflects artistic ways of knowing:

> Strategic judgment grows by listening *artistically* for the music one is interpreting and performing; by weighing musical choices in action; by adjusting one's musical thinking-in-action according to one's choices; by assessing the artistic results of one's choices; and by considering alternative strategies during further efforts to make music well.[25]

Musical problem-solving mirrors "creative problem-solving," a common strategy used in gifted education.[26] The terminology for this problem-solving process can be aligned with the development of a creative artistic or musical product or project as follows:

Creative Problem-solving	*Artistic or Musical Problem-solving*
1. A problem exists— an undefined "mess"	1. ? A vague idea
2. Data Finding: clarify the problem by collection information	2. Exploration of the senses: connection with art form, imagining possibilities (perceptual discrimination, metaperception)
3. Problem finding: stating the problem	3. Problem finding: stating the artistic project
4. Idea finding: generating solutions	4. Idea finding: metaperceptive choices, structuring ideas, interpretive reworking (creative interpretation)
5. Select a solution: decision-making	5. Develop a product/performance: practice, rehearsing, refining (dynamic of performance)
6. Acceptance finding: Implementing the solution	6. Critiquing for further improvement (critiquing)

The product/performance differentiation map in figure 14.5 reflects most of the ideas discussed earlier in relation to the private studio, with accelerated performing experiences (↑) that include all-state performances available to students in music programs in schools. The extension of products beyond performance (←→) offers the advantage of creating a more comprehensive approach to instruction for all students and the opportunity to differentiate for talented students.

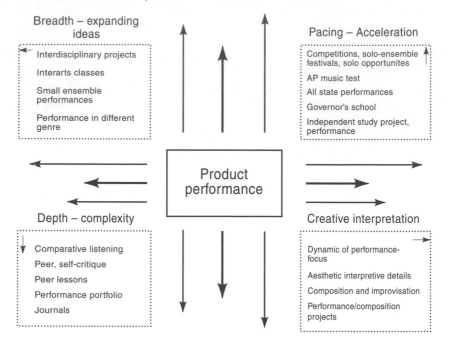

FIGURE 14.5. Product/performance differentiation map for school music programs.

Effective interdisciplinary projects (←) can be exciting creative ventures for music teachers seeking ways to collaborate creatively with colleagues. It is essential that the project not relegate music to the position of a means of learning another discipline. Its value lies in realizing the depth of understanding that can evolve from collaborative creation across disciplines. Thoms describes a fine arts course that explored the definition of "line" through a rich artistic content in music, dance, and visual arts. The resulting project was a creative multimedia, multiarts presentation involving the students' own creative work in dance, film, and music. Talented students relish the experience of creative breadth using their musical knowledge and performance capabilities.[27]

An elementary band director chose to differentiate curriculum by seeking multicultural connections to extend learning beyond instrumental instruction. Students sought out national anthems from their native countries using Internet resources. Music was notated and arranged by the teacher to include differentiated solos and challenging parts for talented students. The project included student inquiry about accurate lyrics from family members newly arrived in this country. Extensions included social studies research of these countries, interviews with family members to learn about customs, and the performance and presentation of the project at the school's international night. An added musical bonus was the enticement of family support of musical practice and instruction through this project.[28]

The use of music technology in school creates an ideal setting to enhance compositional efforts (→), attract students who may not be part of music performance classes, and guide students in areas of music that can pragmatically lead to a career beyond musical performance. The computer has jump-stepped the process of notating musical ideas onto paper through modern notational software. The music education literature notes a number of promising studies and strategies that effectively use this technology to help students understand the structure and process of composing.[29]

Students who are comfortable creating sounds with the synthesizer in rock bands can reach a step further using the vast array of sounds and sequencing programs available on the computer. A computer-savvy student with interest in music and a keen ear can extend musical talents through the development of a creative "real" software product utilizing combined musical and computer skills.

Schools are in the unique position of offering a breadth of curricular options that can truly stretch musical talent in all directions if curricula reflect the guidelines of *National Standards for Arts Education*. These standards offer proficient and advanced levels of achievement from grades 9–12. The following list includes excerpts from each content standard, with advanced achievement standards exemplifying differentiation in music for the talented music student.[30]

National Standards for Arts Education—Grades 9–12:

Content Standard	Advanced Achievement Standard (9–12)
1. Singing alone and with others, a varied repertoire of music	1. Sing in small ensembles, with one student on a part
2. Performing on instruments, alone and with others, a varied repertoire of music	2. Perform with expression and with technical accuracy a large and varied repertoire of instrumental literature with a level of difficulty of 5, on a scale of 1 to 6
3. Improvising melodies, variations, and accompaniments	3. Improvise original melodies in a variety of styles, over given chord progressions, each in a consistent style, meter, and tonality
4. Composing and arranging music within specified guidelines	4. Compose music, demonstrating imagination and technical skill in applying the principles of composition

5. Reading and notating music

5. Demonstrate the ability to read a full instrumental or vocal score by describing how the elements of music are used and explaining all transpositions and clefs

6. Listening to, analyzing, and describing music

6. Analyze and describe uses of the elements of music in a given work that make it unique, interesting, and expressive

7. Evaluating music and music performances

7. Evaluate a given musical work in terms of its aesthetic qualities and explain the musical means it uses to evoke feelings and emotions

8. Understand relationships between music, the other arts, and disciplines outside the arts.

8. Explain how the roles of creators, performers, and others involved in the production and presentation of the arts are similar to and different from one another in the various arts

9. Understanding music in relation to history and culture

9. Identify and explain the stylistic features of a given musical work that serve to define its aesthetic tradition and its historical and cultural context

A music curriculum that offers content in all of these nine areas will provide a rich breadth of musical knowledge for the musically talented student. The selected achievement standards show individualized skills within an ensemble (one person per part), extension of musical understanding to creative improvisation and composition, and analysis skills that expand into interdisciplinary applications. This array of skill development will not be taught in a private studio. Musically talented students can profit from creative exploration and interdisciplinary work available through school. If the music program predominantly rests on performance classes, differentiation will be limited in scope for talented students. By stretching the curriculum beyond performance, we gain the opportunity to nuture student talents through composition, improvisation, musicological interests, critique, and music technology.

Teenage Years

Everything you learn in those teenage years is essential to your development; you can draw on it the rest of your life.

Yo Yo Ma

During the advanced stage of musical development, arriving in the teen years, the talented student has developed impressive technical skills and is learning to make musical decisions regarding style and aesthetic subtleties.[31] The emphasis in training during these years lies on the development of creative interpretation or personal expression communicated through music. The goal is to develop a musical young artist by the end of high school.

Students work with master teachers to attain artistry of expression and technical flamboyance. They begin to build their lives around music. There is daily practice, no matter what. There are multiple musical activities in school and in the private studio, often extending to summer or weekend offerings. Performance opportunities are more prestigious, requiring demanding repertoire performed at a high caliber of refinement.

The talented teenager's social world is an equally musical world, connecting with friends who share their love of music. An intimate circle of friends who share their musical capabilities affords them a chance to compare musical ideas. One's identity as a musician is taken for granted and is equivalent in time allotment to a half-time job plus school. Adapting schedules to provide flexibility to meet the demands of school academic subjects plus the continuance of advanced musical study creates a challenging situation for the outstanding teenage musician.

Some musically talented teenagers arrive at high school with an array of musical talents. They may have private instruction in their principal instrument, with active participation in several school performance groups. These are students who show a breadth of musical interest, filling their lives with a variety of musical activities. Other students may be singularly focused to their principal instrument, with minimal participation in school performing groups. A few students may have decided that their goal in life is to be a professional performer as early as middle school.

The career-oriented student has zeroed into the field of music, with school social and academic work of secondary importance. Parents aggressively seek ways to link these students with prestigious teachers who can prepare them for a career.

The Master Teacher

The master teacher is a pivotal influence in the development of advanced musical talent. These teachers are usually performers themselves and are often connected with a college or conservatory. They primarily teach only talented students, with some concentrating on all ages and others only teaching advanced teenagers and college level students. They have acquired expertise in their specialized field of performance and are equipped to share their knowledge with their students. Talented teenagers working with certain master teachers may find themselves thrust into the conservatory regimen before they finish their formal high school education.

The master teacher persona is both revered and feared in the musical field. Their influence on their students can be immensely rewarding or devastatingly damaging. Master teachers demand a high caliber of commitment from their students. It is not unusual for practice to extend to four hours per day. For many students, these teachers become lasting role models. Students learn the attitudes and habits of a professional musician, from a professional musician. "I absorbed it, every word, like a sponge. . . . I learned integrity, devotion, and a complete dedication to making music and being an artist."[32]

Sosniak describes the stereotypical master teacher as one who does not tolerate sloppiness or laziness, valuing music above the musician and being short and curt to students. One student describes an impossible taskmaster. "He would just intimidate you out of your mind. He would sit there. . . . You played a concert, you didn't play a lesson. You walked in prepared to play a performance. . . . You would get torn apart for an hour." Studying with this type of teacher requires patience, inner strength, and self-discipline. Students gain the advanced technical and interpretive skills of performance through this instruction, but the psychological impact on self-confidence may produce increased performance anxiety.[33]

Persson conducted a study of teachers at a conservatory to investigate the teaching strategies of master teachers who are experts in performance but have limited background in educational psychology. He found that most teachers used a demanding "right or wrong" teaching style with minimal, if any, chance for student-initiated musical decision-making. Interestingly, students *expected* this type of instruction and were often confused if the teacher did not specify performance guidelines. Instruction took the form of "a series of instructions rather than the meaning of an artistic expression." However, he found that these teachers expected their students somehow to be "imaginative, creative, and independent" through this instruction.[34]

Rezits, a successful survivor of a "get-tough" master teacher, was intrigued with the rationale behind the reverence of these teachers in the profession. It seemed paradoxical that a teacher who can often bring out the best at the advanced stages of musical learning can be "unkind, disagreeable, inflexible, uncompromising, hard-headed, and unbelievably strict." Reflective interviews by artists who had studied with these teachers showed that students believed the teachers created an environment that would force the student to excel farther than expected—a master teacher's definition of "growth." "You went to the lesson knowing you were inferior, and you wanted to get better." Lessons were permeated with the sense of working with a person in a position of power that was intoxicating to the student. Resitz's interviews did reveal some positive attributes of master teachers, including "a vital interest in the student, realizing a means of getting the student to work, and teaching the student to listen and ultimately judge himself effectively."[35]

These research and anecdotal entries extend to college and conservatory training and give a dismaying portrait of music teaching at the advanced level. To counterbalance this negative picture, I will examine excellence in teaching at the master teaching level—specifically working with impressionable teenagers.

The field of music pedagogy recognizes the delicate balance of guiding the technical development of a student through both modeled strategies and metaperceptive decision-making by the student. Berenson discusses the issues of competition repertoire and pressures that can often influence teachers to take the short-cut in molding student performance. She suggests establishing a continuum of challenging performance standards, working as a team, with feedback worded productively for improvement. Master teachers of teenagers must take into account the psychological needs of these students in regard to issues of independence, self-esteem, and acceptance.[36]

Again seeking the opinion of experts in the field, I interviewed three master teachers from the Interlochen Arts Academy, a private specialized high school for talented students in the arts, including music. They jointly believed that the level of performance in talented musicians today has increased to an extent that the choreographed, "dictated" performances of the past will no longer be acceptable. Colleges, conservatories, and judges behind the competition table are looking for high school students who have "something to say" musically. They shared their views on the most important aspects of instruction for talented teenagers who are seeking a career in music:

> I try to set them up with a creative personal process toward music so that when they go to college, they have acquired the necessary tools to solve technical problems on their own and make informed musical decisions. . . . I don't try to produce competition winners per se. It is not that I don't respect the value of competitions, but I feel it is a real trap in our society. I think it is much healthier to take a talented student and try to put them on a track where they will learn to be independent and creative musically. (CC)

> One of the most important things that we have to do is to train them to listen—to be able to hear what they are actually playing, the music that they are making. They must be able to hear the musical idea that they want to have physically realized in performance. If they have that idea and they totally love that idea, they are going to be much happier than if they really want to do what their teacher told them to do. (TL)[37]

The role of a nurturing master teacher is to ensure that the student's growing musical ideas have a chance to be explored, questioned, and critiqued. Students who are allowed to question musical ideas grow through this inquiry. The master teacher for teenage years requires instruction that understands the needs of the teenager, as a *person*, first, then as a blossoming young artist. Instruction develops artistic reasoning and technical proficiency through challenging instructional goals, mutually set by teacher and student. There are too many cases of counseling problems and teenage depression of gifted students in music for it to make sense to revere teaching that will exacerbate these conditions. The goal of musical talent development at the advanced level is:

- To nurture creative interpretation through student-initiated decision-making
- To develop technical intricacy that creates an aural vocabulary of musical sound
- To understand stylistic differences and mold personal interpretations to reflect these styles
- To understand the structure of music, through performance, analysis, theory, and listening
- To develop confidence in performance and effectively portray creative interpretations
- To develop sensitivity and subtlety in the critique of music performed by others and by oneself

Talented Teens and School

Parents of a musically talented student often perform a balancing act in the musical school education of their child. Their love for music makes them staunch supporters of school music education for all students. They seek out opportunities to expand their child's musical education. Rarely does a school performance group provide adequate challenge for a musically talented student. However, this student enjoys the experience of working through music with peers in the school setting, especially enjoying leadership roles that often come with this experience.

By the time this student has reached middle school, the discrepancy between the school performance level and individual performance level widens (unless the school program is outstanding). Parents who seek more challenging performance opportunities through outside resources, such as community youth orchestras, feel obligated to support school music by keeping their child in school performance groups. The child now must allot time to practice consistently for private lessons (middle phase of instruction), practice and rehearse for the challenging community youth group, and maintain practice for school performances. By high school, this student's time is stretched pretty thin, and we have not included growing academic demands.

Musically talented teenagers arrive at high school with a set of highly individualized skills in their field. They have learned how to solve complex musical problems through practice and have attained a work ethic that seeks adequate practice time to increase performance skills. Some of these teenagers may be comfortably managing instruction on several instruments, playing in a variety of school performance classes, as well as academically achieving at an above average or higher level in school work. This sounds like an ideal student, with lots of potential for the full development of talent, possibly extending to a career in music. Adjustment and flexibility of demands put on students at this age will determine the success or failure of this full development.

Students who felt quite "special" in the beginning stages of talent development now find problems with peers who view them as "different." Sloboda and Howe's teenagers faced difficulties of peers making fun of their interest in classical music and their outstanding abilities. When students continue in performing groups in high school, there is bound to be inner frustration when they realize the difference between their performance abilities and those of peers. Being a leader, for a sensitive teenager, may not always be a positive position to hold. The study showed that students who had family support and strong commitment to musical studies were more likely to work through these problems. Students less committed to musical study or with minimal family support often discontinued musical studies because of this ridicule.[38]

Academic excellence takes precedence in high school, with talented students trying to balance their advanced musical studies with school work. An either/or choice between music and academics may ultimately cause these students to discontinue lessons. Students are faced with the decision to give up an activity that has been their constant companion through practice and performance for many years. They have reached rewarding repertoire with a level of abstract reasoning in music that may exceed levels of learning in academics. The void of leaving music at this time is often traumatic for these students. Reasonable adjustments by parents, teachers, and schools can allow talented students to complete musical development to a point of closure upon graduation.

School administrators can meet the distinct needs of talented music students through flexible curricular options and awareness of opportunities beyond school walls.[39] The independent study options discussed earlier in this chapter offer some solutions for differentiating the needs of these talented students. Students can receive academic credit for private study that includes assessment through judged competitions and school procedures. Students can independently take the advanced placement music theory or literature examinations, mentored by their school band/orchestra director or private teacher, if no suitable course exists in the school to prepare for the exam. Some students may choose to look into the International Baccalaureate program in music, a comprehensive advanced curriculum stretching over a number of years.

Opportunities linking gifted programs and area colleges are an excellent way to merge high school and early college credit for these students. Many colleges offer admission for these "special students" in academic areas, usually to meet the needs of students with advanced math, science, or computer skills. These opportunities should also extend to talented music students who seek college level coursework in theory, ear training, private instruction, or composition to differentiate currculum not available in their high schools. Parents can work with gifted coordinators ot guidance counselors to arrange these challenging experiences for their talented teenagers.

Additional opportunities for talented students outside of school include community youth orchestras, chamber groups, choirs, or bands and summer music programs. These more selective groups allow students to share music with peers at comparable talent levels who enjoy intensive work in music. There is no better way for a student to gauge interest in pursuing music as a career than by attending a residential summer music camp, away from home. This intensive experience of music-making, where everyone practices, rehearses, and works toward a finished performance after only a week or two of practice gives them a taste of the real world of the professional musician. There are different levels of summer music camps. Parents of talented students in middle to high school should seek out programs that include rigorous schedules of activities in music, with instruction by supportive master teachers.

Chapter 11 included a brief overview of Governor's School programs in the arts, offered through gifted education programs in a number of states. These programs provide four or five weeks of disciplinary and interdisciplinary work during the summer. They are highly selective, relying on school nomination and auditions. These programs emphasize collaborative creativity across the arts, an experience uniquely different from studio or school offerings. They use gifted strategies that incorporate student-centered learning emphasizing student responsibility and decision-making. Music students have a taste of real-world collaborative creation across the arts, working with their talented peers in dance, theater, and the visual arts.

Major cities that have conservatories or schools of music often have a precollegiate program of Saturday classes and instruction that reach demanding levels for talented students. Probably the most prestigious program internationally is found at Juilliard in New York City. Subtonik interviewed students, faculty members, and alumni from the Pre-College Program there to explore the prototype of "elite level talent development." She discovered that one of the most important components of the program was "providing opportunities for young, gifted musicians to socialize with others who share their same passions and interests."[40]

A student who lives, breathes, and craves music and the arts may be more suited to a high school that is devoted to artistic learning. Chapter 11 included an overview of these schools. There are many specialized schools in the arts, both private and public, that offer advanced level academics and advanced arts instruction. There is a rising number of magnet high schools that offer half-day classes in the arts, with students attending their home schools for academic subjects. These schools are especially helpful for students who may not be able to afford private instruction with a master teachers.

Seeking challenging opportunities for talented musical teenagers requires a bit of research into available options offered by the school, community offerings, independent advanced curricular options, and possible specialized schooling or coursework at colleges or conservatories. The appendix includes list of resources to contact for information about advanced curricula, visual and performing arts schools, summer music camps, Governors' Schools, colleges of music, and conservatories.

Talent Profiles

By high school there is quite a mix of student talent profiles. Some students may function well within the normal school setting, selecting challenging curricular options and community activities to nurture their talents. Others may require specialized training or schooling for full development of their skills. Students who do not fit the mold of performance-oriented talents require a bit of creative curricular management by parents, students, and teachers.

Any serious student who has reached an advanced level of private study will require some adjustment in scheduling to accommodate repertoire and practice needs. Parents, students, and private teachers can discuss the options of practice and repertoire to retain the *quality* of musical work, adjusting the *quantity* of work to alleviate frustration for all involved. Most talented students can easily attend a normal high school, seeking ways to differentiate curriculum within school or through community or college offerings to challenge their specific talents. These students may be headed toward majoring in music in college or combining these advanced skills with an academic area as a "double major" in college.

The career-oriented student who is immersed in the field and studying with a master teacher requires extensive time to accommodate a rigorous practice regimen and performance schedule. This student is a prime candidate for early acceptance into a conservatory, independent study, specialized schooling, or home schooling to provide adequate concentration on musical skill development.

Multi-talented music students may be at an advanced level of instruction on a principal instrument, while playing a second instrument or singing in a school performance group. Their breadth of interests and social interaction in musical activities works beautifully in a healthy music program at the high school level. Their multiple musical capabilities make them likely candidates for majoring in music education at the college level.

Some students enjoy multiple interests in music, with no principal strength in a single area, with talent indicated by a breadth of musical knowledge. These students may compose and arrange and play several instruments in different school performance groups, while taking private lessons with a middle-stage teacher on one instrument. They spend hours creating music and sounds on the computer. Differentiation for these students may include advanced music-computer skills for sequencing and notation plus "real" performance opportunities for arrangements and compositions by school performing groups. Mentorship with professional composers or college coursework can augment school curricular offerings.

The musical listener and historian may perform comfortably in school groups, with talents surfacing through fascination with theory, analysis, and historical ideas connected with music. This student may remain hidden in a performance-oriented curriculum, only revealed if analysis and critique activities are included in music classes. This student could also be readily identified as academically gifted and talented, with a strong interest in musical activities. Independent study options that emphasize in-depth analysis of musical style, structure, and historical-cultural connections will allow these unique talents to grow. This student may seek a musicology major or a double major in music and history.

The student who writes songs and plays an instrument in a rock band but does not take private lessons or participate in the school music program is our musical challenge. These talented students have reached a level of self-taught musical skills that may plateau rather than grow through these years without an interested adult to offer guidance. A band director with keen ears and an open personality may be the key figure in this teenager's musical future. Talent development will require lessons that are informal and friendly, allowing students the freedom to create on their own but providing scaffolding of musical ideas for growth beyond the basics gleaned from recordings. Further differentiation can include outside mentorship with a professional musician in the pop, rock, or jazz field.

Final Steps

There is an old joke about a tourist in New York asking how to get to Carnegie Hall. The wise New Yorker simply says, "Practice." Many of the students who attend prestigious conservatories such as the Curtis Institute of Music in Philadelphia and the Juilliard School of Music in New York will most likely seek that route to Carnegie Hall. Parents, students, and school administrators may not realize exactly what level of repertoire and technical skill is necessary to audition for a conservatory level of study. School administrators and parents also may not realize the minimal importance given to academic records or advanced placement classwork in most conservatory settings. The following chart compares entrance requirements to these two major conservatories. Note the SAT requirements and compare them with normal college entrance requirements. The audition repertoire requirements for piano and violin are given as examples of the level of repertoire for entry to these conservatories. Most auditions normally include technical work such as scales and arpeggios, even if they are not noted here.[41]

Entrance Requirements:

Juilliard School	*Curtis Institute of Music*
• High school diploma or GED	No minimum age, no high school diploma required
• SAT score not required	SAT: 500 verbal (no math score required) TOEFL:550 (for foreign students)
• Audition: primary basis of acceptance	Audition: weight of 85–90 percent in acceptance

Piano:
1. Bach Prelude and Fugue
2. Beethoven sonata–all movements (excluding op. 14, 49, 79)

3. Substantial work by Chopin, Schumann, Brahms, Liszt, or Mendelssohn (etudes, nocturnes, short dances, or comparable pieces are not acceptable)
4. A work by a representative twentieth-century composer

Piano:
1. Bach Prelude and Fugue
2. Beethoven or Mozart sonata—all movements (excluding Beethoven op. 49 and Mozart K.545)

3. Two contrasting works by Chopin

Violin:
1. Fast and slow movement from any concerto in the standard repertoire

Violin:
1. Mozart concerto—all movements

2. Bach—unaccompanied sonata or partita, any movement

2. Bach—unaccompanied sonata or partita, complete

3. Two contrasting brilliant concert pieces

3. Concerto of the standard repertoire—complete

4. One Paganini caprice, Dont op. 35, Wienawski op. 10, or Paganini op. 1

4. Paganini caprice

5. Major and minor scales and arpeggios in three octaves with double stops

I vividly remember sitting in the dean's office of a leading conservatory with my daughter on audition day, discussing the role of academic records for entry to the school. He showed me a pile of file folders about five inches high on his desk. "These are the files of academic records for the students we will be auditioning today. They won't be looked at until after students have been initially selected through auditions."

High school administrators must be aware that outstanding students who have decided to enter a conservatory do not need a great deal of advanced placement coursework, and, in some cases, *don't even need a high school diploma*. Obviously, I am not recommending that musically talented students need not do well in the academics. There is a growing trend to change the microscopic focus of the conservatory, even at Juilliard.

Many conservatories or colleges of music offer lessons and classes for advanced musical instruction for precollege students, accepting students of all ages, depending on their musical abilities. Gary Graffman was the youngest student ever to be accepted at the Curtis Institute of Music, as a seven-year-old piano prodigy. His commitment and connection to the conservatory continues, currently serving as director of the Curtis Institute.

As the musically talented student heads off to college, we can look back at a comprehensive team effort in the development of talent. The parents have provided a lasting support system, often running interference to allow their child ample opportunities to enjoy learning through music. Teachers have been a guiding force in this development, with their personalities and musical interpretive ideas guiding the student. Musical peers have shared a love for music that may have inspired this student to continue studies through high school, when increasing demands begin to pull in multiple directions.

Now comes an adult journey through music, in the intense atmosphere of a conservatory or the exploring atmosphere of a university or college. So many students arrive at college with no clue of interests, goals, or future career aims. Music students are at an advantage, arriving at this beginning stage of adulthood with skills well honed in a specialized field they love. It doesn't really matter if this student completes a college education as a performer, music major, or heads for law school. Music will be a vital part of the future, because the "spark" that shone in the eyes of a toddler now has produced a musician.

Questions for Discussion:

1. The intermediate stage of development emphasizes effective practice habits. What are some tools and strategies teachers and parents can provide that can assist in this development?
2. What are the positive and negative aspects of competition, from your personal experience in music or in other areas? Do you agree that competition does not produce superior performance? Why or why not?
3. Develop a personalized differentiation map in content, process, and product/performance, resulting in a lesson plan, unit, or studio project reflecting the "stretched" curricular options presented in this chapter.
4. Describe how the five-step process of artistic problem-solving presented in this chapter can be used to solve a specific musical problem.
5. Why do you believe the music profession reveres the master teacher, even though teaching approaches are didactic and stress negative criticism?

FINAL REFLECTIONS

When you start on a long journey, trees are trees, water is water,
and mountains are mountains. After you have gone some distance,
trees are no longer trees, water no longer water, mountains no longer
mountains. But after you have traveled a great distance, trees are
once again trees, water is once again water, mountains are once
again mountains.

Zen saying

As we reach the end of our journey in search of the "spark," initial perspectives may have been stretched or transformed, resulting in a new level of understanding of the term, musical talent.[1]

During the course of writing this book, I found myself acutely aware of the musical behavior of friends, students, and performers. What do I see and hear that describes the "spark"? The process of exploring the enigma of musical talent allowed me to reflect on past aesthetic musical experiences, still fresh in my memory. Hopefully, as you paused between chapters of this book, you found your ears focusing on surrounding sounds and your mind reflecting on past musical experiences as well. There are still unanswered questions to ponder and research to pursue, but the basics of musical talent remain constant. The spark of talent is experienced when someone expresses himself or herself through music, making a personal aesthetic statement to others.

We have learned that capacities underlying this personal statement can be measured objectively and that the process of developing this interpretation requires metaperceptive reasoning. Students who show potential talent are motivated to learn, eager to hurdle over the next musical challenge. They may have different technical levels, training, and music aptitude scores, but their desire to express themselves through music is readily observable.

Can it really be this simple? In looking back at the hundreds of children, teenagers, and adults I have worked with in my studio and classrooms, I visualize a collage of musical capabilities, each unique in its own way. I remember the sensitive, creative seven-year-old who sought out independent ideas from the first lesson, developing into a highly individual composer and musician as an adult. There was the young boy who arrived at the audition/interview with the *Moonlight* Sonata under his tiny fingers, self-taught, with nuances closely matching the recording he had used as a "teacher." He reached his goal of playing the *Emperor* Concerto as a teenager, still craving more Beethoven. I remember the student who naturally took to the instrument, technically and musically, boggling the mind at how quickly a child can learn and captivating audiences with this musical ease. There is always the quiet student who uses music as a unique emotional outlet, safely expressing emotions through the instrument—an intimate escape from surrounding problems. The student whose iridescent personality craves performance, speed, and technical obstacles savors the experience of sharing this energetic flamboyance with others. These are special students who spoke to me through their musical talents.

The students I have encountered through the MUSICLINK program provide additional portraits of potential. I have seen students who save their allowance to buy a tiny keyboard so they can practice at home as well as at school. One student arrives with music in hand to play for a senior citizen's home each week, with the appreciative audience keeping time with gestures and clapping as she "practices." An audition committee may not see this commitment and desire to communicate; yet these students show potential talent that will surely develop through individualized instruction. Teachers in our schools should keep a focused eye and ear out for these future musicians.

The purpose of this book has been to share information concerning musical talent from multiple sources and specialized fields, described in terms understandable to parents, students, teachers, and musicians. The notes and bibliography will assist persons seeking more scientific inquiry about the topic. There is an impressive number of studies concerning musical perception and abilities that analyze what goes on "inside" when someone is engaged in musical tasks. The examples cited in this book offer some possibilities to explore.

Gnawing questions remain. Exactly what role should creativity play in the recognition of musical talent? Is there a way to clarify the "creativity" inherent in the creative interpretation of performance? How can we broaden our views to recognize the potential of the creative listener and the self-trained musician? Will we ever be able to expand the traditional view of performance as the key element in musical talent?

In chapter 14, I described the development of talent with a teenager in the throes of making future decisions concerning college, music, and a career. The final stage of development showed the constriction of instruction at the advanced level, with some master teachers disallowing personal creative input in lessons. Should this be revered as essential to advanced study? Or are we ready to acknowledge the importance of seeking teaching approaches that encourage students to have "something to say" through personally creative interpretations?

Should we disregard the breadth of talent discussed throughout this book and align with traditional conservatory perspectives? I argue that the reverse is in order. There are a growing number of articles that call for a change of teaching approaches in the field of musical performance and pedagogy. Music education is broadening perspectives beyond performance through the *National Standards for Arts Education*. Even Juilliard is recognizing the importance of developing potential talent in new populations of students through its MAP program. The climate is ripe for a broader view of potential talent and creative approaches to its development. I envision a healthier, cooperative student-teacher approach in college and conservatory instruction within the next decade.

The Sparkler Experiences and Activities in this book were designed to bring the reader into the experience of music-making and perception. Hopefully you have used these experiences personally, or with students, reflecting on the process of musical knowing. If these experiences helped you realize what *metaperception* means in musical functioning, they have done their job. As you close the book, please venture further in your own personal quest to seek out potential talent in your home, studio, and school. Feel free to use ideas and activities in chapter 10 as well as the identification framework in the appendix to assist in this quest. I guarantee that you will enjoy the experience of seeking out that spark. It is easy to recognize. Simply look into the eyes of the next eager child who wants to share music with you.

Appendix

MUSIC APTITUDE TESTS

Author(s)/Dates	Grade/Age	Title/Publisher	Contents	Time to administer	Reliability	Validity
C. Seashore, D. Lewis, J. Saetveit 1919–60	Age 10–adult	*Seashore Measures of Musical Talents* New York: Psychological Corporation	*Discrimination:* pitch, time, timbre, dynamics *Memory:* tone, rhythm *Interpretation:* consonance preference	1 hour	pitch: .82–.84 loudness: .64–.69 rhythm: .64–.69 time: .63–.72 timbre: .55–.68 tonal memory: .81–.84	Questionable, except for pitch, rhythm, and tonal memory
J. Kwalwasser, P. Dykema 1931	Age 10–adult	*Kwalwasser-Dykema Music Tests* New York: Carl Fischer	*Discrimination:* pitch, time, timbre, dynamics *Memory:* tone, rhythm *Interpretation:* tonal movement, melodic taste *Achievement:* tonal and rhythmic notation	1 hour	no information in test manual	Doubtful, except for discriminating most musical from least musical of a group
H.D. Wing 1939–61	Age 8–adult	*Standardized tests of Musical Intelligence* Sheffield, England: City of Sheffield Training College	*Memory:* tonal, pitch, chord *Interpretation:* rhythmic, harmonic, dynamic, phrasing preferences	1 hour	Whole test .91 tests 1–3, .89 tests 4–7, .84	Good, with teachers' ratings .64 to .90
E.T. Gaston 1957	Age 10–adult	*Test of Musicality* Lawrence, Kan.: Odell's Instrumental Service	*Memory:* musical, chord *Interpretation:* tonal movement *Achievement:* tonal and rhythmic notation	40 min.	grades 4–6, 7–9: .88 grades 10–12: .90 grade 12: .84	Association between teachers' ratings and scores significant at .05 level for grades 10–12, 4–12

A. Bentley 1966	Age 7–14	*Musical Abilities in Children and Its Measurement* London, UK: Harrap	*Discrimination:* pitch *Memory:* tonal, rhythm, chord	20 min.	pitch: .74 tonal memory: .53 chord analysis: .71 rhythmic memory: .57 total: .84.	Significant associations between test scores and teachers' estimates of musical ability
E. Gordon 1965	Grades 4–12	*Musical Aptitude Profile* Chicago: GIA	*Memory:* melodic, harmonic, tempo, meter imagery *Interpretation:* phrasing, tonal/rhythmic balance, style preferences	Each section takes 20 min. 2 hours 50 min. total	tonal imagery: .80–.92 rhythm imagery: .82–.91 sensitivity: .84–.90 composite: .90–.96.	Compared with achievement test: .73 composite score
E. Gordon 1979	Grades K–3	*Primary Measures of Music Audiation* Chicago: GIA	*Discrimination:* tonal, rhythmic	12 min. each test 24 min. total	tonal: .85–.89 rhythm: .72–.76 composite: .90–.92	Compared with instrumental achievement ratings: .73 composite score
E. Gordon 1982	Grades 1–4	*Intermediate Measures of Music Audiation* Chicago: GIA	*Discrimination:* tonal, rhythmic	12 min. each test 24 min. total	tonal: .72–.76 rhythm: .70–.72 composite: .80–.81	Compared with instrumental achievement ratings: .67–.70
E. Gordon 1989	Grade 9–adult	*Advanced Measures of Music Audiation* Chicago: GIA	*Discrimination:* tonal, rhythmic	20 min.	toral: .80–.86 rhythm: .80–.87 composite: .81–.89	Predictive validity studies available from publisher

Resources for Talent Development

The following references may be helpful in guiding parents, teachers, and students in opportunities for talented music students:

School Information:

Music Educators National Conference (MENC)
1806 Robert Fulton Dr.
Reston, VA 22091
800-336-3768
  • Information regarding school music programs, National Standards for the Arts, music advocacy

Donald Waldrip
Director of Magnet Schools of America
P.O. Box 8152
The Woodlands, TX 77387
281-296-9813
  • Information regarding magnet school locations and offerings

International NETWORK of Performing and Visual Arts Schools
5505 Connecticut Ave., NW #280
Washington, DC 20015
  • Pertinent information describing over 400 specialized arts schools

Differentiated Curricular Offerings in Music:

The Advanced Placement Program
The College Board
CNN6670
Princeton, NJ 08541-6670
  • Advanced placement tests available in music listening and literature and music theory

International Baccalaureate
200 Madison Ave.
Suite 2007
New York, NY 10016
  • Comprehensive four-year program in music

Music Teacher Information:

Music Teachers National Association
The Carew Tower, Suite 505
441 Vine St.
Cincinnati, OH 45202-2814
www.mtna.org

- Free directory of nationally certified teachers available on request

American String Teacher Association (ASTA)
1806 Robert Fulton Dr.
Reston, VA 22091
703-476-1316
www.astaweb.com
- Will provide the name of state presidents who can locate a teacher in your community

National Association of Teachers of Singing (NATS)
2800 North University Boulevard
Jacksonville, FL 32211
904-744-9022
www.nats.org
- Voice training does not normally begin until middle school. This organization can provide you with a list of teachers by state or by city.

National Association for Music Therapy (NAMT)
8455 Colesville Rd., Suite 1000
Silver Springs, MD 20910
301-589-3300
- For children with special needs. This organization can provide a list of music therapists in your area and a general information packet.

National Guild of Community Schools of the Arts (NGCSA)
Lolita Mayada, Director
Box 8018
Englewood, NJ 07631
201-871-3337
www.natguild.org
- Provides a list of accredited community music schools and their course offerings.

College Information:

Carole J. Everett and Muriel Topaz, *Guide to Performing Arts Programs and Profiles of over 600 Colleges, High Schools, and Summer Programs* (New York: Random House, 1998)
- reference for college and conservatories offering arts major, with audition advice.

Nancy Uscher, *Schirmer Guide to Schools of Music and Conservatories throughout the World* (New York: Schirmer Books, 1988)
- References for schools of music, conservatories, and universities, including those with preparatory divisions.

Summer Programs:

American Music Teacher (AMT)
Music Teachers National Association
The Carew Tower, Suite 505
441 Vine St.
Cincinnati, OH 45202-2814

- Ask for a copy of the issue that includes a listing of summer music programs and camps offered across the country.

National Conference on Governors' Schools
www-pgss.mcs.cmu.edu/MCoGS

- Information regarding Governor's School locations and offerings, summer programs as well as residential schools

Rating Scales from the Research Survey Form

Assessment of Musical Performance: The list below represents common criteria used within auditions in specialized music programs. If your audition process includes criteria not listed please fill it in at the bottom of the page.

Please rank each requirement from 1–5 according to its usefullness in assessing performance for the purposes of your program.

5	4	3	2	1	X
Absolutely essential	Important	Helpful	Not necessary	Of no Importance	Unfamiliar term

_____ Rhythmic accuracy   _____ Poised stage presence

_____ Pitch/note accuracy   _____ Originality

_____ Appropriate tempo   _____ Confident memory

_____ Steady rhythmic pulse   _____ Technical fluency

_____ Sensitivity to mood   _____ Detailed articulation/bowing

_____ Creativity in interpretation   _____ Stylistic awareness

_____ Dynamic contrasts   _____ Tonal color

Other criteria: _____

Assessment of Musical Potential: The list below contains characteristics used within checklists and rating scales in assessing **potential** talent in music. Again rate these characteristics in the same manner as in the performance listing and add suggestions:

5	4	3	2	1	X
Absolutely essential	Important	Helpful	Not necessary	Of no Importance	Unfamiliar term

_____ shows sustained interest in musical activities

_____ is highly creative

_____ shows commitment in arts area

_____ can perceive fine differences in musical tone (pitch, loudness, timbre)

_____ responds discriminately to rhythm, melody, harmony

_____ shows confidence in performing

_____ Can express emotions through sound or music

_____ Moves well to rhythm & music

_____ is self critical: sets high standards

_____ evokes emotional responses from audience

_____ can sing in tune well

_____ can remember melodies and reproduce them accurately

_____ Can identify a variety of sounds heard at a given moment

_____ Has a high degree of tonal memory

_____ is self-disciplined

_____ shows sensitivity to aesthetic elements of music-mood, style

_____ is gifted in academic areas

Other suggestions: _____

FIGURE APP. 1. Rating scales from the research survey form.

Persons Interviewed in the Research Study

The following individuals were interviewed in the research study in chapter 9. Their initials in parentheses are used in the text to identify sources of quotations from interview transcripts.

From the field of research:

Lyle Davidson: Does research in cognitive developmental psychology through Project Zero, Harvard Graduate School of Education; was an integral part of Arts PROPEL and Project Spectrum; is on the theory faculty of New England Conservatory.

Edwin Gordon: Does research in music aptitude; is distinguished music psychologist and psychometrician who has guided research in the area of music aptitude for over thirty years; is the author of many music aptitude and achievement measures; is Professor Emeritus of Temple University.

Peter Webster: Does research in creative thinking in music and music education; is author of a measure for creative thinking and text on music technology; is Professor of Music Education at Northwestern University.

From the field of musical performance:

Yvonne Caruthers (group): Cellist in the National Symphony Orchestra; is the mother of three musically talented children.

William Haroutounian (group): Violinist in the National Symphony Orchestra; was a child prodigy and is the father of a talented singer and musician.

Martha Smith (group): Independent music teacher in Arlington, Virginia; at time of interview was working toward a Master of Music degree in piano pedagogy from Catholic University.

Scott McBride Smith: Director of the International Institute for Young Musicians; is an independent music teacher of outstanding students and an editor of *Keyboard Companion.*

Marienne Uszler: Editor of *Piano and Keyboard;* was formerly on the piano pedagogy faculty department of the University of Southern California, Los Angelas, CA; is author of texts on piano teaching and musical development.

From the field of education (gifted and music):

Larry Bohnert (group): Supervisor of Music and Fine Arts for Arlington County, Virginia, Public Schools; is a bassist in a jazz combo.

Sandra Phaup: Director of Gifted/Fine Arts for Arlington County, Virginia, Public Schools; is also a visual artist.

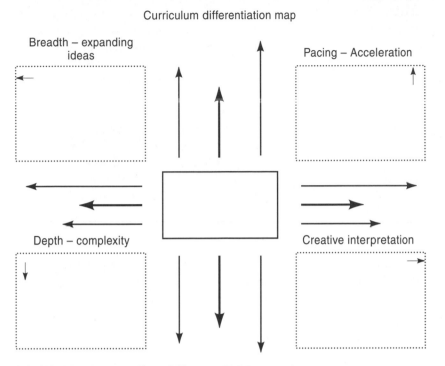

FIGURE APP. 2. Curriculum differentiation map.

Laura Sokeld: Elementary general music teacher in Arlington County, Virginia, Public Schools.

Theresa Bailey: Music associate specialist, Virginia State Department of Education.

Janie Craig: Gifted education specialist, Virginia State Department of Education; is director of the Virginia Governor's School for the Arts.

David Thurmond: Director of the Kentucky Governor's School of the Arts.

Framework for the Identification of Musical Talent

The *Framework for the Identification of Musical Talent* is the outgrowth of my research quest to understand and describe the "spark" of talent that emanates from musical behavior and performance, from toddler to concert artist. There is emerging interest in multiple talents and intelligences in the field of education. Artistic domains are manifest in these intelligences. Arts educators are collaborating to establish national standards and assessment procedures in the areas of music, dance, theater, and visual arts. This inter-est in intelligences that include musical intelligence and in music assessment necessitates the development of instruments and procedures to effectively identify students with potential musical talent. The *Framework* contains criteria and procedural guidelines for the assessment of potential musical talent that can serve as a research-based framework for the development of instruments for talent identification in music.

The framework is based on a research study conducted at the University of Virginia, working with data from the National Research Center on the Gifted and Talented, specialized arts programs and schools, and professional gifted/arts and music organizations. The study sought to develop an identi-fication framework that could be used comfortably in planning sessions by groups of specialists across the gifted and arts fields. The criteria in the frame-work, therefore, must contain understandable terminology across these fields and encompass attributes recognized as indicators of talent by experts in music and gifted/arts areas. Recommended procedures in this framework must effectively highlight these talent criteria and be pragmatically feasible across a variety of educational settings and program purposes.

Background Analysis and Literature Review

A background content analysis of existing identification instruments and procedures provided the starting, status quo position for the study. Analysis began with data pertaining to gifted identification sent to the National Re-search Center on the Gifted and Talented at the University of Virginia. Of over 1,200 folders of identification procedures at the research center, less than 15 included specific procedures for musical talent identification. This data was augmented by mailings to music and gifted/arts organizations, provid-ing analysis of a total of 92 documents, sent from 48 locations.

The literature across music and gifted fields recommends a multistaged and multifaceted procedure for the identification of musically talented students. This identification process includes initial collection of nomination data from a variety of sources, possible testing for music aptitude, and the observation and assessment of musical performance.

The identification of musical talent, fundamentally, requires the assess-ment of musical performance. To encourage the recognition of potential musical talent, the music/gifted literature recommends musical performance assessment that expands beyond demonstrated performance in an audition setting. In the framework, the concept of musical performance is expanded to one of *behavior/performance,* which includes listening, aesthetic reaction to music, and creative improvisation.

Pertinent criteria of potential musical talent evolved from the analysis of instruments and review of the literature across the fields of music psychology, music education, and gifted education. The different perspectives of musical talent used as criteria in the study fell into the basic categories of *musical awareness and discrimination, creative interpretation,* the *dynamic of performance,* and *commitment and self-motivation.*

Method

The study began with a review of the literature and content analysis of a sample of existing identification instruments and procedures used in gifted programs and in specialized arts programs or schools across the country. A survey form was developed from this review and analysis that contained rating scales of categorized characteristics of potential musical talent, criteria of musical performance, and current music performance assessment procedures. The survey was distributed to a sample of music educators, private studio teachers, gifted/arts specialists, performing arts school specialists, and professional musicians representing 30 states. The results of the survey were statistically analyzed and summarized, establishing a list of behavioral characteristics, a list of performance criteria, and recommended procedures found to be most effective for the identification of potential talent by the survey population.

Qualitative inquiry gathered recommendations from experts, administrators, and teachers across the music and gifted fields for a practical gifted identification procedure that would assess potential musical talent in student behavior/performance. Interviews with experts in the fields of music, music psychology, music research, and gifted education afforded different perspectives of potential talent assessment. A group interview with teachers and administrators that represented a purposeful sample population of the survey contributed information regarding pragmatic implementation of identification procedures in a real-world school setting.

Findings

Identification Procedures

The most prevalent form of initial identification of musically talented students is by teacher nomination, used in 54 percent of locations in the background analysis and in 50 percent of the survey locations. Survey and interview respondents recommended nominations by multiple sources, including the private music instructor (45 percent) and other sources in the home and community. Survey locations show minimal use of structured rating scales and checklists in this nomination (9–13 percent), in comparison to the locations in the background analysis (33 percent).

There is minimal use of testing in the identification process (9 percent), with specific music aptitude testing found in 9 percent (survey) to 16 percent (analysis) of the locations. All but one location used music aptitude tests measuring normal rather than high music aptitude. Both analysis and survey findings show evidence of the misuse of standardized achievement, IQ, and general creativity testing for musical talent identification. Interview respondents stressed that identification should not be based solely on music aptitude or other test scores but should include observation of students in the process of music-making.

The audition of individualized performance is currently the most prevalent procedure used for musical talent identification (survey—63 percent; analysis—62 percent). Survey respondents recommended student interviews (63 percent) accompanying these auditions. Experts and teachers suggested a basic change to this process, unanimously recommending that students should *not* be placed in an individualized audition setting. They recommended periodic observation of students working in small groups within a classroom.

All of the interview respondents believed assessment should recognize potential talent beyond musical performance. Student activities should include performing, experiences with creating through music, listening, and interpretive responding to music. Survey results did not reflect this interest in creative activities. The checklist of performance assessment activities showed that tasks that elicit creative and aesthetic musical behavior/performance were used in less than 25 percent of the respondents' locations and were marked as inadequate for assessment by 11 percent–20 percent of the respondents. The activities circled as inadequate for talent assessment by survey respondents included *creating new sounds, improvising, describing mood, style, and color from listening,* and *responding creatively to listening.*

Interview respondents recommended multiple observations over a period of time to allow assessment of the creative/interpretive process on improving work. Observers in the identification process should receive training in the specific techniques of observing musical talent. Ideally, observation should include a team of at least three persons, with at least one observer being a music specialist, musician, or private studio teacher. If general classroom teachers are included in this observation, they will require prior training in the recognition of musical talent.

Identification Criteria—Survey Results

The Assessment of Musical Potential Scale rated behavioral characteristics of potential musical talent for their usefulness in identification on a five-point scale (table 9.1). The survey sample of respondents viewed the characteristics of *sustained interest in music* (4.35), *self-discipline* (4.26), and *perceptual discrimination of rhythm and tone* (4.23, 4.17) as "important (4.00) to absolutely essential *(5.00)*" indicators of musical talent. The characteristic of *giftedness in academic areas*, received the lowest rating (2.92) in the musical potential scale, indicated as "not necessary (2.00)" to "helpful (3.00)" in usefulness.

In the Assessment of Musical Performance Scale (table 9.2), performance criteria rated as "important to absolutely essential" by the survey sample include *pitch/note and rhythmic accuracy* (4.73, 4.65), *steady rhythmic pulse* (4.41), *dynamic contrasts* (4.02), and *technical fluency* (4.02). *Originality* received the lowest rating, with a group mean of 3.04.

A Framework for the Identification of Musical Talent

Findings from the background content analysis, literature review, survey, and interviews were summarized and synthesized to create the following framework for musical talent identification. My goal in developing this framework was to present a clear-cut, understandable outline for use as a starting point in discussions by musicians, educators, and gifted specialists, meeting together to begin their own personal quest—seeking ways to unveil the "spark" of talent in the children in their own classrooms and studios.

Recommended Procedures and Criteria

Rationale for the Identification of Musical Talent

Current educational documents in the field of gifted education and music education recognize the need to identify and provide programming for students who are musically gifted and talented. The U.S. Department of Education established a new definition of students with outstanding talent in 1993 that emphasizes the need to include students in the arts in this identification. The rising interest in Howard Gardner's multiple intelligence theory in education provides the impetus to develop sound identification procedures to recognize outstanding talent in the specific domain of music intelligence.

Identification Procedures

Initial identification: Musical talent identification procedures should reflect the recognition and assessment of potential as well as demonstrated musical talent. This identification should include musical talents beyond overt performance and recognize different types of musical performance styles or genre. The process should include data from sources in the school, home, and community. Biographical information from the parent and student is important to include in musical talent identification, because musical activities may readily take place outside the school setting.

- *Nomination from multiple sources*
  classroom teacher
  school music teacher
  school guidance counselor
  parent
  peer
  student
  private studio music teacher
  church/synagogue choir directors
  scout leaders and other community sources
- *Biographical information from parent and student*
- *Recognition of multiple musical performance styles or genre*
  classical
  jazz, pop, rock
  folk, ethnic
- *Consideration of multiple musical talent areas*
  performance
  improvisatory styles
  composition
  critiquing
  interpretive listening

Testing: Effective identification requires assessment of the sensory capacities of musical aptitude or music intelligence. This assessment requires the observation of students engaged in activities requiring perceptive listening or listening combined with musical performance. Musical *behavior/performance* describes the breadth of musical abilities that include performance, listening, aesthetic reaction to music, and creative musical work.

The administration of standardized music aptitude tests may also be used for this assessment. Music aptitude test scores should not be used as the sole determination of musical talent. However, these tests are useful in uncovering students who may have potential musical talent but do not demonstrate this talent in performance. The level of music aptitude testing should reflect measurement of high music aptitude for the age of the students involved in the identification process. Several measures for creative thinking in music, still in the developmental stages, are listed as measures to consider in identification procedures.

Avoid the use of standardized testing of intelligence, achievement, or general creativity as a screening procedure for musical talent.

- *Assessment of musical activities involving perceptive listening*
- *Assessment of musical activities involving perceptive listening and performance*
- *Optional administration of standardized music aptitude tests* refer to the list of published music aptitude tests on page 290.
- *Optional administration of music creativity tests* *Measures of creativity in Sound and Music* (Wang, 1985) *Measures of Creative Thinking in Music* (Webster, 1989)

Observation and assessment of musical behavior/performance: Identification should include observation of students in the process of music-making in a music or general classroom. Observation should be done over a period of time to view developing musical work. Observation by a team of two or three observers is recommended, including at least one music specialist, musician, or private studio teacher. All persons involved in observation should receive training in techniques of identifying potential musical talent in student behavior/performance. Observers from music fields should be acquainted with the purpose and process of talent identification.

The assessment of musical behavior/performance should seek students with potential as well as demonstrated talent in musical performance. Evidence should be sought of a student's creative, expressive involvement in the music. It should be recognized that physical and technical facility in musical performance requires prior training. The performance setting should be comfortable for the student so as to encourage a musical performance indicative of the student's abilities. Identification procedures should include observation and assessment of musical activities outside of performance, such as interpretive response to listening, and creative work in music.

The assessment instrument should be balanced in format, including specific performance criteria and space for a written critique. Some type of quantified component may be built into the assessment instrument if this facilitates selection.

- *Observers:*
  require training in techniques of observing potential musical talent
  should understand the purpose and process of talent identification
  observe in a natural classroom setting
  observe more than once, assessing improvement of musical work
  include music specialists, musicians, or private studio teachers
  include general classroom teachers, trained in observing musical talent
- *Observation of students:*
  performing in small groups (five to ten)

involved in tasks involving musical decision-making by students
reworking and refining musical performance
engaged in listening activities
working creatively through music
may include the use of videotaped musical activities
- *Assessment of musical behavior/performance:*
seeks recognition of potential as well as demonstrated musical talent
recognizes creative, expressive involvement in music
recognizes that physical or technical ability in music depends on prior training
includes assessment of potential talent in areas outside of performance
is not based solely on individualized performance and technical ability
uses a balanced assessment instrument that includes specific criteria and wholistic written critique.

Identification Criteria

The identification of musically gifted and talented students requires recognition and assessment of the perceptive sensory capacities of music aptitude or musical intelligence as well as the behavioral characteristics observable in musical behavior/performance. There are four categories of criteria indicative of musical talent:

- Musical awareness and discrimination
  perceptual awareness of sound
  rhythmic sense
  sense of pitch
- Creative interpretation
- Dynamic of performance
- Commitment and self-motivation

The framework includes specific procedures to observe or assess these criteria, which are based on recommendations from experts, specialists, musicians, and teachers across the music and gifted fields. A number of suggested activities from these sources are included that will highlight these criteria in student behavior/performance.

Musical Awareness and Discrimination

This criterion refers to the ability to listen carefully and hear or sense differences in musical components. These inherent capacities are described as music aptitude by music psychologists and music intelligence by educational and cognitive psychologists. The psychometric measurement of these capacities can be done through the administration of a music aptitude test. These capacities can also be assessed through activities that focus on aural perception, rhythmic movement, and tonal memory of melodies or songs. Music aptitude/music intelligence consists of three basic sensory components—the perceptual awareness of sound, a rhythmic sense, and a sense of pitch.

Perceptual awareness of sound: The musically gifted and talented student is keenly aware of sounds, both musical and environmental. This student will listen with focused concentration, showing an inward sensing of these sounds. This inner sensing describes the tonal or rhythmic memory of sounds, which may be repeated through singing or performing. This inner sensing is also at work when a student is internally manipulating musical ideas in interpretive decision-making through music.

The musically gifted and talented student is aware of slight differences in melodies, rhythms, tempo (speed), and tonal qualities of sounds. This student can isolate and identify individual sounds in a complex musical or sound context. Look for a student who "tunes in" when listening.

The student who is perceptually aware of sound:
- is keenly aware of sounds
- listens with focused concentration
- can sense sound inwardly and remember it
- can hear slight differences in sounds, melodies, rhythms
- can isolate and identify individual sounds or musical ideas in a complex musical or sound context

Rhythmic sense: The musically gifted and talented student instinctively responds to rhythm. This response is manifest in a sensing of the steady beat of the rhythm as well as a flowing sense of the rhythmic pulse. This student can maintain a steady pulse when performing and can repeat and creatively extend rhythmic ideas. This student will recognize and react to slight changes in the tempo (speed) and meter (sense of two-, three-, four-beat patterns) of the music. This internal rhythmic sense allows this student to remember rhythms and discriminate subtle differences in rhythms heard. Look for a student who instinctively "feels" a rhythmic pulse.

The student with a fine rhythmic sense:
- physically responds to rhythm in a fluid manner
- can feel and maintain a steady pulse in performance
- can internally discriminate differences in rhythms
- recognizes and adjusts to slight changes in tempo or meter
- can repeat and creatively extend rhythmic ideas

Sense of pitch: The musically gifted and talented student hears pitches moving up or down in melodies and can remember this melodic shape. The student can repeat these melodies and creatively extend them. If given the opportunity to explore an instrument, this student can pick out a tune "by ear," transferring the inner sense of pitch onto an instrument. The ability to match pitches and sing in tune is helpful to consider in identification but should not be used as an excluding factor of this talent capacity. Look for a student who enjoys fooling around with tunes.

The student who has a fine sense of pitch:
- Can internally discriminate differences in pitch
- Can remember melodies and repeat them
- Can repeat and creatively extend melodic ideas
- Can pick out tunes on an available instrument

Recommended procedures for the identification of music aptitude/music intelligence:
- Administration of a standardized music aptitude test
- Observation of students involved in perceptive listening tasks
- Observation of students involved in listening and performance activities.

Suggested activities:
- Listening to musical selections that have complexity of sounds or form
- Listening for subtle environmental sounds
- Listening for specific musical elements in compositions
- Listening for specific musical qualities in peer performance
- Listening for specific musical qualities in student's own performance
- Discovering the harmonies that match songs on an autoharp, guitar, and so on
- Echo-clapping, chanting, singing, body percussion (tap legs, stamp, snap)
- Call-and-response clapping or body percussion with creative extensions
- Call-and-response singing or chanting with creative extensions
- Combined singing and body percussion
- Use of Orff or percussion instruments in improvisation, ostinato (short repeated pattern throughout a song)

Creative Interpretation

The musically gifted and talented student creatively interprets through music, communicating a uniquely personal musical performance or product. This creative interpretation may be a spontaneous manipulation of sounds, a carefully refined performance, or a musical composition. It may also be evident in an insightful critique of a musical performance or an interpretive impression in direct response to listening.

The interpretive process requires internal musical decision-making. The gifted and talented student can sense sound inwardly and manipulate these sounds through a perceptual/cognitive process. Each interpretive decision combines personal expression and sound-sensing. The framework describes this inner perceptive/cognitive manipulation as *metaperception*—the artistic parallel to metacognition, recognized in cognitive thinking skills. The musically gifted and talented student enjoys extending, manipulating, and experimenting with sounds. This student is eager to express himself or herself through music and shows a personal involvement in the music when performing. There is an obvious sensing/thinking process at work when engaged in practice or refining musical work. This student is aesthetically sensitive to the mood of music in listening as well as in performance. This student enjoys revising and reworking ideas and shows insight in self-assessment of work as well as the critiquing of the musical performance of others. Look for a student who enjoys expressing personal ideas through the manipulation of sounds.

The student who creatively interprets:
- Enjoys extending, manipulating, and experimenting with sound
- Spontaneously sings and moves to music
- Is sensitive to the mood of music heard and performed
- Is eager to express ideas through music
- Enjoys shaping and refining musical ideas
- Works metaperceptively in revising musical work
- Shows a sense of personal involvement in performance

Recommended procedures for the identification of creative interpretation:
- Observation of students working creatively through music (improvisation, call-and-response extensions, composition, etc.)
- Observation of students engaged in creative decision-making in musical tasks
- Observation of students practicing and revising musical work
- Assessment of student ability to critique musical selections, the performance of others, and self
- Assessment of verbal, written, or artistic responses to listening (seeking evidence of interpretive response to music rather than talents in written and artistic work)

Suggested activities:
- Call and response of melodies and rhythms with creative extension
- Picking out a tune on an available instrument
- Making up songs, compositions (shows evidence of revision and memory but does not require notation)
- Developing a musical performance through metaperceptive practice (Practice shows evidence of creative decision-making toward improvement)

- Creative body percussion or Orff improvisation as an introduction or between sections of songs
- Creating melodies on a MIDI computer program
- Creating melodies on an electronic keyboard with sequenced background sounds
- Sequencing sounds into an electronic keyboard, synthesizer, or computer
- Mapping ideas on paper that describe listening
- Reflecting on performance of others or self through written and verbal critiques
- Writing interpretive ideas about musical experiences or describing musical ideas in journals
- Working on problem-finding and -solving projects through music

Dynamic of Performance

The identification of musically gifted and talented students will, understandably, include the assessment of musical performance. The framework extends the concept of performance to one of behavior/performance to ensure assessment of the full breadth of musical activities, including listening, creative response to listening, and creative improvisation.

Musical performance is a combined process and product because it occurs over time. The performance process/product creates a dynamic between the performer and the audience. The performer communicates an interpretation through performance to the listener. The listener shares this interpretive experience. The mutual aesthetic experience of listener and performer creates the dynamic of performance. This dynamic is significant in identification procedures because it explains the subjectivity of musical performance assessment by observers.

The musically gifted and talented student shows a natural, physical ease in movement, singing, and performing on an instrument. The student communicates a personal interpretation to the audience by showing evidence of sensing sounds and decision-making (metaperception) in performance. The process/product shows evidence of student awareness of sound, sense of rhythm and pitch, and emotional involvement in the music. In essence, the student communicates the criteria of musical talent to the listener through performance.

The musically gifted and talented student also shows evidence of keen listening skills. The student can hear musical intricacies and interpret ideas in response to music in personal ways that shows an ability to listen in depth. Look for a student who captures your attention when performing or describing interpretive musical ideas.

The student who shows potential talent through musical behavior/performance:
- Shows a natural, physical ease in movement, or performance

- Is eager to express emotion through performance or interpretive response to music
- Shows evidence of listening and shaping interpretive ideas while performing
- Communicates a personal involvement in the music to the listener
- Communicates interpretive sensitivity in performance and in response to music
- Performs with a fluid sense of rhythmic pulse
- Seeks to improve physical performance capabilities

The assessment of musical performance recognizes the performance process/ product as well as the behavior of the student in the process of performance.

The musical performance process/product:
- Displays natural ease in performance
- Shows understanding of accuracy in notes and rhythm
- Projects interpretive elements of performance indicative of the age of the student (dynamics, phrasing, tonal colors, articulation, etc.)
- Communicates a sense of personal involvement in music

Recommended procedures for the identification of potential talent in musical behavior/performance:
- Observation of students practicing and revising musical work
- Observation of students rehearsing
- Observation of students in creative performance (improvisation)
- Videotaped observation of students practicing, rehearsing, or creating music
- Assessment of students along a continuum of performances
- Assessment of a revised, reworked performance

Suggested activities:
- Independent practice of musical work toward a refined performance
- Student decision-making in musical skill-building activities (rehearsal, practice)
- Student-led rehearsals
- Progressive student self-assessment of audio- or videotaped performances
- Peer critiquing and peer lessons
- Student self-monitoring performance improvement through practice journals
- Activities that encourage exploration of the instrument or musical sounds
- Listening and critique of comparative performances on records, CDs, tapes

Commitment and Self-Motivation

The musically gifted and talented student displays a number of behavioral characteristics that are not music specific but are motivational factors that play a vital part in the development of musical talent. They describe this student's overall working style. This student can focus intently while engaged in musical tasks and often can concentrate over extended periods of time in musical practice. Musical practice requires a certain persistence and perseverance to conquer physical drills and musically reshape interpretive ideas.

The musically gifted and talented student is comfortable working independently in music and knows how to organize tasks. This self-critical student sets high standards, assessing his or her own musical work as well as critiquing the musical work of others. Look for a student who works through music with internal motivation and drive.

The student who shows internal motivation in musical work:
- Focuses intently while engaged in musical tasks
- Can concentrate for extended periods of time during musical practice
- Shows persistence and perseverance in musical tasks
- Enjoys working independently in musical tasks
- Refines and critiques musical work of self and other
- Sets high standards

Recommended procedures for the identification of motivation in music:
- Observation of student involved in revision and refinement of musical work
- Observation of peer critiquing activities
- Observation of students in problem-finding and -solving activities
- Observation of students working independently on musical tasks
- Assessment of musical products resulting from problem-solving in music
- Assessment of revised performance products

Suggested activities:
- Group and individual problem-solving projects in music
- Independent practice of musical work toward a refined performance
- Progressive student self-assessment of audio- or videotaped performances
- Peer critiquing and peer lessons
- Self-monitoring performance improvement through practice journals
- Developing a musical composition using written or computer notation
- Developing a musical composition from creative exploration or improvisation on an instrument

NOTES

INTRODUCTION

1. Edwin Gordon, *The Nature, Description, Measurement and Evaluation of Music Aptitudes* (Chicago: GIA, 1986); John Sloboda, *The Musical Mind: The Cognitive Psychology of Music* (Oxford: Oxford University Press, 1985); Carl E. Seashore, *Psychology of Music* (New York: McGraw-Hill, 1938); Bennett Reimer, *Philosophy of Music Education* (Englewood Cliffs, NJ: Prentice Hall, 1970); Peter Webster, "Creativity as Creative Thinking," *Music Educators Journal* 76, no. 9 (1990): 22–28.

2. Elliot W. Eisner, *Cognition and Curriculum Reconsidered* (New York: Teachers College Press, 1994), ix.

3. Elliot W. Eisner, "The Role of the Arts in Cognition and Curriculum," in *Developing Minds: A Resource Book for Teaching Thinking*, ed. A. Costa (Alexandria, VA: Association for Supervision and Curriculum Development, 1991); Rudolf Arnheim, *Visual Thinking* (Berkeley: University of California Press, 1969).

CHAPTER 1. PERSPECTIVES

1. This opening scene was inspired by Eisner's description of a minister, real estate broker, and cowboy viewing the Grand Canyon with differing perspectives, in Elliot W. Eisner, *Educating Artistic Vision* (New York: Macmillan, 1972), 69.

CHAPTER 2. TALENT AS MUSIC APTITUDE

1. J. P. Lecanuet et al., "Decelerative Cardiac Responsiveness to Acoustical Stimulation in the Near Term Foetus," *Quarterly Journal of Experimental Psychology* 44b (1992): 279–303. Refer to J. P. Lecanuet, "Prenatal Auditory Experience," in *Musical Beginnings: Origins and Development of Musical Competence*, ed. Irene Deliège and John Sloboda (Oxford: Oxford University Press, 1996), 1–34.

2. Scientific interest in discovering the earliest point at which a fetus can perceive and discriminate sound is apparent in a listing of over 240 studies of prenatal auditory perception in the references cited in Deliège and Sloboda's *Musical Beginnings*.

3. Refer to Deliège and Sloboda, *Musical Beginnings*, for details of the following studies: J. Feijoo, "Le foetus, Pierre et le Loup," in *L'Aube des Sens, Cahiers du Nouveau-né*, ed. E. Herbinet and M. C. Busnel (Paris: Stock, 1981), 192–209; P. G. Hepper, "Fetal 'Soap' Addiction," *Lancet* 1 (1988): 1147–48; quotation from J. P. Lecanuet, "Prenatal Auditory Experience," 25.

4. Both Papoušek studies are included in Deliège and Sloboda, *Musical Beginnings*: Hanuš Papoušek, "Musicality in Infancy Research: Biological and Cultural Origins of Early Musicality," 37–55; Mechthild Papoušek, "Intuitive Parenting: A Hidden Source of Musical Stimulation in Infancy," 88–112.

5. Augustine, *Musik: De Musica libri sex*, trans. Carl Johann Perl (Paderborn, Germany: F. Schoningh, 1962).

6. Rich chronological accounts of early texts and experimental research in the field of music psychology can be found in Rosamunde Shuter-Dyson and Clive Gabriel, *The Psychology of Musical Ability* (London: Methuen, 1968) and Charles T. Eagle, Jr., "An Introductory Perspective on Music Psychology," in *Handbook of Music Psychology*, ed. Donald A. Hodges (Lawrence, KS: National Association for Music Therapy, 1980), 1–15.

7. Carl Seashore, *Psychology of Music* (New York: McGraw-Hill, 1938), 3.

8. Seashore, *Psychology of Music*, 6.

9. For more detailed listening experiences, refer to the listening lessons in Joanne Haroutounian, *Explorations in Music*, books 1–7, with teacher guides and CDs (San Diego: Kjos Music, 1993–99).

10. An overview of the contents of the Seashore tests is in the appendix. For a complete description of the statistics of these measures, refer to J. David Boyle and Rudolf E. Radocy, *Measurement and Evaluation of Musical Experiences* (New York: Schirmer Books, 1987), or appendix 1 of Shuter-Dyson and Gabriel, *Psychology of Musical Ability*.

11. James L. Mursell, *The Psychology of Music* (Westport, CT.: Greenwood Press, 1964), 300.

12. Edwin Gordon, *The Nature, Description, Measurement, and Evaluation of Music Aptitudes* (Chicago: GIA, 1987), 13; Seashore, *Psychology of Music*, 5.

13. Refer to Shuter-Dyson and Gabriel, *Psychology of Musical Ability*, for specific music aptitude studies, including validity and reliability studies of music aptitude tests; J. Meyer, "The Dependence of Pitch on Harmonic Sound Spectra," *Psychology of Music* 6, no. 1 (1978): 3–12; F. Nelson, A. Barresi, and J. Barrett, "Musical Cognition within an Analogical Setting: Toward a Cognitive Component of Musical Aptitude in Children," *Psychology of Music and Music Education* 20 (1992): 70–79; M. Hassler, N. Birbaumer, and A. Feil, "Musical Talent and Visual-Spatial Abilities: A Longitudinal Study," *Psychology of Music* 20 (1992): 99–113. Test instrument information: John Grashel, "Test Instruments Used by *Journal of Research in Music Education* Authors from 1980–1989," *Update: Applications of Research in Music Education* 14, no. 2 (1996). 24–30.

14. A. E. Kemp, *The Musical Temperament: Psychology and Personality of Musicians* (Oxford: Oxford University Press, 1996): 22.

15. John Sloboda, *The Musical Mind: The Cognitive Psychology of Music* (Oxford: Clarendon Press, 1985): 238.

16. Music Educators National Conference, *National Standards for Arts Education: What Every Young American Should Know and Be Able to Do in the Arts* (Reston, VA: Music Educators National Conference, 1994), 7.

17. Ibid., 4, 11, 19.

18. A. Dorhout, "Identifying Musically Gifted Children," *Journal for the Education of the Gifted* 5, no. 1 (1982): 56–65; Joanne Haroutounian, "Talent Identification and Development in the Arts: An Artistic/Educational Dialogue," *Roeper Review* 18, no. 2 (1995): 112–17; Joanne Haroutounian, "The Assessment of Potential Talent in Musical Behavior/Performance: Criteria and Procedures to Consider in the Identification of Musically Gifted and Talented Students" (Ph.D. diss., University of Virginia, 1995); Joseph Khatena, *Educational Psychology of the Gifted* (New York: Wiley, 1982); Carol P. Richardson, "Measuring Musical Giftedness," *Music Educators Journal* 76, no. 7 (1990): 46–49.

19. Haroutounian, "The Assessment of Potential Talent," 16.

20. Edwin Gordon, telephone interview by author, February 24, 1995.

CHAPTER 3. TALENT AS MUSICAL INTELLIGENCE

1. J. P. Guilford, "Three Faces of Intellect," *American Psychologist* 14 (1959): 469–79; J. P. Guilford, *The Nature of Human Intelligence* (New York: McGraw-Hill, 1967).

2. Robert Sternberg, *Beyond IQ: A Triarchic Theory of Human Intelligence* (New York: Cambridge University Press, 1985).

3. Howard Gardner, *Frames of Mind: The Theory of Multiple Intelligences* (New York: Basic Books, 1983), 9.

4. Gardner, *Frames of Mind*, 105.

5. Howard Gardner, *The Unschooled Mind: How Children Think and How Schools Should Teach* (New York: Basic Books, 1991), 145.

6. For a complete description of assessment activities across intelligences for preschool students, refer to Mara Krechevsky, *Project Spectrum: Preschool Assessment Handbook* (Cambridge: Harvard Project Zero, Graduate School of Education, 1994).

7. Refer to: Lyle Davidson and Larry Scripp, "Education and Development in Music from a Cognitive Perspective," in *Children and the Arts*, ed. D. Hargreaves (Philadelphia: Open University Press, 1989), 59–86; Lyle Davidson, "Tools and Environments for Musical Creativity," *Music Educators Journal* 76, no. 9 (1990): 47–51; Lyle Davidson, Larry Scripp, and Patricia Welsh, "'Happy Birthday': Evidence for Conflicts of Perceptual Knowledge and Conceptual Understanding," *Journal of Aesthetic Education* 22, no. 1 (1988): 65–74.

8. Davidson and Scripp, "Education and Development in Music," 61.

9. Ellen Winner, Lyle Davidson, and Larry Scripp, eds., *Arts PROPEL: A Handbook for Music* (Cambridge: Harvard Project Zero and Educational Testing Service, 1992), 5.

10. Davidson, Scripp, and Welsh, "Happy Birthday."

11. Jeanne Bamberger, *The Mind behind the Musical Ear: How Children Develop Musical Intelligence* (Cambridge: Harvard University Press, 1995), 3–4.

12. Haroutounian, "The Assessment of Potential Talent in Musical Behavior/Performance: Criteria and Procedures to Consider in the Identification of Musically Gifted and Talented Students" (Ph.D. diss., University of Virginia, 1995), 164.

13. Ibid., 164.

14. The following content standards in *National Standards for Arts Education* (1994) reflect interdisciplinary instruction: content standard 8: Understanding relationships between music, the other arts, and disciplines outside the arts; content standard 9: Understanding music in relation to history and culture.

15. Aaron Copland, *What to Listen For in Music* (New York: Penguin Books, 1957), 13.

CHAPTER 4. TALENT AS PERFORMANCE

1. This judging scenario and the student performance styles are inspired by Marienne Uszler, "Must the Fittest Just Survive?" *Piano and Keyboard* 160 (1993): 62–65

2. John Sloboda, "The Acquisition of Musical Performance Expertise: Deconstructing the 'Talent' Account of Individual Differences in Musical Expressivity," in *The Road to Excellence: The Acquisition of Expert Performance in the Arts and Sciences, Sports, and Games*, ed. K. A. Ericsson (Mahwah, NJ: Erlbaum, 1996), 108; Also refer to John Sloboda, Jane Davidson, and Michael Howe, "Is Everyone Musical?" *Psychologist* 7, no. 8 (1994): 349–54.

3. M. Davis, "Folk Music Psychology," *Psychologist* 7, no. 12 (1994): 537; Sloboda, "The Acquisition of Musical Performance Expertise," 108.

4. John Sloboda and Michael Howe, "Biographical Precursors of Musical Excellence: An Interview Study," *Psychology of Music* 19 (1991): 3–21; Michael Howe and John Sloboda, "Early Signs of Talents and Special Interests in the Lives of Young Musicians," *European Journal for High Ability* 2 (1992): 102–11.

5. Lauren A. Sosniak, "Learning to Be a Concert Pianist," *Developing Talent in Young People*, ed. Benjamin Bloom (New York: Ballantine Books, 1985).

6. Sloboda, "The Acquisition of Musical Performance Expertise," 119.

7. John Sloboda, "Music Performance: Expression and the Development of Excellence," in *Musical Perceptions*, ed. R. Aiello and J. Sloboda (New York: Oxford University Press, 1994), 153–69.

8. Judith Kogan, *Nothing but the Best: The Struggle for Perfection at the Juilliard School* (New York: Limelight Editions, 1989).

9. Sloboda, "The Acquisition of Musical Performance Expertise," 175. For detailed analysis of the performance and practice process, including automaticity, refer to John Sloboda, *The Musical Mind: The Cognitive Psychology of Music* (Oxford: Clarendon Press, 1985).

10. Sloboda and Howe, "Biographical Precursors"; "Early Signs of Talent"; Sosniak,

"Concert Pianist"; Michael Howe et al., "Are There Early Childhood Signs of Musical Ability?" *Psychology of Music* 23, no. 2 (1994): 162–76.

11. Shinichi Suzuki, *Nurtured by Love: A New Approach to Education* (New York: Exposition Press, 1969), 7, 11.

12. For further reference to Suzuki's background, philosophy, and methods, see ibid.; Ray Landers, *The Talent Education School of Shinichi Suzuki: An Analysis* (New York: Exposition Press, 1980).

13. Instructions quoted from Linda Gutterman, interviewed by author, February 16, 1999. I thank her for these instructions. She is the director of the Greater Washington Suzuki Piano Institute and teaches Suzuki piano at the Peabody Conservatory preparatory division in Baltimore.

14. Ronda Cole, interviewed by author, February 4, 1999.

15. Seashore, *Psychology of Music* (New York: McGraw-Hill, 1938), 11.

16. Renshaw, "Talented Young Musicians and the Yehudi Menuhin School," *Gifted Education International* 1 (1992): 22–25; Other accounts of the importance of commitment include: Reneé B. Fisher, *Musical Prodigies: Masters at an Early Age* (New York: Association Press, 1973); I. C. Moon and M. Neeley, "Remarks by the Gifted on the Gifted," *American Music Teacher* 41, no. 4 (1992): 22–24; P.; Sloboda and Howe, "Biographical Precursors"; Howe and Sloboda, "Early Signs of Talent"; Marienne Uszler, "Musical Giftedness," *American Music Teacher* 41, no. 4 (1990): 20–21, 69–73.

17. K. A. Ericsson, R. T. Krampe, and C. Tesch-Romer, "The Role of Deliberate Practice in the Acquisition of Expert Performance," *Psychological Review* 100 (1993): 363–406.

18. R. T. Krampe and K. A. Ericsson, "Deliberate Practice and Elite Musical Performance," in *The Practice of Performance: Studies in Musical Interpretation*, ed. J. Rink (Cambridge, England: Cambridge University Press, 1995), 86.

19. Sloboda, "The Acquisition of Musical Performance Expertise," 114. The Leverhulme Project is described in Sloboda, Davidson, and Howe, "Is Everyone Musical?"

CHAPTER 5. TALENT AS CREATIVITY

1. Resources for further examination of Guilford's pioneering work in creativity research: J. P. Guilford, *The Nature of Human Intelligence* (New York: McGraw-Hill, 1967); J. P. Guilford, "Traits of Creativity," in *Creativity*, ed. P. E. Vernon (Harmondsworth: Penguin, 1970), 167–78; J. P. Guilford, *Way beyond the IQ: Guide to Improving Intelligence and Creativity* (Buffalo: Creative Education Foundation, 1977).

2. E. P. Torrance, "Some Products of Twenty-five Years of Creativity Research," *Educational Perspectives* 22, no. 3 (1984): 3–8.

3. L. Abeel, C. Callahan, and S. Hunsaker, *The Use of Published Instruments in the Identification of Gifted Students* (Washington, DC: National Association of Gifted Children, 1994); Howard Gardner, "Multiple Intelligences: Implications for Art and Creativity," in *Artistic Intelligences: Implications for Education*, ed. W. Moody (New

York: Teachers College Press, 1990): 11–27; G. Clark and E. Zimmerman, *Issues and Practices Related to the Identification of Gifted and Talented Students in the Visual Arts* (Storrs, CT: National Research Center on the Gifted and Talented, 1992).

4. Creativity testing procedures are found in: M. Wallach and N. Kogan, *Modes of Thinking in Young Children* (New York: Holt, 1965); J. W. Getzels and P. W. Jackson, *Creativity and Intelligence* (New York: Wiley, 1962); Gary Davis, *Creativity Is Forever* (Dubuque, IA: Kendall Hunt, 1992).

5. G. Wallas, *The Art of Thought* (New York: Harcourt Brace and Jovanovich, 1926).

6. A. F. Osborn, *Applied Imagination* (New York: Scribner's, 1963); S. J. Parnes, *The Magic of Your Mind* (New York: Bearly Limited, 1981); D. Treffinger, S. Isaksen, and R. Firestien, *Handbook for Creative Learning* (Williamsville, NY: Center for Creative Learning, 1982).

7. David Perkins, "The Nature and Nurture of Creativity," in *Dimensions of Thinking and Cognitive Instruction*, ed. B. Jones and L. Idol (Hillsdale, NJ: Associated, 1990), 422.

8. Mihaly Csikszentmihalyi, *Flow: The Psychology of Optimal Experience* (New York: HarperCollins, 1990), 4.

9. Mihaly Csikszentmihalyi, Kevin Rathude, and Samuel Whalen, *Talented Teenagers: The Roots of Success and Failure* (Cambridge, England: Cambridge University Press, 1993), 194, 224.

10. M. Vaughan, "Musical Creativity: Its Cultivation and Measurement," *Bulletin of the Council for Research in Music Education* 50 (1977): 72–77.

11. W. Gorder, "Divergent Production Abilities as Constructs of Musical Creativity," *Journal of Research in Music Education* 28, no. 1 (1980): 34–42; Peter Webster, "Relationship between Creative Behavior in Music and Selected Variables as Measured in High School Students," *Journal of Research in Music Education* 27, no. 4 (1979): 227–42.

12. S. Baltzer, "A Validation Study of a Measure of Musical Creativity," *Journal of Research in Music Education* 36, no. 4 (1988): 232–49; S. Baltzer, "A Factor Analytic Study of Musical Creativity in Children in the Primary Grades" (Ph.D. diss., Indiana University, 1990); Peter Webster, "Refinement of a Measure of Creative Thinking in Music," *Applications of Research in Music Behavior*, ed. C. Madsen and C. Pricket (Tuscaloosa: University of Alabama Press, 1987), 257–71; D. Swanner, "Relationships between Musical Creativity and Selected Factors including Personality, Motivation, Musical Aptitude and Cognitive Intelligence as Measured in Third Grade Children" (Ph.D. diss., Case Western Reserve University, 1985).

13. Peter Webster, "Research on Creative Thinking in Music: The Assessment Literature," in *Handbook of Research on Music Teaching and Learning*, ed. R. Colwell (New York: Schirmer Books, 1992), 266–80.

14. Peter Webster, "Rethinking Music Aptitude and its Assessment," *Sound Ideas: Assessment in Music Education*, 2, no. 2 (1998): 6–16.

15. Peter Webster interviewed by author, November 29, 1994.

16. Refer to *Dimensions of Musical Thinking*, ed. Eunice Boardman (Reston, VA: Music Educators National Conference, 1989). Specific chapters in this volume:

Hilary Apfelstadt, "Musical Thinking in the Choral Rehearsal," 73–82; Richard Kennell, "Musical Thinking in the Instrumental Rehearsal," 83–90.

17. Quotation from: Peter Webster, "Research on Creative Thinking in Music," 276; D. Pond, "A Composer's Study of Young Children's Innate Musicality," *Bulletin of the Council for Research in Music Education* 68 (1981): 1–12.

18. V. Cohen, "The Emergence of Musical Gestures in Kindergarten Children" (Ph.D. diss., University of Illinois, Urbana, 1980).

19. Sloboda, *The Musical Mind: The Cognitive Psychology of Music* (Oxford: Oxford University Press, 1985), 139.

20. Leonard Bernstien, *The Infinite Variety of Music* (New York: Simon and Schuster, 1966), 271. The closing chapter, "Something to Say" (265–86), presents a personal statement about his own creative process of work that is quite engaging.

21. Hector Berlioz, *The Life of Hector Berlioz, as Written by Himself in his Letters and Memoirs,* trans. Katharine F. Boult (New York: Dutton, 1923), 232.

22. Aaron Copland, *Music and Imagination* (Cambridge: Harvard University Press, 1952), 42–43. Chapter 3, "The Creative Mind and the Interpretive Mind" (40–57), presents an intriguing picture of the creative process of the composer and performer.

23. In Tom Russell and Sylvia Tyson, *And Then I Wrote: The Songwriter Speaks* (Vancouver: Arsenal Pulp Press, 1996), 85–87.

24. Copland, *Music and Imagination,* 43.

25. In Russell and Tyson, *And Then I Wrote,* 104.

26. Robert Schumann, *Music and Musicians,* trans. F. R. Ritter, 5th ed. (London: William Reeves, 1915), 250–51.

27. Sloboda, *The Musical Mind,* 114. The chapter "Composition and Improvisation" (102–50) presents a comparison of the creative process across these generative musical areas.

28. Jean Bamberger, "In Search of a Tune," in *The Arts and Cognition,* ed. D. Perkins and B. Leondar (Baltimore: Johns Hopkins University Press, 1977), 284–317; J. Kratus, "A Time Analysis of the Compositional Processes Used by Children Aged Five to Thirteen," *Contributions to Music Education* 12 (1985): 1–8.

29. Sloboda, *The Musical Mind,* 136.

30. Some studies using computer-based composition: L. Scripp, J. Meyaard, and L. Davidson, "Discerning Musical Development: Using Computers to Discover What We Know," *Journal of Aesthetic Education* 22, no. 1 (1988): 75–88; L. Daignault, "Children's Creative Thinking within the Context of a Computer-Supported Improvisational Approach to Composition" (Ph.D. diss., Northwestern University, 1997); M. Hickey, "Qualitative and Quantitative Relationships between Children's Creative Musical Thinking Processes and Products" (Ph.D. diss., Northwestern University, 1995); B. Younker, "Thought Processes and Strategies of Eight, Eleven, and Fourteen-Year-Old Students" (Ph.D. diss., Northwestern University, 1998).

31. Susan Langer, *Feeling and Form* (New York: Scribner's, 1953), 138. An excellent summary of Langer's ideas, along with those of many other philosophers and musicians, can be found in *On the Nature of Music Experience,* ed. Bennett Reimer and Jeffrey Wright (Niwot: University of Colorado Press, 1992).

32. John Sloboda, "The Acquisition of Musical Performance Expertise: Deconstructing the 'Talent' Account of Individual Differences in Musical Expressivity," in *The Road to Excellence: The Acquisition of Expert Performance in the Arts and Sciences, Sports, and Games* ed. K. A. Ericsson (Mahwah, NJ: Erlbaum, 1996), 116.

33. Ibid., 119–21.

34. Langer, *Feeling and Form*, 139.

35. Ibid., 141.

36. Susan Langer, *Problems of Art* (New York: Scribner's, 1957), 25.

37. Ibid., 59.

38. Susan Langer, *Philosophy in a New Key: A Study in the Symbolism of Reason, Rite, and Art* (New York: Mentor Books, 1956), 197.

39. Copland, *Music and Imagination* (Cambridge: Harvard University Press, 1952), 42.

40. Ibid., 49.

41. Ibid., 51.

42. S. Feinberg, "Creative Problem-solving and the Music Listening Experience," *Music Educators Journal* 61, no. 1 (1974): 53–59.

43. C. Pfeil, "Creativity as an Instructional Mode for Introducing Music to Nonmusic Majors at the College Level" (Ph.D. diss., Michigan State University, 1972).

44. Carlos Zavier Rodriguez, "Development of Children's Verbal Interpretive Responses to Music Listening," *Bulletin of the Council for Research in Music Education* 134 (1997): 9–31.

45. P. Flowers, "The Effect of Instruction in Vocabulary and Listening on Nonmusicians' Descriptions of Changes in Music," *Journal of Research in Music Education* 31 (1983): 179–89; P. Flowers, "Attention to Elements of Music and Effect of Instruction in Vocabulary on Written Descriptions of Music by Children and Undergraduates," *Psychology of Music* 12 (1984): 17–24; P. Flowers, "The Effects of Teacher and Learning Experiences, Tempo, and Mode on Undergraduates' and Children's Symphonic Music Preferences," *Journal of Research in Music Education* 36 (1988): 19–34; P. Flowers, "Listening: The Key to Describing Music," *Music Educators Journal* 77 (1990): 21–23; David Hargreaves, "The Development of Aesthetic Reactions to Music,"*Psychology of Music,* special issue (1982): 51–54; Rudolf Radocy, "Toward Measuring Aesthetic Sensitivity: Classifying Students' Initial Verbal Reactions to Music" (paper presented at the national convention of Music Educators National Conference, Washington, DC, March 1990).

46. Aaron Copland, *What to Listen For in Music* (New York: Mentor Books, 1953).

47. Igor Stravinsky, *Poetics of Music* (Cambridge: Harvard University Press, 1970), 63.

CHAPTER 6. TALENT AS GIFTEDNESS

1. Otto E. Deutsch, *Mozart: A Documentary Biography*, trans. Eric Blom, Peter Branscombe, and Jeremy Noble, 2nd ed. (Stanford: Stanford University Press, 1965), 24.

2. *The Letters of Mozart and His Family*, ed. and trans. Emily Anderson, 21st ed., vol. 1 (New York: Macmillan, 1938), 47–48.

3. Excellent resources for information about prodigies in different fields: David Feldman, *Nature's Gambit: Child Prodigies and the Development of Human Potential* (New York: Basic Books, 1986); Victor Goertzel and Mildred G. Goertzel, *Cradles of Eminence* (Boston: Little, Brown, 1962); John Radford, *Child Prodigies and Exceptional Early Achievers* (New York: Free Press, 1990); Michael J. Howe, *The Psychology of High Abilities* (New York: New York University Press, 1999).

4. David Feldman, "Child Prodigies: A Distinctive Form of Giftedness," Gifted Child Quarterly 37, no. 4 (1993): 188. Feldman, *Nature's Gambit*, p. 16. Renée Fisher, *Musical Prodigies: Masters at an Early Age* (New York: Association Press, 1973), 10.

5. Radford, *Child Prodigies*, p. 39.

6. Biographical information about musical prodigies: Claude Kenneson, *Musical Prodigies: Perilous Journeys, Remarkable Lives* (Portland, OR: Amadeus Press, 1998), 37, 44, 153, 319, Feldman, *Nature's Gambit* 24–27, 81–82, 94–95, 156–58; Fisher, *Musical Prodigies*, 37–40, 51–55.

7. In Fisher, *Musical Prodigies*, 40.

8. Benjamin Bloom, ed., *Developing Talent in Young People* (New York: Ballantine Books, 1985); Michael Howe and John Sloboda, "Young Musicians' Accounts of Significant Influences in their Early Lives. I. The Family and the Musical Background," *British Journal of Music Education* 8 (1991): 39–52.

9. Kenneson, *Musical Prodigies*, 53.

10. Yehudi Menuhin, *Unfinished Journey* (London: MacDonald and Jane's, 1977), 42.

11. Biographic information about Louis Armstrong and Stevie Wonder: Fisher, *Musical Prodigies*, 137–42, 160–61.

12. Radford, *Child Prodigies and Exceptional Early Achievers*, 108; Michael Howe et al., "Are There Early Childhood Signs of Musical Ability?" *Psychology of Music* 23, no. 2 (1994): 162–76.

13. Bloom, *Developing Talent in Young People*.

14. Jean Bamberger, "Growing Up Prodigies: The Mid-Life Crisis," in *Developmental Approaches to Giftedness and Creativity*, ed. David Feldman (San Francisco: Jossey-Bass, 1982).

15. Article in *Newsweek*, July 1973, 75, reprinted in Kenneson, *Musical Prodigies: Perilous Journeys*, 2.

16. Quaintance Eaton, "Hoffman's Golden Jubilee," *Musical America* 25 (November 1937): 7.

17. Radford, *Child Prodigies and Exceptional Early Achievers*, 106.

18. For a historical overview of the gifted field, refer to Nicholas Colangelo and Gary A. Davis, *Handbook of Gifted Education* (Boston: Allyn and Bacon, 1991), 3.

19. Joseph S. Renzulli and Sally M. Reis, "The Schoolwide Enrichment Model: A Comprehensive Plan for the Development of Creative Productivity," in Davis, *Handbook of Gifted Education*, 99–110.

20. Quotation from Françoys Gagné, "Nature or Nurture? A Re-examination of Sloboda and Howe's (1991) Interview Study on Talent Development in Music," *Psychology of Music* 27 (1999): 39–40; See also Françoys Gagné, "Constructs and Models Pertaining to Exceptional Human Abilities," in *International Handbook of Research and Development of Giftedness and Talent*, ed. K. A. Heller, F. J. Mönks, and A. H. Passow (Oxford: Pergamon Press, 1993); 60–87; Françoys Gagné, "Toward a Differentiated Model of Giftedness and Talent," in Davis *Handbook of Gifted Education*, 65–80.

21. U.S. Department of Education, *National Excellence: A Case for Developing America's Talent* (Washington, DC: U.S. Department of Education, 1993).

22. Michael J. Howe, "The Childhoods and Early Lives of Geniuses: Combining Psychological and Biographical Evidence," in *The Road to Excellence: The Acquisition of Expert Performance in the Arts and Sciences, Sports, and Games*, ed. K. Anders Ericsson (Mahwah, NJ: Erlbaum, 1996), 260.

23. Ibid., 257.

24. Ellen Winner, "The Rage to Master: The Decisive Role of Talent in the Visual Arts," in Ericsson, *The Road to Excellence*, 271–74.

25. Joanne Haroutounian, "Talent Identification and Development in the Arts: An Artistic/Educational Dialogue," *Roeper Review* 18, no. 2 (1995): 112–16; Joanne Haroutounian, "Drop the Hurdles and Open the Doors: Fostering Talent Development through School and Community Collaboration," *Arts Education Policy Review* 99, no. 6 (1998): 15–25.

26. Results of the first study showed that students who listened to music scored eight or nine points higher on the spatial IQ reasoning subtest of the Stanford-Binet Intelligence Scale. The second study showed significant improvement for the Mozart group from day 1 to day 2 versus no improvement for the silence group. The five days naturally included a learning curve, which showed no significant difference between groups after day 2. For specifics, refer to: Frances H. Rauscher, Gordon L. Shaw, and Katherine Ky, "Music and Spatial Task Performance," *Nature* 365 (1995): 611; Frances H. Rauscher et al., "Music and Spatial Task Performance: A Causal Relationship," paper presented at the 102nd annual meeting of the American Psychological Association, Los Angeles, CA, 1994 (ERIC Document Reproduction Service No. ED 390 733).

27. Xiaodan Leng and Gordon L. Shaw, "Toward a Neural Theory of Higher Brain Function Using Music as a Window," *Concepts in Neuroscience* 2 (1991): 231.

28. Frances H. Rauscher and Gordon L. Shaw, "Key Components of the Mozart Effect," *Perceptual and Motor Skills* 86 (1998): 836.

29. B. Rideout, S. Dougherty, and L. Wernert, "The Effect of Music on Spatial Performance: A Test of Generality," *Perceptual and Motor Skills* 86 (1998): 512-14; Kristin M. Nantais and E. Glenn Schellenberg, "The Mozart Effect: An Artifact of Preference," *Psychological Science* 10, no. 4 (1999): 370–73; Christopher F. Chabris, "Prelude or Requiem for the 'Mozart Effect'?" *Nature* 400, no. 6747 (1999): 826–27; Frances H. Rauscher, K. D. Robinson, and J. J. Jens, "Improved Maze Learning through Early Music Exposure in Rats," *Neurological Research* 20 (1998): 427–432; B. E. Rideout and C. M. Laubach, "EEG Correlates of Enhanced Spatial Perfor-

mance Following Exposure to Music," *Perceptual and Motor Skills* 82 (1996): 427–32; J. Sarnthein et al., "Persistent Patterns of Brain Activity: An EEG Coherence Study of the Positive Effect of Music On Spatial-Temporal Reasoning," *Neurological Research* 19 (1997): 107–11.

30. Joan Newman et al., "An Experimental Test of 'The Mozart Effect': Does Listening to His Music Improve Spatial Ability?" *Perceptual and Motor Skills* 81 (1995): 1379–87; Kenneth Steele et al., "Failure to Confirm the Rauscher and Shaw Description of Recovery of the Mozart Effect,"*Perceptual and Motor Skills* 88 (1999): 843–48.

31. Rauscher, "Prelude or Requiem for the 'Mozart Effect'?" 828.

32. The preschool students were given four spatial reasoning tasks from the *Wechsler Preschool and Primary Scale of Intelligence—Revised* (New York: The Psychological Corporation, 1989): object assembly, for spatial-temporal; geometric design, for visual recognition; block design, for pattern matching; animal pegs—matching colored pegs with animal pictures, and the absurdities task, requiring verbal answers from The *Stanford-Binet Intelligence Scale* (4th ed). ed. Robert L. Thorndike, Elizabeth P. Hagen & Jerome M. Sattler, (Chicago, The Riverside Publishing Co., 1986). For further reference to this study: Frances H. Rauscher et al., "Music Training Causes Long-Term Enhancement of Preschool Children's Spatial-Temporal Reasoning," *Neurological Research* 19 (1997): 2–8.; Rauscher et al., "Music and Spatial Task Performance."

33. David Hodges, "Neuromusical Research: A Review of the Literature," *Handbook of Music Psychology*, 2nd ed. (San Antonio, TX: IMR Press, 1996), 197–284; Bruce Bower, "Brain Images Reveal Cerebral Side of Music," *Science News* (April 1994): 145, 260; Leng and Shaw, "Toward a Neural Theory of Higher Brain Function; G. Schlaug, L. Jäncke, Y. Huang, and H. Steinmetz, "In Vivo Evidence of Structural Brain Asymmetry in Musicians," *Science* 267 (1995): 699–701. A summary of this research and other neurological studies is found in Debra Malina, "Cerebral Symphony," *Harvard Medical Alumni Review* 73, no. 1 (1999), 20–27.

34. David Feldman, "Child Prodigies: A Distinctive Form of Giftedness," *Gifted Child Quarterly* 37, no. 4 (1993): 188–93.

35. C. Cox, *Genetic Studies of Genius*, vol. 2, *The Early Mental Traits of Three Hundred Geniuses* (Stanford: Stanford University Press, 1926).

36. A resource to summarized *positive* studies across all of these extra-musical areas is Robert Cutietta, Donald L. Hamann, and Linda Miller Walker, *Spin-Offs: The Extra-Musical Advantages of a Musical Education* (Elkhart, IN: United Musical Instruments USA, 1995); S.A.T. information, 13, 18. Additional sources: Matt Martin, "S.A.T.'s and Music," *American Music Teacher* 44, no. 5 (1995); 16–117; Jerry Trusty and Giacomo M. Oliva, "The Effect of Arts and Music Education on Students' Self-Concept," *Update: Application of Research in Music Education* 11, no. 1 (1994): 23–27.

37. The music industry is quick to promote and publicize the linkage of music and intelligence. The Florida example is from a widely distributed newsletter from Yamaha, *KeyAction* 7, no. 9 (1999): 19. Source of the Massachusetts example: Susan Black, "The Musical Mind," *American School Board Journal* January (1997): 20–22.

38. D. Treffert, *Extraordinary People: Understanding "Idiot Savants"* (New York: Harper and Row, 1989).

39. Martha Morelock and David Henry Feldman, "Prodigies and Savants: What They Have to Tell Us about Giftedness and Human Cognition," in *International Handbook of Research and Development of Giftedness and Talent*, ed. Kurt Heller, Franz J. Mönks, and A. Harry Passow (Oxford: Pergamon Press, 1993), 161–67.

40. Ellen Winner, *Gifted Children* (New York: Basic Books, 1996), 133.

41. Fisher, *Musical Prodigies*, 69–72.

42. J. Sloboda, B. Hermelin, and N. O'Connor, "An Exceptional Musical Memory," *Music Perception* 3 (1985): 155–70.

43. L. K. Miller, *Musical Savants: Exceptional Skill in the Mentally Retarded* (Hillsdale, NJ: Erlbaum, 1989); quotation from Morelock and Feldman, "Prodigies and Savants," 169.

44. B. Hermelin, N. O'Connor, and S. Lee, "Musical Inventiveness of Five Idiots Savants," *Psychological Medicine* 17 (1987): 685–94.

45. Alan J. Klein et al., "Hyperacusis and Otitis Media in Individuals with Williams Syndrome," *Journal of Speech and Hearing Disorders* 55 (1990): 339–44; Daniel J. Levitin and Ursula Bellugi, "Musical Abilities in Individuals with Williams Syndrome," *Music Perception* 15, no. 4 (1998): 357–89; Dave Scheiber, "Music Lights a Fire," *St. Petersburg Times* (Lenox, MA), September 6, 1998.

46. Don's preliminary study is discussed in Levitin and Beluggi, "Musical Abilities in Individuals with Williams Syndrome"; Howard M. Lenhoff et al., "Williams Syndrome and the Brain," *Scientific American* 277, no. 6 (1997): 68–73; Howard M. Lenhoff, "Information Sharing: Insights into the Musical Potential of Cognitively Impaired People Diagnosed with Williams Syndrome," *Music Therapy Perspectives* 16, no. 1 (1998): 33–36.

47. Laura Staumbaugh, "Special Learners with Special Abilities," *Music Educators Journal* 83, no. 3 (1996): 19–23. For additional information about Williams Syndrome: Williams Syndrome Association, P.O. Box 297, Clawson, MI, 48017–0297.

48. Quotation from Levitin and Bellugi, "Musical Abilities in Individuals with Williams Syndrome," 379; Lenhoff, "Williams Syndrome and the Brain."

49. Gary Larson, *In Search of the Far Side* (Kansas City, Andrews and McNeel, 1984), 35.

CHAPTER 8. PERSPECTIVES OF TALENT IDENTIFICATION

1. National Coalition for Music Education, *Growing Up Capable: The Imperative for Music Education* (Reston, VA: Music Educators National Conference, 1989), 6.

2. S. Marland, *Education of the Gifted and Talented: Report to the Congress of the United States by the U.S. Commissioner of Education* (Washington, DC: U.S. Government Printing Office, 1972).

3. E. Susanne Richert, L. Alvino, and R. McDonnel, *National Report on Identification: Assessment and Recommendations for Comprehensive Identification of Gifted and Talented Youth* (Sewell, NJ: Educational Information Resource Center, U.S. Department of Education, 1982).

4. E. Susanne Richert has a number of valuable publications on identification issues: "Rampant Problems and Promising Practices in Identification," in *Handbook of Gifted Education*, ed. N. Colangelo and G. Davis (Boston: Allyn and Bacon, 1991): 81–96; E. Susanne Richert, "Identification of Gifted Students: The Need for Pluralistic Assessment,"*Roeper Review* 8 (1985): 68–72; Richert, Alvino, and McDonnel, *National Report on Identification*. Joseph R. Renzulli, "What Makes Giftedness?" Reexamining a Definition, Phi Delta Kappa, 60, no. 3 (1978): 180–184, 261. Information about the gifted music survey: Betty W. Atterbury, "The Musically Talented: Aren't They Also Gifted?" *Update: Applications of Research in Music Education* 9, no. 3 (1991): 21–23.

5. U.S. Department of Education. *National Excellence: A Case for Developing America's Talent* (Washington, DC: U.S. Government Printing Office, 1993), 26.

6. Music Educators National Conference, *National Standards for Arts Education* (Reston, VA; Music Educators National Conference, 1994); Music Educators National Conference, *Opportunity-to-learn Standards for Music Instruction, Grades PreK–12* (Reston, VA: Music Educators National Conference, 1994), 4, 11,19.

7. *Music Educators Journal* 76, no. 7 (1990) is a focus issue on musical giftedness. *American Music Teacher* 41, no. 4 (1992), includes: Ick-Choo Moon and Marilyn Neeley, "Remarks by the Gifted on the Gifted," 22–24, 75; M. Uszler, "Musical Giftedness," 20–21, 69–73.

8. J. Renzulli et al., *Scales for Rating the Behavioral Characteristics of Superior Students* (Mansfield Center, CT: Creative Learning Press, 1976).

9. L. Abeel, C. Callahan, and S. Hunsaker, *The Use of Published Instruments in the Identification of Gifted Students* (Washington, DC: National Association for Gifted Children, 1994).

10. B. Johnson, "Gifted and Talented Screening Form," in *Assessment in Gifted Education*, ed. F. Karnes and E. Collins (Springfield, IL: Charles Thomas, 1981), 32; M. Karnes, *Music Checklist* (ERIC Document Reproduction Service no. ED 160 226, 1978).

11. J. Khatena and D. Morse, "Preliminary Study of the Khatena-Morse Multitalent Perception Inventory," *Perceptual and Motor Skills* 64 (1987): 1187–90; Karnes and Collins, *Assessment in Gifted Education*.

12. My thanks to the Kentucky Governor's School for the Arts for the use of their Instrumental Governor's School for the Arts Adjudication Form. J. David Boyle and Rudolf E. Radocy, *Measurement and Evaluation of Musical Experiences* (New York: Schirmer Books, 1987), 172.

13. My thanks to the Virginia Music Teachers Association and the Washington, DC, Music Teachers Association for the use of performance forms used in their festivals and competitions.

14. My thanks to the Center for Creative Youth at Wesleyan University for the use of this form.

15. My thanks to ArtsConnection for the use of their identification tally sheet.

16. Boyle and Radocy, *Measurement and Evaluation of Musical Experiences*.

17. G. Wenner, "Discovery and Recognition of the Artistically Talented," *Journal for the Education of the Gifted* 18, no. 3 (1985): 221–38.

18. J. Mills, "Assessment of Solo Musical Performance: A Preliminary Study," *Bulletin of the Council for Research in Music Education* 91 (1987): 119–25; D. Elliot, "Assessing Musical Performance,"*British Journal of Music Education* 4, no. 2 (1987): 157–83; J. Levinson, "Evaluating Musical Performance," *Journal of Aesthetic Education* 21, no. 1 (1987): 75–88.

19. Lauren A. Sosniak, "Learning to Be a Concert Pianist," in *Developing Talent in Young People,* ed. Benjamin Bloom (New York: Ballantine Books, 1985), 19–67. Benjamin Bloom, "Generalizations about Talent Development," in Bloom, *Developing Talent in Young People,* 544.

20. Mihaly Csikszentmihalyi, Kevin Rathune, and Samuel Whalen, *Talented Teenagers: The Roots of Success and Failure* (Cambridge, England: Cambridge University Press, 1993), 26.

21. Ibid., 243–60.

22. John Sloboda and Michael Howe, "Biographical Precursors of Musical Excellence: An Interview Study," *Psychology of Music* 19 (1991): 3–21; John Sloboda and Michael Howe, "Young Musician's Accounts of Significant Influences in their Early Lives: The Family and Musical Background," *British Journal of Music Education* 8 (1991): 39–52; Michael Howe and John Sloboda, "Young Musician's Accounts of Significant Influences in their Early Lives. II. Teachers, Practicing and Performing," *British Journal of Music Education* 7 (1991): 53–63; John Sloboda and Michael Howe, "Problems Experienced by Talented Young Musicians as a Result of the Failure of Other Children to Value Musical Accomplishments," *Gifted Education International* 8, no. 1 (1992): 16–18.

23. S. L. Logsdon, "Teacher Perceptions of Musical Giftedness in Fifth and Sixth Grade Children Compared with a Theoretical Model of Musical Giftedness" (Ph.D. diss., University of Iowa, 1984).

24. Roland S. Persson, "Complementary Studies of Musical Reality: The Phenomenological Concept of Musical Talent: A Pilot Study" (Department of Music, University of Huddersfield, 1994).

25. Moon and Neeley, "Remarks by the Gifted on the Gifted," *American Music Teacher* 41, no. 4 (1992): 22–24.

26. Marienne Uszler, "Musical Giftedness," *American Music Teacher* 41, no. 4 (1990): 20–21, 69–73.

27. Uszler, "Musical Giftedness," 69.

28. ArtsConnection, "Talent beyond Words: Identifying and Developing Talent through Music and Dance in Economically Disadvantaged, Bilingual, and Handicapped Children," report submitted to the United States Department of Education Jacob Javits Gifted and Talented Program (Brooklyn: ArtsConnection, 1992).

CHAPTER 9. THE QUEST

1. Complete reference for this study: J. Haroutounian, "The Assessment of Potential Talent in Musical Behavior/Performance" (Ph.D. diss., University of Virginia, 1995).

2. The NRC G/T is a repository for identification instruments requested from over five thousand gifted consultants nationwide. Additional data was received from specialized performing arts schools. Governors Schools, and gifted/arts programs nationwide.

3. This quantitative study is summarized in J. Haroutounian, "The Assessment of Musical Potential and Musical Performance," *National Research Center on the Gifted and Talented Newsletter* (winter 1993): 12–13.

4. Additional reference for this qualitative study: J. Haroutounian, "Perspectives of Musical Talent: A Study of Identification Criteria and Procedures," *High Ability Studies* 11, no. 2 (2000): 137–60.

CHAPTER 10. THE SPARK

1. Gordon recommends the use of the *Primary Measures of Music Audiation* (*PMMA*) for measuring normal music aptitude in children in grades K–3. The *Intermediate Measures of Music Audiation* (*IMMA*) is more appropriate for measuring high music aptitude for these grades. If students score very high on the *IMMA* below grade 5, the *Music Aptitude Profile* (*MAP*) can discriminate exceptional music aptitude.

2. Adapted from Joanne Haroutounian, *Explorations in Music*, book 3, *Teacher Guide* (San Diego, CA: Kjos Music, 1993), 36.

3. C. Wang, "Measures of Creativity in Sound and Music" (Lexington, KY: School of Music, University of Kentucky, 1985), combines creative improvisation with spontaneous expressive performance and rhythmic pulse. Scores indicate musical fluency and imagination. P. Webster's "Measures of Creative Thinking in Music: Administrative Guidelines (Evanston, IL: School of Music, Northwestern University, 1989), experiments with sounds using a microphone, temple blocks, and a nerf ball on a keyboard with pictures to structure creative activities. Scores indicate originality, extensiveness, flexibility, and musical syntax.

4. Creative problem-solving methods are widely used in gifted education. For problem-solving resources see B. Eberle and B. Stanish, *CPS for Kids* (Carthage, IL: Good Apple, 1985); S. G. Isaksen and D. J. Treffinger, *Creative Problem Solving: The Basic Course* (Buffalo: Bearly Limited, 1985); S. J. Parnes, *The Magic of Your Mind* (New York: Bearly Limited, 1981).

5. MUSICAL KALEIDOSCOPE is adapted from Joanne Haroutounian, *Explorations in Music*, book 3, *Teacher Guide*, 37.

CHAPTER 11. UNVEILING THE SPARK

1. The criteria and format of this form and the *Music Interest Form* have been used as nomination forms to the MusicLink program since 1993. Statistical analysis shows that high correlations between items on the forms indicate internal consistency.

2. Refer to chapter 5 for Wang and Webster music creativity testing resources. Torrance tests: E. P. Torrance, *Thinking Creatively in Action and Movement* (Bensenville, IL: Scholastic Testing Service, 1981); E. P. Torrance, J. Khatena, and

B. F. Cunningham, *Thinking Creatively with Sounds and Words* (Bensenville, IL: Scholastic Testing Service, 1973).

3. P. R. Lehman, "Review of Music Achievement Tests," *The Seventh Mental Measurements Yearbook,* vol. 1, ed. O. K. Buros (Highland Park, NJ: Gryphon Press, 1972), 521–22; Richard Colwell, *Music Achievement Tests* (Chicago, IL: Follett, 1970).

4. Edwin Gordon, *Iowa Tests of Music Literacy* (Iowa City: Bureau of Educational Research and Service, University of Iowa, 1971).

5. P. R. Lehman, "Review of the *Iowa Test of Music Literacy,*" in *The Eighth Mental Measurements Yearbook,* vol. 1, ed. O. K. Buros (Highland Park, NJ: Gryphon Press, 1978), 526–27.

6. J. G. Watkins and S. E. Farnum, *The Watkins-Farnum Performance Scale* (Winona, MN: Hal Leonard Music, 1954); S. E. Farnum, *The Farnum String Scale* (Winona, MN: Hal Leonard Music, 1969).

7. Telephone interview with David Thurmond, director of the Kentucky Governor's School, October 10, 1991.

8. Felice A. Kaufman, Thomas C. Tews, and Cheryl P. Milam, "New Orleans Center for the Creative Arts: Program Descriptions and Student Perceptions,"*Journal for the Education of the Gifted* 8, no. 3 (1985): 211–19.

9. Bruce W. Galbraith, "Interlochen Arts Academy: Its Guidelines for Success," *Journal for the Education of the Gifted* 8, no. 3 (1985): 199–210.

10. University of Virginia Summer Enrichment Program in the Arts (SEPIA), *Audition Schedule and Forms* (Charlottesville, VA: University of Virginia Summer Enrichment Program, 1991).

11. For more information about the Arlington Public Schools Apprentice Program, contact the Director of the Fine Arts Program for the Gifted, Arlington County Public Schools, 1426 N. Quincy St., Arlington, VA 22207.

12. Jim Cross, "Art Renaissance in South Carolina," *Gifted Child Today* (January/February 1990): 41–42.

13. Information about Governors' Schools is in the appendix.

14. For more information: New Orleans Center for Creative Arts, 6048 Perrier St., New Orleans, LA 70118.

15. For more information: The Ellington Fund–Duke Ellington School of the Arts, 3500 R St. NW, Suite 100, Washington, DC 20007.

16. For more information: The Juilliard Pre-Collegiate Division, The Juilliard School, 60 Lincoln Center Plaza, New York, NY 10023-6588.

17. William Grimes, "A New Juilliard for a More Challenging Era," *New York Times,* June 2, 1993, C3.

18. For this crystallizing inspiration, my thanks go to: Kenneth Kreitner and Ann W. Engin, "Identifying Musical Talent," in *Psychology and Education of the Gifted,* ed. J. Renzulli and W. Barbe (New York: Irvington, 1981), 192–205.

19. An analysis of variance procedure revealed parent ratings significantly lower, with $p < .001$ to $.0001$. Findings also showed significant differences between private music teachers and school music teachers in tonal memory ($p < .001$), perseverance in musical tasks ($p < .003$), and refining and critiquing work ($p < .032$). Complete statistical

information is found in: Joanne Haroutounian, "MUSICLINK: Nurturing Potential and Recognizing Achievement," *Arts Education Policy Review* 100, no. 6 (2000); 12–20.

20. Of the 142 analyzed parent forms, 78 percent contained added comments about their child's activities. Percentages of comments: church activities, 35 percent; spontaneous singing, 28 percent; experimenting with instruments, 23 percent; picking up or making up tunes, 21 percent.

CHAPTER 12. KINDLING THE SPARK

1. Rosamunde Shuter-Dyson and Clive Gabriel, *Psychology of Musical Ability* (London: Methuen, 1968) 103–07; Irène Deliège and John Sloboda, *Musical Beginnings: Origins and Development of Musical Competence* (Oxford: Oxford University Press, 1996), 3–55.

2. S. C. Woodward, "The Transmission of Music into the Human Uterus and the Response to Music of the Human Fetus and Neonate" (Ph.D. diss., University of Cape Town, South Africa, 1992). For numerous prenatal studies, refer to Deliège and Sloboda, *Musical Beginnings*, 3–55.

3. L. Salk, "The Effects of the Normal Heartbeat Sound on the Behavior of Newborn Infants: Implications for Mental Health," *World Mental Health* 12 (1960): 1–8; L. Salk, "Mother's Heartbeat as an Imprinting Stimulus," *Transactions of the New York Academy of Sciences*, series 2, 4 (1962): 753–63: A. Yoshida and Y. Chiba, "Neonate's Vocal and Facial Expression and Their Changes during Experimental Playbacks of Intra-uterine Sounds," *Journal of Ethology* 7 (1989): 153–56.

4. Deliège and Sloboda, *Musical Beginnings*, 20–25.

5. D. N. Stern, *The Interpersonal World of the Infant* (New York: Basic Books, 1985).

6. Joshua Kahn and Geri Fox, "Normal Musical Development: A Review," *Medical Problems of Performing Artists* 12, no. 3 (1997): 83–88.

7. H. Chang and S. E. Trehub, "Auditory Processing of Relational Information by Young Infants," *Journal of Experimental Child Psychology* 24 (1977): 324–31: S. E. Trehub, "Infants' Perception of Musical Patterns," *Perception and Psychophysics* 41 (1987): 635–41; S. E. Trehub, L. J. Trainor, and A. M. Unyk, "Music and Speech Processing in the First Year of Life," *Advancement of Child Development Behavior* 24 (1993): 2–35; A. J. Cohen, A. Leigh, and S. E. Trehub, "Infants' Perception of Melodies: The Role of Melodic Contour," *Child Development* 55 (1984): 821–30.

8. S. E. Trehub, "Infants' Perception of Musical Patterns"; W. Kessen, J. Levine, and K. A. Wendrick, "The Imitation of Pitch in Infants," *Infant Behavior Development* 11 (1965): 95–127.

9. H. Moog, *The Musical Experience of the Pre-school Child*, trans. C. Clarke (London: Schott, 1976).

10. Mechthild Papoušek, "Intuitive Parenting: A Hidden Source of Musical Stimulation in Infancy," in Deliège and Sloboda, *Musical Beginnings*, 104.

11. Ibid., 88–112.

12. Lyle Davidson and Larry Scripp, "Conditions of Giftedness: Musical Development in the Preschool and Early Elementary Years," in *Beyond Terman: Con-*

temporary Longitudinal Studies of Giftedness and Talent, ed. Rena F. Subotnik and Karen D. Arnold (Norwood, NJ: Ablex, 1994), 155–85.

13. P. E. McKernon, "The Development of First Songs in Young Children," *New Directions in Child Development* 3 (1979): 43–58.

14. Moog, *The Musical Experience of the Pre-school Child.*

15. N. L. Ries, "An Analysis of the Characteristics of Infant-child Singing Expressions" (Ph.D. diss., Arizona State University, 1982).

16. Refer to numerous rhythmic studies in Shuter-Dyson and Gabriel, *Psychology of Musical Ability,* 110–16; Davidson and Scripp, "Conditions of Giftedness," 174; Arnold Bentley, *Musical Ability in Children and Its Measurement* (New York: October House, 1966).

17. Summaries of the following Pillsbury studies are found in Shuter-Dyson and Gabriel, *Psychology of Musical Ability,* 97–128; G. E. Moorehead and D. Pond, *Music of Young Children* (Santa Barbara: Pillsbury Foundation for Advancement of Music, 1941–51; reprint 1978); D. Pond, S. J. Shelley, and B. D. Wilson, "The Pillsbury Foundation School Revisited," paper presented at the twenty-sixth national conference of the Music Educators National Conference, Chicago, March 1978; M. Prével, "Helping Children Build Their Own Music," in *Challenges in Music Education: ISME* edited by F. Calloway (Perth: Department of Music, University of Western Australia, 1976.

18. Davidson and Scripp, "Conditions of Giftedness."

19. An excellent overall resource for parents seeking guidance in ways to enhance and develop the musical abilities of their children: Wilma Machover and Marienne Uszler, *Sound Choices: Guiding Your Child's Musical Experiences* (New York: Oxford University Press, 1996).

20. For more information about early instrumental instruction: Suzuki Association of the Americas, Box 17310, Boulder, CO 80308; Yamaha Corporation of America–Music Education System, P.O. Box 6600, Buena Park, CA, 90622-6600; Music for Young Children, 39 Leacock Way, Kanata, Ontario, K2K 1T1, Canada.

21. Claire-Lise Dutoit, *Music, Movement Therapy* (Surrey: Dalcroze Society, 1971), 10; For a glimpse at a Dalcroze class, refer to: Anne Farber and Lisa Parker, "Discovering Music through Dalcroze Eurythmics," *Music Educators Journal* 74, no. 3 (1987): 43–45.

22. Carl Orff and Gunild Keetman, *Orff Schulwerk: Music for Children* (Mainz: B. Schott, 1956), i.

23. Ibid., ii.

24. Philip Tacka and Micheal Houlahan, *Sound Thinking: Developing Musical Literacy* (New York: Boosey and Hawkes, 1995), 4–11.

CHAPTER 13. FROM SPARK TO FLAME

1. J. Piaget and B. Inhelder, *The Psychology of the Child* (London: Routledge and Kegan Paul, 1969).

2. David J. Hargreaves, *The Developmental Psychology of Music* (London: Cambridge University Press, 1986), 35.

3. Pflederer identified five types of music conservation: thematic indentity, metrical groupings, augmentation and diminution, transposition, and inversion. M. Pflederer, "The Responses of Children to Musical Tasks Embodying Piaget's Principle of Conservatism," *Journal of Research in Music Education* 12 (1964): 19–36.

4. M. P. Zimmerman and L. Sechrest, "How Children Conceptually Organize Musical Sounds," in *Cooperative Research Project No. 5-0256* (Evanston, IL: Northwestern University, 1968).

5. R. L. Larsen, "Levels of Conceptual Development in Melodic Permutation Concepts Based on Piaget's Theory," *Journal of Research in Music Education* 21 (1973): 256–63; refer to numerous other studies relating to Piaget's theory in Shuter-Dysen and Gabriel, *The Psychology of Musical Ability*, 129–51.

6. David Hargreaves, "The Development of Artistic and Musical Competence," in *Musical Beginnings: Origins and Development of Musical Competence*, ed. Irène Deliège and John Sloboda (Oxford: Oxford University Press, 1996), 145–170.

7. John Sloboda, *The Musical Mind: The Cognitive Psychology of Music* (Oxford: Oxford University Press, 1985), 210.

8. Jerome S. Bruner, *The Process of Education* (New York: Vintage Books, 1963); Jerome S. Bruner, *On Knowing: Essays for the Left Hand* (New York: Atheneum, 1962).

9. Howard Gardner, *The Arts and Human Development* (New York: Basic Books, 1994), xxii.

10. Ibid., 39.

11. E. Ziegfeld, ed., *Education and Art* (Paris: UNESCO, 1953), 22.

12. Sosniak, "Phases of Learning," in *Developing Talent in Young People*, ed. Benjamin Bloom (New York: Ballantine Books, 1985), 434.

13. Alfred North Whitehead, *The Aims of Education* (New York: Free Press, 1929).

14. Sosniak, "Phases of Learning," 412–13; Michael Howe and John Sloboda, "Young Musicians' Accounts of Significant Influences in the Early Lives. II: Teachers, Practicing and Performing," *British Journal of Music Education* 7 (1991): 53–63; David Henry Feldman, *Nature's Gambit: Child Prodigies and the Development of Human Potential* (New York: Basic Books, 1986).

15. Jane W. Davidson et al., "Characteristics of Music Teachers and the Progress of Young Instrumentalists," *Journal of Research in Music Education* 46, no. 1 (1998): 141–60.

16. Wilma Machover and Marienne Uszler, *Sound Choices: Guiding Your Child's Musical Experiences* (New York: Oxford University Press, 1996), 283.

17. Marienne Uszler, "The Independent Music Teacher: Practice and Preparation," *American Music Teacher* 45, no. 8 (1996): 20–29, 62–63.

18. Joanne Haroutounian, *Rhythm Antics* (San Diego: Kjos Music, 1989).

19. Lauren Sosniak, "Learning to Be a Concert Pianist," in Bloom, "Developing Talent in Young People," 38.

20. Davidson et al., "Characteristics of Music Teachers;" Howe and Sloboda, "Young Musicians' Accounts of Significant Influences in their Early Lives."

21. Practice strategies reflect ideas from J. R. Anderson, "Acquisition of Cognitive Skill," *Psychology Review* 89 (1982): 339–46.

22. Barbara Clark, *Growing Up Gifted*, (Columbus, OH: Charles E. Merrill, 1983), 91–99; J. T. Webb, "Nurturing Social-Emotional Development of Gifted Children," in *International Handbook of Research and Development of Giftedness and Talent*, ed. K. A. Heller, F. J. Mönks, and A. Harry Passow (Oxford: Pergamon Press), 525–38.

23. Elliot W. Eisner, *The Educational Imagination: On the Design and Evaluation of School Programs* (New York: Macmillan, 1985), 87–108.

24. June Maker, *Curriculum Development for the Gifted* (Rockville, MD: Aspen, 1982); Carol Ann Tomlinson, *How to Differentiate Instruction in Mixed-Ability Classrooms* (Alexandria, VA: Association for Supervision and Curriculum Development, 1995); S. Winebrenner, *Teaching Gifted Kids in the Regular Classroom: Strategies Every Teacher Can Use to Meet the Needs of the Gifted and Talented* (Minneapolis: Free Spirit, 1992); Sandra N. Kaplan, "The Grid: A Model to Construct Differentiated Curriculum for the Gifted," in *Systems and Models for Developing Programs for the Gifted and Talented*, ed. Joseph S. Renzulli (Mansfield Center, CT: Creative Learning Press, 1986).

25. Tomlinson, *How to Differentiate Instruction*, 61.

26. Marienne Uszler, Stewart Gordon, and Elyse Mach, *The Well-Tempered Keyboard Teacher* (New York: Schirmer, 1991); R. Fred Kern and Marguerite Miller, *Projects for Piano Pedagogy*, vols. 1 and 2 (San Diego: Kjos Music, 1988).

27. Josef Levinne, *Basic Principles in Pianoforte Playing* (New York: Dover, 1972); Walter Gieseking and Karl Leimer, *Piano Technique* (New York: Dover, 1972); P. Bernac, *The Interpretation of French Song* (London: Victor Gollancz, 1978); P. Hurford, *Making Music on the Organ* (Oxford: Oxford University Press, 1988); G. Mantel, *Cello Technique: Principles and Forms of Movement*, trans. B. Haimberger-Thiem (London: Indiana University Press, 1975); R. Morley-Pegge, *The French Horn: Some Notes on the Evolution of the Instrument and its Technique* (London: Benn, 1973).

28. Eloise Ristad, *A Soprano on Her Head: Right-side-up Reflections on Life and Other Performances* (Moab, UT: Real People Press, 1982); Seymour Bernstein, *With Your Own Two Hands: Self-Discovery through Music* (New York: Schirmer Books, 1981); quotation from Stewart Gordon, *Etudes for Piano Teachers: Reflections on the Teacher's Art* (New York: Oxford University Press, 1995), 24.

29. Sally M. Reis and Joseph S. Renzulli, "The Secondary Triad Model," in *Systems and Models for Developing Programs for the Gifted and Talented*, ed. Joseph S. Renzulli (Mansfield Center, CT: Creative Learning Press, 1986), 267–305.

30. Joanne Haroutounian, "Talent Identification and Development in the Arts: An Artistic/Educational Dialogue," *Roeper Review* 18, no. 2 (1995): 112–17. Joanne Haroutounian, "The Academics of Artistic Thinking," *Think* 5, no. 2 (1994): 17–20.

31. Robert Woody, "Getting into Their Heads," *American Music Teacher* 49, no. 3 (1999–2000): 24–27.

32. Lucinda Mackworth-Young, "Pupil-centered Learning in Music Classes," *American Music Teacher* 40, no. 5 (1991): 26–31.

33. Joanne Haroutounian, "The Recital Project—A Creative Performance Alternative," *American Music Teacher* 43, no. 2 (1993): 34; Joanne Haroutounian, Cre

atively Teaching the Artist Within," *American Music Teacher* 42, no. 3 (1992–93): 20–23, 75–80.

34. This creative contemporary project is from the studio of Carolyn Diann Clark of Vienna, Virginia.

35. *A Seven Piece Puzzle* contained compositions and art work by Hannah Calvert, Christopher Wood, Sarah Kormann, James DeWire, Robert Glaubitz, Grace Jean, and Joanna Kohan. All of these creative "youngsters" are now college graduates.

36. Jodi Domer and Joyce Eastlund Gromko, "Qualitatative Changes in Preschoolers' Invented Notations following Music Instruction," *Contributions to Music Education* 23 (1996): 62–78; Jeanne Bamberger, "Revisiting Children's Drawings of Simple Rhythms: A Function for Reflection-in-Action," in *U-Shaped Behavioral Growth*, ed. S. Strauss (New York: Academic Press, 1982), 191–226.

37. For more information concerning musical dimensions: Jeanne Bamberger, "Cognitive Issues in the Development of Musically Gifted Children," in R. Sternberg and J. Davidson, *Conceptions of Giftedness* (New York: Cambridge University Press, 1986), 389–413. For additional musical tasks across multiple dimensions, refer to Joanne Haroutounian, *Explorations in Music* (San Diego: Kjos Music, 1993–99). The series has seven levels of exploratory theory, composition, listening, eartraining, and creative activities from primary concepts through advanced placement levels.

CHAPTER 14. THE FLAME

1. The epigraph to this chapter is from Stephen Gray-Lewis, "Children and Art— An Interview with Mark Schubart," in *The Gifted Child, The Family, and the Community*, ed. Bernard Miller and Merle Price (New York: Walker, 1981), 195. Mark Shubart was the director of Lincoln Center's arts education programs at the time of this interview.

2. Lauren Sosniak, "Learning to Be a Concert Pianist," in *Developing Talent in Young People*, ed. Benjamin Bloom (New York: Ballantine Books, 1985), 19–67; Michael Howe and John Sloboda, "Young Musician's Accounts of Significant Influences in their Early Lives. II. Teachers, Practicing and Performing," *British Journal of Music Education* 7 (1991): 53–63.

3. Sosniak, "Learning to be a Concert Pianist," 61.

4. Ibid., 63.

5. Sloboda and Howe, "Young Musician's Accounts of Significant Influences in their Early Lives," 56.

6. Joanne Haroutounian, "MTNA Winners after a Decade: Portraits of Commitment and Excellence," *American Music Teacher* 47, no. 2 (1997): 20–25, 66.

7. Bruce Berr, "Transformational Practice Technique for Piano," *American Music Teacher* 44, no. 5 (1995): 12–15, 93–95.

8. Pianist: Emely Phelps; clarinetist: Stefanie Schmitz.

9. Resources for practice strategies: Malva Freymuth, "Mental Practice: Some Guidelines for Musicians," *American Music Teacher* 43, no. 5 (1994): 18–21; Siw G. Nielsen, "Learning Strategies in Instrumental Music Practice," *British Journal of Music Education* 15, no. 3 (1999): 275–91; J. R. Anderson, "Acquisition of Cog-

nitive Skill, *Psychology Review* 89 (1982): 339–46; Barry Green with W. Timothy Gallwey, *The Inner Game of Music* (New York: Anchor Press, 1986); George Leonard, *Mastery: The Keys to Success and Long-term Fulfillment* (New York: Plume, 1992).

10. The Performance Portfolio was used in a pedagogy project involving eight private studios to develop terminology and format suitable for a variety of student ages and developmental levels. Refer to: Joanne Haroutounian, "Judge for Yourself," *Piano and Keyboard* 181 (July/August 1996): 46–50.

11. Sosniak, "Learning to Be a Concert Pianist," 51–53.

12. Alfie Kohn, *No Contest: The Case against Competition* (New York: Houghton Mifflin, 1986).

13. Marienne Uszler, "Must the Fittest Just Survive?" *Piano and Keyboard* 160 (1993): 62–66.

14. Paul Pollei, "What Role Should Competitive Activities Play in a Piano Student's Development? Damage to the Ego Is Sometimes Difficult to Reconcile," *Keyboard Companion* 3, no. 2 (1992): 5–8.

15. Joanne Haroutounian, "The Assessment of Potential Talent in Musical Behavior/Performance" (Ph.D. diss., University of Virginia, 1995), 178.

16. Jeanne Bamberger, "Cognitive Issues in the Development of Musically Gifted Children," in *Conceptions of Giftedness*, ed. Robert Sternberg and Janet Davidson (Cambridge, England: Cambridge University Press, 1986), 388–89.

17. Jenny Boyd, *Musicians In Tune: Seventy-five Contemporary Musicians Discuss the Creative Process* (New York: Simon and Schuster, 1992), 37.

18. Liona Bresler, "Music in a Double-Bind: Instruction by Non-Specialists in Elementary Schools," *Bulletin of the Council for Research in Music Education* 115 (1993): 1–13.

19. Bennett Reimer, "Beyond Performing: The Promise of the New National Standards in Music Education," *Quarterly Journal of Music Teaching and Learning* 6, no. 2 (1995): 23–32.

20. Charles Fowler, "Finding the Way to Be Basic: Music Education in the 1990s and Beyond," in *Basic Concepts in Music Education II*, ed. Richard J. Colwell (Niwot: University Press of Colorado), 13.

21. Description of a differentiated curriculum in music developed by Mary Hannah Klontz of Arlington, Virginia.

22. Eunice Boardman, ed., *Dimensions of Musical Thinking* (Reston, VA: Music Educators National Conference, 1989); Lenore Pogonowski, "Developing Skills in Critical Thinking and Problem Solving," *Music Educators Journal* 73, no. 6 (1987): 37–41; Carol P. Richardson and Nancy L. Whitaker, "Critical Thinking and Music Education," in *Handbook of Research on Music Teaching and Learning*, ed. Richard Colwell (New York: Schirmer Books, 1992): 546–57; Paul Woodford, "Musical Intelligence in the World: Negotiating the Social World of Music," *Quarterly Journal of Music Teaching and Learning* 7, no. 2 (1995): 49–59.

23. For a description of the musical problem-solving process, refer to: Joanne Haroutounian, "Creatively Teaching the Artist Within," *American Music Teacher* 42, no. 3 (1992–93): 20–23, 76–80; Jeannine W. Hamburg, *Where Is That Music*

Coming From? A Path to Creativity (Cherry Hill, NJ: Myrte Press, 1989); Pogonowski, "Developing Skills in Critical Thinking and Problem Solving"; Richardson and Whitaker, "Critical Thinking and Music Education."

24. L. C. DeLorenzo, "An Exploratory Field Study of Sixth Grade Students' Creative Musical Problem Solving Processes in the General Music Class" (Ph.D. diss., Columbia University, 1987).

25. David J. Elliot, "Musicing, Listening, and Musical Understanding," *Contributions to Music Education* 20 (1993): 72.

26. D. Treffinger and S. Isaksen, *Creative Problem Solving: An Introduction* (Sarasota, FL: Center for Creative Learning, 1991).

27. Hollis Thoms, "Encouraging the Musical Imagination through Composition," *Music Educators Journal* 73, no. 5 (1987): 27–30.

28. Description of a differentiated music curriculum developed by Estelle Roth of Arlington, Virginia.

29. Timothy S. Brophy, "Building Music Literacy with Guided Composition," *Music Educators Journal* 83, no. 3 (1996): 15–18; Sam Baltzer, "Enhancing Aural Lessons with Multimedia Programs," *Music Educators Journal* 81, no. 3 (1996): 33–36; W. Berz and J. Bowman, *Applications of Research in Music Technology* (Reston, VA: Music Educators National Conference); T. Rudolph, *Teaching Music with Technology* (Chicago: GIA, 1996); David Brian Williams and Peter R. Webster, *Experiencing Music Technology* (New York: Schirmer Books, 1996).

30. Music Educators National Conference, *National Standards for Arts Education: What Every Young American Should Know and Be Able to Do in the Arts* (Reston, VA: Music Educators National Conference, 1994), 98–109.

31. The quotation from Yo Yo Ma is from Edith Eisler, "Chalk Talk: A Lifelong Music Teacher Discusses Pedagogy, Imitation and the Creative Spirit," *Classical Pulse* (February 1995): 12.

32. Sosniak, "Learning to Be a Concert Pianist," 61.

33. Ibid., 63.

34. Roland S. Persson, "Concert Musicians as Teachers: Good Intentions Falling Short," in *Fostering Growth of High Ability: European Perspectives*, ed. Arthur J. Cropley and Detlev Dehn (Norwood, NJ: Ablex, 1996), 305–17; Roland S. Persson, "Survival of the fittest of the Most Talented? Deconstructing the Myth of the Musical Maestro," *Journal of Secondary Gifted Education* 12, no. 1 (2000): 25–38.

35. Joseph Rezits, "Those Get-Tough Famous Teachers," *Piano and Keyboard* 175 (1997): 40–44.

36. Gail Berenson, "The Performer or the Performance?" *Piano and Keyboard* 176 (1997): 69–71.

37. The interviewees were Chris Campbell, Hal Grossman, and T. J. Lymenstull. Refer to: Joanne Haroutounian, "An Interview with Three Master Teachers from the Interlochen Arts Academy," *Journal of Secondary Gifted Education* 12, no. 1 (2000): 39–42.

38. John Sloboda and Michael Howe, "Problems Experienced by Talented Young Musicians as a Result of the Failure of Other Children to Value Musical Accomplishments, *Gifted Education International* 8, no. 1 (1992): 16–18.

39. For additional ideas, refer to J. Haroutounian, "Drop the Hurdles and Open the Doors," *Arts Education Policy Review* 99, no. 6 (1998), 15–25; "The Delights and Dilemmas of the Musically Talented Teenager," *Journal of Secondary Gifted Education*, 12, no. 1 (2000): 3–16.

40. Rena Subotnik, "Developing Young Adolescent Performers at Juilliard: An Educational Prototype for Elite Level Talent Development in the Arts and Sciences," in *Developing Talent across the Lifespan*, ed. C. F. M. Van Lieshout and P. G. Heymans (Philadelphia: Psychology Press, 2000), 249–75.

41. Information is from the 1999 application forms to the Juilliard School and the Curtis Institute of Music.

CHAPTER 15. FINAL REFLECTIONS

1. David Bayles and Ted Orland, *Art and Fear: Observations on the Perils (and Rewards) of Artmaking* (Santa Barbara: Capra Press, 1993), 109.

BIBLIOGRAPHY

Abeel, L., C. Callahan, and S. Hunsaker.*The Use of Published Instruments in the Identification of Gifted Students*. Washington, DC: National Association of Gifted Children, 1994.

Aiello, Rita, and John Sloboda. *Musical Perceptions*. New York: Oxford University Press, 1994.

Anderson, Emily, ed. and trans. *The Letters of Mozart and His Family*. 21st ed. Vol. 1. New York: Macmillan, 1938.

Anderson, J. R. "Acquisition of Cognitive Skill." *Psychology Review* 89 (1982): 339–46.

Apfelstadt, Hilary. "Musical Thinking in the Choral Rehearsal." In *Dimensions of Musical Thinking*, edited by Eunice Boardman. Reston, VA: Music Educators National Conference, 1989, 73–82.

Arnheim, Rudolf. *Visual Thinking*. Berkeley: University of California Press, 1969.

ArtsConnection. "Talent beyond Words: Identifying and Developing Talent through Music and Dance in Economically Disadvantaged, Bilingual, and Handicapped Children." Report submitted to the United States Department of Education Jacob Javits Gifted and Talented Program. Brooklyn: ArtsConnection, 1992.

Atterbury, Betty W. "The Musically Talented: Aren't They Also Gifted?" *Update: Applications of Research in Music Education* 9, no. 2 (1991): 21–23.

Augustine. *Musik: De Musica libri sex*. Translated by Carl Johann Perl. Paderborn Germany: F. Schoningh, 1962.

Balk, H. Wesley. *Performing Power: A New Approach for the Singer-Actor*. Minneapolis: University of Minnesota Press, 1985.

Baltzer, S. "Enhancing Aural Lessons with Multimedia Programs." *Music Educators Journal* 83, no. 3 (1996): 33–36.

———. "A Factor Analytic Study of Musical Creativity in Children in the Primary Grades." Ph.D. diss., Indiana University, 1990.

————. "A Validation Study of a Measure of Musical Creativity." *Journal of Research in Music Education* 36, no. 4 (1988): 232–49.

Bamberger, Jeanne. "Cognitive Issues in the Development of Musically Gifted Children." In *Conceptions of Giftedness,* edited by Robert Sternberg and Janet Davidson. Cambridge, England: Cambridge University Press, 1986, 389–413.

————. "Growing Up Prodigies: The Mid-Life Crisis." In *Developmental Approaches to Giftedness and Creativity,* edited by David Feldman. San Francisco: Jossey-Bass, 1982, 265–79.

————. "In Search of a Tune." In *The Arts and Cognition,* edited by David Perkins and Barbara Leondar. Baltimore: Johns Hopkins University Press, 1977, 284–317.

————. *The Mind behind the Musical Ear: How Children Develop Musical Intelligence.* Cambridge: Harvard University Press, 1995.

————. "Revisiting Children's Drawings of Simple Rhythms: A Function of Reflection-in-Action." In *U-Shaped Behavioral Growth,* edited by S. Strauss. New York: Academic Press, 1982, 191–226.

Barrett, Carolyn. *The Magic of Matsumoto: The Suzuki Method of Education.* Palm Springs: ETC 1995.

Bartlett, John. *Familiar Quotations.* Little, Brown, 1980.

Bayles, David, and Ted Orland. *Art and Fear: Observations on the Perils (and Rewards) of Artmaking.* Santa Barbara: Capra Press, 1993.

Bennett, Stan. "The Process of Musical Creation: Interviews with Eight Composers." *Journal of Research in Music Education* 24, no. 1 (1976): 3–11.

Bentley, Arnold. *Musical Ability in Children and its Measurement.* New York: October House, 1966.

Berenson, Gail. "The Performer or the Performance?" *Piano and Keyboard* 176 (1997): 69–71.

Berlioz, Hector. *The Life of Hector Berlioz, as Written by Himself in his Letters and Memoirs.* Translated by Katharine F. Boult. New York: Dutton, 1923.

Bernac, P. *The Interpretation of French Song.* London: Victor Gollancz, 1978.

Bernstein, Leonard. *Findings.* New York: Simon and Schuster, 1982.

————. *The Infinite Variety of Music.* New York: Simon and Schuster, 1966.

Bernstein, Seymour. *With Your Own Two Hands: Self Discovery through Music.* New York: Schirmer Books, 1981.

Berr, Bruce. "Transformational Practice Techniques for Piano." *American Music Teacher* 44, no. 5 (1995): 12–15, 93–95.

Berz, W., and J. Bowman. *Applications of Research in Music Technology.* Reston, VA: Music Educators National Conference, 1994.

Black, Susan. "The Musical Mind." *American School Board Journal* (January 1997): 20–22.

Bloom, Benjamin, ed. *Developing Talent in Young People.* New York: Ballantine Books, 1985.

————. *Taxonomy of Educational Objectives: The Classification of Educational Goals. Handbook 1: Cognitive Domain.* New York: Longmans, Green, 1956.

Boardman, Eunice, ed. *Dimensions of Musical Thinking.* Reston, VA: Music Educators National Conference, 1989.

Boettcher, Wendy S., Sabrina S. Hahn, and Gordon L. Shaw. "Mathematics and Music: A Search for Insight into Higher Brain Function." *Leonardo Music Journal* 4 (1994): 53–58.

Bower, Bruce. "Brain Images Reveal Cerebra Side of Music." *Science News* (April 1994): 145, 260.

Boyd, Jenny. *Musicians in Tune: Seventy-five Contemporary Musicians Discuss the Creative Process.* New York: Simon and Schuster, 1992.

Boyle, J. David, and Rudolf E. Radocy. *Measurement and Evaluation of Musical Experiences.* New York: Schirmer Books, 1987.

Bresler, Liora. "Music in a Double-Bind: Instruction by Non-Specialists in Elementary Schools." *Bulletin of the Council for Research in Music Education* 115 (1993): 1–13.

Brophy, Timothy S. "Building Music Literacy with Guided Composition." *Music Educators Journal* 83, no. 3 (1996): 15–18.

Bruner, Jerome S. *On Knowing: Essays for the Left Hand.* New York: Atheneum, 1962.

———. *The Process of Education.* New York: Vintage Books, 1963.

Bruscia, Kenneth. "Building Effective Student-Teacher Relationships in the Private Music Studio." *American Music Teacher* 39, no. 2 (1989): 12–15.

Burns, Kimberly. "Invented Notation and the Compositional Processes of Children." *Update: Applications of Research in Music Education* 14, no. 3 (1997): 12–16.

Carson, Rachel. *The Sense of Wonder.* New York: Harper and Row, 1956.

Cary, Emily P. "Music as a Prenatal and Early Childhood Impetus to Enhancing Intelligence and Cognitive Skills." *Roeper Review* 9, no. 3 (1987): 155–60.

Chabris, Christopher F. "Prelude or Requiem for the 'Mozart Effect'?" *Nature* 400, no. 6747 (1999): 826–27.

Chang, H., and S. E. Trehub. "Auditory Processing of Relational Information by Young Infants." *Journal of Experimental Child Psychology* 24 (1977): 324–31.

Clark, Barbara. *Growing Up Gifted.* Columbus, OH: Charles E. Merrill, 1983.

Clark, G., and E. Zimmerman. *Issues and Practices Related to the Identification of Gifted and Talented Students in the Visual Arts.* Storrs, CT: National Research Center on the Gifted and Talented, 1992.

Cohen, A. J., A. Leigh, and S. E. Trehub. "Infants' Perception of Melodies: The Role of Melodic Contour." *Child Development* 55 (1984): 821–30.

Cohen, V. "The Emergence of Musical Gestures in Kindergarten." Ph.D. diss., University of Illinois, Urbana, 1980.

Colangelo, Nicholas, and Gary A. Davis. *Handbook of Gifted Education.* Boston: Allyn and Bacon, 1991.

Colwell, Richard. *Music Achievement Tests.* Chicago: Follett, 1970.

———, ed. *Basic Concepts in Music Education II.* Niwot: University Press of Colorado, 1991.

Copland, Aaron. *Music and Imagination.* Cambridge: Harvard University Press, 1952.

———. *What to Listen For in Music.* New York: Penguin Books, 1957.

Cox, C. *Genetic Studies of Genius. Vol. 2. The Early Mental Traits of Three Hundred Geniuses.* Stanford: Stanford University Press, 1926.

Cropley, Arthur J., and Detlev Dehn, eds. *Fostering the Growth of High Abilitiy: European Perspectives*. Norwood, NJ: Ablex, 1996.

Cross, Jim. "Art Renaissance in South Carolina." *Gifted Child Today* (January/February 1990): 41–42.

Csikszentmihalyi, Mihaly. *Creativity: Flow and the Psychology of Discovery and Invention*. New York: HarperCollins, 1996.

———. *Flow: The Psychology of Optimal Experience*. New York: HarperCollins, 1990.

Csikszentmihalyi, Mihaly, Kevin Rathude, and Samuel Whalen. *Talented Teenagers: The Roots of Success and Failure*. Cambridge, England: Cambridge University Press, 1993.

Cutietta, Robert, Donald L. Hamann, and Linda Miller Walker. *Spin-Offs: The Extra-Musical Advantages of a Musical Education*. Elkhart, IN: United Musical Instruments USA, 1995.

Daignault, L. "Children's Creative Thinking within the Context of a Computer-Supported Improvisational Approach to Composition." Ph. D. diss., Northwestern University, 1997.

Davidson, Jane, Derek Moore, John Sloboda, and Michael Howe. "Characteristics of Music Teachers and the Progress of Young Instrumentalists." *Journal of Research in Music Education* 46, no. 1 (1998): 141–60.

Davidson, Lyle. "Songsinging by Young and Old: A Developmental Approach to Music." In *Musical Perceptions*, edited by Rita Aiello and John Sloboda. New York: Oxford University Press, 1994, 99–130.

———. "Tools and Environments for Musical Creativity." *Music Educators Journal* 76, no. 9 (1990): 47–51.

Davidson, Lyle, and Larry Scripp. "Conditions of Giftedness: Musical Development in the Preschool and Early Elementary Years." In *Beyond Terman: Contemporary Longitudinal Studies of Giftedness and Talent*, edited by Rena F. Subotnik and Karen D. Arnold. Norwood, NJ: Ablex, 1994, 155–85.

———. "Education and Development in Music from a Cognitive Perspective." In *Children and the Arts*, edited by D. Hargreaves. Philadelphia: Open University Press, 1989, 59–86.

———. "Surveying the Coordinates of Cognitive Skills in Music." In *Handbook of Research on Music Teaching and Learning*, edited by Richard Colwell. New York: Schirmer Books, 1992, 392–400.

Davidson, Lyle, Larry Scripp, and Patricia Welsh. "'Happy Birthday': Evidence for Conflicts of Perceptual Knowledge and Conceptual Understanding." *Journal of Aesthetic Education* 22, no. 1 (1988): 65–74.

Davies, John B. *The Psychology of Music*. Stanford: Stanford University Press, 1978.

Davis, Gary. *Creativity Is Forever*. Dubuque, IA: Kendall Hunt, 1992.

Davis, M. "Folk Music Psychology." *Psychologist* 7, no. 12 (1994): 537.

Deliège, Irène, and John Sloboda. *Musical Beginnings: Origins and Development of Musical Competence*. Oxford: Oxford University Press, 1996.

———. *Perception and Cognition of Music*. East Sussex: Psychology Press, 1997.

DeLorenzo, L. C. "An Exploratory Field Study of Sixth Grade Students' Creative Musical Problem Solving Processes in the General Music Class." Ph.D. diss., Columbia University, 1987.

Deutsch, Otto E. *Mozart: A Documentary Biography*. 2nd ed. Translated by Eric Blom, Peter Branscombe, and Jeremy Noble. Stanford: Stanford University Press, 1965.

Dinnocenti, Susan T. "Differentiation: Definition and Description for Gifted and Talented." *National Research Center on the Gifted and Talented Newsletter* (spring 1998): 10–11.

Domer, Jodi, and Joyce Eastlund Gromko. "Qualitative Changes in Preschoolers' Invented Notations following Music Instruction." *Contributions to Music Education* 23 (1996): 62–78.

Dorhout, A. "Gifted Education in the Arts." *NJEA Review* 55, no. 9 (1982): 20–21.

———. "Identifying Musically Gifted Children." *Journal for the Education of the Gifted* 5, no.1 (1982): 56–65.

Dutoit, Claire-Lise. *Music, Movement Therapy*. Surrey: Dalcroze Society, 1971.

Eagle, Charles T., Jr. "An Introductory Perspective of Music Psychology." In *Handbook of Music Psychology*, edited by Donald A. Hodges. Lawrence, KS: National Association for Music Therapy, 1980, 1–15.

Eaton, Quaintance."Hoffman's Golden Jubilee." *Musical America* 25 (November 1937): 7.

Eberle, B., and B. Stanish. *CPS for Kids*. Carthage, IL: Good Apple, 1985.

Eisler, Edith. "Chalk Talk: A Lifelong Music Teacher Discusses Pedagogy, Imitation and the Creative Spirit." *Classical Pulse* (February 1995): 12.

Eisner, Elliot W. *Cognition and Curriculum Reconsidered*. New York: Teachers College Press, 1994.

———. *Educating Artistic Vision*. New York: Macmillan, 1972.

———. *The Educational Imagination: On the Design and Evaluation of School Programs*. New York: Macmillan, 1985.

———. "The Role of the Arts in Cognition and Curriculum." In *Developing Minds: A Resource Book for Teaching Thinking*, edited by A. Costa. Alexandria, VA: Association for Supervision and Curriculum Development, 1991, 169–75.

Elliott, David J. "Assessing Musical Performance." *British Journal of Music Education* 4, no. 2 (1987): 157–83.

———. "Musicing, Listening, and Musical Understanding." *Contributions to Music Education* 20 (1993): 64–83.

———. *Music Matters: A New Philosophy of Music Education*. New York: Oxford University Press, 1995.

Ericsson, K. A. *The Road to Excellence: The Acquisition of Expert Performance in the Arts and Sciences, Sports, and Games*. Mahwah, NJ: Erlbaum, 1996.

Ericsson, K. A., R. T. Krampe, and C. Tesch-Romer. "The Role of Deliberate Practice in the Acquisition of Expert Performance." *Psychological Review* 100 (1993): 363–406.

Farber, Anne, and Lisa Parker. "Discovering Music through Dalcroze Eurythmics." *Music Educators Journal* 74, no. 3 (1987): 43–45.

Farnum, S. E. *The Farnum String Scale*. Winona, MN: Hal Leonard Music, 1969.

Feijoo, J. "Le foetus, Pierre et le Loup." In *L'Aube des Sens, Cahiers du Nouveau-né*, edited by E. Herbinet and M. C. Busnel. Paris: Stock, 1981, 192–209.

Feinberg, S. "Creative Problem-solving and the Music Listening Experience." *Music Educators Journal* 61, no. 1 (1974): 53–59.

Feldman, David. "Child Prodigies: A Distinctive Form of Giftedness." *Gifted Child Quarterly* 37, no. 4 (1993): 188–93.

———. *Nature's Gambit: Child Prodigies and the Development of Human Potential*. New York: Basic Books, 1986.

Fisher, Renée. *Musical Prodigies: Masters at an Early Age*. New York: Association Press, 1973.

Fiske, Harold E. *Music Cognition and Aesthetic Attitudes*. Lewiston, NY: Edwin Mellen Press, 1993.

Flowers, P. "Attention to Elements of Music by Children and Undergraduates." *Psychology of Music* 12 (1984): 17–24.

———. "The Effect of Instruction in Vocabulary and Listening on Nonmusicians' Descriptions of Changes in Music." *Journal of Research in Music Education* 31 (1983): 179–89.

———. "The Effects of Teacher and Learning Experiences, Tempo, and Mode on Undergraduates' and Children's Symphonic Music Preferences." *Journal of Research in Music Education* 36 (1988): 19–34.

———. "Listening: The Key to Describing Music." *Music Educators Journal* 77 (1990): 21–23.

Fowler, Charles. "Finding the Way to Be Basic: Music Education in the 1990s and Beyond." In *Basic Concepts in Music Eduation II*, edited by Richard J. Colwell. Niwot: University Press of Colorado, 1991, 3–26.

Frahm, Robert A. "Music and Minds: UConn Program Explores Genetic Connection." *Hartford Courant*, June 29, 1998, A1.

Freeman, Joan. "Talent in Music and Fine-Art." *Gifted Education International* 2, no. 2 (1984): 107–10.

Freymuth, Malva. "Mental Practice: Some Guidelines for Musicians." *American Music Teacher* 43, no. 5 (1994): 18–21.

Gagné, Françoys. "Constructs and Models Pertaining to Exceptional Human Abilities." In *International Handbook of Research and Development of Giftedness and Talent*, edited by Kurt A. Heller, Franz J. Mönks, and Harry A. Passow. Oxford: Pergamon Press, 1993.

———. "Nature or Nurture? Re-examination of Sloboda and Howe's (1991) Interview Study on Talent Development in Music." *Psychology of Music* 27 (1999): 38–51.

———. "Toward a Differentiated Model of Giftedness and Talent." In *Handbook of Gifted Education*, edited by Nicholas Colangelo and Gary A. Davis. Boston: Allyn and Bacon, 1991, 65–80.

Galbraith, Bruce W. "Interlochen Arts Academy: Its Guidelines for Success." *Journal for the Education of the Gifted* 8, no. 3 (1985): 199–210.

Gardner, Howard. *The Arts and Human Development*. New York: Basic Books, 1994.

———. *Frames of Mind: The Theory of Multiple Intelligences*. New York: Basic Books, 1983.

———. "Multiple Intelligences: Implications for Art and Creativity." In *Artistic Intelligences: Implications for Education*, edited by W. Moody. New York: Teachers College Press, 1990, 11–27.

———. *Multiple Intelligences: The Theory in Practice*. New York: Basic Books, 1993.

———. *The Unschooled Mind: How Children Think and How Schools Should Teach*. New York: Basic Books, 1991.

Getzels, J. W., and P. W. Jackson. *Creativity and Intelligence*. New York: Wiley, 1962.

Gieseking, Walter, and Karl Leimer. *Piano Technique*. New York: Dover, 1972.

Giomo, Carla. "The Studio Teacher as Aesthetic Educator." *American Music Teacher* 44, no. 4 (1995): 14–17.

Goertzel, Victor, and Mildred G. Goertzel. *Cradles of Eminence*. Boston: Little, Brown, 1962.

Gorder, W. "Divergent Production Abilities as Constructs of Musical Creativity." *Journal of Research in Music Education* 28, no. 1 (1980): 34–42.

Gordon, Edwin. *Advanced Measures of Music Audiation*. Chicago: GIA, 1989.

———. *Intermediate Measures of Music Audiation*. Chicago: GIA, 1982.

———. *Iowa Tests of Music Literacy*. Iowa City: Bureau of Educational Research and Service, University of Iowa, 1971.

———. *Musical Aptitude Profile*. Chicago: GIA, 1965.

———. "Musical Child Abuse." *American Music Teacher* 37, no. 5 (1988): 14–17, 59.

———. *The Nature, Description, Measurement, and Evaluation of Music Aptitudes*. Chicago: GIA, 1986.

———. *Primary Measures of Music Audiation*. Chicago: GIA, 1979.

Gordon, Stewart. *Etudes for Piano Teachers: Reflections on the Teacher's Art*. New York: Oxford University Press, 1995.

Grashel, John. "Test Instruments Used by *Journal of Research in Music Education* Authors from 1980–1989." *Update: Applications of Research in Music Education* 14, no. 2 (1996): 24–30.

Gray-Lewis, Stephen. "Children and Art—An Interview with Mark Schubart." In *The Gifted Child, the Family, and the Community*, edited by Bernard Miller and Merle Price. New York: Walker, 1981, 192–98.

Green, Barry, with W. Timothy Gallwey. *The Inner Game of Music*. New York: Anchor Press, 1986.

Grilli, Susan. *Preschool in the Suzuki Spirit*. Tokyo: Harcourt Brace Jovanovich, 1987.

Grimes, William. "A New Juilliard for a More Challenging Era." *New York Times*, June 2, 1993, C13.

Gromko, Joyce Eastlund, and Allison Smith Poorman. "The Effect of Music Training on Preschoolers' Spatial-Temporal Task Performance." *Journal of Research in Music Education* 46, no. 2 (1998): 173–81.

Guilford, J. P. *The Nature of Human Intelligence*. New York: McGraw-Hill, 1967.

———. "Three Faces of Intellect." *American Psychologist* 14 (1959): 469–79.

———. "Traits of Creativity." In *Creativity*, edited by P. E. Vernon. Harmondsworth: Penguin, 1970, 167–78.

———. *Way Beyond the IQ: Guide to Improving Intelligence and Creativity.* Buffalo: Creative Education Foundation, 1977.

Guilmartin, Kenneth K. *Music Together: Teacher Education.* Princeton: Center for Music and Young Children, 1999.

Hallam, Susan. "Predictors of Achievement and Dropout in Instrumental Tuition." *Psychology of Music* 26 (1998): 116–32.

Hamburg, Jeannine W. *Where Is That Music Coming From? A Path to Creativity.* Cherry Hill, NJ: Myrte Press, 1989.

Hargreaves, David. "The Development of Aesthetic Reactions to Music." *Psychology of Music*, special issue (1982): 51–54.

———. "The Development of Artistic and Musical Competence." In *Musical Beginnings: Origins and Development of Musical Competence*, edited by Irene Deliège and John Sloboda. Oxford: Oxford University Press, 1996, 145–68.

———, ed. *Children and the Arts.* Philadelphia: Open University Press, 1989.

———. *The Developmental Psychology of Music.* Cambridge, England: Cambridge University Press, 1986.

Haroutounian, Joanne. "The Academics of Artistic Thinking." *Think* 5, no. 2. (1994): 17–20.

———. "The Assessment of Potential Talent in Musical Behavior/Performance: Criteria and Procedures to Consider in the Identification of Musically Gifted and Talented Students." Ph.D. diss., University of Virginia, 1995.

———. "Creatively Teaching the Artist Within." *American Music Teacher* 42, no. 3 (1992–93): 20–23, 76–80.

———. "The Delights and Dilemmas of the Musically Talented Teenager." *Journal of Secondary Gifted Education* 12, no.1 (2000): 3–16.

———. "Drop the Hurdles and Open the Doors: Fostering Talent Development through School and Community Collaboration." *Arts Education Policy Review* 99, no. 6 (1998): 15–25.

———. *Explorations in Music.* 7 books. San Diego: Kjos Music, 1993–99.

———. "How Mozart *Really* Makes You Smarter." *Piano and Keyboard* 208 (2001): 40–44.

———. "An Interview with Three Master Teachers from the Interlocken Arts Academy." *Journal of Secondary Gifted Education* 12, no. 1 (2000): 39–42.

———. "Judge for Yourself." *Piano and Keyboard* 181 (1996): 46–50.

———. "Kindling a Musical Spark: The MusicLink Collaboration." *Communicator* 29, no. 2 (1998): 1, 24–27.

———. "MTNA Winners after a Decade: Portraits of Commitment and Excellence." *American Music Teacher* 47, no. 2 (1997): 20–25, 66.

———. "MusicLink: Nurturing Potential and Recognizing Achievement." *Arts Education Policy Review* 101, no. 6 (2000): 12–20.

———. "Perspectives of Musical Talent: A Study of Identification Criteria and Procedures." *High Ability Studies* 11, no. 2 (2000): 137–60.

———. "The Recital Project—A Creative Performance Alternative." *American Music Teacher* 43, no. 2 (1993): 34.

———. *Rhythm Antics*. San Diego: Kjos Music, 1989.

———. "Talent Identification and Development in the Arts: An Artistic/Educational Dialogue." *Roeper Review* 18, no. 2 (1995): 112–17.

———. "Teaching Talented Teenagers at the Interlochen Arts Academy: An Interview with Three Master Teachers." *Journal of Secondary Gifted Education* 12, no. 1 (2000): 39–42.

Hassler, Marianne. "The Critical Teens: Musical Capacities Change in Adolescence." In *Fostering the Growth of High Ability: European Perspectives*, edited by Arthur J. Cropley and Detlev Dehn. Norwood, NJ: Ablex, 1996, 247–62.

Hassler, M., N. Birbaumer, and A. Feil. "Musical Talent and Visual-Spatial Abilities: A Longitudinal Study." *Psychology of Music* 20 (1992): 99–113.

Heller, Kurt A., Franz J. Mönks, and Harry A. Passow. *International Handbook of Research and Development of Giftedness and Talent*. Oxford: Pergamon Press, 1993.

Hepper, P. G. "Fetal 'Soap' Addiction." *Lancet* 1 (1988): 1147–48.

Hermelin, B., N. O'Connor, and S. Lee. "Musical Inventiveness of Five Idiots Savants." *Psychological Medicine* 17 (1987): 685–94.

Heyge, Lorna and Audrey Sillick. *The Cycle of Seasons: A Musical Celebration of the Year for Young Children*. Greensboro, NC: Musicgarden/MusicMatters (1994).

Hickey, M. "Qualitative and Quantitative Relationships between Children's Creative Musical Thinking Processes and Products." Ph.D. diss., Northwestern University, 1995.

Hodges, David. "Neuromusical Research: A Review of the Literature." *Handbook of Music Psychology*. 2nd ed. San Antonio, TX: IMR Press, 1996, 197–284.

Hodges, Donald A., ed. *Handbook of Music Psychology*. Lawrence, KS: National Association of Music Therapy, 1980.

Howe, Michael J. "The Childhoods and Early Lives of Geniuses: Combining Psychological and Biographical Evidence." In *The Road to Excellence: The Acquisition of Expert Performance in the Arts and Sciences, Sports, and Games*, edited by K. Anders Ericsson. Mahwah, NJ: Erlbaum, 1996, 255–70.

———. *The Psychology of High Abilities*. New York: New York University Press, 1999.

Howe, Michael J., J. Davidson, D. Moore, and J. Sloboda. "Are There Early Childhood Signs of Musical Ability?" *Psychology of Music* 23, no. 2 (1994): 162–76.

Howe, Michael, and John Sloboda. "Early Signs of Talents and Special Interests in the Lives of Young Musicians." *European Journal for High Ability* 2 (1992): 102–11.

———. "Young Musicians' Accounts of Significant Influences in Their Early Lives. I. The Family and the Musical Background." *British Journal of Music Education* 8 (1991): 39–52.

———. "Young Musician's Accounts of Significant Influences in Their Early Lives. II. Teachers, Practicing and Performing." *British Journal of Music Education* 7 (1991): 53–63.

Hughes, William. "General Music in Secondary Schools: Beyond the Performing Arts." *NASSP Bulletin* 76, no. 544 (1992): 5–10.

Hurford, P. *Making Music on the Organ.* Oxford: Oxford University Press, 1988.

Isaksen, S. G., and D. J. Treffinger. *Creative Problem Solving: The Basic Course.* Buffalo: Bearly Limited, 1985.

Johnson, B. "Gifted and Talented Screening Form." In *Assessment in Gifted Education* , edited by F. Karnes and E. Collins. Springfield, IL: Charles Thomas, 1981, p. 32.

Jones, Mari Riess, and Susan Holleran, eds. *Cognitive Bases of Musical Communication.* Washington, DC: American Psychological Association, 1992.

Kahn, Joshua, and Geri Fox. "Normal Music Development: A Review." *Medical Problems of Performing Artists* 12, no. 3 (1997): 83–88.

Kaplan, Sandra N. "The Grid: A Model to Construct Differentiated Curriculum for the Gifted." In *Systems and Models for Dveloping Programs for the Gifted and Talented,* edited by Joseph S. Renzulli. Mansfield Center, CT: Creative Learning Press, 1986, 180–93.

Karnes, F., and E. Collins. *Assessment in Gifted Education.* Springfield, IL: Charles Thomas, 1981.

Karnes, M. *Music Checklist.* ERIC Document Reproduction Service no. ED 160 226, 1978).

Kaufman, Felice A., Thomas C. Tews, and Cheryl P. Milam. "New Orleans Center for the Creative Arts: Program Descriptions and Student Perceptions." *Journal for the Education of the Gifted* 8, no. 3 (1985): 211–19.

Kemp, A. E. *The Musical Temperament: Psychology and Personality of Musicians.* Oxford: Oxford University Press, 1996.

Kennell, Richard. "Musical Thinking in the Instrumental Rehearsal." In *Dimensions of Musical Thinking,* edited by Eunice Boardman. Reston, VA: Music Educators National Conference, 1989, 83–90.

Kenneson, Claude. *Musical Prodigies: Perilous Journeys, Remarkable Lives.* Portland. OR: Amadeus Press, 1998.

Kern, R. Fred, and Marguerite Miller. *Projects for Piano Pedagogy.* 2 vols. San Diego: Kjos Music, 1988.

Kessen, W., J. Levine, and K. A. Wendrick. "The Imitation of Pitch in Infants." *Infant Behavior Development* 11 (1965): 95–127.

Khatena, Joseph. *Educational Psychology of the Gifted.* New York: Wiley, 1982.

Khatena, Joseph, and D. Morse. "Preliminary Study of the Khatena-Morse Multitalent Perception Inventory." *Perceptual and Motor Skills* 64 (1987): 1187–90.

Klein, Alan J., B. L. Armstrong, M. K. Green, and F. R. Brown. "Hyperacusis and Otitis Media in Individuals with Williams Syndrome." *Journal of Speech and Hearing Disorders* 55 (1990): 339–44.

Kogan, Judith. *Nothing but the Best: The Struggle for Perfection at the Juilliard School.* New York: Limelight Editions, 1989.

Kohn, Alfie. *No Contest: The Case against Competition.* New York: Houghton Mifflin, 1986.

Krampe, R. T., and K. A. Ericsson. "Deliberate Practice and Elite Musical Performance." In *The Practice of Performance: Studies in Musical Interpretation*, edited by J. Rink. Cambridge, England: Cambridge University Press, 1995, 84–101.

Kratus, J. "A Time Analysis of the Compositional Processes Used by Children Aged 5 to 13." *Contributions to Music Education* 12 (1985): 1–8.

Krechevsky, Mara. *Project Spectrum: Preschool Assessment Handbook*. Cambridge: Harvard Project Zero, Graduate School of Education, 1994.

Kreitner, Kenneth, and Ann W. Engin. "Identifying Musical Talent." In *Psychology and the Education of the Gifted*, edited by J. Renzulli and W. Barbe. New York: Irvington, 1981, 193–204.

Kroeker, Charlotte. "Adolescents and Piano Study: The Two Can Mix." *Clavier* 26, no. 5 (1987): 38–40.

Landers, Ray. *The Talent Education School of Shinichi Suzuki: An Analysis*. Smithtown, NY: Exposition Press, 1980.

Langer, Susan. *Feeling and Form*. New York: Scribner's, 1953.

———. *Philosophy in a New Key: A Study in the Symbolism of Reason, Rite, and Art*. New York: Mentor Books, 1956.

———. *Problems of Art*. New York: Scribner's, 1957.

Larsen, R. L. "Levels of Conceptual Development in Melodic Permutation Concepts Based on Piaget's Theory." *Journal of Research in Music Education* 21 (1973): 256–63.

Larson, Gary. *In Search of the Farside*. Kansas City: Andrews and McMeel, 1984, 35.

Lecanuet, J. P., C. Granier-Deferre, A. Y. Jacquet, and M. C. Busnel. "Decelerative Cardiac Responsiveness to Acoustical Stimulation in the Near Term Foetus." *Quarterly Journal of Experimental Psychology* 44b (1992): 279–303.

Lehman, P. R. "Review of the *Iowa Test of Music Literacy*." In *The Eighth Mental Measurements Yearbook*, vol. 1, edited by O. K. Buros. Highland Park, NJ: Gryphon Press, 1978, 526–27.

———. "Review of Music Achievement Tests." In *The Seventh Mental Measurements Yearbook*, vol. 1, edited by O. K. Buros. Highland Park, NJ: Gryphon Press, 1972, 521–22.

Leng, Xiaodan, and Gordon L. Shaw. "Coding of Musical Structure and the Trion Model of Cortex." *Music Perception* 8, no. 1 (1990): 49–62.

———. "Toward a Neural Theory of Higher Brain Function Using Music as a Window." *Concepts in Neuroscience* 2 (1991): 229–58.

Lenhoff, Howard M. "Information Sharing: Insights into the Musical Potential of Cognitively Impaired People Diagnosed with Williams Syndrome." *Music Therapy Perspectives* 16, no. 1 (1998): 33–36.

———. "Mentally Asymmetric." *Ability Network* 3 (1995): 15–16.

Lenhoff, Howard M., Paul P. Wang, Frank Greenberg, and Ursula Bellugi. "Williams Syndrome and the Brain." *Scientific American* 277, no. 6 (1997): 68–73.

Leonard, George. *Mastery: The Keys to Success and Long-Term Fulfillment*. New York: Plume, 1992.

Levine, Josef. *Basic Principles in Pianoforte Playing*. New York: Dover, 1972.

Levine, Karen. "Williams Syndrome Information for Teachers." Clawson, MI: Williams Syndrome Association, n.d.

Levinson, J. "Evaluating Musical Performance." *Journal of Aesthetic Education* 21, no. 1 (1987): 75–88.

Levitin, Daniel J., and Ursula Bellugi. "Musical Abilities in Individuals with Williams Syndrome." *Music Perception* 15, no. 4 (1998): 357–89.

Lincoln, W., and M. Suid. *The Teachers Quotation Book*. Palo Alto, CA: Dale Seymour, 1986.

Logan, Kay. "Changing Roles: Artists and Educators." *American String Teacher* 47, no. 1 (1997): 85–88.

Logsdon, S. L. "Teacher Perceptions of Musical Giftedness in Fifth and Sixth Grade Children Compared with a Theoretical Model of Musical Giftedness." Ph.D. diss., University of Iowa, 1984.

Machover, Wilma, and Marienne Uszler. *Sound Choices: Guiding Your Child's Musical Experiences*. New York: Oxford University Press, 1996.

Mackworth-Young, Lucinda. "Pupil-Centered Learning in Music Classes." *American Music Teacher* 40, no. 5 (1991): 26–31, 57.

Maker, June. *Curriculum Development for the Gifted*. Rockville, MD: Aspen, 1982.

Malina, Debra. "Cerebral Symphony." *Harvard Medical Alumni Bulletin* 73, no. 1 (1999): 20–27.

Mallonee, Richard L. "Goals, Motivations, and Performance." *American String Teacher* 49, no. 3 (1999): 66–67, 69–70.

Mantel, G. *Cello Technique: Principles and Forms of Movement*, translated by B. Haimberger-Thiem. London: Indiana University Press, 1975.

Manturzewska, Maria. "Identification and Promotion of Musical Talent." In *Fostering the Growth of High Ability: European Perspectives*, edited by Arthur J. Cropley and Detlev Dehn. Norwood, NJ: Ablex, 1996, 271–86.

Marek-Schroer, Marilyn F., and Nathan A. Schroer. "Identifying and Providing for Musically Gifted Young Children." *Roeper Review* 16, no. 1 (1993): 33–36.

Marland, S. *Education of the Gifted and Talented: Report to the Congress of the United States by the U.S. Commissioner of Education*. Washington, DC: U.S. Government Printing Office, 1972.

Martin, Matt. "S.A.T.'s and Music." *American Music Teacher* 44, no. 5 (1995): 16–17.

McKernon, P. E. "The Development of First Songs in Young Children." *New Directions in Child Development* 3 (1979): 43–58.

Menuhin, Yehudi. *Unfinished Journey*. London: MacDonald and Jane's, 1977.

Meyer, J. "The Dependence of Pitch on Harmonic Sound Spectra." *Psychology of Music* 6, no. 1 (1978): 3–12.

Miller, L. K. *Musical Savants: Exceptional Skill in the Mentally Retarded*. Hillsdale, NJ: Erlbaum, 1989.

Millman, Dan. *Sacred Journey of the Peaceful Warrior*. Tiburon, CA: Kramer, 1991.

Mills, J. "Assessment of Solo Musical Performance: A Preliminary Study." *Bulletin of the Council for Research in Music Education* 91 (1987): 119–25.

Monk, Dennis C. "Who Will Teach the Understanding of Music?" *American Music Teacher* 43, no. 3 (1994–95): 16–19, 78–79.

Moog, H. *The Musical Experience of the Pre-school Child,* translated by C. Clarke. London: Schott, 1976.

Moon, Ick-Choo, and Marilyn Neeley. "Remarks by the Gifted on the Gifted." *American Music Teacher* 41, no. 4 (1992): 22–24.

Moorehead, G. E., and D. Pond. *Music of Young Children.* Santa Barbara: Pillsbury Foundation for Advancement of Music, 1941–51; reprint, 1978.

Morelock, Martha, and David Henry Feldman. "Prodigies and Savants: What They Have to Tell Us about Giftedness and Human Cognition." In *International Handbook of Research and Development of Giftedness and Talent,* edited by Kurt Heller, Franz J. Mönks, A. Harry Passow. Oxford: Pergamon Press, 1993, 161–69.

Morley-Pegge, R. *The French Horn: Some Notes on the Evolution of the Instrument and Its Technique.* London: Benn, 1973.

Mozart, W. A. *The Letters of Mozart and His Family.* Vol. 1. 21st ed. Edited and translated by Emily Anderson. New York: Macmillan, 1938.

Murphy, Frank. "Music and the Gifted." *Gifted Education International* 7, no. 1 (1990): 33–35.

———. "Success with Programmes for the Musically Gifted: Illusion or Reality?" *Studies in Educational Evaluation* 19 (1993): 35–40.

Mursell, James L. "Growth Processes in Music Education." In *Basic Concepts in Music Education II,* edited by Richard J. Colwell. Niwot: University Press of Colorado, 1991.

———. *The Psychology of Music.* Westport, CT: Greenwood Press, 1964.

Music Educators National Conference. *National Standards for Arts Education: What Every Young American Should Know and Be Able to Do in the Arts.* Reston, VA: Music Educators National Conference, 1994.

———. *Opportunity-to-learn Standards for Music Instruction, Grades PreK–12.* Reston, VA: Music Educators National Conference, 1994.

Nantais, Kristin M., and E. Glenn Schellenberg. "The Mozart Effect: An Artifact of Preference." *Psychological Science* 10, no. 4 (1999): 370–73.

National Coalition for Music Education. *Growing Up Capable: The Imperative for Music Education.* Reston, VA: Music Educators National Conference, 1989.

Nelson, F., A. Barresi, and J. Barrett. "Musical Cognition within an Analogical Setting: Toward a Cognitive Component of Musical Aptitude in Children." *Psychology of Music and Music Education* 20 (1992): 70–79.

Newman, Joan, John Rosenbach, Kathryn Burns, Brian Latimer, Helen Matocha, and Elaine Rosenthal Vogt. "An Experimental Test of 'The Mozart Effect': Does Listening to His Music Improve Spatial Ability?" *Perceptual and Motor Skills* 81 (1995): 1379–87.

Nielsen, Siw G. "Learning Strategies in Instrumental Music Practice." *British Journal of Music Education* 16, no. 3 (1999): 275–91.

Oestreich, James R. "Do Contests Need a Winner?" *New York Times,* June 13, 1995, H1, 27.

Orff, Carl, and Gunild Keetman. *Orff Schulwerk: Music for Children*. Mainz: Schott, 1956.

Osborn, A. F. *Applied Imagination*. New York: Scribner's, 1963.

Overy, Katie. "Can Music Really 'Improve' the Mind?" *Psychology of Music* 26 (1998): 97–99.

Papoušek, Hanuš. "Musicality in Infancy Research: Biological and Cultural Origins of Early Musicality." In *Musical Beginnings: Origins and Development of Musical Competence*, edited by Irène Deliège and John Sloboda. Oxford: Oxford University Press, 1996, 37–55.

Papoušek, Mechthild. "Intuitive Parenting: A Hidden Source of Musical Stimulation in Infancy." In *Musical Beginnings: Origins and Development of Musical Competence*, edited by Irène Deliège and John Sloboda. Oxford: Oxford University Press, 1996, 88–112.

Parnes, S. J. *The Magic of Your Mind*. New York: Bearly Limited, 1981.

Patton, M. Q. *Qualitative Evaluation Methods*. Beverly Hills: Creative Education Foundation, 1980.

Perkins, David. *The Mind's Best Work*. Cambridge: Harvard University Press, 1981.

———. "The Nature and Nurture of Creativity." In *Dimensions of Thinking and Cognitive Instruction*, edited by B. Jones and L. Idol. Hillsdale, NJ: Associated, 1990, 410–25.

Perkins, David, and Barbara Leondar, eds. *The Arts and Cognition*. Baltimore: John Hopkins University Press, 1977.

Persson, Roland S. "Complementary Studies of Musical Reality: The Phenomenological Concept of Musical Talent: A Pilot Study." W. Yorkshire: UK Department of Music, University of Huddersfield, 1994.

———. "Concert Musicians as Teachers: Good Intentions Falling Short." In *Fostering Growth of High Ability: European Perspectives*. Norwood, NJ: Ablex, 1996, 305–17.

———. "Survival of the Fittest or the Most Talented? Deconstructing the Myth of the Musical Maestro." *Journal of Secondary Gifted Education* 12, no. 1 (2000): 25–38.

Persson, Roland S., George Pratt, and Colin Robson. "Motivational and Influential Components of Musical Performance: A Qualitative Analysis." *European Journal for High Ability* 3 (1992): 206–17.

Pfeil, C. "Creativity as an Instructional Mode for Introducing Music to Non-music Majors at the College Level." Ph.D. diss., Michigan State University, 1972.

Pflederer, M. "The Responses of Children to Musical Tasks Embodying Piaget's Principle of Conservatism." *Journal of Research in Music Education* 12 (1964): 19–36.

Piaget, Jean. *Play, Dreams and Imitation in Childhood*. London: Routledge and Kegan Paul, 1951.

Piaget, J., and B. Inhelder. *The Psychology of the Child*. London: Routledge and Kegan Paul, 1969.

Piirto, Jane. *Talented Children and Adults: Their Development and Education*. New York: Macmillan, 1994.

———. *Understanding Those Who Create.* Dayton, OH: Ohio Psychology Press, 1992.

Pogonowski, Lenore. "Developing Skills in Critical Thinking and Problem Solving." *Music Educators Journal* 73, no. 6 (1987): 37–41.

Pollei, Paul C. "What Role Should Competitive Activities Play in a Piano Student's Development? Damage to the Ego Is Sometimes Difficult to Reconcile." *Keyboard Companion* 3, no. 2 (1992): 5–8.

Pond, D. "A Composer's Study of Young Children's Innate Musicality." *Bulletin of the Council for Research in Music Education* 68 (1981): 1–12.

Pond, D., S. J. Shelley, and B. D. Wilson. "The Pillsbury Foundation School Revisited." Paper presented to the twenty-sixth National conference of the Music Educators National Conference, Chicago, March, 1978.

Prevel, M. "Helping Children Build Their Own Music." In *Challenges in Music Education,* edited by F. Calloway. Perth: Department of Music, University of Western Australia, 1976.

Radford, John. *Child Prodigies and Exceptional Early Achievers.* New York: Free Press, 1990.

Radocy, Rudolf. "Toward Measuring Aesthetic Sensitivity: Classifying Students' Initial Verbal Reactions to Music." Paper presented at the national convention of Music Educators National Conference, Washington, DC, March 1990.

Radocy, Rudolf, and J. David Boyle. *Psychological Foundations of Musical Behavior.* 3rd ed. Springfield, IL: Charles C. Thomas, 1997.

Rauscher, Frances H. "Prelude or Requiem for the 'Mozart Effect?'" *Nature* 400, no. 6747 (1999): 828.

Rauscher, Frances H., K. D. Robinson, and J. J. Jens. "Improved Maze Learning through Early Music Exposure in Rats." *Neurological Research,* 20 (1998): 427–432.

Rauscher, Frances H., and Gordon Shaw. "Key Components of the Mozart Effect." *Perceptual and Motor Skills* 86 (1998): 835–41.

Rauscher, Frances H., Gordon Shaw, and Katherine Ky. "Music and Spatial Task Performance." *Nature* 365 (1995): 611.

Rauscher, Frances H., Gordon Shaw, Linda Levine, Katherine Ky, and Eric Wright. "Music and Spatial Task Performance: A Causal Relationship." Paper presented at the 102nd annual convention of the American Psychological Association, Los Angeles, August, 1994.

Rauscher, Frances H., Gordon Shaw, Linda Levine, and Eric Wright. "Music Training Causes Long-Term Enhancement of Preschool Children's Spatial-Temporal Reasoning." *Neurological Research* 19 (1997): 2–8.

Reimer, Bennett. "Beyond Performing: The Promise of the New National Standards in Music Education." *Quarterly Journal of Music Teaching and Learning* 6, no. 2 (1995): 23–32.

———. *Philosophy of Music Education.* Englewood Cliffs, NJ: Prentice Hall, 1970.

Reimer, Bennett, and Jeffrey Wright, eds. *On the Nature of Musical Experience.* Niwot: University of Colorado Press, 1992.

Reis, Sally M., and Joseph S. Renzulli, "The Secondary Triad Model." In *Systems and Models for Developing Programs for the Gifted and Talented,* edited by Joseph S. Renzulli. Mansfield Center, CT: Creative Learning Press, (1986) 267–305.

Renshaw, P. "Talented Young Musicians and the Yehudi Menuhin School." *Gifted Education International*, 1 (1992): 22–25.

Renzulli, Joseph S. "What Makes Giftedness?: Reexamining a Definition." *Phi Delta Kappan* 60, no. 3 (1978): 180–184, 261

Renzulli, Joseph S., L. Smith, A. White, C. Callahan, and R. Hartman. *Scales for Rating the Behavioral Characteristics of Superior Students*. Mansfield Center, CT: Creative Learning Press, 1976.

Renzulli, Joseph R., and Sally M. Reis. "The Schoolwide Enrichment Model: A Comprehensive Plan for the Development of Creative Productivity." In *Handbook of Gifted Education*, edited by Nicholas Colangelo and Gary A. Davis. Boston: Allyn and Bacon, 1991, 111–41.

Rezits, Joseph. "Those Get-Tough Famous Teachers." *Piano and Keyboard* 175 (1997): 40–44.

Richardson, Carol P. "Measuring Musical Giftedness." *Music Educators Journal* 76, no. 7 (1990): 46–49.

Richardson, Carol P., and Nancy L. Whitaker. "Critical Thinking and Music Education." In *Handbook of Research on Music Teaching and Learning*, edited by Richard Colwell. New York: Schirmer Books, 1992, 546–57.

Richert, E. Susanne. "Identification of Gifted Students: The Need for Pluralistic Assessment." *Roeper Review* 8, no. 2 (1985): 68–72.

————."Rampant Problems and Promising Practices in Identification." In *Handbook of Gifted Education* , edited by Nicholas Colangelo and Gary A. Davis. Boston: Allyn and Bacon, 1991, 81–96.

Richert, E. Susanne, L. Alvino, and R. McDonnel. *National Report on Identification: Assessment and Recommendations for Comprehensive Identification of Gifted and Talented Youth*. Sewell, NJ: Educational Information Resource Center, U.S. Department of Education, 1982.

Rideout, B. E., and C. M. Laubach. "EEG Correlates of Enhanced Spatial Performance Following Exposure to Music." *Perceptual and Motor Skills* 82 (1996): 427–32.

Rideout, B., S. Dougherty, and L. Wernert. "The Effect of Music on Spatial Performance: A Test of Generality." Perceptual and Motor Skill 86 (1998): 512–14.

Ries, N. L. "An Analysis of the Characteristics of Infant-child Singing Expressions." Ph.D. diss., Arizona State University, 1982.

Ries, Sally M., and Joseph S. Renzulli. "The Secondary Triad Model." In *Systems and Models for Developing Programs for the Gifted and Talented*, edited by Joseph S. Renzulli. Mansfield Center, CT: Creative Learning Press, 1986, 267–305.

Rink, John. *The Practice of Performance: Studies in Musical Interpretation*. Cambridge, England: Cambridge University Press, 1995.

Ristad, Eloise. *A Soprano on Her Head: Right-side-up Reflections on Life and Other Performances*. Moab, UT: Real People Press, 1982.

Rodriguez, Carlos Xavier, and Peter Richard Webster. "Development of Children's Verbal Interpretive Responses to Music Listening." *Bulletin of the Council for Research in Music Education* 134 (1997): 9–30.

Royal Swedish Academy of Music. *Basic Musical Functions and Musical Ability*. No. 32. Stockholm: Royal Swedish Academy of Music, 1981.

Rudolph, T. *Teaching Music with Technology*. Chicago: GIA, 1996.

Russell, Tom, and Sylvia Tyson. *And Then I Wrote: The Songwriter Speaks*. Vancouver: Arsenal Pulp Press, 1996.

Rutkowski, Joanne. "A Comparison of Adolescents' In-School and Out-of-School Music Experiences and Involvement." *Update: Applications of Research in Music Education* 11, no. 1 (1994): 17–21.

Sarafine, Mary Louise. *Music as Cognition: The Development of Thought in Sound*. New York: Columbia University Press, 1988.

Salk, L."The Effects of the Normal Heartbeat Sound on the Behavior of Newborn Infants: Implications for Mental Health." *World Mental Health* 12 (1960): 1–8.

———. "Mother's Heartbeat as an Imprinting Stimulus." *Transactions of the New York Academy of Sciences*, Series 2, 4 (1962): 753–63.

Sarnthein, J., A. von Stein, P. Rappelsberger, H. Petsche, F. H. Rauscher, and G. L. Shaw. "Persistent Patterns of Brain Activity: An EEG Coherence Study of the Positive Effect of Music On Spatial-Temporal Reasoning." *Neurological Research* 19 (1997): 107–11.

Sawyer, R. Keith. "Improvised Conversations: Music, Collaboration, and Development." *Psychology of Music* 26 (1999): 192–216.

Scheiber, Dave. "Music Lights a Fire." *St. Petersburg Times (Lenox, MA)*, September 6, 1998, A1.

Schlaug, G., L. Jäncke, Y. Huang, and H. Steinmetz. "In Vivo Evidence of Structural Brain Asymmetry in Musicians." *Science* 267 (1995): 699–701.

Schmidt, Charles P., and Jean Simor. "An Investigation of the Relationships Among Music Audiation, Musical Creativity, and Cognitive Style." *Journal of Research in Music Education* 34, no. 3 (1986): 160–72.

Schopp, Steven. "Stressing Performance Classes as Part of the School Curriculum." *NASSP Bulletin* 76, no. 544 (1992): 11–16.

Schuman, William. "The Performing Arts in the Curriculum." In *Dance: An Art in Academe*, edited by M. Haberman and T. G. Meisel. New York: Teachers College Press, 1970, 110–20.

Schumann, Robert. *Music and Musicians*. 5th ed. Translated by F. R. Ritter. London: William Reeves, 1915.

Scripp, L., J. Mcyaard, and L. Davidson. "Discerning Musical Development: Using Computers to Discover What We Know." *Journal of Aesthetic Education* 22, no. 1 (1988): 75–88.

Seashore, Carl E. *Psychology of Music*. New York: McGraw-Hill, 1938.

Shakespeare, William. *Twelfth Night*. In *The Complete Works of William Shakespeare*, edited by William Aldis Wright. New York: Doubleday, 1936.

Shuler, Scott. "Reaching At-Risk Students through Music Education." *NASSP Bulletin* 76, no. 544 (1992): 30–35.

Shuter-Dyson, Rosamunde, and Clive Gabriel. *The Psychology of Musical Ability*. London: Methuen, 1968.

Single, Nancy. "A Summary of Research-Based Principles of Effective Teaching." *Update: Application of Research in Music Educaiton* 8, no. 2 (1991): 3–10.

Sloboda, John. "The Acquisition of Musical Performance Expertise: Deconstructing the 'Talent' Account of Individual Differences in Musical Expressivity." In *The Road to Excellence: The Acquisition of Expert Performance in the Arts and Sciences, Sports, and Games*, edited by K. A. Ericsson. Mahwah, NJ: Erlbaum, 1996, 107–27.

———. *Generative Processes in Music*. Oxford: Clarendon Press, 1988.

———. *The Musical Mind: The Cognitive Psychology of Music*. Oxford: Oxford University Press, 1985.

———. "Music Performance: Expression and the Development of Excellence." In *Musical Perceptions* , edited by Rita Aiello and John Sloboda. New York: Oxford University Press, 1994, 153–69.

Sloboda, John, Jane Davidson, and Michael Howe. "Is Everyone Musical?" *Psychologist* 7, no. 8 (1994): 349–54.

Sloboda, John, B. Hermelin, and N. O'Connor. "An Exceptional Musical Memory." *Music Perception* 3 (1985): 155–70.

Sloboda, John, and Michael Howe. "Biographical Precursors of Musical Excellence: An Interview Study." *Psychology of Music* 19 (1991): 3–21.

———. "Problems Experienced by Talented Young Musicians as a Result of the Failure of Other Children to Value Musical Accomplishments." Gifted Education International 8 no. 1 (1992): 16–18.

Sosniak, Lauren A. "Learning to Be a Concert Pianist." In *Developing Talent in Young People*, edited by Benjamin Bloom. New York: Ballantine Books, 1985, 19–67.

———. "Phases of Learning." In *Developing Talent in Young People*, edited by Benjamin Bloom. New York: Ballantine Books, 1985, 409–38.

Staumbaugh, Laura. "Special Learners with Special Abilities." *Music Educators Journal* 83, no. 3 (1996): 19–23.

Steele, Kenneth M., Joshua D. Brown, and Jaimily A. Stoecker. "Failure to Confirm the Rauscher and Shaw Description of Recovery of the Mozart Effect."*Perceptual and Motor Skills* 88 (1999): 843–48.

Stern, D. N. *The Interpersonal World of the Infant*. New York: Basic Books, 1985.

Sternberg, Robert. *Beyond IQ: A Triarchic Theory of Human Intelligence*. New York: Cambridge University Press, 1985.

Sternberg, Robert, and J. Davidson. *Conceptions of Giftedness*. New York: Cambridge University Press, 1986.

Stravinsky, Igor. *Poetics of Music*. Cambridge: Harvard University Press, 1970.

Subotnik, Rena. "Developing Young Adolescent Performers at Juilliard: An Educational Prototype for Elite Level Talent Development in the Arts and Sciences." In *Developing Talent across the Lifespan*, edited by C. F. M. Van Lieshout and P. G. Heymans. Philadelphia: Psychology Press, 2000, 249–75.

Suzuki, Sinichi. *Ability Development from Age Zero*. Translated by Mary Louise Nagata. Athens, OH: Ability Development Associates, 1969.

———. *Nurtured by Love: A New Approach to Education*. Ttranslated by Waltraud Suzuki. New York: Exposition Press, 1969.

———. *Where Love Is Deep*. Translated by Kyoko Selden. New Albany, IN: World-Wide Press, 1982.

Swanner, D. "Relationships between Musical Creativity and Selected Factors including Personality, Motivation, Musical Aptitude and Cognitive Intelligence as Measured in Third Grade Children." Ph.D. diss., Case Western Reserve University, 1985.

Tacka, Philip, and Micheal Houlahan. *Sound Thinking: Developing Musical Literacy*.
New York: Boosey and Hawkes, 1995.

Thompson, Brad. "It's Only a Phase: Teaching Adolescents." *American Music Teacher*
45, no. 1 (1995): 22–25, 72.

Thompson, Keith. "Integrating Music into the Curriculum: A Recipe for Success."
NASSP Bulletin 76, no. 544 (1995): 47–51.

Thoms, Hollis. "Encouraging the Musical Imagination through Composition." *Music
Educators Journal* 73, no. 5 (1987): 27–30.

Thorndike, R. L., E. P. Hagen, and M. S. Jerome. *The Stanford-Binet Intelligence
Scale*. Chicago: Riverside, 1986.

Tomlinson, Carol Ann. *How to Differentiate Instruction in Mixed-Ability Classrooms*. Alexandria, VA: Association for Supervision and Curriculum Development, 1995.

Torrance, E. P. "Some Products of Twenty-five Years of Creativity Research." *Educational Perspectives* 22, no. 3 (1984): 3–8.

———. *Thinking Creatively in Action and Movement*. Bensenville, IL: Scholastic
Testing Service, 1981.

Torrance, E. P., J. Khatena, and B. F. Cunningham. *Thinking Creatively with Sounds
and Words*. Bensenville, IL: Scholastic Testing Service, 1973.

Treffert, D. *Extraordinary People: Understanding "Idiot Savants."* New York:
Harper and Row, 1989.

Treffinger, D., and S. Isaksen. *Creative Problem Solving: An Introduction*. Sarasota,
FL: Center for Creative Learning, 1991.

Treffinger, D., S. Isaksen, and R. Firestien. *Handbook for Creative Learning*.
Williamsville, NY: Center for Creative Learning, 1982.

Trehub, S. E. "Infants: Perception of Musical Patterns." *Perception and Psychophysics* 41 (1987): 635–41.

Trehub, S. E., L. J. Trainor, and A. M. Unyk. "Music and Speech Processing in the
First Year of Life." *Advancement of Child Development Behavior* 24 (1993): 2–35.

Trusty, Jerry, and Giacomo M. Oliva. "The Effects of Arts and Music Education on
Students' Self-Concept." *Update: Applications of Research in Music Education*
11, no. 1 (1994): 23–27.

University of Virginia Summer Enrichment Program in the Arts (SEPIA). *Audition
Schedule and Forms*. Charlottesville, VA: University of Virginia Summer Enrichment Program, 1991.

U. S. Department of Education. *National Excellence: A Case for Developing America's
Talent*. Washington, DC: U.S. Government Printing Office, 1993.

Uszler, Marienne. "The Independent Music Teacher: Practice and Preparation."
American Music Teacher 45, no. 8 (1996): 20–29, 62–63.

———. "Musical Giftedness." *American Music Teacher* 41, no. 4 (1990): 20–21,
69–73.

———. "Must the Fittest Just Survive?" *Piano and Keyboard* 160 (1993): 62–65.

Uszler, Marienne, Stewart Gordon, and Elyse Mach. *The Well-Tempered Keyboard Teacher*. New York: Schirmer Books, 1991.

Vaughan, M. "Musical Creativity: Its Cultivation and Measurement." *Bulletin of the Council for Research in Music Education* 50 (1977): 72–77.

Wallach, M., and N. Kogan. *Modes of Thinking in Young Children*. New York: Holt, 1965.

Wallas, G. *The Art of Thought*. New York: Harcourt Brace and Jovanovich, 1926.

Walters, Darrel, and Cynthia C. Taggart. *Readings in Music Learning Theory*. Chicago: GIA, 1989.

Walters, Joseph, and Howard Gardner. "The Crystallizing Experience: Discovering an Intellectual Gift." In *Conceptions of Giftedness*, edited by Robert Sternberg and Janet Davidson. New York: Cambridge University Press, 1986, 302–18.

Wang, C. "Measures of Creativity in Sound and Music." Lexington, KY: School of Music, University of Kentucky 1985.

Warren, George E., and Donald A. Hodges. "The Nature of Musical Attributes." In *Handbook of Music Psychology*, edited by David A. Hodges. Lawrence, KS: National Association for Music Therapy, 1980, 401.

Warrener, John J. "Applying Learning Theory to Musical Development: Piaget and Beyond." *Music Educators Journal* 72, no. 3 (1985): 22–27.

Watkins, J. G., and S. E. Farnum. *The Watkins-Farnum Performance Scale*. Winona, MN: Hal Leonard Music, 1954.

Webb, J. T. "Nurturing Social-Emotional Development of Gifted Children." In *International Handbook of Research and Development of Giftedness and Talent*, edited by Kurt A. Heller, Franz J. Mönks, and Harry A. Passow. Oxford: Pergamon Press, 525–38.

Webster, Peter. "Creativity as Creative Thinking." *Music Educators Journal* 76, no. 9 (1990): 22–28.

———. "Measures of Creative Thinking in Music: Administrative Guidelines." Evanston, IL: School of Music, Northwestern University, 1989.

———. "The Preschool Child and Creative Thinking." *American Music Teacher* 40, no. 6 (1991): 16–19.

———. "Refinement of a Measure of Creative Thinking in Music." *Applications of Research in Music Behavior*, edited by C. Madsen and C. Pricket. Tuscaloosa: University of Alabama Press, 1987, 257–71.

———. "Relationship between Creative Behavior in Music and Selected Variables as Measured in High School Students." *Journal of Research in Music Education* 27, no. 4 (1979): 227–42.

———. "Research on Creative Thinking in Music: The Assessment Literature." In *Handbook of Research on Music Teaching and Learning*, edited by R. Colwell. New York: Schirmer Books, 1992, 266–80.

———. "Rethinking Music Aptitude and Its Assessment." In *Sound Ideas: Assessment in Music Education* 2, no. 2 (1998): 6–16.

Webster, Peter, and Maud Hickey. "Rating Scales and Their Use in Assessing Children's Music Compositions." *Quarterly Journal of Music Teaching and Learning* 17, no. 4 (1995): 28–44.

Wechsler, D. *Wechsler Preschool and Primary Scale of Intelligence*. Rev. ed. New York: Psychological Corporation, 1989.

Wenner, G. "Discovery and Recognition of the Artistically Talented." *Journal for the Education of the Gifted* 18, no. 3 (1985): 221–38.

Whitehead, Alfred North. *The Aims of Education*. New York: Free Press, 1929.

Wiggins, Jacqueline H. "Children's Strategies for Solving Compositional Problems with Peers." *Journal of Research in Music Education* 42, no. 3 (1994): 232–52.

Williams, David Brian, and Peter R. Webster. *Experiencing Music Technology*. New York: Schirmer Books, 1996.

Winebrenner, S. *Teaching Gifted Kids in the Regular Classroom: Strategies Every Teacher Can Use to Meet the Needs of the Gifted and Talented*. Minneapolis: Free Spirit, 1992.

Winner, Ellen. *Gifted Children* . New York: Basic Books, 1996.

———. "The Rage to Master: The Decisive Role of Talent in the Visual Arts." In *The Road to Excellence: The Acquisition of Expert Performance in the Arts and Sciences, Sports, and Games*, edited by K. Anders Ericsson. Mahwah, NJ: Erlbaum, 1996, 271–85.

Winner, Ellen, Lyle Davidson, and Larry Scripp, eds. *Arts PROPEL: A Handbook for Music*. Cambridge: Harvard Project Zero and Educational Testing Service, 1992.

Wolfe, Delores M., Susan Mondschein, and B. Keith Eicher. "Governors' Schools: Spinning Webs for Educational Change." *Gifted Child Today* 14, no. 3 (1991): 28–30.

Woodford, Paul. "Musical Intelligence in the World: Negotiating the Social World of Music." *Quarterly Journal of Music Teaching and Learning* 7, no. 2 (1995): 49–59.

Woodward, S. C. "The Transmission of Music into the Human Uterus and the Response to Music of the Human Fetus and Neonate." Ph.D. diss., University of Cape Town, South Africa, 1992.

Woody, Robert. "Getting into Their Heads." *American Music Teacher* 49, no. 3 (1999–2000): 24–27.

Yamaha Corporation. "Music is the Key to Brain Fitness," *Key Action* 7 no. 9. (1999): 1, 19.

Yoshida, A., and Y. Chiba. "Neonate's Vocal and Facial Expression and Their Changes during Experimental Playbacks of Intra-uterine Sounds." *Journal of Ethology* 7 (1989): 153–56.

Younker, B. "Thought Processes and Strategies of Eight, Eleven, and Fourteen-Year Old Students." Ph.D. diss., Northwestern University, 1998.

Ziegfeld, E., ed. *Education and Art*. Paris: UNESCO, 1953.

Zimmerman, Marilyn P. *Musical Characteristics of Children*. Washington, DC: Music Educators National Conference, 1971.

———. "Psychological Theory and Music Learning." In *Basic Concepts in Music Education II*, edited by Richard J. Colwell. Niwot: University Press of Colorado, 1991, 157–74.

Zimmerman, Marilyn P., and L. Sechrest, "How Children Conceptually Organize Musical Sounds." Evanston, IL: Cooperative Research Project no. 5-0256, Northwestern University, 1968.

INDEX